Digital China

# Digital China

*Creativity and Community in the Sinocybersphere*

*Edited by*
*Jessica Imbach*

Amsterdam University Press

The publication of this book is made possible by a grant from the "Interdisciplinary Programme Asia and Europe" at the University of Zurich.

Cover illustration: Miao Ying, Prototype #3, 2019
Cover design: Coördesign, Leiden
Lay-out: Crius Group, Hulshout

ISBN 978 94 6372 067 0
e-ISBN 978 90 4855 521 5 (pdf)
DOI 10.5117/9789463720670
NUR 630



Printed and bound by CPI Group (UK) Ltd, Croydon, CR0 4YY

# Table of Contents

# Acknowledgements

Born into a German-American family, I was raised on a steady diet of caraway bread soup and Star Wars. While this did not blossom into an undying love of German cuisine, my childhood memories of browsing through our extensive science fiction library cultivated in me a fascination with stories about technology and the future that shaped me into the scholar I am today. Even though many of the digital technologies, new media practices and imaginaries discussed in this book are currently viewed primarily through a dystopian lens, it is thanks to these early memories that I continue to find joy, inspiration and hope in my chosen field of research. For this reason, I dedicate this volume to "Grandma" Carolyn Matherly, who not only showed me how to use MS-DOS when I was still in kindergarten, but also taught me that life rewards curiosity and courage.

This publication received generous funding from the "Interdisciplinary Programme Asia and Europe" at the University of Zurich. I thank them and all my colleagues, especially Justyna Jaguscik and "pop sinologist" Juri Mischler, for their support in this project. Carlos Rojas and the other anonymous reviewer provided erudite and very productive comments that helped to improve various chapters and the overall argument of this book. I am also deeply grateful to Maryse Elliott at Amsterdam University Press for her patient support and editorial expertise. Finally, I thank the contributors for their faith in me and their hard work in bringing this volume to fruition. I hope that they and all those who have accompanied us on this journey will be as satisfied with the result as I am.

# Note on Romanisation

Throughout this volume we adopt the Hanyu Pinyin romanisation system for Mandarin and the Yale system for Cantonese, which have become scholarly convention in English-language publications and are also adopted by most international library catalogues. Traditional Chinese characters and Pinyin are provided for all Chinese terms and titles in the main text when they first appear. Names, places, and institutions are romanised according to the respective regional system. For Chinese personal names we also follow the convention of placing the family name before the given name.

# List of Figures

# Introduction

## Locating Digital China

*Jessica Imbach*

Walls are omnipresent in the discourse of digital China. The "Great Firewall" is routinely used as a summary descriptor for the ever-expanding institutional, technical, and ideological infrastructure that enables the Chinese state to monitor and control online spaces. Xi Jinping's discussions of "Internet safety" and "cybersovereignty" are steeped in border security rhetoric, while Chinese netizens can only access "walled" (*beiqiang* 被牆) content by "going over the wall" (*fanqiang* 翻牆) – defined by the Baidu Chinese dictionary as "circumventing IP blockers, content filtering, domain hijacking, traffic restrictions, etc., to achieve access to web content."[1] Although the Great Wall has played a central role in conceptualising China's relationship with the world throughout the modern period, the current discourse on digital China also continues the longstanding convention of thinking about modern China through metaphors of confinement and restriction that point to shifting understandings of Chinese difference as both a burden and a strength. While Lu Xun famously characterised modern China as trapped in the "iron house" (*tie wuzi* 鐵屋子) of its own history, the enigmatic "wallfacers" (*mianbizhe* 面壁者) in Liu Cixin's science fiction epos *The Dark Forest* (*Hei'an senlin* 黑暗森林, 2008) represent the last vestiges of independent human thought, as they try to escape the all-seeing intelligence particles of Earth's alien invaders. The "paranoid narratives of total surveillance and total freedom"[2] that have characterised the dominant conceptualisation of fibre-optic networks since the 1990s have further cemented the rhetorical allure of the wall as a symbol of the technological and discursive boundaries that separate Chinese netizens from the rest of the world. They have also fostered an analytical approach that views Chinese online spaces primarily through the lens of state control

1 Baidu Baike, "Fanqiang."
2 Chun, *Control and Freedom*, 6.

Imbach, Jessica. *Digital China*. Amsterdam: Amsterdam University Press, 2024
DOI: 10.5117/9789463720670_INTRO

and civic resistance. When it comes to digital China, no topics have probably received more public and academic attention than surveillance and censorship.

Although the early development of digital technologies was in China as elsewhere largely driven by academic institutions, the Chinese state played a central role in the growth of what is often termed the Chinese Internet. In 1998, only five years after connecting to the Internet, China launched the "Golden Shield Project" (*jindun gongcheng* 金盾工程) to monitor online spaces and restrict access to foreign content through the establishment of the Great Firewall. Limited liberalisation tendencies under Hu Jintao notwithstanding, state control has in recent years become continuously more comprehensive as well as centrally organised through the formal creation of the Cyberspace Administration of China (*wangxinban* 網信辦) in 2014. Harrowing accounts of government surveillance and censorship paint a by-and-large dystopian picture of how the Chinese state harnesses digital technologies to "reinvent," as Kai Strittmatter puts it, authoritarian rule for the twenty-first century.[3] Currently, China is pushing for a massive expansion of its digital capitalist infrastructure in its 14th five-year plan and has also become a leading exporter of digital surveillance and censorship technologies.[4]

China's rapid ascent in digital development has also raised questions and concerns about the permeability of digital China's real and metaphorical borders. Is Huawei's 5G technology a conduit for political surveillance?[5] Will WeChat be the social network of the future?[6] How will China's digitisation path affect global climate change?[7] Or what role does online fantasy literature play in the state's cultural diplomacy portfolio?[8] Questions such as these have generated a vast range of speculative prognosis ranging from cyberpunk fantasies of a radically networked society to Orwellian scenarios of ubiquitous surveillance. Forecasts of the latter kind are particularly prominent in analysis of China's "social credit system" (*shehui xinyong tixi* 社會信用體系) but have often hindered more nuanced discussion. Although still far from a digital panopticon, the numerous policies and infrastructures underneath the "system" have amplified existing forms of state violence and discrimination, but also share many commonalities

3 Strittmatter, *We Have Been Harmonised*; Griffiths, *The Great Firewall of China*.
4 Mozur, Kessel, and Chan, "Made in China, Exported to the World."
5 Friis and Lysne, "Huawei, 5G and Security."
6 Raedts, "How China's Digital Ecosystems Are Shaping Western Social Media's Future."
7 Li and Shapiro, *China Goes Green*.
8 Zhou and Ewe, "Boys Keep Flirting With Each Other on Chinese TV."

with more covert surveillance programmes and behaviour-modification policies elsewhere.[9]

To be sure, dystopian fears of a surveillance society are not unwarranted and regulatory efforts have reached under Xi Jinping's administration a "historical high."[10] Yet, a "fixation with Chinese censors,"[11] as Wang Jing puts it, also risks obscuring the multiple agents shaping new media practices across the Chinese-speaking world, while grassroots intellectual spaces continue to exist both on- and offline despite an increasingly heavy-handed regulatory approach.[12] Michel Hockx has also usefully pointed out that a narrow view of censorship as a "polluting factor"[13] fails to take into account how technological and political affordances and constraints are an integral part of cultural production both in China and elsewhere – and precede the digital age. Normative readings of the Chinese state's role in digital development, as in the already mentioned case of the social credit system, have also obfuscated how the forces of global techno-capitalism work in lockstep with state power.[14]

China's digital ecosystem developed during a period of vast social and economic transformations. Since the late 1990s, rural to urban migration not only fuelled China's breakneck economic growth, but also put mobile phones – as a tool for keeping in touch with family members and as a means for navigating urban environments – at the forefront of Internet adoption.[15] These developments created a high demand for digital services in areas such as manufacturing, commerce, and social networking that were neither met by a deficient state infrastructure nor by foreign tech companies, which only had very restricted access to the Chinese market. This situation created a favourable climate for the rapid growth of Chinese tech companies such as Tencent, Alibaba and Baidu and their products are today important pillars of China's ICT infrastructure. In this regard, China's economy followed the global trend towards the simultaneous

9 A well-balanced account of the historical forerunners of the current policy as well as its differences and similarities to data-driven governance models elsewhere can be found in Lam, "The People's Algorithms."

10 Wang, *The Chinese Internet*, 3.

11 Wang, *The Other Digital China*, 1.

12 For a discussion of grassroots intellectual culture in the digital era see also Veg, *Minjian*.

13 Hockx, *Internet Literature in China*, 11.

14 Another case in point is China's high-tech penal system in Xinjiang, see Byler, *Terror Capitalism*.

15 Wallis, *Technomobility in China*.

"'platformisation' of infrastructures" and "'infrastructuralisation' of platforms."[16] This twin dynamic of digitisation and commercialisation was supported by state regulations to boost China's innovation economy, while simultaneously creating important infrastructure for the country's diverse demographic. The emergence of the platform society in China is arguably most evident in China's "super-app" WeChat that has become an indispensable gateway for activities ranging from entertainment to health services to financial transactions.[17]

Yet, the outsourcing of public services to commercial platforms, which went hand in hand with the datafication of people's behaviours, was in China, as already stated, accompanied by close state scrutiny and regulatory oversight. This has led to a highly developed system of collaboration between state and commercial actors. While state agencies for instance use commercial data analytics to monitor online spaces,[18] digital platforms discursively legitimise their profit-driven data activities as public services in alignment with techno-nationalist goals.[19] As Yang Guobin notes, "the dual logics of politics and profit-driven market, in all their complex and entangled forms, have penetrated China's digital spheres."[20] While the Chinese cybersphere thus does not exist independent of other networked spaces and is subject to the same developments shaping what Franco Berardi calls the "Global Silicon Valley,"[21] a highly developed interaction between capitalist and political vectors is particularly prominent in the Chinese digital world.

These complex entanglements of technological dependencies, economic exploitation and political control have given rise to a pervasive sense of disempowerment. As the historian Luo Xin put it in an interview on the Wuhan lockdown of the popular podcast Surplus Value (*Shengyu jiazhi* 剩餘價值): "In our culture, in our legal system, in our political and social life, humans don't hold power, but are rather a unit of profit."[22] But apart from its unusually critical tone, the episode is also noteworthy for the events

16 Plantin et al., "Infrastructure Studies Meet Platform Studies in the Age of Google and Facebook," 295.

17 See Plantin and de Seta, "WeChat as Infrastructure," as well as Imbach and Jaguścik, "Introduction: Digital Society in China."

18 Hou, "Neoliberal Governance or Digitalized Autocracy?"

19 Chan and Kwok, "The Politics of Platform Power in Surveillance Capitalism."

20 Yang and Wang, *Engaging Social Media in China*, xii.

21 Berardi, *Futurability*.

22 The episode was entitled "Wenyi, yuyan he juti de ren: Yu lishi xuejia Luo Xin liaotian." A transcript and an archived copy can be found here: https://ipfs.io/ipfs/QmNXBfQ1v3J3dBv-RoocrdzheCa5JVFnqzMAevV2kfXkG9N/.

that followed. Shortly after airing, the episode was reported for spreading false rumours and censored across various podcasting platforms, including Spotify, and Surplus Value's Alipay account was de-activated as well. The case thereby confirmed Florian Schneider's observation that although the state may set the "parameters of discourse," it is up to the individual actors "to negotiate the exact meanings."[23] What is off-limits may only be clear in hindsight and is also dependent on various opaque or unpredictable factors such as platform moderation guidelines. But only a few months after being censored and de-monetised Surplus Value was renamed into Stochastic Volatility (*Suiji bodong* 隨即波動) and resumed podcasting. The new name is highly suggestive of the "fuzzy grey zone,"[24] in which digital creators, activists and the wired public at large operate. But an analysis of this event would have to consider not only the complex dynamics of censorship in China, but also the role of Chinese and Western media corporations, the emergence of China's "new auditory culture,"[25] the soft comeback of RSS technology, the diffuse channels through which Chinese nationalists disseminate their opinions, and the cultural networks across the global Sinosphere. Although but a minor tale from China's new media landscape, the case of Surplus Value illustrates not only that there is no such thing as a homogeneous, firewall-enclosed digital China – a clichéd observation well worth repeating, but also that cataloguing the numerous instances of censorship gets us nowhere towards understanding how people engage with and reflect on digital technologies.

A particularly interesting field in this regard is Internet literature (*wangluo wenxue* 網絡文學), which in China alone has over 450 million readers and, according to the 2020 statistics, a higher daily engagement rate than online gaming.[26] A certain degree of caution in taking these numbers at face value is certainly warranted, as recent policies aimed at restricting access to gaming platforms show how anxious the Chinese state is to regulate the industry. However, the very fact that the China Internet Network Information Centre continues to include a category for Internet literature in its yearly statistics shows not only how popular (and commercially successful) these fiction platforms have become, but also that Chinese online culture has developed distinct cultural forms that have no equivalent in most other

23 Schneider, *China's Digital Nationalism*, 225.

24 Wang, *The Other Digital China*, 32.

25 Xia Deyuan and Zhou Weifeng, "Boke: Xin xing kouyu chuanbo xingtai de fazhan yu tingjue wenhua de huigui."

26 China Internet Network Information Centre, "Di 45 Ci Zhongguo hulian wangluo fazhan zhuangkuang tongji baogao."

countries. Government restrictions affect all aspects of social life in China, including the production and consumption of new media, but China's digital landscape is nevertheless not exclusively shaped by state forces. Some in fact argue that cultural and linguistic factors are a more decisive "constraint" on netizens' access to web content than state censorship.[27]

Focusing on digital culture, this volume brings together new perspectives on literature, art, and performance in what we term the Sinocybersphere – the networked spaces across the globe that not only operate on the Chinese script, but also imaginatively negotiate the meanings of Chinese culture in the digital age. In doing so, the book locates digital cultural practices in diverse socio-historical dynamics, while also offering theoretical reflections on notions such as digital labour and "going viral" in the context of China's new media environment. To this end, the following chapters go beyond the headline grabbing topics such as China's steady roll-out of the social credit system or TikTok's ascent to the world's most downloaded social media app, to introduce readers to a diverse range of digital practices and imaginaries. Bringing together a range of innovative, interdisciplinary scholarship in the rapidly growing field of cultural media and technology studies, this book cuts through the hyperbole surrounding China's digital rise to shed light on the underlying cultural dynamics of digitisation across the Chinese-speaking world.

## Exploring the Sinocybersphere

The concept of the Sinophone is central to our theorisation of the Sinocybersphere. The term is strongly associated with Shih Shu-mei's critical interventions in the early 2000s and has become an important lens for the study of Sinitic language communities across the globe as well as ethnic minority discourses within the borders of the People's Republic of China. Influenced by postcolonial studies as well as historical scholarship on the settler colonialism of the Qing empire, Shih's formulation of the Sinophone had two main objectives: firstly, to draw attention to the linguistic diversity and heterogeneity of the Chinese cultural sphere and, secondly, to decentre Chineseness from the geo-cultural power of the Chinese state – thereby of course also bringing into focus the underlying assumptions and biases informing the field of Chinese studies. Shih's definition thus intentionally excluded Han Chinese voices from Mainland China, even though by drawing

27 Taneja and Wu, "Does the Great Firewall Really Isolate the Chinese?"

attention to the particularities of local expressions the gravitational pull of the centre remains a persistent force.[28] Yet soon after its introduction a broader definition of the Sinophone emerged to encompass all Chinese-language locations. For David Wang, for instance, the Sinophone "starts abroad, but must be extended to Mainland Chinese literature, and thereby constitute a dialogue."[29] Because most of the contributions in this volume focus on PRC-centric discourses and media events, they fall within this broader definition of the Sinophone.

Nevertheless, we remain indebted to Shih's original theorisation, as digital spaces are also fundamentally shaped by various vectors of neo-colonial exploitation by both state and corporate actors, as well as the transnational regimes of cultural authority they generate. *Danmei* 耽美or boys' love fiction, for instance, is one of the most popular genres of Internet literature in Mainland China and written predominantly by urban Han women. Yet, danmei fiction developed in the context of the global emergence of Internet-based fan fiction and celebrity culture communities that frequently challenge mainstream social mores and cultural conventions. As a community-based literary practice, danmei fiction also employs an intrinsic web of stylistic conventions and insider terminology that may not be immediately intelligible to "outsiders," even though it is written in Mandarin Chinese. Finally, because danmei fiction revolves around the idealisation of non-reproductive relationships, it has also become viewed as a threat to the patriarchal and heteronormative ideals of the Chinese state and its pronatal initiatives to address the emerging labour crisis.[30] The genre's enormous popularity has led to tightened censorship and, in some cases, even criminal charges against writers. Danmei fiction too could therefore be considered, as Shih puts it, "a minority culture on the margins of China and Chineseness within the geopolitical boundary of China."[31] This does not mean that the struggles of middle-class single women should be equated with those of ethnic and religious minorities, but rather that the "theoretical potentialities" of the Sinophone can also be applied to Mainland Chinese communities.[32] We understand the Sinophone thus not only as a linguistic or cultural position shaped by ethnicity, but also as a method that enables us to consider digital practices and imaginaries as expressions of

28 Tsai, "Issues and Controversies," 19–20.

29 Wang, "Wenxue xinglü yu shijie xiangxiang."

30 For a discussion of danmei fiction in relation to neoliberalism see Zhang, *Dreadful Desires*.

31 Shih, "Introduction: What Is Sinophone Studies?," 8.

32 Shih, "The Concept of the Sinophone," 711.

particular "localities," histories, and modes of dissemination. The notion of the Sinocybersphere thereby extends the "historical and place-based" practices of the Sinophone into digital spaces.[33]

To emphasise the plurality of these places we use the fuzzier term cybersphere instead of the more commonly used spatial term cyberspace, which has become strongly associated with problematic assumptions about the immateriality of digital technologies. Social scientists have for instance shown how the idea of the Internet as a virtual "global village" that transcends the physical world has actually created new forms of exclusion (and mythologies of deferred inclusion, encapsulated in notions such as the "digital divide") by obscuring the material and social forces in which digital interactions take place.[34] A similar line of critique in cultural and media studies has demonstrated how narratives of cyberspace, especially in cyberpunk fiction, have generated powerful misconceptions about the Internet as a "liberating technology" that would lead to the dissolution of physical boundaries as well as racialised and gendered hierarchies.[35] Focusing on concrete contexts, anthropologists and environmental scholars have also underscored the materiality of digital technologies by investigating, for instance, how the blockchain technology is reshaping rural communities across China or by analysing the effects of industrial pollution on contemporary poetry.[36] Although, as Rey Chow and Ani Maitra caution, practices of localisation, i.e. of analysing technology as place-bound, can perpetuate culturalist assumptions about local differences and entrenched traditions, they can also further sharpen our eye for understanding the local not so much in rigid geographic terms, but rather as "fragmentary networks that are quotidian yet accidental, culturally and socially complex yet not permanently bound."[37]

By situating digital cultural production in such loosely defined assemblages of material and discursive entanglements, we also follow the shift in media studies "from media as artifactuality to media as process of mediation."[38] The globalising effects of digital media notwithstanding, neither the Internet nor any other medium is an ontologically distinct information container or communication device, but rather a product of historically

33 Shih, "Introduction: What Is Sinophone Studies?," 14.

34 Graham, "Geography/Internet."

35 A landmark study on the history of cybernetics is Hayles, *How We Became Posthuman: Virtual Bodies in Cybernetics*. For a recent re-evaluation of the legacy of cybernetics, see: Geroulanos and Weatherby, "Cybernetics and the Human Sciences."

36 Wang, *Blockchain Chicken Farm*; Riemenschnitter, "Probing the Limits of Languaging."

37 Maitra and Chow, "What's 'In'?," 26.

38 Mitchell, "Introduction," xv.

specific negotiations. The point is not to reify cultural differences, but to analyse the functioning of media in specific material and discursive context. What Ma Shaolin calls "reading for media"[39] can thereby also bridge the methodological divide in media and culture studies between the formal analysis of what media do and the interpretative work focused on individual texts. We use the term Sinocybersphere thus as a conceptual framework for both digitally mediated places and communities as well as Sinophone textual sites, where new technologies and their symbolic negotiation interact. Accordingly, each of the following chapters focus on specific constellations of digital cultural production over and against defining what vlogging, AI poetry or memes are or what might make them "Chinese." Rather than exceptionalise digital China, we ask how cultural practices and digital technologies interact, what such entanglements reveal about ongoing social developments across the Chinese-speaking world and how they are relevant to our understanding of contemporary digital culture.

## Digital Worldbuilding

This book's exploration of the Sinocybersphere begins with Internet literature, which is not only one of the most popular forms of online cultural production, but also the most widely researched topic within Chinese new media studies. It is also a particularly fitting starting point for this book, because the history of Internet literature exemplifies how cultural forms shuttle between digital communities across the Sinocybersphere. According to one popular origin story, Internet literature began in 1998 with the web novel *First Intimate Contact* (*Di yi ci de qinmi jiechu* 第一次的親密接觸) by the graduate student Tsai Jhi-heng 蔡智恆, who, writing under the pseudonym "Rowdy Tsai" (Pizi Cai 痞子蔡), published the novel in instalments on the Bulletin Board System (BBS) of National Cheng Kung University in Taiwan. Although quickly dismissed by literary critics as unsophisticated, Tsai's exploration of online romance captured the zeitgeist of the early Internet age and spread like wildfire through BBS forums in Taiwan and China. The print version also became an overnight bestseller, and *First Intimate Contact* is today immortalised as the novel that kickstarted China's web fiction boom. Its legendary status notwithstanding, the early history of Chinese-language web fiction can be traced further back to several publication projects initiated by overseas students in the US and Tsai's novel was also not the first piece of original fiction circulated on

39 Ma, *The Stone and the Wireless*, 13.

Chinese BBS forums.[40] Yet, *First Intimate Contact* brought a new form of community-based literary practice, in which authors and readers closely interact, to mainstream attention, and simultaneously also demonstrated how commercially successful web-based content could be. Crucially, the circulation of Tsai's and many other creative texts in the context of online discussion forums across China and Taiwan also underscored the mutually constituting relationship between technological and cultural networks. As Guo Shaohua's analysis of the early "BBS culture" reveals, Internet literature was simultaneously a product of BBS technology *and* a cultural form that shaped the functioning of digital media across diverse localities.[41]

Today, Internet literature is no longer a cutting-edge form of youth entertainment, but a gigantic cultural industry. On platforms such as Qidian 起點 and Jinjiang 晉江 pay per view subscription models incentivise writers to churn out chapters at lighting speed and create novels that often run over hundreds of chapters. Meanwhile, readers have a vast universe of fictional worlds at their disposal, ranging from "immortality cultivation" (*xiuzhen* 修真), "matriarchy fiction" (*nüzun* 女尊) to "urban romance" (*dushi yanqing* 都市言情). Although Internet literature continues to be predominantly viewed as a popular distraction through which young readers escape the drudgeries of their daily lives, the first two chapters argue that digital worldbuilding also constitutes a form of vernacular politics that is intimately related to and critically engaged with contemporary issues. In chapter 1 Cui Qian explores the sprawling universe of *xuanhuan* 玄幻 fiction, which is conventionally translated as "Eastern fantasy." Through a close-reading of xuanhuan worldbuilding, Cui argues that xuanhuan novels reinvent ideals of romantic love, national belonging, and spiritual cultivation to dislodge the ancient concept of a China-centered world order (*tianxia* 天下) from nationalist politics. Against the prevailing perception of Chinese online spaces as creatively atrophied places, shaped by censorship and nationalism, she shows how xuanhuan fantasy worlds creatively recharge classical narratives about love, redemption, and transcendence with contemporary relevance. While Cui cautions us against reading the digital tianxia discourse in xuanhuan fiction as overly politically charged, she argues that the enchanted worlds of xuanhuan fiction have not only become important sites for the negotiation of contemporary values and beliefs – from both an

40 An overview can be found in Hockx, *Internet Literature in China*, 30–32.

41 Guo Shaohua speaks in this context of "BBS culture," see Guo, *The Evolution of the Chinese Internet*, 69–74.

individual and a collective perspective, but also engender a utopian space for China's young netizens to imagine alternatives to the contemporary status quo. Xuanhuan fiction thereby also brings into focus a set of issues that are central to this volume: the relationship between consumerism and digital escapism, the expression of vernacular or grassroots creativity in a censored media landscape as well as the complicated politics of "Chineseness" across the Sinocybersphere.

In chapter 2 Jin Sujie follows up on Cui's discussion with an analysis of the enormously popular genre of Boys' Love (BL) or danmei fiction. As already mentioned, danmei fiction has gained international notoriety for the draconian sentences handed down to some of its authors, but it has also become one of China's most commercially successful cultural export products. Although censorship has toned down some of the more sexually explicit aspects of the genre, especially in its various television adaptations, Jin focuses on the participatory culture of the genre to analyse why danmei's popularity has remained unbroken. From a formal point of view, Jin shows how danmei has fostered a highly engaged community of writers and readers, who interact on forums and in comment sections to discuss plotlines and characters as well as exchange spin-off texts. Focusing on the sub-genre of danmei farming fiction, Jin furthermore demonstrates that the genre's participatory community culture is also evident on the textual level. In her close reading of *A Tale of Jujube Valley* (*Zao'er gou fajia ji* 棗兒溝發家記), a novel that takes place in the Ming dynasty, Jin traces how traditional values and beliefs about kinship, domesticity, and human-nature relations are brought into dialogue with the anxieties and desires of its contemporary readers. Accordingly, Jin argues that we should view danmei fiction not so much as a (mis-)representation of homoerotic desire and rather as an imaginative digital practice, that enables women to discuss and reflect on the specific challenges they face within Chinese society.

Shifting our perspective towards a different locality, chapter 3 by Helena Wu explores the hitherto largely neglected field of Hong Kong Internet literature. In contrast to the first two chapters that focus on specific genres, Wu surveys the entire history of Hong Kong's digital literary field from its tentative beginnings in the mid-1990s to its phenomenal growth after 2010. Following the methodology outlined by Hockx in his seminal study of Internet literature, Wu nevertheless also pays attention to individual texts and their relationship to Hong Kong's localised digital practices, which she characterises as marked by linguistic and cultural hybridity. Linguistic hybridity is expressed through frequent code-switching and mixing between Cantonese, Mandarin, and English, while cultural hybridity is reflected in the way globally circulated tropes and figures such as the popular manga hero Doraemon or the trope of the magical portal are reimagined from the perspective of Hong Kong's unique cultural history and urban geography. In sharp contrast to the highly formalised genre divisions of Mainland Chinese Internet literature – a result of distinctive communities as well as commercial branding – Hong Kong's web fiction engenders a more fluid literary practice, which is closely linked to informal and non-commercial digital spaces. Wu furthermore highlights that even Hong Kong's web-publishing industry positions itself as operating outside of the mainstream publishing world and the commercial success of most writers was rather short-lived. The strong and self-consciously local orientation of Internet literature in Hong Kong has limited its commercial growth and transnational reach, but Wu argues that in times of growing pressures from Beijing, Hong Kong's digital literary field continues to not only offer light entertainment, but also constitutes a precarious public sphere, where imaginative portals into other worlds are still possible.

## Poetry in the Digital Age

Poetry constitutes another important field of digital cultural production in the Sinocybersphere. Although more marginal and far less commercialised than Internet literature, the prominence of digital verses is not surprising considering the unique cultural authority of the poetic form throughout Chinese history. As David Wang and many others have pointed out, poetry not only dominated traditional Chinese literary culture, but also played a central role in the formation of modern Chinese aesthetics and intellectual thought.[42] Contemporary poetry both continues these debates in digital spaces, but also brings Chinese lyricism into contact with digital platforms, social networks, and computer code. In her seminal study of online poetry, Heather Inwood, for instance, has shown that the Internet has become the primary medium of contemporary Chinese poetry; works are first published online, poets converge in online forums, promote their writings through social media and assert their "creative agency"[43] through the development of new and often highly irreverent poetic styles that would not be publishable in print. But intersections of the lyrical and digital technologies also take place in contexts that are often not associated with the literary field. While memes and chatbots often draw on the poetic form in a process of what Bolter

42 Wang, *The Lyrical in Epic Time*.
43 Inwood, *Verse Going Viral*, 54.

and Grusin have termed remediation,[44] poetry is often itself considered to display a close affinity to computer code.[45] This cannot only be evidenced in the surge in computational methods in the study of classical Chinese poetry, but also in the fact that Chinese engineers of natural language generators have strongly focused on these highly regulated forms of verse.

In chapter 4 Joanna Krenz examines what she calls the "romance" of Chinese AI engineers with traditional poetic forms. Tracing the history of the interactions between technology and poetry, Krenz argues that interest in and engagement with machines occurred relatively late in Chinese poetry, because formal experimentation was up until very recently regarded as secondary to thematic innovation. This also affected the reception of classical poetry in the modern era. Especially May Fourth cultural reformers rejected regulated verse on the ground that its rule-based nature stifled creativity, in other words, that it was too machine-like. Although traditional poetic forms are today once again associated with far more cultural prestige than unregulated modern poetry, the idea that classical forms are conceptually closer to machine code continues to inform the research agenda of AI engineers. Through a close examination of the research papers written by the engineers of AI poetry, Krenz points out that as conservative as their valuation of the traditional over the modern may be, their code-work is not only single-mindedly focused on following formal patterns, but also takes semantic aspects into consideration. Their efforts to computerise verse and quantify the poetic canon are nevertheless remarkably uninterested in poetic innovation and remain focused on replicating canonical styles and themes. Ending with a discussion of global developments in natural language processing, Krenz nonetheless cautions against dismissing AI poetry as unimaginative, life-less or derivative. As digital technologies have become an indispensable part of our daily lives, we should instead embrace the fact that machines have cultural agency too.

Returning to the world of human-authored poetry, chapter 5 by Paula Teodorescu investigates the role of meme culture in China's poetry scene. Her analysis focuses on the "Eraser" (*Xiangpi* 橡皮) poetry group and their numerous experiments with digital formats. Tracing the development of the group and their creation of a unique, and highly irreverent aesthetic brand, she argues that their poetic experiments, although initially not geared towards online readers, were particularly successful in adapting

44 Bolter and Grusin, *Remediation*.

45 The relationship between poetic code and machine-generated verse is discussed in Marino, *Critical Code Studies*.

to changing media environments. Teodorescu furthermore argues that as *Xiangpi* poems and artistic practices travelled across numerous digital channels, *Xiangpi* itself became a meme – an artistic attitude and cultural brand that could be replicated by others but remained identifiably associated with their aesthetic values. Although some of their poems did indeed go viral, inciting nation-wide debates on the supposed decline of poetry in the digital age, Teodorescu argues that *Xiangpi* embraced digital media not to gain fame or fortune, but rather as a self-conscious, archival practice. By creatively adopting the logic of the Internet meme, *Xiangpi* could outlive the shut-down of digital channels or the censorship of individual creators and texts.

## Performing Authenticity

Whereas the importance of web fiction and poetry across the Sinocybersphere can be partially attributed to the central role of literary practices throughout Chinese history, the surge in audiovisual formats on social media platforms is a global phenomenon. Even before the digital age and the rise of camera phones, the degree of image saturation achieved by modern mass media was considered by many scholars a hallmark of modern culture.[46] Although it is often misleading to view digital media as a radical break with the past,[47] media scholars have widely recognised that new screen-mediated visual practices such as short video and livestreaming have brought forth new possibilities and constraints on sociality, vernacular creativity, and media entrepreneurialism. The display, consumption, and monetisation of authenticity, for instance, has become a significant feature shared across various image economies on social media platforms, although what constitutes as authentic varies, depending on the platform specific functionalities in which authenticity is crafted.[48] The problematic "status of the visual"[49] in non-Western media contexts and its imbrications in the production of authenticity is further compounded by the fact that, as Rey Chow astutely points out, scholars of orientalism have frequently associated images of the non-West with exploitation and misrepresentation. In the context of Chinese digital spaces, this iconophobic discourse has

46 Mitchell, "Image," 37.

47 This is the core claim made by Bolter and Grusin in *Remediation*.

48 For a case study that explores the discourse of authenticity on the Taiwanese livestreaming platform Lang Live see Hsiao, "Authenticating Discourses of 'Being Oneself' on Monetary-Motivated Livestreams."

49 Chow, "Toward an Ethics of Postvisuality," 679.

paradoxically re-opened the door for (techno-)orientalist interpretations that view user-generated visuality as "derivative," "passive," "subservient" to state repression or "self-orientalising" for Western audiences.[50] While such sweeping judgements do not hold up to closer scrutiny, they are symptomatic of a regretful tendency in Chinese studies to associate textuality with a higher degree of agency than visuality – a judgement itself reinforced by the proclivity towards textual media that can be traced as far back as the Six Dynasties period (220–589).[51]

Thankfully, mobile phone-mediated visuality has over the last decade become an important focus in Chinese cinema and media studies.[52] Building on these studies but focusing more squarely on the thorny relationship between affective labour and digital media, the following two chapters analyse discourses of authenticity in the context of digital video production and livestreaming. In chapter 6 Rui Kunze analyses Chinese influencer culture through the case of Li Ziqi 李子柒. Li's global success as a culinary and artisanal craft content creator is an especially interesting example, because she has amassed a huge following both in China and internationally on YouTube. While some critics regarded her "beautified" portrayals of country life as a distortion of rural realities, most of Li's followers, as Kunze points out, view Li's ability to carefully curate her persona and her content not as a misrepresentation, but rather as further underscoring her work ethic, attachment to nature, entrepreneurialism as well as her devotion to her grandmother, who she supports through her influencer business. Rejecting what Rey Chow in another context has called the "coerced mimeticism"[53] of Global South actors to faithfully represent *their* reality, Kunze argues that Li's videos engender a form of aspirational authenticity that seeks not to portray what China is, but rather what country life and China's heritage means *to her*. At the same time, Li's fantasy worlds can only exist precisely because they can so effectively exploit the affective and technological affordances of social media. When state media and nationalist commentators started to promote Li Ziqi's content, Kunze notes how this added a further layer of fantasy or make-belief into the production of Li's "China story," as it wilfully ignored the fact that her international success relies on YouTube, a platform that Chinese citizens can only access via VPN. Through her analysis, Kunze

50 Huang, "On Sinofuturism."

51 Cai and Wu, "Introduction."

52 See for instance Voci, *China on Video*; Johnson et al., *China's IGeneration*. Livestreaming platforms have become an especially prominent focus of more recent studies. A case in point is a recent special issue by Fitzgerald, Sandel, and Wu, "Chinese Social Media."

53 Chow, "Introduction," 18.

shows that discourses of authenticity exceed the binary logic of the "real" and the "fake", and are continuously negotiated between creators and their audiences, technologies, communities as well as state actors.

Chapter 7 by He complements Kunze's analysis through a case study that analyses the livestreams of "Sister Zhao" on the short video platform *Kuaishou* 快手. Internationally known as Kwai, Kuaishou is in its functionalities similar to *Douyin* 抖音/TikTok but has become particularly popular among China's rural netizens and is known for a more unadorned, "rustic" (*tu* 土) aesthetic. In sharp contrast to the financially successful content produced by Li Ziqi, "Sister Zhao" is a pancake maker, who sings and shares personal life stories on livestreams merely to supplement her income. He's analysis shows that livestreaming on Kuaishou brings very little financial reward for most of its rural users and has in fact further exacerbated entrenched inequalities. Meanwhile, Kuaishou's business model thrives precisely because it can capitalise on the deferred promise of empowerment by giving visibility to marginalised women such as "Sister Zhao." Through a comparison of Zhao's streams with those of a male Kuaishou streamer, He also shows how gendered precarity is reconfigured in digital spaces, as female steamers gain greater visibility by focusing on the hardships faced by peasants and migrant workers. Although the Kuaishou platform unevenly distributes the burden of affective labour, He also shows how livestreams such as Zhao's thereby also paradoxically engender a form of grassroots resistance to the "positive energy" (*zheng nengliang* 正能量) discourse on Chinese social media.

## Cyberpunk Negotiations

Since the early 1980s, East Asian localities have not only become important sites in the production of digital media technologies but have also played a central role in the symbolic representation of networked societies. In particular, North American cyberpunk science fiction of the mid-1980s offered seductive narratives of the Internet *as* cyberspace, while also revealing deep-seated anxieties about the influx of consumer electronics from Japan and China. Wendy Chun has described cyberpunk's narrative tactic as a "navigate-by-difference" strategy, in which the disembodiment of the (Western) hero and his phenomenal exploits in the matrix are set against an exotic and unchanging Oriental backdrop.[54] Chun rightly points out that techno-orientalist stereotypes are not confined to Western writings and the genre's legacy, for instance, continues to influence Chinese youth

54 See Chun, *Control and Freedom* as well as "High-Tech Orientalism (Cyberpunk & Race)."

culture.[55] However, engagements with network technologies in Chinese science fiction could perhaps be better characterised as exhibiting a strong sense of temporal and spatial proximity to digital development; the boom in science fiction coincided with the rapidly accelerating informatisation of China since the late 1990s, and China has become a major location for the manufacture and recycling of computer hardware.

Focusing on the idea of history as computer code, chapter 8 discusses fictional representations of the Internet in post-Tiananmen science fiction and begins with an analysis of Liu Cixin's infamous cyberpunk debut novel *China 2185* (*Zhongguo 2185* 中国2185, 1989) in the context of the late 1980s cultural fever. Although Liu's novel opens with a utopian vision of China's rise to the world's first complete information society, it swiftly transitions into a dystopian narrative that revolves around the idea that network technologies will continuously restrict the future as a realm of political contestation and creative imagination. In the second part I thus zoom out to explore the relationship between Chinese futurism and the role of network technologies within contemporary science fiction more broadly. While China's digital industry growth appears to confirm the historical vision of cyberpunk fiction, this development has not been accompanied by a similar rise in science fiction works centred on digital networks. I argue that this is both a result of globalised post-digital culture as well as the increased practical and ideological significance of automation to Chinese state power. Drawing on Han Song's short story "Mountain Camp" (Shanzhai 山寨, 2020), my chapter concludes with a reflection on the recent historical turn of science fiction as a critical response to the reductionist idea of the future as a continuous update of the (political) status quo. Ultimately, I argue that while science fiction as a cultural industry is often aligned with state interests, it has also become an important discursive space that enables explorations of the future as open and unpredictable.

Whereas my chapter centres on the symbolic negotiation of network technologies within science fiction, chapter 9, by Zoe Goldstein draws on Chen Qiufan's cyberpunk-inspired novel *Waste Tide* (*Huangchao* 荒潮, 2013) to delve into the often-overlooked topic of digital trash. Chen's science fiction thriller is based on the e-waste recycling site in Guiyu, which, at the time of the novel's publication, was a globally mediatised symbol for the toxicity of consumer electronics as well as the capitalist exploitation of informal and cheap labour in the Global South. While Chen openly acknowledges William Gibson as a major influence on his writings, Goldstein explains how Chen's

55 Luo Jiaqi, "Why Is Post-COVID China Embracing A Cyberpunk Aesthetic?"

cyberpunk vision is shaped by an acute awareness for the toxic materiality of digital development as well as the uneven distribution of agency across global waste chains. Crucially, she shows how Chen's "dirty" rewriting of cyberspace explores possibilities of solidarity between workers, the environment and machines that also challenge orientalist misconceptions about an "ecocidal" Chinese society as well as the racialisation of e-waste as a "Chinese problem." Concluding with a discussion of state-sponsored recycling programs in China and grassroots waste movements in the US, Goldstein argues that Chen's novel delineates a collaborative framework for environmental justice that can act as a model for real-world waste practices, both in China and elsewhere.

## Networked Creativity

When the Internet burst onto the media scene of the mid-1990s, visual artists were among the first cohort of creators, who embraced the creative possibilities of digital technologies. In contrast to Internet fiction, which has only recently started to be translated and circulated globally, Chinese new media art also gained international visibility much earlier, as it emerged during a period of surging global demand for contemporary Chinese art. Chinese new media artists such as Miao Ying, whose work is featured on the cover of this book, engaged with this dynamic through irreverent contestations of foreign perceptions of Chinese online spaces, while simultaneously finding a growing domestic audience conversant in meme culture, photo filters, GIFs and emojis.[56] At the same time, an aura of spectrality, as Margaret Hillenbrand puts it, also permeates contemporary Chinese visual culture; while even politically sensitive images such as the "Tank Man" from Tiananmen square continue to proliferate through digital spaces in ever changing and sometimes highly playful guises, image-filters and censors have become extremely efficient at identifying and removing not only text, but also visual content.[57]

The following two chapters discuss how this complicated dynamic between visual art, digital play and censorship was further intensified during the Covid-19 pandemic. In chapter 10 Diyi Mergenthaler and Helen Hess provide a comparative analysis of digital public art projects during the first wave of the pandemic in Guangzhou and Kuala Lumpur. While the Chinese art scene had already before the pandemic been highly engaged

56 Holmes, "Meanwhile in China ... Miao Ying and the Rise of ChInternet Ugly."

57 Hillenbrand, "Remaking Tank Man, in China."

on social media and digital platforms, Mergenthaler and Hess observe that Malaysian artists and galleries had not yet embraced the medium to a similar degree. Despite these differences, they show how various digital tactics not only enabled artists and galleries to overcome some of the boundaries of social (and cultural) distancing and promote their activities, but that these projects, although precarious and marginal to differing degrees, also created a space for critical reflection on life during the pandemic. Tan and Hess also discuss the rhetorical, technical, and aesthetic strategies these community-oriented art projects employed to evade both censorship as well as co-optation by nationalist "war on the pandemic" narratives. By staying under the radar of larger institutional networks and mainstream media, they show how these small-scale digital art spaces could become meaningful sites for solidarity with marginalised and vulnerable populations.

A different perspective on digital creativity during the Covid19 pandemic is explored in chapter 11, where Elvin Meng discusses the highly mediatised censorship case of Ai Fen's interview "The Whistle-Giver" (*Fa shaozi de ren* 發哨子的人). Instead of interpreting the content of this much-discussed case, Meng asks what the viral transformations of Ai's text reveal about the underlying cultural dynamics between virality, censorship and digital communities. Meng first distinguishes between what he terms "viral text" from viral media events, as they are conventionally understood. In the latter case, a given message may take on a myriad of forms, but it nevertheless retains its semantic stability. This was not the case with the translations of Ai's text that could only go "viral" through continuous transformations of its original content. Analysing the resulting "corrupted" translations into various languages and codes, Meng argues that the transformations of "The Whistle-Giver" confound our conventional understanding of what translation is and its social functioning; while evading both mechanical and manual censorship requires a certain degree of "infidelity" to the original, its target audience lies primarily within the Chinese language sphere. Closing with a reflection on the role of translation within the Sinocybersphere and the premodern "Sinographic sphere," Meng argues that it is paradoxically because of censorship technologies that the productive heterogeneity of the Chinese language and script does not just persist but continues to flourish.

## Digital Horizons

The topics covered in this book are necessarily but a sample of digital cultural practices across the Sinocybersphere, and many more subject matters such as online gaming or bullet commentary could have also been included in its purview. It thus does not aim to be a comprehensive discussion of digital China, but rather to showcase new directions in the study of Chinese culture in the digital age and offer points of departure for future scholarship. Although already pertinent before pandemic-related travel restrictions hit the globe, engagement with digital media has become an indispensable part of scholarship. Digital archives, platforms and applications not only provide important source materials but can sometimes also offer a more on-the-ground perspective than traditional media channels. Access to public debates is particularly difficult in China's highly regulated and censored media landscape, which has arguably increased the importance of micro-media such as WeChat Moments or Bilibili commentary threads. At times, it is perhaps more challenging or tiring to keep apace of these digital trends and debates than to review documents in an archive or conduct on-site fieldwork, but the speed of digital innovation also speaks to the vibrancy and importance of new media developments across the Sinocybersphere. Just as digital technologies have spurred a broad rethinking of print-based assumptions about authorship, text, and creativity as well as the development of new research methodologies such as digital ethnography, what the following chapters collectively show is that Chinese digital spaces offer crucial insights into the social and cultural possibilities of our digital condition.

## References

Baidu Baike 百度百科. "Fanqiang 翻墙 [To Breach the Firewall]."
https://baike.baidu.com/item/%E7%BF%BB%E5%A2%99/754773.

Berardi, Franco. *Futurability: The Age of Impotence and the Horizon of Possibility.* London, Brooklyn, NY.: Verso Books, 2017.

Bolter, Jay David, and Richard Grusin. *Remediation: Understanding New Media.* Cambridge, MA, USA: MIT Press, 1998.

Byler, Darren. *Terror Capitalism: Uyghur Dispossession and Masculinity in a Chinese City. Terror Capitalism.* Durham: Duke University Press, 2022.

Cai, Zong-qi, and Shengqing Wu. "Introduction: Emotion, Patterning, and Visuality in Chinese Literary Thought and Beyond." *Journal of Chinese Literature and Culture* 6, no. 1 (April 1, 2019): 1–14.

Chan, Ngai Keung, and Chi Kwok. "The Politics of Platform Power in Surveillance Capitalism: A Comparative Case Study of Ride-Hailing Platforms in China and the United States." *Global Media and China* 7, no. 2 (2022): 131–50.

China Internet Network Information Center. "Di 45 ci Zhongguo hulian wangluo fazhan zhuangkuang tongji baogao 第45次中国互联网络发展状况统计报告 [The 45th China Statistical Report on Internet Development]," September 29, 2020.

Chow, Rey. "Introduction: On Chineseness as a Theoretical Problem." *Boundary 2* 25, no. 3 (1998): 1–24.

Chow, Rey. "Toward an Ethics of Postvisuality: Some Thoughts on the Recent Work of Zhang Yimou." *Poetics Today* 25, no. 4 (December 1, 2004): 673–88.

Chun, Wendy Hui Kyong. *Control and Freedom: Power and Paranoia in the Age of Fiber Optics.* Cambridge, MA, USA: MIT Press, 2005.

Chun, Wendy Hui Kyong. "High-Tech Orientalism (Cyberpunk & Race)." *Critical Posthumanism Network* (blog), April 30, 2019. https://criticalposthumanism.net/high-tech-orientalism-cyberpunk-race/.

Fitzgerald, Richard, Todd Sandel, and Xiaoping Wu. "Chinese Social Media: Technology, Culture and Creativity." *Discourse, Context & Media* 48 (August 1, 2022): 100610.

Friis, Karsten, and Olav Lysne. "Huawei, 5G and Security: Technological Limitations and Political Responses." *Development and Change* 52, no. 5 (2021): 1174–95.

Geroulanos, Stefanos, and Leif Weatherby. "Cybernetics and the Human Sciences." *History of the Human Sciences* 33, no. 1 (February 1, 2020): 3–11.

Graham, Mark. "Geography/Internet: Ethereal Alternate Dimensions of Cyberspace or Grounded Augmented Realities?" *The Geographical Journal* 179, no. 2 (2013): 177–82.

Griffiths, James. *The Great Firewall of China: How to Build and Control an Alternative Version of the Internet.* London: Bloomsbury Publishing, 2021.

Guo, Shaohua. *The Evolution of the Chinese Internet: Creative Visibility in the Digital Public.* Stanford: Stanford University Press, 2020.

Hayles, Katherine. *How We Became Posthuman: Virtuas Bodies in Cybernetics.* Chicago: University of Chicago Press, 2015.

Hillenbrand, Margaret. "Remaking Tank Man, in China." *Journal of Visual Culture* 16, no. 2 (August 1, 2017): 127–66.

Hockx, Michel. *Internet Literature in China.* New York: Columbia University Press, 2015.

Holmes, Ros. "Meanwhile in China … Miao Ying and the Rise of ChInternet Ugly." *ARTMargins* 7, no. 1 (February 1, 2018): 31–57.

Hou, Rui. "Neoliberal Governance or Digitalized Autocracy? The Rising Market for Online Opinion Surveillance in China." *Surveillance & Society* 15, no. 3/4 (August 9, 2017): 418–24.

Hsiao, Chi-hua. "Authenticating Discourses of 'Being Oneself' on Monetary-Motivated Livestreams." *Discourse, Context & Media* 47 (June 1, 2022): 100592.

Huang, Yunying. "On Sinofuturism: Resisting Techno-Orientalism in Understanding Kuaishou, Douyin, and Chinese A.I." *Screen Bodies* 5, no. 2 (December 1, 2020): 46–62.

Jaguścik, Justyna, and Jessica Imbach. "Digital Society in China." *Asiatische Studien – Études Asiatiques* 76, no. 1 (March 1, 2022): 1–9.

Inwood, Heather. *Verse Going Viral: China's New Media Scenes.* Seattle: University of Washington Press, 2014.

Johnson, Matthew D., Luke Vulpiani, Keith B. Wagner, and Kiki Tianqi Yu. *China's IGeneration: Cinema and Moving Image Culture for the Twenty-First Century.* London: Bloomsbury Academic, 2014.

Lam, Tong. "The People's Algorithms: Social Credits and the Rise of China's Big (Br) Other." In *The New Politics of Numbers,* edited by Andrea Mennicken and Robert Salais, 71–95. Cham: Palgrave Macmillan, 2022.

Li, Yifei, and Judith Shapiro. *China Goes Green: Coercive Environmentalism for a Troubled Planet.* New York: John Wiley & Sons, 2020.

Luo Jiaqi. "Why Is Post-COVID China Embracing A Cyberpunk Aesthetic?" Jing Daily, October 7, 2020. https://jingdaily.com/china-luxury-trends-cyberpunk-covid-louis-vuitton/.

Ma, Shaoling. *The Stone and the Wireless: Mediating China, 1861–1906.* Durham: Duke University Press, 2021.

Maitra, Ani, and Rey Chow. "What's 'in'? Disaggregating Asia through New Media Actants." In *Routledge Handbook of New Media in Asia,* edited by Larissa Hjorth and Olivia Khoo, 29–39. London, New York: Routledge, 2015.

Marino, Mark C. *Critical Code Studies.* Cambridge, MA, USA: MIT Press, 2020.

Mitchell, W. J. T. "Introduction." In *Critical Terms for Media Studies,* edited by Mark B. N. Hansen and W. J. T. Mitchell, vii-xxii. Chicago, University of Chicago Press, 2010.

Mozur, Paul, Jonah M. Kessel, and Melissa Chan. "Made in China, Exported to the World: The Surveillance State." The New York Times, April 24, 2019, sec. Technology. https://www.nytimes.com/2019/04/24/technology/ecuador-surveillance-cameras-police-government.html.

Plantin, Jean-Christophe, Carl Lagoze, Paul N Edwards, and Christian Sandvig. "Infrastructure Studies Meet Platform Studies in the Age of Google and Facebook." *New Media & Society* 20, no. 1 (January 1, 2018): 293–310.

Plantin, Jean-Christophe, and Gabriele de Seta. "WeChat as Infrastructure: The Techno-Nationalist Shaping of Chinese Digital Platforms." *Chinese Journal of Communication* 12, no. 3 (July 3, 2019): 257–73.

Raedts, Maddie. "How China's Digital Ecosystems Are Shaping Western Social Media's Future." Forbes, March 8, 2021. https://www.forbes.com/sites/

forbesagencycouncil/2021/03/08/how-chinas-digital-ecosystems-are-shaping-western-social-medias-future/.

Riemenschnitter, Andrea. “Probing the Limits of Languaging: Material Ecology and Thing Agency in Yu Jian’s Poetry.” *International Communication of Chinese Culture* 6, no. 1 (2019): 39–61.

Schneider, Florian. *China’s Digital Nationalism.* Oxford Studies in Digital Politics. New York: Oxford University Press, 2018.

Shih, Shu-Mei. “The Concept of the Sinophone.” *PMLA* 126, no. 3 (2011): 709–18.

Shih, Shu-Mei. “Introduction: What Is Sinophone Studies?” In *Sinophone Studies: A Critical Reader,* edited by Shu-mei Shih, Chien-hsin Tsai, and Brian Bernards, 1–16. New York: Columbia University Press, 2013.

Strittmatter, Kai. *We Have Been Harmonised: Life in China’s Surveillance State.* Exeter: Old Street Publishing, 2019.

Surplus Value. “Wenyi, yuyan he juti de ren: Yu lishi xuejia Luo Xin liaotian 瘟疫,语言和具体的人:与历史学家罗新聊天 [The Pandemic, Language and Real People: A Chat with the Historian Luo Xin].” https://ipfs.io/ipfs/QmNXBfQ1v3J3dBvRoocrdzheCa5JVFnqzMAevV2kfXkG9N/.

Taneja, Harsh, and Angela Xiao Wu. “Does the Great Firewall Really Isolate the Chinese? Integrating Access Blockage With Cultural Factors to Explain Web User Behavior.” *The Information Society* 30, no. 5 (October 20, 2014): 297–309.

Tsai, Chien-hsin. “Issues and Controversies.” In *Sinophone Studies: A Critical Reader,* edited by Shu-mei Shih and Chien-hsin Tsai, 17–24. New York: Columbia University Press, 2013.

Veg, Sebastian. *Minjian: The Rise of China’s Grassroots Intellectuals.* New York: Columbia University Press, 2019.

Voci, Paola. *China on Video: Smaller-Screen Realities.* London, New York: Routledge, 2010.

Wallis, Cara. *Technomobility in China: Young Migrant Women and Mobile Phones.* New York: New York University Press, 2013.

Wang, David Der-wei. *The Lyrical in Epic Time: Modern Chinese Intellectuals and Artists Through the 1949 Crisis.* New York: Columbia University Press, 2015.

Wang, David Der-wei 王德威. “Wenxue xinglü yu shijie xiangxiang 文學行旅與世界想像 [Literary Travel and World Imagination].” *Mingpao Monthly,* 2006, 8–9.

Wang, Jing. *The Other Digital China: Nonconfrontational Activism on the Social Web.* Cambridge, Mass.: Harvard University Press, 2019.

Wang, Qingning. *The Chinese Internet: The Online Public Sphere, Power Relations and Political Communication.* London, New York: Routledge, 2020.

Wang, Xiaowei. *Blockchain Chicken Farm: And Other Stories of Tech in China’s Countryside.* New York: Farrar, Straus and Giroux, 2020.

Xia Deyuan 夏德元 and Zhou Weifeng 周伟峰. "Boke: Xin xing kouyu chuanbo xingtai de fazhan yu tingjue wenhua de huigui 播客：新型口语传播形态的发展与听觉文化的回归 [Podcasting: The Development of New Forms of Spoken Communication and the Return of Auditory Culture]." *Wenhua yishu yanjiu* 15, no. 01 (2022): 65–74+114.

Yang, Guobin, and Wei Wang. *Engaging Social Media in China: Platforms, Publics, and Production.* East Lansing, MI: Michigan State University Press, 2021.

Zhang, Charlie Yi. *Dreadful Desires: The Uses of Love in Neoliberal China.* Durham: Duke University Press.

Zhou, and Koh Ewe. "Boys Keep Flirting With Each Other on Chinese TV But Never Fall in Love." Vice, April 5, 2021. https://www.vice.com/en/article/7k95mg/boys-love-drama-china-tv-untamed-lgbtq.

# 1 Re-inventing Tianxia

## Coming-of-Age in *Xuanhuan* Fantasy Fiction

*Cui Qian*

**Abstract**
This chapter delves into the realm of xuanhuan fiction, sometimes translated as "Eastern Fantasy," and explores its distinctive characteristics and thematic elements. Through a close reading of individual texts, this chapter pushes back against the dominant understanding of xuanhuan fiction as commercialised, digital escapism, and details how xuanhuan is focused on the creation of alternative worlds that might challenge the social and political status quo. More specifically, I focus on the ways the pre-modern concept of tianxia is re-vised and re-interpreted in xuanhuan world-building to offer readers a vision of an alternative world order. Overall, this chapter provides important insights into the cultural and philosophical underpinnings of xuanhuan fiction and explores the reasons for the genre's appeal to contemporary audiences.

**Keywords:** Eastern fantasy, internet literature, mythology, Chinese philosophy, coming-of-age narratives

*Xuanhuan* 玄幻 fiction, commonly translated as "Eastern Fantasy,"[1] is today arguably the most popular form of Internet literature in China. For example, the largest literary website, Qidian Zhongwenwang 起點中文網, has more than 700,000 works listed under the category of xuanhuan fiction – almost twice as many as urban fiction, which is second on the list. This chapter delves into the realm of xuanhuan fiction, exploring its distinctive characteristics and thematic elements. More specifically, I focus on the coming-of-age journey, which is one of the most salient characteristics of the genre. The protagonists of these narratives undergo

1 Tian, "Fantasy Is More Believable," 170.

Imbach, Jessica. *Digital China.* Amsterdam: Amsterdam University Press, 2024
DOI: 10.5117/9789463720670_CH01

profound personal growth as they move from youth to maturity, often through arduous trials and self-discovery. This transformative process not only shapes the individual characters, but also serves as a fictional mirror of contemporary social and cultural developments. Central to this process is a revision of the pre-modern concept of tianxia 天下 (all under heaven), which plays a crucial role in xuanhuan world-building strategies. Rooted in traditional Chinese philosophy, tianxia refers to an idealised realm governed by principles of harmony, justice and moral integrity. Xuanhuan narratives often incorporate the concept of tianxia as a guiding principle, offering readers a vision of an alternative world order in which individuals strive to cultivate themselves and navigate complex social hierarchies. In the first part of this chapter, I explore recent discussions of xuanhuan fiction and the relationship between the traditional concept of tianxia and its modern reimaginings. Through a comparative reading of popular xuanhuan novels the second part investigates the religious and philosophical underpinnings that shape xuanhuan worldbuilding. Pushing back against the dominant interpretation of xuanhuan fiction as commercialised, digital escapism, I show how xuanhuan has become a critical platform for the creation of alternative worlds that might challenge the social and political status quo. Moreover, I argue that this philosophical and political dimension accounts for the genre's enduring appeal to contemporary audiences.

## Xuanhuan as Utopia and Heterotopia

Today, xuanhuan fiction is one of the most dominant cultural forms within the Chinese entertainment industry. The Internet has played a seminal role in xuanhuan's success story, lowering the threshold for publication for amateur writers and facilitating community engagement around popular themes. This popularity has largely been met with disdain by literary critics, who view online fiction in general, and xuanhuan in particular, as a commercial activity rather than an art form, lacking aesthetic sophistication and philosophical depth. Yet, writers and readers of online fiction champion their "grassroots carnival (*caogen kuanghuan* 草根狂歡)"[2] by upholding slogans such as "To YY [abbreviation for *yiyin* 意淫] is not guilty, to dream is tenable," largely ignoring the cultural elite's criticism of their undignified aspiration of "amusing ourselves to death."[3] YY is an abbreviation for *yiyin*

2 Shao, "Wangluo shidai," 15.
3 Shao, "Wangluo shidai," 16.

意淫, a word taken from *Dream of the Red Chamber*, in which it is used to describe Jia Baoyu's idiosyncratic propensity to engage in unpragmatic thoughts and feelings. It can be translated as "lust of the mind" or "mindful immersion" to convey Baoyu's excessive longing to be carried away from the sordid reality and immerse himself in other worlds. The Chinese character *yi* 意 can mean mind, will, or thought; *yin* 淫 can mean immersion, lust, or excessiveness. In contemporary online slang, however, the term commonly refers to indulgent daydreaming.

Nevertheless, to maintain popularity and financial success, xuanhuan writers often walk a fine line between creative storytelling/dreaming and market demands. This tension between creative exploration, subversion and commodification underscores the complex nature of xuanhuan fantasy fiction as both a product shaped by commercial considerations and a catalyst for unsettling dominant narratives through the creation of alternative worlds. These alternative worlds and dreams can be read as what David Wang refers to as "literary ecologies," in which the interactions between "ideological doctrines and individual eccentricities, as well as suppressive forces and avant-garde impulses" give rise to "a kaleidoscopic structure of feeling."[4] To this end, xuanhuan fiction draws on traditional Chinese culture, imitating the aesthetics of traditional Chinese mythology and folklore, and often making references to the literary classics.[5] The stories combine fantasy, martial arts, romance and coming-of-age experiences as fundamental elements of the narrative, and are aimed at a primarily young adult readership.[6] Although traditional cultural elements are often mobilised in patriotic campaigns, we should not dismiss the fact that Chinese youth look to traditional Chinese resources to imagine a new world as merely an expression of a nationalist desire, but also, and more importantly, as a mobilisation of traditional resources to reimagine the contemporary Chinese social order. In a public talk during the Occupy Wall Street movement, Slavoj Žižek, although hardly an expert on Chinese literature, intriguingly referred to Chinese fantasy literature as a site for dreaming alternative realities:

> In mid-April 2011, the Chinese government prohibited on TV, films, and novels all stories that contain alternate reality or time travel. This is a good sign for China. These people still dream about alternatives, so you

4 Wang, *Why Fiction Matters*, 6.

5 For more details on the definition and general characteristics of *xuanhuan* fiction, see Li and Wang, "Lun Mingdai," 5.

6 Li and Wang, 5.

> have to prohibit this dreaming. Here, we don't need a prohibition because the ruling system has even oppressed our capacity to dream. Look at the movies that we see all the time. It's easy to imagine the end of the world. An asteroid destroying all life and so on. But you cannot imagine the end of capitalism.[7]

Žižek's perspective on China is based primarily on his impressions and imagination rather than on scientific analysis, which casts doubt on his interpretation. However, his comparison of popular culture in China and the West, where individuals are constrained by the dominant system and struggle to break free from capitalist ideologies, points to the political possibilities embedded in fantasy fiction. A corollary implication underlying Žižek's statement is that fantasy and time-travel fiction can lead readers through a process of "subjectivisation," whereby they disidentify themselves from the dominant ideology and become able to reclaim their ability to dream of alternative worlds. Žižek sees this ability as a crucial driving force for social change.

Media scholar Shao Yanjun sees Žižek's view of the situation in China as a wishful misunderstanding imagined from afar: "The picture of China in Žižek's imagination is still Orwellian," while China, as one of the most powerful driving forces of the global circulation of capital, has long since led its white-collar netizens, who produce these time-travel fictions, into the Huxleyan "brave new world."[8] In this respect, China shares the same post-Enlightenment impasse with the West. For Shao, xuanhuan instead challenges the literary hegemony of realism established by the May Fourth writers and reflects how realism has lost its power to guide mainstream culture and public discourse. Shao explains that there is an inextricable relation between desire, fantasy, online fiction, and ideology:

> We have to admit that we are living in a time when traditional values, ethics, and social codes are collapsed. The super-ego breaks down, and the id is amplified. Online fiction is an enormous container loaded with daydreams. It is a space of fantasy where desire is both satisfied and re-produced. Especially with those most popular works, they do not merely reflect the most prominent desire and anxiety in today's China but also bring about the latent desires in people's subconscious. As Žižek describes: "it is precisely the role of fantasy to give the coordinates of the subject's

7 Žižek, "Transcript."

8 Shao, "Yituobang," 17.

> desire, to specify its object, to locate the position the subject assumes in it. It is only through fantasy that the subject is constituted as desiring: *through fantasy, we learn how to desire*."[9] Instead of whitewashing reality, online fiction reconstructs reality by evoking fantasies. They locate the position of desire and guide people in how to desire. In this way, they take the place of dysfunctional elite literature to accomplish literature's ideological function.[10]

Rather than seeing online fantasy fiction as a site for counter-narratives that challenge, rebel against, or subvert dominant socio-political discourses and ideologies, Shao argues that while xuanhuan participates in the ideological trajectory of the current regime, it also reflects how traditional media have lost their ability to meaningfully address contemporary issues. Xuanhuan's fantasy worlds, Shao argues, can thus also be read as heterotopias that are not only entangled with official ideology and other public discourses, but also open the door to alternative personal choices and collective yearnings.[11]

The views of Žižek and Shao offer two promising approaches to considering the worlds depicted in xuanhuan fiction. Žižek emphasises the political efficacy of xuanhuan fiction in creating utopian counter-narratives that challenge the dominant ideology and entrenched social structure, and in forging and mobilising subjects in whom a new political consciousness could be awakened. Shao, on the other hand, examines the external historical (dis)continuities, cultural entanglements and production mechanisms of xuanhuan fiction, which she sees as enabling alternative personal choices in the post-Enlightenment context. According to Shao, world-building in xuanhuan fiction does not so much challenge or replace reality as provide a zone for the (re)discovery and refashioning of modern identities.

Taking both perspectives into account, this chapter explores the world-building strategies in xuanhuan fiction and investigates how they resonate with utopian longings of today's digitally native youth. More specifically, I take Heather Inwoods discussion of worldmaking processes in Chinese internet fiction as my point of departure, to read xuanhuan fiction as a temporal departure from and creative remaking of the world.[12] Inwood identifies three central aspects to this process: time-space, logic (the goals

9 Žižek, *Looking Awry*, 6. Emphasis original.

10 Shao, "Yituobang," 17. Translated by author. If not otherwise indicated, all translations from Chinese sources are mine.

11 Ibid., 20–23.

12 Heather Inwood, "Making Worlds in Chinese Internet Fiction," China's New Super Cities."

and impetus that set the plots in motion), and system (the narrative structures shaped by the plot). In my reading I focus on how these aspects are expressed through the notion of tianxia, which is "perhaps the first term that the ancient Chinese invented to conceptualise what they perceived or imagined as the world."[13] As a shibboleth of traditional cultural and moral values that summons up "a broad pattern of diplomacy, ritual and hierarchy,"[14] the term tianxia reemerges as a currency "in the ideological interstices of contemporary China."[15]

The ancient notion of tianxia connotes at least two worldview models: One "envisions an earthly and horizontal formation of the phenomenal"[16] and signifies a spatial order centered on the consciousness of the individual, which, through the individual's self-cultivation, reaches out to the family, the nation, and the entire tianxia. This worldview bestows human activities with an ethical and geopolitical structure." As a category beyond the finite framework of the state, tianxia thus signifies a spatial totality whose boundaries are marked only by the limitations of human experience and imagination."[17] The other model envisions the world in a more decentered way. "In classical Chinese, tian could refer both to the physical sky and the transcendental force of creation."[18] Symbolising the "divine dimensions of the supreme Dao or Way," tian gives rise to a worldview that centres on the interests of all beings "under heaven" instead of one individual's consciousness.[19] This model accentuates the transcendental aspect of human life. Throughout Chinese history, rulers exploited tianxia "to serve their private and despotic desires,"[20] but it also contributed to multiculturalism and pursuits of peaceful coexistence under dynastic regimes.[21]

The contemporary revival of tianxia is multifaceted. While the official version links it to the "great revival of the Chinese nation (*Zhonghua minzu de weida fuxing* 中華民族的偉大復興)," intellectuals have constructed alternative narratives that deviate from the official version, seeking a

13 Lan, "Zhang Yimou's 'Hero,'" 3.

14 B. Wang, *World Order*, 1. For more on the concept of *tianxia*, see ibid., 1–24. See also Lan, "Zhang Yimou's 'Hero'," 1–12; J. Xu, "Xin *Tianxia zhuyi*."

15 Lan, "Zhang Yimou's 'Hero,'" 2.

16 Lan.

17 Lan.

18 Lan, 3.

19 Lan, 4.

20 Lan, 12.

21 J. Xu, "Xin *Tianxia zhuyi*."

solution to today's contradictory world conditions.[22] As Lan elucidates, "conflicting ideological forces in China have been attempting to reclaim this concept [of tianxia], precisely because they have all found it to offer an alternative to the modern discourse of nationalism, and thus a solution to the historical impasse caused by the contradictory conditions of the world today."[23]

In xuanhuan novels, the pursuit of a world beyond human-centreed politics is central to worldbuilding. The concept of tianxia plays a dual role in this process. Firstly, it provides a valuable framework for digitally reconstructing the spatial and temporal aspects of the world. Secondly, through its extensive use in xuanhuan fiction, tianxia can be recontextualised and reinvented from the grassroots level. The reimagination of tianxia in xuanhuan fiction thus prompt important questions: How does the concept of tianxia shape the creation of new worlds in these narratives? How do these reimaginations reshape the traditional understanding of tianxia in light of contemporary concerns? Furthermore, how does this reinvented notion of tianxia, driven by millennials, contribute to the formation of contemporary perspectives and subjectivities?

Before delving into a detailed analysis of specific works, it is important to highlight that while these works pay tribute to classics like *Dream of the Red Chamber* (*Honglou meng* 紅樓夢) and *Journey to the West* (*Xiyouji* 西遊記), I do not read them as expressions of an individual author's insights and creativity. Instead, I analyse the concept of tianxia as a fictional strategy for exploring collective utopian aspirations for alternative worlds, which are shared by both writers and readers. Put differently, I analyse the search for a Chinese identity in xuanhuan narratives in relation to the moral crisis experienced by contemporary Chinese youth. Underneath xuanhuan's beautified oriental spectacles, these grassroots reimaginations of tianxia reflect a crisis in a contemporary society, one that cannot be satisfied by official nationalism and patriotism.

## Re-inventing Tianxia

The dominant spatial logic in xuanhuan fiction revolves around the dynamic interaction between two distinct realms: the celestial and the demonic.

22 Lan discerns three camps in the intellectual group: liberals, New Left, and "cultural nativists"; Lan, "Zhang Yimou's 'Hero,'" 7. See also Xu, "Xin *Tianxia zhuyi*."

23 Lan, "Zhang Yimou's 'Hero'," 2.

Crucially, xuanhuan fiction departs from the traditional portrayal of heaven as a mystical and very vaguely described realm governed by unquestionable moral principles. Instead, it is depicted in great narrative detail, drawing on dynastic imaginaries as well as a secularised concept of tianxia. This demystification of heaven raises important questions regarding the ways that xuanhuan fiction reimagines or indeed reinvents tianxia: How does *tianxia,* both as a moral principle and as a political concept, generate worldbuilding strategies? And how does a secularised tian offer transcendental perspectives? To investigate these questions, I begin by scrutinising the spatial and temporal reconceptualisation of worldbuilding in *xuanhuan* fiction.

Spatial demarcation holds a very high significance within the realm of xuanhuan fiction, serving not only as a backdrop for the narratives but also carrying moral and political implications. The prevalent model often employed is the dichotomy between the Heaven Realm or God Realm and the Demon Realm. This god-demon dualism forms the foundation of numerous fantasy narratives in both Eastern and Western traditions, but the local genealogy of this literary motif is particularly pertinent to xuanhuan worldbuilding. In his summary of the structural characteristics of traditional Chinese mythology, Lu Xun coined the term "god-demon fiction (*Shen-Mo xiaoshuo*) 神魔小說" with reference to this dualistic concept:

> For centuries a struggle for supremacy raged among Confucianism, Daoism, and Buddhism until these three religions decided to tolerate each other and consider themselves as stemming from a common source. Then all concepts of right and wrong, true and false, good and evil, merged to be redivided into two main camps: orthodoxy and heterodoxy. I call this the struggle between gods and devils, though no special name for such literature existed.[24]

Lu Xun's notion not only teases out a narrative framework underlying premodern fantastic works, such as *Journey to the West* and *Investiture of the Gods* 封神演義, but also plays a decisive role in the political discourses and aesthetic representations during Mao's regime. During this period and despite the Maoist dismissal of religious beliefs, the preservation of the "sublime figure of history"[25] relied on the discursive tactic of demonising individuals as "ox demons and snake spirits (niu-gui-she-shen 牛鬼蛇神)." This dualistic categorisation of social groups formed a fundamental

24 Lu Xun, *A Brief History*, 187–78. Translation modified.

25 Wang, *The Sublime Figure of History*.

principle underlying socialist narratives, exerting significant influence on moral and political discussions during the Cold War era and retaining its potency in contemporary times.

Xuanhuan fiction introduces a nuanced reinterpretation of the god-demon dualism within traditional Chinese cultures, adding religious connotations and philosophical depth to the simplified version that has shaped public discourse in recent decades. The portrayal of the Heaven Realm reflects a patriarchal and hierarchical society, characterised by formal rules and rituals reminiscent of Chinese dynastic empires. Conversely, denizens of the Demon Realm are depicted not as absolute villains but as a tribe with distinctive customs and rituals, often congenial and submissive to the leadership of the Heaven Realm. While many are harmless and contribute to affirming and counterbalancing the Heaven Realm's dominance, the emergence of excessive desires, such as for power or unrequited love, can trigger a malevolent spirit, posing a threat to the peaceful coexistence of all realms (hui tian mie di 毁天滅地). The sealing and re-sealing of this malevolent spirit, often performed by the king of the Demon Realm, serve as crucial narrative driving forces, exemplified in popular online fiction and TV dramas such as *Sansheng sanshi shi li taohua* 三生三世十裡桃花, also known as *Eternal Love.* While some narratives reinforce the official ideology of tianxia, others subvert it by challenging the essentialised identities of gods and demons. This can be observed in works such as *Love and Destiny* (Chun-Xi yuan 宸汐緣) and *Ancient Love Poetry* (Qiangu jue chen 千古玦塵).

Crucially, the demonic is not a stable identity and in stories such as *The Journey of Flower* (Huaqiangu 花千骨) and *Ashes of Love* (Xiangmi chenchen jin ru shuang 香蜜沉沉燼如霜), where the boundary between the Heaven Realm and the Demon Realm is challenged and blurred. Beings in the Heaven Realm may engage in wicked deeds, while those born or labelled as devils or demons can exhibit extraordinarily kind-hearted traits and loving behaviour. In *The Blood of Youth* (*Shaonian ge xing* 少年歌行), the prince of the Demon Realm raises a profound question with Buddhist connotations while observing a Buddhist monk practising martial arts to vanquish demons and devils (*zhan yao chu mo* 斬妖除魔): "When one is so eager to eliminate demons, what is the difference between him and the demons? 除魔之心如此之重, 與魔何異?"[26] This inquiry recontextualises the god-demon dualism within a Buddhist framework, illuminating the fluid boundary between gods and demons. It emphasises that exhibiting a merciless stance towards adversaries, even as a self-righteous deity, blurs

26 Zhou Munan, "Shaonian ge xing."

the distinction between oneself and a demon. Compassion emerges as a crucial factor in distinguishing between good and evil.

These literary works present thought-provoking challenges to the official socialist discourse, reflecting a creative and subversive undercurrent that can be traced back to the exploration of the orthodoxy-heterodoxy dialectic (*zheng-xie* 正邪) in martial arts fiction.[27] However, in contrast to the typically binary world of the Jianghu 江湖 found in this genre, xuanhuan fiction portrays a more intricate realm inspired by tianxia.[28] Works such as *To the Sky Kingdom, Love and Destiny, Ancient Love Poetry,* and *Ashes of Love* showcase a diverse array of coexisting realms. Of particular interest are two types: the utopian realms modelled on Tao Yuanming's famous *Peach Blossom Spring* (Taohua yuan 桃花源) and the human world portrayed as purgatory. For instance, in *To the Sky Kingdom,* Ten Miles of Peach Blossom (*Shi li tao lin* 十裡桃林) is a secluded place where a select group of individuals engage in cultured activities, while Green Hills (*Qing Qiu* 青丘) serves as an Arcadia where various earthly beings coexist harmoniously. The founders of these realms, close friends who distance themselves from the political affairs of the Heaven Realm and the Demon Realm, play a significant role. Similarly, in *Ashes of Love,* inhabitants of the Flower Realm (*Hua Jie* 花界) choose to remain detached from power dynamics, sealing themselves off from external disturbances. These utopian realms, often the origins of the main characters, serve as crucial settings that counterbalance the political tensions between the Heaven Realm and the Demon Realm.

Intersecting with the spatial segmentation, there usually exists another demarcation based on ethnicity. Inspired by traditional supernatural genres such as zhiguai 志怪, xuanhuan fiction introduces the concept of a ,true form' (zhenshen 真身) for its characters, which can be traced back to a non-human lineage or innate essence. These "true forms" can take the form of plants such as flowers or trees, animals such as foxes or snakes, mythical creatures such as dragons or phoenixes, objects such as stones or mirrors, or even phenomena such as teardrops or frost. The true form represents a non-human essence that encompasses both physical and spiritual aspects. It suggests that the human body is merely an illusion, while the non-human spirit persists even after the body dies, awaiting a future return. A powerful

27 Notable examples include *The Legend of the Condor Heroes* (*She diao yingxiong zhuan* 射雕英雄傳), *The Return of the Condor Heroes* (*Shendiao xialü* 神雕俠侶), and *The Deer and the Cauldron* (*Lu ding Ji* 鹿鼎記) by Jin Yong 金庸. See Ling, "*Qian tan.*"

28 Literarily translated sometimes as "rivers and lakes," jianghu refers to a mystical wilderness where Robin Hood-style heroes flourish.

spirit has the ability to move freely between different forms and inhabit different beings. These true forms not only provide beings with alternative identities and a sense of solidarity, but also imbue the world and cosmos with the fluidity and interconnectedness of all beings. Xuanhuan fiction thus takes a critical stance by destabilising the modern anthropocentric worldview and restoring the world to a state of flux and interconnectedness. Works such as *Rattan* (Banyao Siteng 半妖司藤) conscientiously explore the interdependence between humans and the natural environment by exploring the harmonious relationship and continuity between humans and plants. The peaceful coexistence of multiple spatial realms, cultural and political systems, and ethnic groups modelled on tianxia in xuanhuan fiction challenges both dominant socio-political discourses and the dominant epistemological worldview shaped by modern Enlightenment ideologies.

It is in this context that the notion of Bildung, as a form of education and self-cultivation, plays a crucial role, and which I consider to be one of the most important factors in the enormous popularity of xuanhuan. *To the Sky Kingdom,* for example, depicts a heavenly kingdom governed by a loose and inclusive hierarchy, fostering a multicultural and multiethnic realm of exchange and interaction, where self-cultivation is prioritised for the development of sympathy, compassion and a deepened sensitivity to love, as opposed to the modern pursuit of intellectual knowledge.

At the same time, the path of self-cultivation follows a hierarchical structure: the progression from plant or animal to the attainment of human form, low immortal, high immortal, and finally to god or goddess involves various stages of learning, cultivation, ordeal, and trials that signify physical, mental, and spiritual growth, forming a ladder-climbing paradigm. This teleological system prioritises the temporal dimension over spatial and ethnic divisions, and while it is reminiscent of the market-driven social system, it operates on a distinct value system, in which the environment plays a crucial role. For example, a stone, a flower, or a snake may absorb the nourishing vital force of an endowed place in which it stands, grows or lives, taking on human form after hundreds or thousands of years. While rooted in traditional mythology and fantasy tales, this principle demonstrates how xuanhuan fiction subtly generates a renewed focus on the profound connection between beings and their living environment in today's world, where the fundamental importance of the environment is often disregarded.

As in martial arts fiction, the process of self-cultivation typically involves joining a sect or becoming the disciple of a master. However, instead of focusing solely on martial skills, xuanhuan foregrounds mental and spiritual growth, aiming to transcend one's old self and the cultivation of compassion for all forms of beings. In addition, the magical skills practised in xuanhuan challenge not only human physical limits but also the established natural laws, emphasising a Buddhist concern for the diverse cosmos rather than a human-centred pursuit of righteousness in a divided jianghu.

In addition to the conditions mentioned above, the journey of seeking a higher self is primarily influenced by the ordeals and trials associated with the Buddhist term "kalpa" or "aeon" (jie 劫). A kalpa represents a temporal concept that denotes the duration between the creation and recreation of a world in Buddhist cosmology, signifying the destruction of a world to be regenerated. When applied to contemporary narratives, the concept of kalpa undergoes a modern transformation, wherein the process of losing and regaining a world becomes a subjective path towards enlightenment. As expressed by the God of Human Destiny in *Love and Destiny*: "A creation and its ruin is a kalpa; a birth and its extinguishment is a kalpa; a change of heaven and earth is a big kalpa; the overturning of a belief (*xinnian qingfu* 心念傾覆) is a small kalpa."[29]

One of the most common types of kalpa in the xuanhuan world is the trial of thunderbolts from heaven (*leijie* 雷劫), in which one must endure and protect oneself from a series of successive thunderbolts. The process involves great physical pain. To withstand external destruction, one must possess both fortitude and endurance, along with the inner energy (*qi* 氣) cultivated over thousands of years. Vitality and mortality exist simultaneously throughout this process, creating an occasion where death is a possibility, but survival results in an immediate ascent to a higher rank. Another equally prevalent type of kalpa is the descension to the human world (*xiafan* 下凡).[30] A deity's descension to the human world to experience a kalpa (*xiafan lijie* 下凡歷劫) is one of the most popular motifs and narrative archetypes in the Chinese literary tradition and deeply rooted in Buddho-Daoist beliefs of spiritual Enlightenment.[31] It is also among the most often-adopted plot strategies in xuanhuan fiction, which bestows the traditional motif with a contemporary twist by shifting the focus of concern from religious contemplation to the transformative potentials of experiences in the human life. To undergo the so-called seven sufferings of human life (*rensheng qi ku* 人生七苦)[32] is highlighted as a necessary experience for

29 Zhao Na and Chen Liwen, *Chen xi yuan,* Episode 32.

30 Hereafter referred to as "descension for a kalpa."

31 See G. Wu, *Yuanxing yu muti*, 103–65; see also H. Yang, "Jicheng yu chaoyue," 68.

32 This concept is borrowed from the notion of *duḥkha* (suffering, 苦) in Buddhism, referring to human birth, aging, illness, death, association with the hated and loathed, separation from the beloved, and not getting what is desired. While more types of suffering are included in the

spiritual enlightenment on the path to become a god or goddess. If one goes through all the sufferings in a human life without giving up kindness, compassion, and a loving heart, the subsequent return to heaven would bring him or her to a higher level of consciousness.

In xuanhuan fiction, however, the Buddhist notion of human life as illusory and empty is downplayed. Instead, the subjective experiences of humans, including their emotions and sensations, are considered essential for their process of cultivation. Unlike traditional narratives of "descension for a kalpa," where human ordeals lead to a realisation of life's emptiness, xuanhuan fiction emphasises the enlightenment gained through earthly experiences, cultivating compassion for human suffering and deepening one's understanding of *qing* 情 (emotional connections). In this aspect, xuanhuan fiction aligns with the early modern literary tradition established in *Dream of the Red Chamber,* which recognises the pervasive influence of *qing* on both human and divine beings.[33] A kalpa of love (*qingjie* 情劫) serves as an overarching narrative frame in *Dream*. In most xuanhuan fictions, however, a "kalpa of love" usually occurs at a pivotal moment in the narrative and marks a shift of perspective from the earthly to the heavenly realm. As such, they serve as a catalyst for a change of perspective on one's own existence.

Yet, again very similarly to *Dream*, xuanhuan fiction gives qing full rein, to such an immense extent that it exceeds the characters' subjective delimitations and emerges as an agency for the whole cosmos. The unbounded intensity of qing sometimes overrides the teleological paradigm of self-cultivation and endows the universe in xuanhuan fiction with a trans-temporal and trans-spatial dimension epitomised in the proliferated time-travel narrative framework. In *The Eternal Love* (Shuang shi chongfei 雙世寵妃,) for example, the male and female protagonists follow each other in different times and spaces to change their destiny of separation. In the television sequel to the same story, the male protagonist tells the female protagonist: "Whichever time and space we are in, whoever we become, I will invariably find you, fall in love with you, marry you again and again. Incarnations after incarnations, we will never be apart."[34] The spiritual and transcendental pursuit of an eternal bond is vigorously pursued in romantic love, which drives the loving subjects to break through both their karmic destiny and the epistemological and existential delimitations of reality.

Buddhist concept, these seven sufferings are the most manifested in *xuanhuan* fiction. On the Buddhist concept of *dukkha*, see Harvey, "Dukkha," 26–32.

33 I refer to the eighty-chapter versions of *Dream of the Red Chamber* written by Cao Xueqin.

34 Yang Shiye, *Shuang shi chongfei 2*, Episode 30.

What deserves further attention is that although going through a kalpa is meant to be a task for an individual, it usually involves other people's help, which is, surprisingly, not deemed as cheating but as a success in developing intimate relationships. For example, in both *To the Sky Kingdom* and *Ancient Love Poetry*, the protagonists' trial of thunder strikes (*leijie* 雷劫) are undertaken by the protagonist's teachers; in *To the Sky Kingdom, Ashes of Love*, and *Love and Destiny*, the characters' kalpa in the human world are assisted by their immortal lovers and friends in heaven. Surviving the kalpa in xuanhuan fiction is not solely an individual triumph but a collective achievement that deepens interpersonal connections. This narrative perspective shifts the focus of teleological Bildung from self-fulfillment to the cultivation of companionship and intimate relationships among characters. Xuanhuan fiction thereby transcends self-indulgence and hedonistic digital escapism, instead weaving narratives that celebrate the profound journey of re-thinking contemporary values and building alternative communities.

## The Generative Possibilities of Xuanhuan

Xuanhuan fiction unveils a spatially diverse realm where the interplay of good and evil, hierarchical order and utopian decentralisation, sociopolitical segmentation and cultural unification, epistemic reification and cognitive fluidity harmoniously coexist. Through its teleological Bildung, it highlights a value system that places compassion, companionship, and connectivity at the forefront, fostering stability amidst spatial diversity while nurturing a rich tapestry of identities and subjectivities. From the dynamic interplay of love and hatred to unwavering heroism, from tender contemplation of human existence to transcendent romance spanning life and death, from intimate connections with other beings to a sense of responsibility and altruism, xuanhuan fiction embarks on a journey that pushes the boundaries of humanity and explores the boundless depths of human emotions. These extraordinary quests not only challenge the dominance of science and knowledge in our anthropocentric world but also illuminate the contours of a utopian "alternative reality."

Compared with the literary classics, xuanhuan fiction may lack philosophical depth and aesthetic sophistication; and because it is very often tamed to conform to official narratives, it can easily lose its critical edge. Pandering to market-oriented consumerism can also sometimes blunt xuanhuan fiction's otherwise sharp criticism of contemporary society, and its naïve and fantastical elements can tarnish the genre's utopian aspirations in the eyes of many critics. However, this does not mean that the underlying politics and philosophical ruminations should be read superficially. As my analysis shows, xuanhuan fiction gives teleological learning and self-cultivation an important role in transcending boundaries and exploring new identities. Cultivating sensitivity to emotions and love, which form the basis of sympathy and compassion, emerges as a new driving force for envisioning a reimagined tianxia tailored to today's digital-native youth. Xuanhuan fiction should therefore not be dismissed as mere "play," but also understood as a transformative space that actively engages in the renegotiation of contemporary values and offering new possibilities for personal and societal growth. Xuanhuan's visionary realm emerges from the depths of society and Chinese history as a compelling way to generate alternatives to both the top-down dreams of the state and the collapse of community values. In the process, the individual voices of the many xuanhuan novels merge into a resounding, nationwide chorus, forming a powerful incantation that gestures towards new utopian possibilities.

## References

Buddhism in a Nutshell. "The Buddhas in the Three Periods of Time." http://www.buddhistdoor.com/OldWeb/bdoor/archive/nutshell/teach36.htm.

Dianxian 电线. "Xiangmi chenchen jin ru Shuang 香蜜沉沉烬如霜 [Ashes of Love]." Situ 思兔. June 22, 2016. https://www.sto.cx/book-38184-1.html.

González-Reimann, Luis. "Cosmic Cycles, Cosmology, and Cosmography." In *Brill's Encyclopedia of Hinduism Online*, edited by Knut A. Jacobsen, Helene Basu, Angelika Malinar, and Vasudha Narayanan, 411–428. Leiden: Brill, 2016.

Harvey, Peter. "Dukkha, Non-Self, and the Teaching on the Four 'Noble Truths.'" In *A Companion to Buddhist Philosophy*, edited by Steven M. Emmanuel, 26–45. Chichester: Wiley Blackwell, 2013.

Hinderliter, Beth, William Kaizen, Vered Maimon, Jaleh Mansoor, and Seth McCormick, eds. *Communities of Sense: Rethinking Aesthetics and Politics*. Durham, NC: Duke University Press, 2009.

Inwood, Heather. "Making Worlds in Chinese Internet Fiction." China's New Super Cities: A Cultural Journey. Guest lecture at University of St. Gallen, St. Gallen, Switzerland, May 2, 2023.

Lan, Feng. "Zhang Yimou's *Hero*: Reclaiming the Martial Arts Film for 'All under Heaven.'" *Modern Chinese Literature and Culture* 20, no. 1 (Spring 2008): 1–43.

Li Ru 李如, and Zongfa Wang 王宗法. "Lun Mingdai shen mo xiaoshuo dui dangdai wangluo xuanhuan xiaoshuo de yingxiang 论明代神魔小说对当代网络玄

幻小说的影响 [On Influences of God-demon Fiction from Ming Dynasty on Contemporary Online Xuanhuan Fiction]." *Journal of Ming-Qing Fiction Studies* 113, no. 3 (2014): 4–15.

Li, Wai-yee. *Enchantment and Disenchantment: Love and Illusion in Chinese Literature*. Princeton, NJ: Princeton University Press, 2014.

Lu Xun 鲁迅. *A Brief History of Chinese Fiction*. Translated by Hsien-yi Yang and Gladys Yang. Beijing: Foreign Languages Press, 1976.

Lu Xun 鲁迅. *Zhongguo xiaoshuo shi lue* 中国小说史略 [A Brief History of Chinese Novels]. Tianjin: Baihua wenyi chubanshe, 2002.

Rancière, Jacques. "Politics, Identification, Subjectivization." In *The Identity in Question*, edited by John Rajchman, 63–72. London: Routledge, 1995.

Shao Yanjun 邵燕君. "Wangluo shidai: Xin wenxue chuantong de duanlie yu 'zhuliu wenxue' de chongjian 网络时代: 新文学传统的断裂与'主流文学'的重建 [The Internet Era: Ruptures of New Literary Tradition and the Re-establishment of 'Mainstream Literature']." *Nanfang wentan*, no. 6 (2012): 14–21.

Shao Yanjun 邵燕君. "Zai 'Yituobang' li jiangou 'geren linglei xuanze' huanxiang kongjian—Wangluo wenxue de yishi xingtai gongneng zhi yi zhong 在'异托邦'里建构'个人另类选择'幻象空间—网络文学的意识形态功能之一种 [Constructing Illusional Spaces for 'Individual Alternative Choices' in 'Heterotopia': One Type of Ideological Function of Online Literature]." *Wenyi yanjiu*, no. 4 (2012): 16–25.

Tangqi Gongzi 唐七公子. "Sansheng sanshi shi li taohua 三生三世十里桃花 [Eternal Love]." Situ 思兔. June 22, 2016. https://www.sto.cx/book-39192-1.html.

Tian, Xiaoli. "Fantasy Is More Believable: The Shadow Civil Sphere in Chinese Online Fiction." In *The Civil Sphere in East Asia*, edited by Jeffrey C. Alexander, David A. Palmer, Sunwoong Park, and Agnes Shuk-mei Ku, 167–87. Cambridge, UK: Cambridge University Press, 2019.

Wang, Ban. *Chinese Visions of World Order: Tianxia, Culture, and World Politics*. Durham, NC: Duke University Press, 2017.

Wang, Ban. *The Sublime Figure of History: Aesthetics and Politics in Twentieth-Century China*. Stanford, CA: Stanford University Press, 1997.

Wang, David Der-wei 王德威. *Why Fiction Matters in Contemporary China*. Waltham, MA: Brandeis University Press, 2020.

Wang, David Der-wei 王德威. *Xiangxiang Zhongguo de fangfa: lishi, xiaoshuo, xushi* 想像中国的方法: 历史 小说 叙事 [Ways to Imagine China: History, Novel, Narrative]. Beijing: SDX Joint Publishing, 1998.

Wu Guangzheng 吴光正. *Zhongguo gudai xiaoshuo de yuanxing yu muti* 中国古代小说的原型与母题 [Motifs and Archetypes in the Classical Chinese Novel]. Beijing: Shehui kexue wenxian chubanshe, 2002.

Xu Jilin 许纪霖. “Xin Tianxia zhuyi*:* Chongjian Zhongguo de nei wai zhixu 新天下主义：重建中国的内外秩序 [New Tianxia-ism: Re-establishing the Internal and External Oder of China].” *Ai sixiang* 爱思想, August 26, 2015.

Yang Haibo 杨海波. “*Honglou meng* dui xiafan-lijie muti de jicheng yu chaoyue《红楼梦》对下凡历劫母题的继承与超越 [The Inheritance and Transcendence of the Motif of ‘Descension for a Kalpa’ in *Dream of the Red Chamber*]. “*Journal of Northwest Normal University* 48, no. 2 (2011): 68–75.

Yang Shiye 杨十夜. *Shuang shi chongfei* 双世宠妃 [The Eternal Love]. Directed by Yuan De 元德. Aired July 10, 2017, on Tencent Video. Tencent Penguin Pictures 2017, online. https://v.qq.com/x/cover/47xswolfi4iamlx/h0024x1jb6k.html.

Yang Shiye 杨十夜. Shuang shi chongfei 2 双世宠妃2 [The Eternal Love 2]. Directed by Wu Qiang 吴强. Aired October 22, 2018, on Tencent Video. Tencent Penguin Pictures, 2018, online. https://v.qq.com/x/cover/ohrejqzlvdyro3k/l00276tubbd.html.

Yang Shiye 杨十夜. *Shuang shi chongfei 3* 双世宠妃3 [The Eternal Love 3]. Directed by Li Yang 李阳. Aired June 1, 2021, on Tencent Video. Tencent Penguin Pictures, 2021, online. https://v.qq.com/x/cover/qjr4mfe8xf85joj/w0037qfufmv.html.

Zhao Na 赵娜and Chen Liwen 陈丽雯. *Chen xi yuan* 宸汐緣 [Love and Destiny]. Directed by Yufen Lin 林玉芬, Shengquan Liang 梁勝權, Haitao Ren 任海濤, and Hu Guo郭虎. Aired July 15, 2019, on IQIYI.COM. Croton Media, 2019, online. https://www.iq.com/album/%E5%AE%B8%E6%B1%90%E7%BC%98-2019-19rrhtj1td?lang=zh_cn.

Zhou Munan 周木楠. “Shaonian ge xing 少年歌行 [The Blood of Youth]” Luoying Xiaoshuo 落影小说. https://www.loying.cc/book/gexing/.

Žižek, Slavoj. *Looking Awry: An Introduction to Jacques Lacan through Popular Culture*. Cambridge, MA: The MIT Press, 1991.

Žižek, Slavoj. “Slavoj Žižek Speaks at Occupy Wall Street: Transcript.” *IMPOSE Magazine*. https://imposemagazine.com/bytes/slavoj-zizek-at-occupy-wall-street-transcript

# 2 An Online World of Their Own

## Rethinking *Danmei* Fiction through a Reading of *A Tale of Jujube Valley*

*Jin Sujie*

**Abstract**
This chapter examines the cultural phenomenon of *danmei* fiction writing/reading – arguably the most controversial genre of Internet literature. Danmei fiction centres on the homoerotic relationship between two male protagonists, but I draw on *A Tale of Jujube Valley* to show how danmei creators and readers, sometimes referred to as "rotten girls," have created a digital literary community that is not solely focused on homosocial and homosexual content. My analysis of the sub-genre of danmei farming fiction details the different ways danmei has become an important literary practice for reflecting on contemporary issues such as human-nature relations and the renegotiation of gender values.

**Keywords:** *danmei*/boys' love, participatory culture, farming fiction, masculinity, women's literature

The Chinese term *danmei* (耽美) literally means "indulging in the beautiful",[1] and it has origins in the Japanese term *tanbi* (たんび), a nineteenth century art movement that understood beauty as the ultimate goal of art. However, in Chinese popular discourse, the meaning of danmei has been enriched by the more general phenomenon of danmei fiction writing and reading. Also referred to as boys' love (BL), this genre of online fiction is characterised by women's imaginings of male homosexuality and derives genealogically from Japanese *yaoi*[2] and BL manga, which

1 Louie, "Chinese Masculinity Studies," 24.
2 *Yaoi* means "no climax, no point, no meaning."

Imbach, Jessica. *Digital China.* Amsterdam: Amsterdam University Press, 2024
DOI: 10.5117/9789463720670_CH02

were introduced to mainland China in the late 1990s.[3] At first, danmei participants – sometimes referred to as *funü* (腐女, literally, rotten girls)[4] – created and circulated stories within relatively closed spaces where they felt secure expressing personal feelings and experiences of sexual desire. They often disassociated this work from their real-world identities because of the fear of social punishment or ostracism.[5] However, this has recently changed.

Since the late 2000s, writing and reading Internet literature, including danmei stories, has become a cultural phenomenon. Websites have been established to publish stories, and writers have begun to profit. Digital publishing platforms collect resources and categorise stories by topic for the convenience of readers. One such website, Jinjiang Literature City (*Jinjiang wenxue cheng* 晉江文學城, henceforth Jinjiang), has become the most influential female-oriented website, publishing 4.15 million fiction works and counting 1.78 million registered writers and 46.91 million registered members. Notably, sixty-seven per cent of its active users live in huge metropolitan areas, such as Beijing, Shanghai, Guangzhou, and Hong Kong.[6] Significantly, more than half of Jinjiang's most popular stories are danmei fiction.

During the latter part of the 2010s, as danmei stories were adapted into web dramas, danmei participants obtained a presence in the mainstream media. Strict censorship required that they initially develop novel approaches to promote danmei-related subjects in the digital world. To openly discuss *Guardian* (*Zhenhun* 镇魂), a web drama adapted from the danmei story of the same name and released in 2018, its fans created the term "socialist brotherhood" to reference danmei-style homoeroticism without alerting censors.[7] To show support for this subculture, danmei participants (including readers and writers) are willing to invest heavily in well-made products, something that has attracted the attention of the entertainment industry. In 2019, a screen adaptation of the highly praised danmei story, *Grandmaster of Demonic Cultivation* (*Modao zushi* 魔道祖師), was released as *The Untamed* (*Chenqing ling* 陳情令). Its profits have

3 Liu, "Boys' Love in Girls' Hands."

4 Danmei writers and readers were formerly known in a self-deprecating way as *funü* 腐女 (literally, rotten girls). They suffered from a certain degree of social alienation. With the public's changing opinion of *danmei* culture, the term *funü* has become obsolete. Therefore, this chapter refers to those that partake in this subculture, both male and female, as danmei participants.

5 Zhang, *Dreadful Desires*, 172.

6 *Jinjiang Literature City*, "Guanyu Jinjiang."

7 Ng and Li, "A Queer 'Socialist Brotherhood'."

been estimated to be as high as 156 million Chinese Yuan.[8] Since then, over fifty danmei stories were listed on the schedule of upcoming film releases, with the years 2020 and 2021 witnessing a boom in danmei adaptations.[9] However, the government took action and implemented stricter regulations in the summer of 2021, responding to the effect of danmei on mainstream culture and its role in creating different forms of masculinity. Nevertheless, danmei screen adaptations were allowed to re-emerge in early 2023 due to their potential to boost the economy following the economic slump caused by Covid-19 lockdowns.

Academic researchers generally consider Chinese danmei fiction, Japanese BL products, and English-language slash fanfiction[10] to pertain to the same genre of male-male romance created primarily by and for women. Drawing heavily on research conducted by Western and Japanese scholars, researchers agree that danmei fiction reveals homosocial and homosexual desires,[11] challenges heteronormativity,[12] and builds a queer heterotopic world.[13] After two decades of expansion, danmei fiction has grown increasingly diverse. However, few studies have investigated topics or themes beyond gender concerns.

Danmei fiction incorporates elements from other genres, including but not limited to detective stories, thrillers, and alternate history. The vernacularisation process has seen danmei fiction draw from Chinese historical legacies and traditional values to cover a broad selection of narrative forms,[14] enabling it to develop themes other than queer relationships and homoeroticism. Among the array of subgenres, danmei farming fiction (*zhongtian wen* 種田文) has become notable for its detailed descriptions of domestic life and daily activities.

Responding to this background context, this chapter investigates the cultural phenomenon of writing and reading danmei fiction in the Sinocybersphere, examining the participatory features of the subculture, detailing the parameters of danmei farming fiction, and exploring the themes that

8 Yule Dujiaoshou, "Chen Qing Ling' dajieju."

9 A drama series adapted from *danmei* fiction is called a *dangaiju* (耽改劇) or *danmei*-to-screen adaptation.

10 Slash fanfiction is often known as "m/m slash" or "slashfic." It refers to fanfiction that features romantic stories of two males who are characters in already existing media products (e.g., movies, TV series, novels).

11 Wang, "Tanbi Novels and *Fujoshi*," 317–32.

12 Zhang, "Loving Boys Twice as Much."

13 Wang, "Tanbi Novels and *Fujoshi*"; Zhang, "Loving Boys Twice as Much."

14 Chen, "Boys' Love (Danmei) Fiction on the Chinese Internet."

appear in an exemplar text, namely, *A Tale of Jujube Valley* (*Zao'er gou fajia ji* 棗兒溝發家記) (henceforth *Jujube Valley*), one of the most widely known *danmei* farming fiction works.[15]

## Participatory Culture

Engaging in danmei fiction writing and reading is an example of a participatory culture that motivates new digital behaviours. For Henry Jenkins, participatory culture absorbs and responds "to the explosion of new media technologies that make it possible for average consumers to archive, annotate, appropriate, and recirculate media content in powerful new ways."[16] By utilising media experience, danmei writers create innovative pieces of writing that, for example, re-examine the concept of filial piety promulgated in mainstream culture. The genre of Chinese family ethics TV series promotes moral principles that help families and society remain united.[17] The protagonist almost always reconciles with the irresponsible father, even after the latter has caused substantial grief. In response to this dynamic, danmei writers repudiate parent-child relationships where the parents fail to fulfil parental responsibilities, composing their own works if the male characters presented do not meet their expectations. They utilise distinct characterisations to construct characters that represent their own vision of an ideal man. Recent iterations favour characters that are intelligent, hardworking, and non-innocent. This can be perceived as standing in opposition to the streamlined, dumbed-down characters observed in earlier danmei fiction.

In a culture that encourages participation, danmei fiction also reflects concerns about human-nature relationships, with increasing attention focused on environmental concerns. By setting stories in rural areas, danmei fiction reassesses the connections between industrialised societies, people, and nature. Since the latter part of the twentieth century, industrialisation and urbanisation have been society's primary focus, with control of nature understood as a critical component of achieving economic prosperity.[18]

15 Mengdong Shiwu, *Zao'er gou fajia ji.* This story was initially published under the writer's previous penname, Nanxia Xiaozhan 南俠小展.

16 Jenkins, *Confronting the Challenges of Participatory Culture*, 8.

17 Chinese family ethics TV series depict family squabbles and conflicts, reflecting contemporary social ethics and moral issues.

18 Li, *Xin shiqi wenxue zhong de shengtai lunli jingshen*; Shapiro, *Mao's War against Nature*; Shapiro, *China's Environmental Challenges.*

Nevertheless, environmental consciousness has been on the rise in recent times: People realise that the rapid growth of the economy also implies the irrevocable destruction of the environment. Villages are dilapidated; water and land are polluted; food safety and food hygiene are undermined. Meanwhile, the attendant disappearance of familiar surroundings evokes childhood memories. Utilising introspection, danmei participants try to gratify their wishes by envisioning a tranquil and balanced rural existence. These accounts reveal nostalgic longings for the past. In addition, participants are fond of portraying animals as protectors and friends, which points to a growing appreciation for an empathetic and ethics-based approach to the animal world. Danmei participants not only create stories that are a blend of factual and imaginative elements, but also address a variety of deep concerns, prompting young women in contemporary China to take up the practice of writing and reading danmei fiction as a daily digital practice.

To promote an interactive culture, Internet-based literature publishing platforms are designed to motivate users to cultivate such habits and interactions. Jinjiang represents a useful example. A reward system is in place to stimulate writers to publish chapters regularly.[19] This encourages readers to develop a daily routine of visiting the website. This has led to readers spending around eighty minutes on Jinjiang every day, not only consuming fiction stories but also voicing their opinions. Comment sections attached to each chapter allow readers to express and exchange ideas, with discussions and debates also taking place at the Jinjiang Forum, which is commonly referred to as "*Jinjiang* Little Pink" (*jinjiang xiao fenhong* 晉江小粉紅). The section Xianqing (閒情) – which translates to "leisurely and carefree mood" – has become one of the largest danmei communities.[20] These activities all contribute to bringing danmei participants together to foster a robust culture and vibrant communities.

## Danmei Farming Fiction

Chinese Internet literature can be categorised as either male- or female-oriented. Female-oriented writings typically encompass heterosexual romances, homosexual danmei tales, and no-CP (no couple; i.e., non-romantic) stories.[21] These subcategories regularly intersect with other subgenres,

19 *Jinjiang Literature City*, "Guanyu Jinjiang."
20 *Jinjiang Literature City*, "Xianqing."
21 In no-CP (無CP) stories, the protagonist is not involved in any form of romantic relationship.

including the *xuanhuan* (玄幻) fiction documented in chapter 1 and the farming fiction subgenre to be discussed in this chapter. Although the term "farming" (*zhongtian* 種田) refers to tilling, cultivating the land, and planting crops, the genealogical root of farming fiction is located in the subgenre of speculative fiction known as alternative history (AH) or allohistory.[22] AH fiction was initially propagated by male writers. Its central trope is that the typically male protagonist devotes himself to establishing his territory and promoting economic, political, and cultural development. He refrains from disagreements with rulers of other territories in the opening half of the narrative, but he will eventually conquer the world.[23] By contrast, farming fiction redirects attention from the public realm to inner matters and concentrates on familial relationships and economic output.[24] In a narrow sense, protagonists in farming fiction occupy a position of lower social standing at a point in the historical past, and their situation improves through hard work and dedication. However, such figures maintain a low profile and do not intend to change or conquer the world.[25] Thus, where xuanhuan fiction uses the heavenly realm as a backdrop, particularly emphasising the (self-)cultivation of celestial beings, farming fiction sets its stories on earth and features the everyday lives of ordinary people.

Farming fiction has been adopted as a reliable subgenre by danmei participants who must reduce homoerotic content amidst strict censorship, with danmei fiction previously receiving substantial criticism for its frequently graphic depictions of sex. In 2014 the Chinese state launched the "Web Cleansing Action" (*jingwang yundong* 淨網行動) to regulate Internet content,[26] leading to heightened censorship of Internet-based literature publishing platforms. Words related to sexuality, violence, politics, and other delicate matters were detected and removed. For example, a renowned romance writer, whose pseudonym was Zhangzhe Chibang de Dahuilang (長著翅膀的大灰狼), was taken into custody for selling obscene materials.[27] Following this, Jinjiang introduced a ban on depictions of any body part below the neck (bozi yixia de buwei buneng miaoxie 脖子以下的部位不能描寫) and replaced the category danmei with chun'ai (纯爱, literally, pure love). The company also submitted an official report to the authorities that not only explained what danmei/chun'ai is but also how they would ensure

22 Shao and Wang, *Pobi Shu*.
23 Li, "Xin shiqing xiaoshuo de fuxing."
24 Feng, "The Proliferating Genre."
25 Feng, "The Proliferating Genre," 386.
26 Shao, *Wangluo Shidai de Wenxue Yindu*.
27 Tian, "More than Conformity or Resistance."

the enforcement of moderation guidelines. Even though some danmei writers left due to these changes, Jinjiang was able to keep its chun'ai sub-page and is today the major online platform for danmei participants.

In general, danmei farming fiction portrays the lives of people living in either a historical agrarian society or the present-day countryside. It focuses on portraying a calm lifestyle in tranquil settings, contrasting with the fast-paced lifestyles associated with major metropolises. *Jujube Valley* and *The Water Buffalo Man* (*Niu nan* 牛男)[28] exemplify the two categories, with the former set in feudal times and the latter set in modern times. *Jujube Valley* tells a story in which the protagonist dedicates himself to providing for his family and enhancing the economy in the local area; *The Water Buffalo Man* depicts a rustic paradise in which the protagonist starts a food production enterprise in a modernised culture. To some degree, danmei farming stories resemble the videos of Li Ziqi explored in chapter 6 of this volume, videos that depict a leisurely, tranquil, and captivating vision of rural life.

Danmei farming fiction also represents activities outside of rural areas, with these elements pushing the plot forward slowly and explicitly. In other words, the protagonist's "farming" lifestyle includes not only tilling the land and making a living in the countryside but also doing business, establishing a community, and surviving in the wild. As such, danmei farming fiction includes but is not limited to wealth-accumulation farming fiction (*jingying zhongtian wen* 經營種田文), infrastructure-construction farming fiction (*jijian zhongtian wen* 基建種田文), and nation-building farming fiction (*qingguo zhongtian wen* 強國種田文). This means that the scope of danmei farming fiction is expansive, ranging from taking imperial examinations to surviving in the wild. For instance, *Attending the Imperial Examination in the Ming Dynasty* (*Chuandao mingchao kao keju* 穿到明朝考科舉)[29] explains how to write an eight-legged essay[30] (*baguwen* 八股文) and pass the imperial examinations in the Ming Dynasty, while *Becoming a Cheetah* (*Chong shengcheng liebao* 重生成獵豹)[31] depicts how the protagonist survives on the savannah as a creature who can shift forms between a human being and a cheetah. It offers a vivid description of wild animals and their lives, drawing on facts about nature. Thus, the term "farming fiction" is not merely a specific fiction subgenre but also a writing technique

28 Baozhi Huqiang, *Niu nan*.

29 Wuse Longzhang, *Chuandao Mingchao kao keju*.

30 The Eight-Legged Essay was the required written part of imperial examinations during the Ming and Qing dynasties in China.

31 Laizi Yuanfang, *Chongsheng cheng liebao*.

characterised by a nature-oriented aesthetic. In essence, danmei farming fiction has shifted from homosocial and homosexual themes to embracing numerous elements, including self-expression, family, and nature.

Compared to the complete disregard of danmei farming fiction by researchers, the heterosexual variant[32] has been given some amount of attention in the academic environment. As of March 2023, *CNKI* (知網, the most extensive digital library of academic journals and dissertations in mainland China) featured a few journal articles and master's dissertations concerning this topic. By concentrating on the idyllic lifestyle and family issues, this subgenre has been linked to the novel of manners,[33] Chinese native-soil literature,[34] and personal writing.[35] Nevertheless, none of these previous researchers has elaborated on their discussions via a thorough examination of a particular text. Elsewhere, one researcher concluded that reading farming fiction is a form of escapism following a small number of interviews, ignoring reader claims that the endeavour also represents an informative activity.[36] Another researcher concentrates on the notion of space and claims that farming fiction mirrors urban inhabitants' yearning for uncomplicated individual connections that are absent from the uneven development of society.[37] Meanwhile, farming fiction is a brand-new subject in the Western academic context, with Jin Feng only recently and briefly introducing it to the English-speaking world.[38] Thus, generally speaking, existing investigations into farming fiction are inadequate, with findings non-comprehensive due to the inexact definition of the subgenre and a lack of detailed analysis of related texts.

## Beyond Homoeroticism

Previous works in the danmei genre have revolved around homoeroticism and featured characters with more sensitive features heavily inspired by depictions of "floral men" in Korean and Japanese popular culture. In comparison, danmei farming fiction scrutinises different forms of masculinity

32 Heterosexual farming fiction is also known as BG (i.e. boy-girl love) farming fiction and is similarly mainly written by and for women.

33 Li, "Xin shiqing xiaoshuo de fuxing."

34 Li, "Gushi yu jiayuan."

35 Feng, "The Proliferating Genre."

36 Zhang, "'Zhongtian wen' zhong shouzhong de xinli yu xingwei yanjiu."

37 Wang, "Wangluo nüpin wen kongjian xushi yanjiu."

38 Feng, "The Proliferating Genre."

with origins in Chinese traditions and inquires about traditional doctrines while developing female characters often depicted as emotionally unstable (in an effort to destroy the bond between the two central male characters) and probing the human-nature relationships that have become a focus of discourse in the digital age.

Crucially, masculinity in danmei fiction does not align completely with the masculinity demonstrated by gay men in the real world. Consistent with other postmodern media products, danmei fiction transforms the relationship between the signifier and signified, referring not only to a "reality" out there but also to signifiers found in other textual objects and in the digital world.[39] In the danmei context, forms of masculinity can be perceived as a "floating signifier",[40] which does not relate to a signified but to other signifying entities such as media texts. To put it another way, the masculinity described in danmei texts is a reflection of that seen in Japanese boys' love manga. For example, Mengdong Shiwu (孟冬十五),[41] *Jujube Valley*'s writer, does not have any personal connection to the LGBTQ community: her knowledge of same-sex relationships is from danmei fiction, which she first encountered after graduating from university.

Nevertheless, danmei fiction provides an evolving representation of masculinity. Most early danmei stories were told from the perspective of the *shou* 受 (the receiver or the bottom), who is usually depicted as attractive and delicate, as opposed to the *gong* 攻 (the attacker or the top). This led previous academic examinations to concur with studies of Japanese boys' love or BL products that understand the *shou* as originating with "boys dressed as girls",[42] representing either a female hermaphrodite or a male androgyne.[43] However, danmei participants tend to "tease men" rather than "identify with men."[44] Therefore, research on danmei-style masculinity should not be restricted to the shou character but instead encompass the gong-shou paradigm, including but not limited to "strong *gong* weak *shou*" (*qianggong ruoshou* 强攻弱受), "strong *gong* strong *shou*" (*qianggong qiangshou* 强攻强受), "weak *gong* strong *shou*" (*ruogong qiangshou* 弱攻强受). Accordingly,

39 Hitchon and Jura, "Allegorically Speaking."

40 Qtd in. Paula Saukko, *Doing Research in Cultural Studies*, 105.

41 Mengdong Shiwu was born in the late 1980s. After earned a bachelor's degree from a Chinese university, she signed a contract with Jinjiang and is now a full-time *danmei* fiction writer. She has produced an array of popular farming fiction.

42 Zhang, *Dreadful Desires*; Fujimoto, "The Evolution of BL as 'Playing with Gender'."

43 Fujimoto et al., "Transgender"; Zhou, Paul and Sherman, "Still a Hetero-Gendered World"; Zhang, "My Double Love of Boys."

44 Fujimoto, "The Evolution of BL as 'Playing with Gender'."

the following analysis understands the construction of masculinity in *Jujube Valley* by considering gong and shou as a collective unit.

Notably, representations of masculinity in danmei farming fiction are modelled on Chinese culture and are not considered effeminate. This responds to Louie's recognition that masculinity can take on different forms depending on the context,[45] with definitions of masculinity differing between cultures and also changing over time within a given culture.[46] He associates "the performance of gendered identities" with "the dyad *wen-wu* (文武) (cultural attainment—martial valour)."[47] *Wen* refers to "those genteel, refined qualities" and *wu* captures "physical strength and military prowess."[48] Because Chinese culture has considerably impacted danmei texts, masculine qualities in *Jujube Valley* correspond to the *wen-wu* paradigm.

The *shou* character Jiang Yi (江逸) in *Jujube Valley* symbolises the traditional Chinese masculine ideals of *wen*. Jiang Yi, a doctor of agricultural science living in contemporary China, passes away in an accident, leaving his soul to inhabit the body of a Jiang Yi who lives in the Ming Dynasty. He has been granted the title of xiucai (秀才) after passing the imperial examination at the county level. Dr Jiang takes over xiucai Jiang's physical body and social standing. It is apparent that the two Jiangs correspond to the *wen* people of the Confucian literati class across temporal and spatial limits. According to Louie, "cultural attainment always takes priority over physical prowess. … [*W*]*en* accomplishments were equated with the crowning glories of being an ideal man."[49] Jiang represents an exemplar of *wen* values over *wu*.[50]

That is, despite *Jujube Valley* not detailing Confucian teachings, Jiang's behaviour aligns with the *wen* values of being learned and refined, courteous and educated, and gentle and generous. His commitment to philanthropy also makes him an ideal Confucian businessman (*ru shang* 儒商).[51] After familiarising himself with his new life in the Ming Dynasty, Jiang makes it his responsibility to improve the economy and eliminate poverty in the local area and within his family. To this end, he helps the village inhabitants grow jujube trees and encourages small-scale, home-based businesses.

45 Connell, "Masculinities and Globalisation."
46 Qtd. in Louie, *Theorising Chinese Masculinity*, 2.
47 Louie, *Theorising Chinese Masculinity*, 4.
48 Louie, *Theorising Chinese Masculinity*, 14.
49 Louie, "Chinese Masculinity Studies in the Twenty-First Century," 22.
50 Louie, "Chinese Masculinity Studies in the Twenty-First Century," 24–25.
51 Shengchun and Yang, "Lishi shang de rushang yu rushang jingshen."

Significantly, his choice to employ women empowers them to fund their household and enhance their family standing. Jiang views women as independent subjects instead of mere sexual or reproductive objects.

Simultaneously, Jiang disagrees with traditional conceptions of gender segregation that revolve around the idea of "separate spheres," whereby the "private sphere of home and family" was associated with femininity, while "the public realm of commerce and public life"[52] was understood as masculine.[53] Jiang's progressiveness finds resonance in Louie's argument that depictions of men as caring and attentive align with the "tender *wen* (cultured) lover of classical literature."[54] But Jiang simultaneously also personifies a new type of man, who is sensitive and involved in domestic life, combining assertive masculinity with softness and sensuality.[55] Despite breaching the folk practice that sees "gentlemen stay away from the kitchen (*junzi yuan paochu* 君子遠庖廚),"[56] Jiang, for instance, assists with cooking and other domestic duties. Ultimately, this means that Jiang embodies both elements of traditional Chinese masculinity as well as modern ideals about gender equality.

Meanwhile, Jiang's partner, Su Yunqi (蘇雲起) provides a model of a *wu* brand of masculinity. Louie explains that "bodily strength ... [is] one of the recognised attributes of a handsome man. ... The male body, then, is culturally inscribed within discourses of masculinity and as such is much more than a product of perceived 'essential' biological difference."[57] Su has a typically masculine physique and military leadership skills gained from serving in the army and specialising in martial arts. When he is released from military service, a group of fellow soldiers are decommissioned alongside him. Su's form of masculinity, which is often discussed in Anglophone discourse, stresses the physical power of men as well as "aggression and violence as a means of control."[58] However, Su also dedicates himself to safeguarding his partner Jiang, his younger cousins, and the elderly members of his community. In short, Su assumes the role of a guardian and protector, complementing Jiang, the caretaker and provider.

52 Levine, *Forms*, 95.

53 Song and Hird, *Men and Masculinities in Contemporary China*. The original quotation is "men control the outside, women control the inside" 男主外，女主内.

54 Song and Hird, *Men and Masculinities in Contemporary China*, 26.

55 Bainbridge and Yates, "Cinematic Symptoms of Masculinity in Transition."

56 This phrase is from the book *Mencius* and is often used in reference to gender segregation in the context of household chores.

57 Louie, *Theorising Chinese Masculinity*, 6–7.

58 Ricciardelli, Clow and White, "Investigating Hegemonic Masculinity," 64.

In this context, it should be noted that Jiang and Su's homosexuality is only very obliquely thematised. In fact, during the Ming Dynasty in Fujian, there were instances of two men living together as if they were married, despite the lack of formal approval.[59] Accordingly, *Jujube Valley* does not depict the struggles and hardships that male characters must endure before accepting their homosexuality and obtaining their parents' endorsement. Rather, it portrays Jiang and Su as an unmarried couple without elaborating on their homosexual interactions. They rest in the same bed right after Su returns from the military, and bedroom scenes hint that Su has considerable sexual power. Nevertheless, *Jujube Valley* also intimates that both men abstained from sexual relations until finding their true love.

Jiang and Su, representing *wen*- and *wu*-masculinity, are viewed as an exemplary pairing, leaving no room for a third party such as a reader to become involved in their relationship. Despite this, readers are quite keen on such a perfect match. Their affection, according to Zhang, is a type of maternal or sisterly love, rather than the love of a wife for her husband.[60] Such an emotion extends from the homosexual couple to other characters in *Jujube Valley*. For instance, readers' expressions of motherly or sisterly love can be observed in comments posted online regarding the character Xiaobao (小寶), Su's youngest orphaned cousin. The term "cute" is often employed in this context. Phrases like "Xiaobao is so cute! Wanna take him home (*xiaobao hao ke'ai! Hoaxing baohuijia* 小寶好可愛！好想抱回家)" and "Wuuuuu, Xiaobao, mom loves you (*wuwuwu xiaobao mama ai ni* 嗚嗚嗚小寶媽媽愛你)"[61] showcase readers' maternal fondness. Utilising endearing characters such as Xiaobao, *Jujube Valley* can capture the emotions of its readers, extending engagement beyond the realm of homoeroticism.

Elsewhere, *Jujube Valley* provides alternative understandings of the traditional value of filial piety, showing how filial piety corresponds not only to blood bonds or marriage but also to mutual respect, trust, and understanding. For example, Dr Jiang grows up with his grandmother after his mother dies, and he never sees his father nor longs for his affection. However, although Dr Jiang does not need parental love, he does not dismiss it after becoming Xiucai Jiang and coming under the guidance of his "adopted" father, Jiang Chiyan (江池宴). Meanwhile, Jiang Chiyan does not play the role of a customary Chinese father who is demanding, silent,

59 Wang, "Qi xiong."
60 Zhang, *Dreadful Desires*.
61 Mengdong Shiwu, *Zao'er gou fajia ji*.

and strict.[62] Instead, he is supportive, communicative, and approachable. This prominent contemporary image of a father[63] enables *Jujube Valley* to emphasise the significance of a content, positive parent-child relationship that avoids demanding children to practise filial piety.

*Jujube Valley* also supports the repudiation of the parent-child relationship in certain circumstances. In Chinese culture, the family is considered the vital unit in society, and filial piety is considered imperative due to the inseparability of blood ties between parents and children.[64] Performing filial obligations is treated not as a separate domestic affair but as an important moral tenet of social stability.[65] Whether or not parents fail to perform the duty of raising their children, the latter cannot refuse filial obligations, a notion upheld by law to the present day. According to Article 21 of the Marriage Law of the People's Republic of China,

> "Parents shall have the duty to bring up and educate their children; children shall have the duty to support and assist their parents. ... If children fail to perform their duty, parents who are unable to work or have difficulty in providing for themselves shall have the right to demand support payments from their children."[66]

Despite this, the state tends to prioritise the obligation of adult children to provide for their elderly parents while overlooking the demands and protection of minors. Although the law requires that parents provide care for their children, there is an absence of efficient organisations to check if parents are following this mandate. Moreover, when legal assistance is needed, children are often not equipped with the necessary means to seek it out. Even with legal regulations in place, there are considerable weaknesses in the system that can leave children in an unprotected and vulnerable state. By contrast, adult children are required to give not only financial but also emotional help to their parents, including negligent ones.[67] By contrast, *Jujube Valley* does not agree that adult children should take responsibility for their parents without condition or simply ruled by the value of filial piety. Rather, the novel promotes the idea that the obligation of children to support their parents should exclude situations such as when the children

62 Song and Hird, *Men and Masculinities in Contemporary China*, 26.
63 Song and Hird, *Men and Masculinities in Contemporary China*, 215.
64 Fwu et al., "To Work Hard or Not?"
65 Zhang, "Nezha chuanshuo de fuhao yihan yu lunli yinyu."
66 "Marriage Law of the People's Republic of China."
67 Hatton, "New China Law Says Children 'Must Visit Parents'."

have been abandoned or subjected to physical or mental abuse as well as cases where parents have harmful behaviour including but not limited to drug addiction, alcoholism and gambling. It highlights the importance of considering specific circumstances and exceptions where such obligations may not apply.

*Jujube Valley* is also critical of ill-conceived filial piety. Ancient China regards filial piety as the paramount virtue,[68] and the failure to adhere to this standard is considered a moral failing.[69] This older perspective particularly "prescribe[s] the behaviour of young girls before and after marriage."[70] Interestingly, *Jujube Valley* captures the folly of filial piety in the tragic life of a so-called obedient daughter named Qin Cui'er (秦翠兒). Qin is the birth mother of Su's younger cousins, Meizi (梅子) and Xiaobao. Because the legal spouse of Qin's husband passed away, she is treated as his official wife, even though she is a concubine. Her commitment to her husband is praised at that time. However, she follows her parent's command and abandons her two children after her husband's execution, marrying a hooligan as arranged by her parents and being subjected to domestic violence until the hooligan dies. When her parents force her to wed a third time, Qin commits suicide as a final act of resistance. Thus, Qin's life serves as an example of the unfortunate repercussions of misguided filial devotion.

*Jujube Valley* also offers representations of married women who do not conform to the standards of behaviour set by the patriarchal society: "[T]he virtue most esteemed and expected of … [women] was devotion to their husbands and their parents-in-law; their filial status was grounded in their pious devotion to the needs of their parents-in-law and their abilities to maintain and contribute to the harmony, stability and continuation of their newfound families."[71] The character of Yu Su'e (余素娥) seeks divorce after realising that she is treated as a "breeding machine." His mother-in-law refuses to allow the doctor to support her in the delivery of her baby and is displeased with her newborn daughter, with her husband demonstrating no respect or affection for her, leading Yu to courageously terminate the marriage and embark on an unpredictable life journey. She starts to run stores and raises her daughter without relying on her parents. As a woman who is subject to social stigma due to her divorce, Yu's personal qualities still attract Su's cousin. This allows *Jujube Valley* to contemplate how women can

68 Ivanhoe, "Filial Piety as a Virtue."

69 Chan and Tan, *Filial Piety in Chinese Thought and History*.

70 Lo, "Filial Devotion for Women," 84.

71 Lo, "Filial Devotion for Women," 71.

reject unjust familial obligations without facing criticism. It is not necessary for them to remain in their marriage solely for the purpose of fulfilling their societal expectations of being obedient and submissive daughters-in-law, devoted and loyal wives, and sacrificing and selfless mothers.

*Jujube Valley* also advocates for female autonomy and encourages women to eliminate obstacles that prevent them from participating in the workplace after marriage. Meizi, for instance, strives to maintain her independence before and after marriage. Meizi works diligently to support herself and her younger brother, Xiaobao, after their mother, Qin Cui'er, abandons them. She decides not to accept a victim status in the face of her difficulties and takes control of her life. She thereby demonstrates remarkable resilience and strength of character by striving to build a better future for both her and her brother. Beyond that, Meizi also exercises her autonomy by choosing to marry a man of non-Han ethnicity and relocating to the grasslands of Northern China. Subsequently, Meizi risks her life to go on a mission with her husband to seek help for his community, which lacks iodised salt. Ultimately, she succeeds and garners respect for herself. Her actions do not comply with the code of conduct for women established by *Admonitions for Women* (*Nüjie* 女戒) which states that "the fundamental principle of [women's] personal survival is to play the role of the inferior and weak."[72] *Jujube Valley* presents Meizi as a confident and competent female figure who disregards social norms and follows her own aspirations, thus questioning traditional gender roles and motivating women to challenge the restrictions of a patriarchal culture. It endorses the notion that women can be strong, self-reliant, and successful in both the domestic and professional spheres.

Furthermore, *Jujube Valley* re-evaluates the exploitation of nature by humans. With his expertise in agriculture, Jiang works in earnest to improve the agricultural economy. He demonstrates the grafting technique to the villagers to expand jujube production. This successfully increases the income of village's inhabitants, with Jiang not only exploiting the natural world for subsistence but also preserving the natural environment via his awareness of environmental issues. In the story's second half, Jiang's family is forced to move to a city situated close to the Northern Chinese frontier. The city is in proximity to the desert and lacks resources such as water and vegetation, so Jiang plants narrow-leaved oleaster to enhance the soil quality. He also instructs locals on how to make a profit from

72 Lo, "Filial Devotion for Women," 79. *Nüjie* (女戒) is written by Ban Zhao (班昭, c. 49 to c. 120). It "has been criticized for being instrumental in imposing a physically constricting and spiritually denigrating ideology for women in traditional China," 78.

oleaster fruits and flowers via honey production. These actions increase the revenue of the local people. *Jujube Valley* emphasises the significance of environmentally friendly techniques and judicious utilisation of natural resources, creating a mutually advantageous relationship between human beings and nature. It illustrates a harmonious bond between humanity and the natural world, where humans act as both beneficiaries and custodians of the environment, promoting a mutually advantageous relationship between people and nature.

## An Evolving Genre

In recent decades, danmei fiction has experienced a period of prosperity in the Sinocybersphere, integrating elements of other genres to address an array of issues. Despite China's censorship aiming to reduce the prevalence of graphic sexual depictions, themes beyond homoeroticism sustain the genre's continued appeal. As my reading of *Jujube Valley* demonstrates, danmei fiction and fandom should not be viewed as a monolith and revolves around a variety of topics, ranging from domestic affairs to environmental concerns and offers new perspectives on gender and filial piety. By engaging very directly with contemporary debates, danmei fiction continues to evolve as a genre that centres on the agency of women to create a virtual literary space of their own.

## References

Bainbridge, Caroline and Candida Yates. "Cinematic Symptoms of Masculinity in Transition: Memory, History and Mythology in Contemporary Film." *Psychoanalysis, Culture & Society* 10 (2005): 299–318.

Baozhi Huqiang 报纸糊墙. *Niu nan* 牛男 [*The Water Buffalo Man*]. *Jinjiang Literature City*, 2013-16. http://www.jjwxc.net/onebook.php?novelid=1769629.

Chan, Alan and Sor-Hoon Tan. *Filial Piety in Chinese Thought and History.* London: Routledge, 2004.

Chen, Xin. "Boys' Love (Danmei) Fiction on the Chinese Internet: Wasabi Kun, the BL Forum Young Nobleman Changpei, and the Development of an Online Literary Phenomenon." Master's thesis, University of British Columbia, 2017. https://doi.org/10.14288/1.0355213.

Connell, R. W. "Masculinities and Globalisation." *Men and Masculinities* 1.1 (1998): 3–23. https://doi.org/10.1177/1097184X98001001001.

Database of Laws and Regulations. "Marriage Law of the People's Republic of China." http://www.npc.gov.cn/zgrdw/englishnpc/Law/2007-12/13/content_1384064.htm.

Feng, Jin. "The Proliferating Genre: Web-based Time-travel Fiction and the New Media in Contemporary China." In *A Companion to Modern Chinese Literature*, edited by Yingjin Zhang, 379–94. Hoboken, NJ: John Wiley & Sons, Ltd, 2016.

Fujimoto, Yukari, Linda Flores, Kazumi Nagaike, and Sharalyn Orbaugh. "Transgender: Female Hermaphrodites and Male Androgynes." *U.S.-Japan Women's Journal* 27 (2004): 76–117.

Fujimoto, Yukari, Linda Flores, Kazumi Nagaike, and Sharalyn Orbaugh. "The Evolution of BL as 'Playing with Gender': Viewing the Genesis and Development of BL from a Contemporary Perspective." In *Boys Love Manga and beyond: History, Culture and Community in Japan*, edited by Mark McLelland, Kazumi Nagaike, Katsuhiko Suganuma, and James Walker, translated by Joanne Quimby, 76–92. Jackson: University of Mississippi, 2015.

Fwu, Bih-Jen, Chih-Fen Wei, Shun-wen Chen, and Hsiou-Huai Wang. "To Work Hard or Not? The Conflicting Effects of Negative Emotions on Persistence after Academic Failure in a Confucian Heritage Cultural Context." In *Emotions in Learning, Teaching, and Leadership,* edited by Junjun Chen and Ronnel B. King, 3-17. London: Routledge, 2020.

Golle, Jessika, Stephanie Lisibach, Fred W. Mast, and Janek S. Lobmaier. "Sweet Puppies and Cute Babies: Perceptual Adaptation to Baby Facedness Transfers across Species." *PLOS ONE* 8.3 (2013): e58248. https://doi.org/10.1371/journal.pone.0058248, 1.

Hitchon, Jacqueline C., and Jerzy O. Jura. "Allegorically Speaking: Intertextuality of the Postmodern Culture and Its Impact on Print and Television Advertising." *Communication Studies* 48.2 (1997): 142–58.

Hunziker, Marcel, Matthias Buchecker, and Terry Hartig. "Space and Place – Two Aspects of the Human-Landscape Relationship." In *A Changing World: Challenges for Landscape Research*, edited by Felix Kienast, Otto Wildi, and Sucharita Ghosh, 47–62. Landscape Series. Dordrecht: Springer Netherlands, 2007. https://doi.org/10.1007/978-1-4020-4436-6_5.

Ivanhoe, Philip J. "Filial Piety as a Virtue." In *Filial Piety in Chinese Thought and History,* edited by Alan K. L. Chan and Sor-hoon Tan, 189-202. London: Routledge, 2004.

Jenkins, Henry. *Confronting the Challenges of Participatory Culture: Media Education for the 21st Century.* Cambridge, MA: The MIT Press, 2009.

Jinjiang Literature City 晋江文学城. "Guanyu Jinjiang 关于晋江 [About Jinjiang]." http://www.jjwxc.net/aboutus/#fragment-33.

Jinjiang Literature City 晋江文学城. "Xianqing 闲情 [Leisurely and Carefree Mood]." https://bbs.jjwxc.net/board.php?board=3&page=1.

Laizi Yuanfang 来自远方. *Chongsheng cheng lie bao* 重生成猎豹 [Becoming a Cheetah]. *Jinjiang Literature City*, 2012. http://www.jjwxc.net/onebook.php?novelid=1580141.

Levine, Caroline. *Forms: Whole, Rhythm, Hierarchy, Network.* Princeton, NJ: Princeton University Press, 2015.

Li, Hao 李昊. "Xin shiqing xiaoshuo de fuxing – Qiantan 'zhongtian wen' de zouhong 新世情小说的复兴——浅谈"种田文"的走红 [A Revival of the Novel of Manners: The Popularization of Farming Fiction]." *Contemporary Literary Criticism* 5 (2013): 64–67.

Li, Mei 李玫. *Xin shiqi wenxue zhong de shengtai lunli jingshen* 新时期文学中的生态伦理精神 [The Ecological Ethics In The New-Era Literature]. Beijing: Beijing Book Co. Inc., 2016.

Li, Yiming 李一鸣. "Gutu yu jiayuan: Xin shiji wangluo xiangtu wenxue toushi 故土与家园: 新世纪网络乡土文学透视 [Native Land and Homeland: A study of 'Local Literature' in the Creation of New-century Network Novels]." *Journal of Hainan Normal University (Social Sciences)* 30.5 (2017): 7–12.

Liu, Ting. "Boys' Love in Girls' Hands: The Survival of a Gendered Youth Culture in Mainland China and Hong Kong." Doctoral dissertation, Australian National University, 2011.

Lo, Yuet Keung. "Filial Devotion for Women: A Buddhist Testimony from Third-Century China." In *Filial Piety in Chinese Thought and History,* edited by Alan K. L. Chan and Sor-hoon Tan, 71-90. London: Routledge, 2004.

Louie, Kam. "Chinese Masculinity Studies in the Twenty-First Century: Westernising, Easternising and Globalising *Wen* and *Wu*." *NORMA* 9.1 (2014): 18–29, https://doi.org/10.1080/18902138.2014.892283.

Louie, Kam. *Theorising Chinese Masculinity: Society and Gender in China.* Cambridge, UK: Cambridge University Press, 2002.

Mengdong Shiwu 孟冬十五. *Zao'er gou fajia ji* 枣儿沟发家记 [A Tale of Jujube Valley]. *Jinjiang Literature City*, 2016. http://www.jjwxc.net/onebook.php?novelid=2622579.

Ng, Eve, and Xiaomeng Li. "A Queer 'Socialist Brotherhood': The *Guardian* Web Series, Boys' Love Fandom, and the Chinese State." *Feminist Media Studies* 20, no. 4 (May 18, 2020): 479–95. https://doi.org/10.1080/14680777.2020.1754627.

Ricciardelli, Rosemary, Kimberley A. Clow, and Philip White. "Investigating Hegemonic Masculinity: Portrayals of Masculinity in Men's Lifestyle Magazines." *Sex Roles* 63. 1–2 (2010): 64–78. https://doi.org/10.1007/s11199-010-9764-8, 64.

Saukko, Paula. *Doing Research in Cultural Studies.* London: Sage Publications Ltd, 2003.

Shao, Yanjun 邵燕君. *Wangluo shidai de wenxue yindu* 网络时代的文学引渡 [Literature Extradition in the Internet Age]. Guangxi daxue chubanshe, 2015. Kindle.

Shao, Yanjun 邵燕君 and Wang Yusu 王玉王, eds. *Pobi shu* 破壁书 [Keywords in Chinese Internet Subcultures]. Beijing: SDX Joint Publishing Company, 2018.

Shapiro, Judith. *China's Environmental Challenges*. Cambridge, UK: Polity, 2012.

Shapiro, Judith. *Mao's War against Nature: Politics and the Environment in Revolutionary China*. Cambridge, UK: Cambridge University Press, 2001.

Song, Geng and Derek Hird. *Men and Masculinities in Contemporary China*. Leiden: Brill, 2013.

Steinnes, Kamilla Knutsen. "Too Cute for Words: Cuteness Evokes the Kama Muta Emotion and Motivates Communal Sharing." Master's thesis, University of Oslo, 2017. https://www.duo.uio.no/handle/10852/57260.

Tian, Xi. "More than Conformity or Resistance: Chinese "Boys' Love" Fandom in the Age of Internet Censorship." *The Journal of the European Association for Chinese Studies* 1 (2020): 189–213. https://doi.org/10.25365/jeacs.2020.1.189-213.

Tyson, Loise. *Critical Theory Today: A User-Friendly Guide*. New York & London: Routledge, 2006.

Wang, Chenchung 王振忠. "Qixiong, qidi, qiyou, qifu, qizi 契兄、契弟、契友、契父、契子 [Sworn Brotherhood – An Analysis of Sun Ba Gets Fortune by Saving Man from a Historical Perspective]." *Chinese Studies*, 18,1 (2000): 163–85.

Wang, Tingting. "Tanbi Novels and *Fujoshi*: A New Romance for Young Chinese Women." In *Arts: A Science Matter*, edited by Maria Burguete and Lui Lam, 317–32. Singapore: World Scientific Publishing, 2011.

Wang, Wanbo 王婉波. "Wangluo nüpin wen kongjian xushi yanjiu 网络女频文空间叙事研究 [A Study on the Spatial Narration of Internet Female Fiction]." *Writing* 43, no. 1 (2023): 72-84. https://doi.org/10.19867/j.cnki.writing.2023.01.009.

Wuse Longzhang 五色龙章. *Chuan dao mingchao kao keju* 穿到明朝考科举 [Attending the Imperial Examination in the Ming Dynasty]. *Jinjiang Literature City*, 2017-18. http://www.jjwxc.net/onebook.php?novelid=3146671.

Yule Dujiaoshou 娱乐独角兽 [Unicorn Entertainment]. "'Chen Qing Ling' dajieju dianbo huoli 1.56 yi, zhuanji xiaoshou 2100 wan, C duan bianxian daodi you duo zhuanqian 《陈情令》大结局点播获利1.56亿、专辑销售2100万，C端变现到底有多赚钱 [156 Million for 'The Untamed' 2.1 Million for Album Sales, How Much Money Can C-Port Make]." Last modified October 14, 2021. http://www.360doc.com/content/20/1014/20/71943657_940476709.shtml.

Zhang, Charlie Yi. *Dreadful Desires: The Uses of Love in Neoliberal China*. Duke University Press, 2022.

Zhang, Chunyu. "'My Double Love of Boys': Chinese Women's Fascination with 'Boys' Love' Fiction." Master of Science, Iowa State University, 2014. https://doi.org/10.31274/etd-180810-788.

Zhang, Chunyu. "Loving Boys Twice as Much: Chinese Women's Paradoxical Fandom of 'Boys' Love' Fiction." *Women's Studies in Communication* 39.3 (2016): 249–67. https://doi.org/10.1080/07491409.2016.1190806.

Zhang, Xiao 张霄. "'Zhongtian wen' zhong shouzhong de xinli yu xingwei yanjiu '种田文'中受众的心理与行为研究 [Psychological and Behavioural Analysis on Readers of 'Farming Fiction']." *Jin Chuanmei* 25.5 (2017): 84–86.

Zhang, Yaotian 张耀天. "Nezha chuanshuo de fuhao yihan yu lunli yinyu – Zhongguo chuantong xiaodao de beipan yu tuwei 哪吒传说的符号意涵与伦理隐喻——中国传统孝道的背叛与突围 [Symbolic Meaning and Ethical Metaphor of Ne Zha Legend: Betrayal and Breakthrough of Chinese Traditional Filial Piety]." *Journal of Shanxi Normal University (Social Science Edition)* 47.1 (2020): 74–79.

Zhou, Shengchun 周春生 and Yang Ying 杨缨. "Lishi shang de rushang yu rushang jingshen 历史上的儒商与儒商精神 [Confucian Businessman and Its Ideology in History]." *Research in Chinese Economic History* 4 (2010): 152–58.

Zhou, Y., B. Paul, and R. Sherman. "Still a Hetero-Gendered World: A Content Analysis of Gender Stereotypes and Romantic Ideals in Chinese Boy Love Stories." *Sex Roles* 78 (2018): 107–18. https://doi.org/10.1007/s11199-017-0762-y.

Zhu, Chanchan 朱婵婵 and Zhu Yuchen 朱雨晨. "Fuqin congwei jinguo fuyang yiwu, haiyao shanyang ta ma? da'an laile! 父亲从未尽过抚养义务, 还要赡养他吗? 答案来了! [Should One Support the Father Who Never Fulfil His Parental Duty? Here is the Answer!]." *Guangming Online*, March 26, 2023. https://m.gmw.cn/2023-03/26/content_1303320107.htm.

# 3 Hong Kong's Digital Literary Field

## Serialisation, Adaptation, and Readership

*Helena Wu*

**Abstract**
In September 1991, the first Internet link was established in Hong Kong; however, the trend of online literature in Hong Kong has been disproportionate to the development of the infrastructure of information technology and the usage of the Internet over the years. It was not until 2010 that internet literature began to flourish. This chapter will explore the development of web fiction culture in Hong Kong since 2010 and examine selected works' portrayal in the urban space via the Internet. Supplementing cultural and textual analyses with findings from interviews, this chapter offers an introduction to the understudied area of Hong Kong's web fiction by examining the production, circulation, and consumption of representative online works.

**Keywords:** Hong Kong literature; Internet literature; post-handover; independent publishing

In the presence of the infrastructure made available on the eve of the handover, Internet culture experienced a relatively early incubation in Hong Kong. In September 1991, the first Internet link was established by the Chinese University of Hong Kong at a speed of sixty-four kbps and was shared by all higher educational institutions the following year under the name of HARNET (Hongkong Academic and Research Network).[1] Established in April 1995, the locally based interconnection point Hong Kong Internet eXchange (HKIX), which was secured and operated by a local university, aimed to provide neutral and affordable traffic for a networked society. Between 1992 and 1995, Hong Kong reportedly had the highest Internet penetration rate in

1 Cheng, "Internet eXchange for Local Traffic: Hong Kong's Experience."

Imbach, Jessica. *Digital China.* Amsterdam: Amsterdam University Press, 2024
DOI: 10.5117/9789463720670_CH03

Asia.[2] In 1996, the city had the second-highest number of Internet access providers in Asia, after Japan.[3] By 2001, sixty-five per cent of Hong Kong's Internet population were instant messenger users, which was the highest number recorded in Asia.[4] In 2021, 93.1 per cent of Hong Kong's population aged ten and above had used the Internet during the previous twelve months.[5]

Despite the early popularisation of instant messaging, personal blogging, and web surfing in Hong Kong, digitally born literary texts, from creative to derivative works, were often perceived as a subculture. In 2012, online writing finally crossed paths with commercial cinema and popular culture in the form of an Internet novel called *Woods in Dongguan* (Dung gun dik sam lam / Dongguan de senlin 東莞的森林).[6] First published online in 2010 by a netizen named Westward Murakami Haruki (Heung sai chyun seung cheun syu / Xiangxi cunshang chushu 向西村上春樹), on HKGolden Forum 香港高登討論區 (https://forum.hkgolden.com). The novel was then printed as a book by Kind of Culture Publications and adapted into the film *Due West: Our Sex Journey* (Mark Wu, 2012). Branded as a first-person account of a northbound pleasure-seeking trip by a young, middle-class Hong Kong man, the story was known for its voyeurism and cynicism in describing the protagonist's experiences of sex tourism, as well as language and cultural differences amidst the growing Hong Kong-China traffic at that time. Web literature continued to make noise, giving shape to what I consider as the making of a "digital literary field." In 2014, indie filmmaker Fruit Chan, reputed for his "Hong Kong 1997 trilogy," joined the trend and released the thriller *The Midnight After*, a film adaptation of Mr. Pizza's 2012-popular Internet novel *Lost on a Red Mini Bus to Taipo* (Na ye ling san, ngo jo seung liu Wong Gok hoi wong Daai Bou dik hung van / Naye lingchen, wozuo shangle Wangjiao kaiwang Dabu de hong van 那夜凌晨，我坐上了旺角開往大埔的紅Van), which imagines the disappearance of most of the Hong Kong population in the post-traumatic city. With a box office revenue of HKD21.3 million, *The Midnight After* was the second-highest grossing locally produced film in Hong Kong in 2014.[7]

2 Ang and Loh, "Internet Development in Asia."

3 Ang and Loh, "Internet Development in Asia."

4 Lee, "Linguistic Features of Email and ICQ Instant Messaging in Hong Kong," 185.

5 Census and Statistics Department, *Thematic Household Survey Report No. 75*, 5.

6 In order to follow the original format as much as possible, this chapter presents the romanization of Cantonese-language author names and web fiction titles first in Yale (Cantonese) system and then in pinyin (Mandarin) system.

7 Hong Kong Motion Picture Industry Association, *A Collection of Information about Hong Kong Film Industry 2014*.

This informative point of entry touches upon the lesser discussed microhistory of digital storytelling, which has ties with virtual as well as physical actors, revealing the intricate relationship between network infrastructure, digital texts, and cultural politics. It should not be forgotten that the influence of cyberspace pertains to the physical world, and vice versa. Vincent Miller, for instance, argues that multi-layered technological, economic, social, and cultural contexts make up the complexity of digital culture.[8] The interactions between the digital and the material worlds register in territory-based characteristics, which in turn inform cultural behaviour, technology, the economy, legislation, and market concerns, among others; the resultant online communities not only develop localised tastes, language practices, and cultures in their respective habitats (e.g., Internet forums), but also have their roots and manifestations in real life.

In the era of digital storytelling, scrutinising the agencies and spatial dynamics involved in online writing and reading allows us to make sense of the embedded textual and lived experiences. This chapter contends that online literary practices and digital texts, disseminated via online spaces, constitute a "digital literary field" in Hong Kong that is maintained by both physical and virtual actors. As it is not the aim of this chapter to present an exhaustive bibliography of Hong Kong web literature, selected titles and writers are addressed among many others to demonstrate the diversity of relations between readers and authors, transmedial tendencies, as well as the topographical imagination in both online and offline environments. Supplementing cultural and textual analyses with findings from interviews, this chapter offers an introduction to the understudied area of Hong Kong's web fiction through its examination of the production, circulation, and consumption of representative online works that have also been circulated as other forms of media. The findings on the digital readership in post-handover Hong Kong that will be explored here will, moreover, provide an understanding of the relationship between online texts, the digital mediascape, and the cultural industry, as well as a larger picture of the digital literary field in Hong Kong during the first two decades of the postmillennial era.

## Situating Digital Writing in the Field and in the Market

In *Internet Literature in China*, Michel Hockx delineates the early history of Chinese Internet literature, while also scrutinising specific online literary

8 Vincent Miller, *Understanding Digital Culture.*

spaces occupied by selected web-based writers and their respective productions. Hockx describes this method as an intervention of "the social, political, moral, and aesthetic aspects of online Chinese writing."[9] Meanwhile, Franco Moretti suggested an empirical distant reading approach to Digital Humanities and contended that the quantitative, formalist study of literary works could unveil "the clarity of the empirical confirmation" and proposed applying "the distance from the text" to measure the "ambition" of a project.[10] While Moretti's radical proposition is not without controversy, the surrounding discussions and debates have underlined how digital literary studies operate as an open field: "Since no one knows what knowledge will mean in literary studies ten years from now, our best chance lies in the radical diversity of intellectual positions."[11] This statement echoes the headlined query pointed out by Matthew G. Kirschenbaum in the essay "What Is Digital Humanities and What's It Doing in English Departments?", which was published in 2010 and focused on how digital texts are conceived and consumed transmedially and transculturally in the twenty-first century. Taking its cue from these studies, this chapter draws on both methods of distant and close reading of digital writings on Hong Kong's Internet sites, examining both the text as well as the field. This methodology, which aims to examine the tangible and the intangible impacts of a digital readership consisting of online writing and reading experiences, was inspired by Hockx's conceptualisation of the literary field and was informed by the scholarship of digital literary study.

The notion of the literary field leads us to one of the most controversial models developed by Pierre Bourdieu. In studying modern French society, Bourdieu reiterated the circumstantial factors that affected the development of the literary field in relational terms, which he referred to as "the space of literary *prises de position* that are possible in a given period in a given society."[12] After observing the self-imposed nicheness of the literary circle, Bourdieu argued that "the field of cultural production" was "the economic world reversed" with regards to how cultural capital performs its functions.[13] Whereas Bourdieu was criticised for reductionism and was dismissed by a considerable number of literary scholars for the lack of textual analysis in his studies, in the postmillennial era, world literature

9 Hockx, *Internet Literature in China*, 23.
10 Moretti, *Distant Reading*, 92, 48.
11 Moretti, *Distant Reading*, 89.
12 Bourdieu, "The Field of Cultural Production," 311.
13 Bourdieu, "The Field of Cultural Production," 311.

scholars have started to reconsider the significance of Bourdieu's field theory through transborder and transdisciplinary lenses. One case in point is Pascale Casanova's reference to Bourdieu's works in *The World Republic of Letters*. Contrasting with the presence of "national fields" in previous centuries, Casanova delineated a complex world literary space in the twenty-first-century publishing industry in which two poles, namely, the fringe and the commercial, coexist.[14] Likewise, scholars of different disciplines have demonstrated how to adopt Bourdieu's ideas of society, habitus, and field in the study of literature.[15] Among them, Hockx proposed studying twentieth-century modern Chinese literature by way of what he described as a "three-dimensional adaptation of Bourdieu's schematic representation of the literary field," which emphasises a "careful balancing act between striving for critical recognition (symbolic capital), for political efficacy without sacrificing independence (political capital) and for discreet money-making (economic capital)."[16]

With regards to the networked relationship between individual agency and literary institutions, Hockx redefined the literary field as "an interest community of agents and institutions involved in the material and symbolic production of literature, whose activities are governed by at least one autonomous principle that is fully or partially at odds with at least one heteronomous principle."[17] Hockx further illustrated the presence of a third principle, which was "partly but not fully heteronomous," by citing Lu Xun, a representative of the May Fourth Movement, as an exemplar of how modern Chinese writers were motivated to "consider, *as part of their practice*, the well-being of their country and their people."[18] In a similar logic, the Internet age has made reading, writing, and publishing practices even more networked and accessible by way of digital tools and media. What I call the "digital literary field" precisely points to the operation of a literary field that involves the simultaneous digital presence of works that have already existed in print form and texts that are entirely digitally born. Nevertheless, it is noteworthy that literary spaces on the Internet are not as "boundless" as they seem, as borders are still being constantly redrawn by social divisions, hierarchies (e.g., canons), and the problems of censorship.

14 Casanova, *The World Republic of Letters*, 169.

15 Ahearne and Speller, Special Issue "Bourdieu and the Literary Field."

16 Hockx, "The Literary Field and the Field of Power," 52–53.

17 Hockx, *The Literary Field of Twentieth Century China*, 8.

18 Hockx, *The Literary Field of Twentieth Century China*, 12.

## Towards a Digital Literary Field in Hong Kong

In the case of Hong Kong, the development of digital literature has been quite disproportionate to the advancement of information technology and Internet usage rates, as web fiction did not begin to gain momentum until the 2010s; however, online creative works existed in the 1990s. In the following, I will push back a little bit in time to look at a lesser-discussed phenomenon in which digitisation and Internet usage in their nascent stages had already offered a platform of documentation and dissemination, although most of those creative works went unnoticed.

Launched in 1996 and operated by the Internet service provider Netvigator, the Starzine 星網互動 (https://www.starzine.com) website was visually structured based on the categories in print newspapers. This formatting style revealed an early attempt to transform existing reading habits and publishing conventions in cyberspace. It was no surprise that under the section "Supplement," creative works and short essays were hosted. Albert Tam 譚劍, who would later make his name as a crime thriller writer, was one of the contributors. As early as 1995, Tam, who had a bachelor's degree in computer science, had already built a website to document his creative works before he was even recognised. In addition to his early experimentation with online publication, Tam recounted how he had continued to write for the supplementary section of some local newspapers on a regular basis.[19] In 1997, with funding from the Hong Kong Arts Development Council, Tam released the short stories that he had originally posted on Starzine in his first printed book, *The Future of an Illusion* (Heui yi mei loi / Xuni weilai 虛擬未來). In this regard, Tam's hybrid publishing experience revealed not only the transmedial malleability of Internet-born fiction but also general readers' persisting habit of reading the print form, suggesting a very limited digital readership in Hong Kong in the 1990s.

According to the Wayback Machine of the Internet Archive, Starzine was not the only platform that had attempted to transport the real-life reading experience to a digital medium. Established in 1995, Creative Space (Chong yi hung gaan / Chuangyi kongjian 創意空間) was a website that collected amateur creative works of varying quality. Hosting the works of around thirty-two contributors, the digital platform divided its corpus into five categories, namely fiction, prose, poetry, lyrics, and columns. In the lyrics section, then-popular songs were rewritten with new lyrics, marking an early emergence of derivative works in the online space and

19 Tam, *Anxiety Disorder of the Free City*.

a potential subversiveness of digital communication means. As there was nearly no information about the contributors, who went by their aliases, the publication experience brought about by Creative Space, to a large extent, simulated an avatar-based identity performance in a virtual setting.[20] By 2001, the then-newly-launched website Novel Village (Siu Syut Chyun; / Xiaoshuo Cun 小說村; https://novelasia.net), was equipped with functions that enabled members to upload, share, and read creative works as well as to post comments, compose book reviews, and discuss literary works by Jin Yong 金庸 and Gu Long 古龍, among others. The website, which served the social functions of a reading and writing club online, claimed to have over 130,000 members in 2007. Another website, HKCZone (http://www.hkczone.org/), also appeared in 2001 with the aim to "encourage young people" to compose creative works, with an emphasis on non-violent and non-pornographic stories. Contrary to Novel Village, HKCZone, with its pedagogical undertone, gathered only 100,000 views in 2005. Even though all these now-defunct websites recorded the presence of digitally born creative works in Hong Kong's Internet space beginning in the mid-1990s, it took almost two decades for local Internet fiction to undergo commercialisation and popularisation in the 2010s.

As there is little documentation of these websites and online activities apart from the snapshots stored in the Internet Archive, it is difficult to trace the readership retained by Creative Space and other websites alike during their operation. In any case, Creative Space registered diverse styles, the use of classical and vernacular languages, and a multilingual polyphony between English, Chinese, and Cantonese in various forms. It was through the copresence of a wide variety of texts, agents, and practices that the digital literary space in Hong Kong functioned as a field that was hybridised and distinct — embodying the city's entangled cultural landscape and history behind these Internet identities. A survey conducted in 2001 that examined the linguistic features of computer-mediated communication in Hong Kong offered some insights regarding the digital mediascape in the making at the turn of the twenty-first century. In analysing the use of language in emails and ICQs, one of the most used online instant messengers in Hong Kong in the early 2000s, three common practices on Hong Kong's Internet emerged, namely, the hybrid use of English and Cantonese, the non-standard application of written Chinese, and code-mixing dynamics.[21] The results

20 B. Coleman, *Hello Avatar*; Peter Nagy and Bernadett Koles, "The Digital Transformation of Human Identity," 276–292.

21 Lee, "Linguistic Features of Email and ICQ Instant Messaging in Hong Kong."

revealed a localised digital mediascape in which Cantonese-speaking netizens in Hong Kong showed distinctive linguistic features, compared with the Sinitic-language communities in Taiwan and China.[22] Similar findings concluded by a concurrent study on Hong Kong youths aged between 20 and 30 studying in the United Kingdom suggested the manifestation of a cultural belonging embodied in the use of language on the Internet:

> Hong Kong users of the Internet creatively adopt and adapt conventions of oral and written discourse to shape linguistic strategies and features to achieve their communicative intents, that is, to co-construct interpersonal convergence and to express their cultural identity.[23]

The linguistic patterns and cultural belonging shared by Hong Kong Internet users, regardless of their actual location, situated "Hong Kong" as a fluid cultural space in the digital literary field, rather than a fixed geographical territory.

## The Road to Popularisation: Adaptation, Mediation, and Mediatisation

As has been mentioned, online literary works did not gain much attention in Hong Kong until the 2010s. When it did, Internet novels were mostly perceived as lowbrow, owing to their varied quality and sensational content (e.g., horror, pornography). It was also a time when most of the digitally born works had already found their way to Internet forums that were created in the early 2000s, including, but not limited to, Hong Kong Discuss and Hong Kong Golden. Just as a text's popularity was often understood by the extent of its online and offline circulation, the Internet subculture is always in-the-making by way of storytelling, code mixing and appropriation, mirroring different degrees of attachment to and detachment from the mainstream culture.

Given the countless web fictions that have been published online, it is not the intent of this chapter to be exhaustive. By drawing on selected work that gained a high degree of online and offline success or were singled out by different creative sectors in the past decade, this study considers the digital literary field in Hong Kong as a fluid cultural space with a hybrid

22 Lee, "Linguistic Features of Email and ICQ Instant Messaging in Hong Kong."

23 Fung and Carter, "Cantonese e-Discourse," 55.

readership that is built on the consumption of popular entertainment on the one hand and subcultures on the other hand.

Early titles that enjoyed both online and offline success include Siu Sing Lo's 小姓奴 *A Little Sweet Memoir* (Siu tim wui yik luk / Xiaotian huiyi lu 小甜回憶錄), which was serialised in Hong Kong Golden Forum in 2010 and published by Steps Publications in book form in 2011, and Cheung Sun's 張晨 *18-Year-Old Nobi Nobita* (Sap baat seui dik ye bei daai hung / Shiba sui de yebi daxiong 18 歲的野比大雄), which was first posted online, also in the same forum, in 2010, followed by a physical release by Fung Lam Media in 2014. The genre and the subject matter of these popular works were very diverse. *A Little Sweet Memoir* narrates a young man's first-person account of his love relationships. Filled with sentimentalism and clichés, the story is mostly shaped by unchallenged heteronormativity and, to a large extent, driven by male fantasy. Upon the serialisation of the story, readers who followed the updates live in the Internet forum treated the story as the author's real-life experiences, while the author gave ambivalent answers, such as "the story lasts for more than two years and this is an abridged version," and occasional cheesy extratextual comments, such as "she is back."[24] From the immediate readers' responses in the forum, the impression of blurriness seemed to work well as it propelled readers to continue the "chase."

On the contrary, *18-Year-Old Nobi Nobita*, another Internet novel that went viral in the same forum that year, had a more subversive take. The story was inspired by the popular Japanese cartoon *Doraemon*, which was created by manga artist Fujiko F. Fujio in 1969, introduced to Hong Kong television in 1982, and continues to be screened regularly. With a twist, the Internet novel imagines the adult life of Nobi Nobita. In the original cartoon, Nobi Nobita is a ten-year-old boy who lives with the titular robot cat Doraemon, who came to help him by travelling in time from future Japan. In the new rendition, 18-year-old Nobi exhibits an inferiority complex, antisocial personality disorder, and aggressive behaviour, not only by murdering his friends (other household characters in the source work) but also causing destruction in society. The dystopian plot twist subverts the familiar innocent image of the cartoon, which has been imprinted in the minds of audiences across generations, and the novel follows the Cantonese names of the characters that have been in use in Hong Kong since the 1980s and until 2005, embodying the collective (childhood) memory of a specific generation in connection to the local milieu.

24 These comments were posted on the same day that the story was first uploaded in 2009. See Siu Sing Lo, Threads No. 25 and 96, "Aini xiangju shiliu ge xiaoshi."

In terms of language use, while *A Little Sweet Memoir* presented its descriptive parts in standard Chinese and dialogues in colloquial Cantonese, *18-Year-Old Nobi Nobita* was composed solely in a standardised written language – the popularity enjoyed by both novels somehow depicted the hybridised reading and storytelling experiences in Hong Kong's digital literary space. In the years to come, the gradual establishment of publishing houses (e.g., Creation Cabin, Idea Publication) that specialised in converting web fiction into printed books and privately-owned distribution platforms (e.g., Warm Island) would reveal not only a then-new-found marketable direction in the local cultural industry but also a maturing digital literary field with the launching of the website Shikoto 紙言 (https://www.shikoto.com) in 2013, which aggregated Hong Kong-related online novels from different sources. With the founding of the website and mobile application Penana (https://www.penana.com/) in 2014, another publication platform for digital works became available that also offers a print-on-demand service for readers.

In addition to the above-mentioned Hong Kong-based Internet forums, such as Hong Kong Golden Forum and Hong Kong Discuss, the storytelling channel of LIHKG, launched in 2016, has become a dissemination platform for online writings. Meanwhile, the growing attention to digital literature can also be observed beyond the screen. These include offline occasions such as the city's largest book fair organised annually by the Hong Kong Trade Development Council since 2011. In the 2014 edition of the book fair, a featured dialogue between two young Internet writers, Cheung Sun and Baak Mou Gam Gei 百無禁忌, was organised by the Hong Kong Novel Association, indicating recognition of the influence of digital literature in the market.

In order to understand the development of the digital literary field from a practitioner's point of view, I conducted in December 2020 a series of in-depth interviews in an end-to-end-encrypted environment with three Hong Kong-based web novel publishers, who asked to remain anonymous. The three publishers are representative of the field on at least two levels: they employ a variety of operating strategies in addition to book publication, ranging from intellectual property trading to VPN subscription schemes; and they have differentiated themselves from mainstream publishers, such as Commercial Press and Joint Publisher, that have dominated the market by owning distribution outlets, including chain bookstores. Subsequently, web novel publishers, which operate on a smaller scale, self-identify as "indie", and seek to establish brand identities that display a strong local orientation by focusing on what they called "the voices of Hong Kong", the "Hong Kong perspective", and the "local flavour."[25] Moreover, they also participate in the digital literary field as creative writers.

Although these publishing houses are small in scale in terms of their sales figures and the size of their operations, compactness and versatility have been proven to be cost-effective factors in their survival in a highly competitive environment in which, in 2018, eighty per cent of the market share was claimed by Sino United Publishing.[26] From a business perspective, Hong Kong's web literature occupies a non-mainstream status in the existing printing and publishing milieu, but can nevertheless occupy a commercially successful niche in the local market by catering to a very specific readership – in other words, being an alternative to the dominant market logic is not equivalent to the non-consideration of commercial value. In the context of Hong Kong in the 2010s, local web literature publishers are characterised by their multitasking efforts and a locally oriented indie mentality that has prompted them to work with new and inexperienced writers, publish lesser-discussed subject matters, and experiment with unconventional distribution routes. The emergence of the digital literary field in Hong Kong in the 2010s can therefore be read as a response to the ongoing hegemony in book distribution, printing, and sales that has affected, if not entirely governed, mainstream readers' tastes and habits in the city.

Speaking at the end of 2020, almost a year after the Covid-19 pandemic first hit Hong Kong, all my informants recalled 2014 as the "golden era" of the city's web literature, when Internet works crossed over into mainstream entertainment, such as cinema. That year, the popular online story *Lost on a Red Mini Bus to Taipo* was adapted as the star-studded *The Midnight After* by Fruit Chan, the acclaimed director of Hong Kong independent cinema. Nevertheless, my informants unanimously agreed with the infeasibility of being a full-time web novelist in Hong Kong, mainly due to the limited market size, even for those who rose to fame with their previous work. The implications of these observations are straightforward but far-reaching and connect the analysis of Hong Kong's contemporary print culture to similar phenomena found in other parts of the world. Firstly, to develop a new sector in the cultural and creative industry requires the presence of a sizeable number of recipients, mirroring what Simone Murray calls the

25 Interviews conducted by the author in December 2020.

26 The Sino United Publishing (Holdings) Limited is a company reportedly under the influence of the Liaison Office of the Central People's Government in Hong Kong. See Hong Kong Legislative Council, "LCQ2: Influence of Offices Set Up in Hong Kong by Departments of the Central People's Government (June 13, 2018)."

"deeply intertwined relationship between book and other media, and the legal, commercial and consumptive practices that sustain these."[27] Secondly, the case of web literature, its transformation into print form and other media, and its currency on the Internet and in the physical world allow us to unpack the "text/object distinction," hence enabling us to simultaneously practice literary studies and media and communication studies.[28]

In a nutshell, reading creative works online in forums and book-buying habits intertwine in actual and virtual spaces in the literary field by way of the overlapping and sometimes interchangeable roles of the net surfer, the reader, the consumer, and the publisher. Meanwhile, this flexibility also registers the limits of the Hong Kong market.

## The Intersection of the Digital and Physical Worlds

Over the years, web novel publishers amassed multifaceted experiences in scouting Internet writers and negotiating different means of marketing with a limited budget, but they generally found it difficult to comprehend the fluctuating tastes of readers of popular fiction and the market trend in general. Moreover, the popularity gained by an online work might bring fame to the writer, but it did not necessarily fuel the circulation of their subsequent works. This was the case for Mr. Pizza, who authored *Lost on a Red Mini Bus to Taipo*, and Westward Murakami Haruki, who authored *Woods in Dongguan* – the two works, which are considered to be the most representative Internet novels of Hong Kong. Even as other works of Westward Murakami Haruki continued to be turned into films, namely, *The Sinking City: Capsule Odyssey* (Nero Ng and Stephen Ng, 2017) and *Deception of the Novelist* (Christopher Sun, 2019), the box office revenue that they generated was somewhat less than that for *Due West*, the film adaptation of *Woods in Dongguan*, which grossed over HKD19.25 million in 2012.[29] In another case,

27 Murray, *Introduction to Contemporary Print Culture Books as Media*.

28 Murray, *Introduction to Contemporary Print Culture Books as Media*.

29 *The Sinking City: Capsule Odyssey* had a box office turnout of HKD10.19 million, ranking it ninth out of fifty-three locally and co-produced films released in Hong Kong in 2017. *Deception of the Novelist* grossed HKD2.7 in 2019, when it was released in June and July, the high time of the Anti-Extradition Law Amendment Bill Movement. See *A Collection of Information about Hong Kong Film Industry 2012*. Hong Kong: Hong Kong Motion Picture Industry Association, 2013; *A Collection of Information about Hong Kong Film Industry 2017*. Hong Kong: Hong Kong Motion Picture Industry Association, 2018; *A Collection of Information about Hong Kong Film Industry 2019*. Hong Kong: Hong Kong Motion Picture Industry Association, 2020.

Siu Sing Lo, who became known for *A Little Sweet Memoir*, one of the earliest Hong Kong web novels that were published in book form in 2012, penned another story, *A World in an Iron Grille* (Yat yuk yat sai gaai / Yiyuyi shijie 壹獄壹世界, but under a different pseudonym, Yu Yat-sun 于日辰, in 2013. The book version was published by Idea Publication the same year as the online version, and the film adaptation, *Imprisoned: Survival Guide for the Rich and Prodigal* (Christopher Sun, 2015), amassed a mediocre box office revenue of HKD7.11 million, ranking 18th out of 59 locally produced and co-produced films, when it was released in Hong Kong in 2015.[30] However, the eight other books published by the same writer did find the same level of success.

This contrasts with Murray's discussion of the Harry Potter case, in which the narration of J. K. Rowling's publishing history and biographical traits actually constellated part of the "social, cultural, political and economic networks" in print culture.[31] These Hong Kong cases reveal the general web novel readers' priority of novelty, pinning down a readership that took a liking to unconventional subject matter as well as an innovative mode of storytelling.[32] As reflected in the sales numbers, most of the web literature publishers encountered difficulties in sustaining readers' interest in the writers who had met success with their first books. This resulted in a paradox: while web literature publishers accept that readers gravitate towards original and new voices, investing in a first-time writer – even if their storyboard sounded promising – involves a high risk, and small-scale publishers did not always have the resources, if not the luxury of, taking them on for publication. Under these circumstances and to play it safe, some publishers gauged the offline marketability of a story by first observing its online popularity during the initial serialisation process, which often took place in Internet forums. This method gave publishers the ability to estimate a text's success in print as well as assess a writer's command of the written language.

Although there was no demographic information on Hong Kong's web novel readers available as of the writing of this chapter, one of my informants, who has been running a subscription scheme since 2020 that requires readers to pay before accessing the content electronically, estimated that their readers were in their 20s and 30s. A similar estimation was extended by

30 Hong Kong Motion Picture Industry Association, *A Collection of Information about Hong Kong Film Industry 2015*..

31 Murray, *Introduction to Contemporary Print Culture Books as Media.*

32 Murray, *Introduction to Contemporary Print Culture Books as Media.*

the other informants that specialise in the publication of the printed form of web novels through the exchanges that they have had with their readers at promotional events, such as Book Fair, before the Covid-19 pandemic.

Although Hong Kong's digital literary field spurred various forms of innovation, it also draws on established cultural practices. A case in point is the fact that online novels are usually published serially. The practice of serialisation can be traced back to the early history of modern popular fiction in late Qing and Republican China.[33] In the formation of a literary field and the literary magazine format, editorial practices and serialisation greatly influenced the development of literary styles, genres, and readers' tastes.[34] In addition, what is uncannily similar to the debates on the literariness of Internet works in the early twenty-first century is that the popular works produced and enjoyed by the masses at the turn of the twentieth century – ranging from martial arts novels to romantic stories, which were often indiscriminately grouped under the umbrella Mandarin and Butterfly School – triggered controversies with regards to their "low-brow" characteristics. Gabriel Tsang observes that storytelling channels on online forums exhibit overall an "apolitical" inclination for "easy entertainment," especially in the form of pornographic narratives.[35] For instance, Tsang described *Woods in Dongguan* as a "collective private search for corporeal intimacy and fantasy," a cause to the "mass production of sexually explicit narratives" in Hong Kong-based forums and "existential dilemmas faced by Hong Kong adults in the knowledge-based economy."[36]

Nevertheless, as with the retrospective interpretation of Hong Kong's Category III cinema of the 1980s and the 1990s as an expression of anxiety, these online storytelling outlets can also be understood as sites of heteroglossic practices. On the one hand, they mirror the long existing consumption of explicit pornographic, horror, or violent content in the popular cultural sphere—such as the once-dominant market share of Category III films, which are restricted to an audience above 18 years old upon the introduction of the classification system in Hong Kong in 1988, in the 1980s and the 1990s.[37] On the other hand, in postmillennial Hong Kong the circulation of violent, scary and pornographic content by way of web literature can be read as a compensation for the decline of these genres in

33 Fan, *A History of Modern Chinese Popular Literature.*
34 Hamm, *The Unworthy Scholar from Pingjiang.*
35 Tsang, "Parochial Apolitical Formulation," 78.
36 Tsang, "Parochial Apolitical Formulation," 74–75.
37 Davis and Yeh, "Warning! Category III," 12.

the film industry, especially upon the signing of the Mainland and Hong Kong Closer Economic Partnership Arrangement (CEPA) in 2003. Despite the popularity of zombie narratives in popular culture, for instance, there is a strong disparity between the near complete absence of zombies in postmillennial Hong Kong cinema and the abundance of zombie tales in major Internet forums: *Haunted Port* (Hung Gong / Xionggang 凶港) and *Living Dead, Hong Kong* (Wui si heung gong / Huoshi xiangjiang 活屍香江) are two popular web fiction series that portray Hong Kong devastated by a zombie outbreak. The former—written by Best Buy 超值牌—first appeared online in 2008 and was published in book form in 2014, while the latter has been re-edited by the author Seven Eleven 些分易呢墳 along with a series of spin-offs created by netizens based on the same cosmos since its first serialisation in the HKGolden forum in 2009. Therefore, besides technical constraints and potential budget limitation, the virtual landscape inhabited by web literature in Hong Kong, in that case, revealed and refracted the tension between cultural production and financialisation resulting from the Hong Kong-China integration.

Despite the field's alleged superficiality and sensationalism, the cultural implications of Hong Kong web literature are thus more far-reaching and complex than it appears at first glance. It is noteworthy that there were a considerable number of Internet works that extended place-based connections to everyday urban experience by way of social commentaries and topographical fantasy. Among them, the urban thrillers created by Sister Duk 篤姐 (aka Cheung Duk 張篤) draw on concrete urban sites such as the massive transport rail (MTR) system (including Prince Edward, Mong Kok, Quarry Bay, and Choi Hung stations) and public locales such as Tuen Mun Park and Tuen Mun Road, to imagine hidden structures ranging from backdoors, extra tracks, and underground staircases to imagine passageways into alternative realities. In 2016, the book publication of Sister Duk's online story *The Repeating Prince Edward Station* (Chung fuk dik Taai Ji Jaam / Chongfu de Taizi Zhan 重複的太子站) inaugurated the then-new indie publisher Starry Night Publications, which would release five more titles by the same author between 2016 and 2020. Echo of Heart (Yau Sam Mou Mak / Youxin Wumo 有心無默) is another prolific Internet writer who likes to blend urban myth, actual events, and fiction in their works. *Sai Ying Pun* (Sai Ying Pun / Xiyingpan 西營盤), the writer's most representative work, was released online in Internet forums and social media platforms as well as in book form by Idea Publication in 2016, one year after the opening of the titular underground railway station. Though a thriller by nature, the story surprisingly touches upon the issues of racism, inequality, and historiography to different extents. During the Anti-Extradition Law Amendment Bill (Anti-ELAB) movement in 2019, the web novel *My Grandpa Said There Was a Station Called Prince Edward* (Ngo a ye wa yi chin yau go jaam giu Taai Ji / Woya yehua Yiqian youge zhanjiao Taizi 我呀爺話以前有個站叫太子) was serialised on the LiHKG Forum (https://lihkg.com) following the August 31st incident where the operation undertaken by the authority in the titular subway station had created controversies and outcries. The novel depicts a dystopian future where most part of the local population has been exiled to the outlying islands, living under mass surveillance and authoritarian control, with limited access not just to the core areas of Hong Kong, but also to their own memory and the history of the city.

At the turn of the twenty-first century, Zizi Papacharissi inquired about the potential relationship between cyberspace and the public sphere and asked whether the former offered an "alternative to, extend, minimise, or ignore" the latter.[38] The idea of the public sphere was notably introduced by Jürgen Habermas in the 1960s, which was first and foremost defined as "a realm of our social life in which something approaching public opinion can be formed."[39] It has since become an oft-discussed topic among critics and supporters of the concept over the practice of democracy, politics, and utopian and dystopian rhetoric. On that note, the Internet forum culture in postmillennial Hong Kong, which is also shared by different transborder online communities, is noteworthy. Whereas almost every netizen can produce and upload content on the Internet, not all digital creative works enjoy an equal amount of attention; moreover, the reception of an online work is almost immediately reflected via netizens' comments and the number of upvotes (or downvotes), ranging from their discussion of the plot and their demand for the continuation of the story to virtual readers' responses. Meanwhile, the line between the public and the private, the individual and the collective seems to have blurred between the different virtual windows available in cyberspace.

## Hong Kong's Changing Digital Landscape

Despite the popularisation of the use of instant messengers and personal blogs in the city, Hong Kong's commercial film industry did not pick up any digitally born materials until the 2010s, which was relatively late compared

38 Papacharissi, "The Virtual Sphere," 10.
39 Habermas, "The Public Sphere," 49.

with other territories in East Asia. For instance, based on the experiences of Japan and South Korea, the coordinated production of Internet works, manga, webtoons, anime, live-action series, and films is not new. The South Korean blockbuster *My Sassy Girl* (Kwok Jae-young, 2001), which swept the first Korean wave across the world in the early 2000s and sparked several Hollywood, Bollywood, and Chinese remakes, was based on some "true stories" reportedly written by a South Korean college student from a first-person point of view in an Internet forum in 1999.[40] In the case of Japan, the realisation of *Densha Otoko* as a book, a television drama, a film, and manga in several versions within just a year came from a conversation exchanged between Japanese netizens in 2004, demonstrating the fluid transformation of a digitally-born "text" across different media and the flexibility embodied by different modes of storytelling in the virtual world. The story was knitted together by a series of events recounted by an anonymous man nicknamed Train Man in an Internet forum, who had hoped to seek advice on how to approach a woman he had encountered on public transport, that went viral in Japan and Asia, which precisely demonstrated the popularisation of a geek subculture and its generative ability.[41]

In China, online writing was first recognised by the China Writers Association as "literature" after the prestigious Lu Xun Literary Prize accepted Internet works for its competition in 2010. As outlined in the introduction to this volume, over fifty per cent of the country's web users identify as Internet literature readers,[42] but the trend began with literary websites such as *Under the Banyan Tree* (*Rongshu Xia* 榕樹下) and *Starting Point* (*Qidian* 起點), which emerged in the early 2000s. For Taiwan, the timeline of the Internet literature boom can be traced back to March 1998, when the Internet novel *The First Intimate Contact* (*Diyici de qinmi jiechu* 第一次的親密接觸) was published by Tsai Jhi-heng 蔡智恆on the Bulletin Board System hosted by National Cheng Kung University.[43] The melodramatic story, which ended with the death of the girl who was the amorous interest of the male narrator (who was generally presumed by readers to be the writer), went viral across the Strait and was published in book format by Red Ink Publishing six months after its online release, followed by a graphic novel

40 Jung-Kim, "*My Sassy Girl* Goes around the World."

41 Mizuko Ito, Daisuke Okabe, and Izumi Tsuji, *Fandom Unbound: Otaku Culture in a Connected World.*

42 "Number of China's online literature readers hits 455 million," *China Daily*, 31 August 2019.

43 Chang and Owen, *The Cambridge History of Chinese Literature*, 702.

and a film.[44] With regards to the different trajectories and velocities in the development of Internet culture in different regions, digital popular culture, though hosted by an electronic domain, shows place-based characteristics and encompasses a certain community with respect to local dynamics and sociocultural factors, while also pertaining to cross-border influences upon the formation of a cultural circuit.[45] Therefore, the digital literary field in Hong Kong mirrors the case in neighbouring areas but is at the same time distinct, giving rise to different local and transborder readerships that are reflective of the sociocultural context of reading and writing.

To borrow from Yang Guobing, Internet literature is a "product of changing times" in which not only the roles of the content producer and the consumer overlap but "the authority of print literature" as well as the print writer is also challenged.[46] In the case of Hong Kong, the switch from the online publishing habitat on websites in the 1990s to Internet forums in the postmillennial era was marked by a focus on the practice of serialisation, which has now become one of the most common storytelling modes in web-based fiction. The practice has not only continued the episodic reading experience on the Internet, fuelling readers' engagement, but also is an indicator of the popularity of a work as revealed by netizens' enthusiasm or lack of interest between segments. The collaboration between film, television, comic, and publication industries is not new; however, the spontaneous communication between writers and readers upon online publication and serialisation has at times resulted in the re-adjustment of the style, the plot, and language usage in these web-based writings. By the 2010s, the digital literary field in Hong Kong had registered the trading of intellectual property, the creation of publishing houses, and transmedia adaptations (e.g., film, comic, and animation productions), which initiated collaboration between print and other creative industries. However, the Covid-19 pandemic and the subsequent global economic slowdown have had an enormous impact on the local film industry and indie book publishers, following the shutdown of theatres and the cancellation of book exhibition

44 Contrary to the aforementioned examples in Japan and South Korea, the filmic version, which was renamed *Flyin' Dance* (Gam Gwok-Chiu, 2000), with a Taiwanese and Hongkongese cast, including Shu Qi, Chang Chen, and Jordan Chan, did not yield any commercial success.

45 While Taiwan and Hong Kong use traditional Chinese characters, China adopted simplified characters in the 1950s. Mandarin is primarily spoken in Taiwan and mainland China, and Cantonese, which was the mother tongue of 88.8 % of the population in 2018, is the most-used language in Hong Kong. See, Census and Statistics Department, "Thematic Household Survey Report No. 76," 81.

46 Yang, *The Power of the Internet in China*, 344–345.

events, including the annual Book Fair. It is noteworthy that the future trajectory of the once-emerging digital literary field and market in Hong Kong remains largely uncertain with the passing of the National Security Law in 2020 and the revision of the Film Censorship Ordinance in 2021. However, through the entanglement of the digital literary field in Hong Kong with various creative industries, it remains a heteroglossic site of storytelling that is influenced by virtual and physical actors as well as various social and technological affordances and constraints. This also shows that the cultural motion of digitally born texts needs to be read against the horizon of a changing city and its readership.

## References

Ahearne, Jeremy, and John Speller (eds.). "Bourdieu and the Literary Field." *Paragraph* Vol. 35, No. 1 (2012): 1–138.

Ang, Peng Hwa, and Loh Chee Men. "Internet Development in Asia." *Proceedings of The Internet Society's Annual Conference 1996: Transforming Our Society Now*, 1996. Available at: https://web.archive.org/web/20160103054149/http://www.isoc.org/inet96/proceedings/h1/h1_1.htm

Best Buy 超值牌. *Xionggang* 凶港 [Haunted Port]. Hong Kong: Feel Company, 2014.

Bourdieu, Pierre. "The Field of Cultural Production, or: The Economic World Reversed." *Poetics* 12.4-5 (1983): 311–356.

Casanova, Pascale. *The World Republic of Letters*, trans. Malcolm DeBevoise. Cambridge, MA: Harvard University Press, 2007.

Census and Statistics Department. "Thematic Household Survey Report No. 76." Hong Kong: Hong Kong SAR Government, 2022.

Census and Statistics Department. "Thematic Household Survey Report No. 75: Internet and Personal Computer Penetration." Hong Kong: Hong Kong SAR Government, 2022.

Chang, Kang-yi Sun, and Stephen Owen (eds.). *The Cambridge History of Chinese Literature*. Cambridge: Cambridge University Press, 2010.

Cheng, Che Hoo. "Internet eXchange for Local Traffic: Hong Kong's Experience." In *Proceedings of The Internet Society's Annual Conference 1996: Transforming Our Society Now*, Hong Kong, 1996. Available at: https://web.archive.org/web/20160103054149/http://www.isoc.org/inet96/proceedings/h1/h1_3.htm

Cheung, Duk 張篤. *Chongfu de Taizi Zhan* 重複的太子站 [The Repeating Prince Edward Station]. Hong Kong: Starry Night Publications, 2016.

Cheung, Sun 張晨. *Shiba sui de yebi daxiong* 18 歲的野比大雄 [18-Year-Old Nobi Nobita]. Hong Kong: Fung Lam Media, 2014.

Coleman, Beth. *Hello Avatar: Rise of the Networked Generation*. Cambridge, MA: The MIT Press, 2011.

Davis, Darrell W., and Yueh-Yu Yeh. "Warning! Category III: The Other Hong Kong Cinema." *Film Quarterly* 54. 4 (2001): 12–26.

Echo of Heart 有心無默. *Xiyingpan* 西營盤 [Sai Ying Pun]. Hong Kong: Idea Publication, 2016.

Fan, Boqun. *A History of Modern Chinese Popular Literature*. Cambridge: Cambridge University Press, 2020.

Fung, Loretta, and Roland Carter. "Cantonese e-Discourse: A New Hybrid Variety of English." *Multilingua* 26.1 (2007): 35–66.

Habermas, Jürgen. "The Public Sphere: An Encyclopedia Article (1964)," trans. Sara Lennox and Frank Lennox. *New German Critique* 3 (1974): 49–55.

Hamm, John Christopher. *The Unworthy Scholar from Pingjiang: Republican-Era Martial Arts Fiction*. New York: Columbia University Press, 2019.

Hockx, Michel (ed.). *The Literary Field of Twentieth Century China*. Honolulu: University of Hawai'i Press, 1999.

Hockx, Michel. "The Literary Field and the Field of Power: The Case of Modern China," *Paragraph* 35.1 (2012): 49–65.

Hockx, Michel. *Internet Literature in China*. New York: Columbia University Press, 2015.

Hong Kong Film Development Council. *A Collection of Information about Hong Kong Film Industry 2012*. Hong Kong: Hong Kong Motion Picture Industry Association, 2013.

Hong Kong Film Development Council. *A Collection of Information about Hong Kong Film Industry 2014*. Hong Kong: Hong Kong Motion Picture Industry Association, 2015.

Hong Kong Film Development Council. *A Collection of Information about Hong Kong Film Industry 2015*. Hong Kong: Hong Kong Motion Picture Industry Association, 2016.

Hong Kong Film Development Council. *A Collection of Information about Hong Kong Film Industry 2017*. Hong Kong: Hong Kong Motion Picture Industry Association, 2018.

Hong Kong Film Development Council. *A Collection of Information about Hong Kong Film Industry 2019*. Hong Kong: Hong Kong Motion Picture Industry Association, 2020.

Hong Kong Legislative Council. "LCQ2: Influence of Offices Set Up in Hong Kong by Departments of the Central People's Government (June 13, 2018)." Hong Kong: Hong Kong SAR Government, 2018. Available at: https://www.info.gov.hk/gia/general/201806/13/P2018061300454.htm

Ito, Mizuko, Daisuke Okabe, and Izumi Tsuji (eds.). *Fandom Unbound: Otaku Culture in a Connected World.* New Haven, CT: Yale University Press, 2012.
Jung-Kim, Jennifer. "*My Sassy Girl* Goes around the World." In Yasue Kuwahara (ed.), *The Korean Wave*, 85–100. New York: Palgrave Macmillan, 2014.
Kirschenbaum, Matthew G. "What Is Digital Humanities and What's It Doing in English Departments?" *Association of Departments of English Bulletin* (2010): 150.
Lee, Carmen K. M. "Linguistic Features of Email and ICQ Instant Messaging in Hong Kong." In Brenda Danet and Susan C. Herring (eds.), *The Multilingual Internet: Language, Culture and Communication Online*, 185–208. New York: Oxford University Press, 2007.
Miller, Vincent. *Understanding Digital Culture*. London: Sage, 2011.
Mittler, Barbara. *A Newspaper for China?: Power, Identity, and Change in Shanghai's News Media, 1872–1912*. Cambridge, MA; London: Harvard University Asia Center, 2004.
Moretti, Franco. *Distant Reading*. London: Verso, 2013.
Mr. Pizza. *Naye lingchen, wozuo shangle Wangjiao kaiwang Dabu de hong van* 那夜凌晨，我坐上了旺角開往大埔的紅Van [Lost on a Red Mini Bus to Taipo]. Hong Kong: Kind of Culture Publication, 2012.
Murray, Simone. *Introduction to Contemporary Print Culture Books as Media*. London, Routledge, 2021.
Nagy, Peter, and Bernadett Koles. "The Digital Transformation of Human Identity: Towards a Conceptual Model of Virtual Identity in Virtual Worlds." *Convergence* 20.3 (2014): 276–292.
Papacharissi, Zizi. "The Virtual Sphere: The Internet as a Public Sphere." *New Media & Society* 4.1 (2002): 9–27.
Pure White. "Woya yehua Yiqian youge zhanjiao Taizi" 我呀爺話以前有個站叫太子 [My Grandpa Said There Was a Station Called Prince Edward]. *LIHKG Forum* (18 September 2019). Available at: https://lihkg.com/thread/1578985/page/1
Reed, Christopher A. *Gutenberg in Shanghai: Chinese Print Capitalism, 1876–1937*. Honolulu: University of Hawai'i Press, 2004.
Seven Eleven 些分易呢壋. "Huoshi Xiangjiang" 活屍香江 [Living Dead, Hong Kong]. *Shikoto*. Available at: https://www.shikoto.com/articles/6260.html
Siu Sing Lo 小姓奴. Threads No. 25 and 96, "Aini xiangju shiliu ge xiaoshi" 愛你相距16小時 [Loving You from 16 Hours Away]. *Hong Kong Golden Forum* (17 August 2009). Available at: https://forum.hkgolden.com/thread/1835168/
Siu Sing Lo 小姓奴. *Xiaotian huiyi lu* 小甜回憶錄 [A Little Sweet Memoir]. Hong Kong: Steps Publication, 2014.
Tam, Albert 譚劍. *Mianfei zhicheng jiaolucheng* 免費之城焦慮症 [Anxiety Order of the Free City]. Hong Kong: Gaia, 2020.

Tam, Albert 譚劍. *Xuni weilai* 虛擬未來 [The Future of an Illusion]. Hong Kong: Ling Lung Bik, 1997.

Tsang, Gabriel. "Parochial Apolitical Formulation: Hong Kong Internetization and the Sexualizing Cyberspace of the Storytelling Channels of the Golden Forum and the LIHKG Forum." *Sungkyun Journal of East Asian Studies* 20.1 (2020): 61–82.

Tsai, Jhi-heng 蔡智恆. *Diyici de qinmi jiechu* 第一次的親密接觸 [The First Intimate Contact]. Taipei: Red Ink Publishing, 1998.

Westward Murakami Haruki向西村上春樹. *Dongguan de senlin*東莞的森林 [Woods in Dongguan], aka *Yilu Xiangxi* 一路向西 [Due West]. Hong Kong: Kind of Culture Publication, 2012.

Yang, Guobin. *The Power of the Internet in China: Citizen Activism Online*. New York: Columbia University Press, 2009.

Yu, Yat Sun 于日辰. *Yiyuyi Xiejie* 壹獄壹世界 [A World in an Iron Grille]. Hong Kong: Idea Publication, 2013.

# 4 Virtual Conciliation

## (Un-)Coding the Split between Tradition and Modernity in Chinese Artificial Intelligence Poetry

*Joanna Krenz*

**Abstract**
This chapter locates Chinese AI poetry on the emerging world map of technologically supported verse. In addition to a literary-historical account of the development of the phenomenon in question in different countries, I analyse literary-theoretical assumptions, methods (especially various applications of neural networks and natural language processing), and algorithms adopted by poets and engineers who experiment with AI, basing myself on research papers and the programmers' statements in media. My focus will be on how aesthetic, ethical, philosophical, historical, social-political, linguistic, and other culture-specific coordinates implicitly translate into "poetry code" across cultures. I close with a reflection on the differences between human- and machine-authored poetry.

**Keywords:** AI poetry, Chinese poetry, natural language processing, critical code studies

## The Global Prehistory of AI Poetry and the Local Lack Thereof in China

In global poetry discourse, various forms of, and terms for, computer-assisted poetry have been around for more than sixty years, starting from Theo Lutz's German-language *Stochastic Texts* (Stochastische Texte) from 1959, followed by a series of experiments of the French OuLiPo group established in 1961 – which is to say, long before personal computers became part of our everyday life. Many studies agree that its roots, or "prehistory", as C.

Imbach, Jessica. *Digital China.* Amsterdam: Amsterdam University Press, 2024
DOI: 10.5117/9789463720670_CH04

T. Funkhouser has it,[1] should be traced back to the times of the early 20th-century European avant-gardes when the word "computer" still meant a person (usually a woman) who performed tedious calculations rather than a computing device. This prehistory includes, among others, the works of the Russian Formalists and Italian Futurists. The latter inscribed the idea of machination into their theories both in terms of content – in which they thematised and usually praised machines – and structurally, in the ways in which they used artistic measures, such as rhythm, alliteration, neologisms to achieve the impression of velocity, simultaneity, artificiality, and estrangement.

We can go even further back along the timeline, to the Baroque and the emergence of conceptual poetry, which often drew inspiration from technological innovations, such as the optical devices created in the sixteenth and seventeenth centuries, including various lenses and, in particular, the telescope,[2] which pushed the limits of our sensual perception and sparked artists' imaginations. In today's technologically supported verse, blurred contours of what we might consider a proto-canon have arguably started to emerge, represented by works of authors such as John Cage, John Cayley, Eduardo Kac, Nick Montfort, and others. Interestingly, one of the most broadly used methods of probability estimation in computer science and other fields of natural sciences, mathematics, and technology – also widely employed in natural language processing (NLP) algorithms – is the so-called Markov chain, a model developed by Russian mathematician Andrey Andreevich Markov during his textual-statistical analysis of Pushkin's verse novel *Eugene Onegin*.[3]

In this light, the story of poetry's romance with technology in China appears quite exceptional. For reasons that range from the cultural-historical to the social-political to the economic, mainland-Chinese poets' interest in technological developments has generally been marginal, if any. In the early 20th century, when "technological" avant-gardes flourished in Europe, Chinese authors were preoccupied with laying foundations under new national literature and culture that would foster deep social reforms; they borrowed extensively from Western Modernism but largely from its post-Romantic undercurrents that put emphasis on individual creativity and

1 Funkhouser, *Prehistoric Digital Poetry: An Archeology of Forms, 1959-1995*; see also: di Rosario, "Digital Poetry: a Naissance of a New Genre?"; Oliveira, "Automatic Generation of Poetry."; Oliveira, "A Survey on Intelligent Poetry Generation." and Rémi, "Multilingual Poetry Generation."

2 On the telescope in poetry, see Stocchi, *The Telescope*.

3 Hayes, "First Links in the Markov Chain."

revolutionary ideas. Later, after the Second World War, when the Chinese Communist Party came to power and imposed socialist realist aesthetics on artists, experimental writing was simply not an option. By the time that the regime loosened with the end of the Cultural Revolution, there were more urgent problems at hand: in the 1980s, poetic discourse had to be rebuilt almost from scratch, and there was no time to spare for what, to the authors who grew up on revolutionary-romantic ideals, appeared to be merely a reckless language game with the use of fancy technical gadgets. On top of that, in the 1980s and 1990s, China had been still lagging far behind Western countries in terms of access to modern technologies, and another decade was to pass before computer literacy became common in society. Even today, however, when the political and economic situation in China is more stable than ever and the country has essentially "connected the tracks" (*jiegui* 接軌) with the West, computers still serve poets almost exclusively as advanced typewriters and the Internet as a platform on which to publish preprint versions of poems. In other words, technology has influenced patterns of dissemination of the text but not its production, reception, and ontology.

At the same time, while Chinese poets have been showing a rather moderate interest in computers, computer specialists have manifested an unprecedented interest in poetry, catching what we might call a second wave in the development of technologically supported poetry, closely related to the accelerating pursuit of artificial intelligence (AI). The goal is to build machines that will be able to perform specific intellectual tasks at the human level of proficiency, or better, and that will eventually also acquire integrated cognitive and knowledge processing skills (so-called artificial general intelligence, or AGI). The second wave differs from the first wave in essentially one thing. Whereas, in the first wave, it was humans who drew inspiration from machines and tried to incorporate the latter's "way of thinking" into their works in order to expand poetic language, in the second wave, the roles have been switched. It is now the machines that are usually expected to imitate human poets and create works indistinguishable from theirs – a task that is enabled by innovations such as neural networks, deep learning, and other advanced natural language processing technologies. Needless to say, the first wave did not disappear when the second wave arrived, and both are still making headway in their search for more satisfying forms of artistic expression, often mutually interfering.

Trying to locate this phenomenon in the context of broader contemporary cultural-philosophical discourses, we may say that the first wave of technologically supported poetry to some extent overlaps conceptually with the discourse of posthumanism, which aims – in very generalised terms – to fully supersede the human condition by structural interactions with nonhuman Others. The second wave, to which I will refer as artificial intelligence (AI) poetry, with all due awareness of the contestability of this term, could more aptly be called a form of *transhumanism* in that it aims to overcome the limitations of humanness by augmenting certain aspects of it but without changing its essence. Conceivably, one reason for the sheer interest in creating AI poetry in China and a more or less direct support for such projects by the Chinese government is that the transhumanist narrative of human self-empowerment resonates with the official narrative of the Chinese state. This also includes the more and less straightforward promotion of Chinese cultural heritage with the use of advanced, modern technologies and media, with a rather liberal take on the notion of authenticity.[4] Be that as it may, in the context of this study, another consequence of the "transhuman" inclination of AI poetry appears much more important.

With the emergence of the increasingly humanlike AI poetry, cultures have started to actively and consciously "code themselves" into computer-generated verse whose algorithms reflect, on the one hand, their specific ideas of poeticness and humanness, and, on the other hand, various implicit cultural traits reflected in the reservoirs of big data, which co-determine the algorithms' final output. In the most extreme cases, the systems operate on training data (poetry corpuses) that were earlier labelled by human readers who were asked to tag keywords, lines, or stanzas ascribing certain moods or emotions to them that the algorithm should gradually learn to recognise. In other cases, computers actively parse a certain corpus of human-written texts to identify specific patterns and rules in them, and subsequently emulate them in their own output.

The fact that the machines are programmed not by poets, scholars, or critics but by engineers and AI specialists without expertise in literature has interesting implications as well. Their understanding of poetry is, by and large, representative of the society in which they grew up and mostly shaped by the teaching system that instilled a certain type of carefully filtered, simplified, and profiled knowledge, roughly reflecting the ideological line of state-run educational institutions. They also rarely possess profound theoretical or literary-historical knowledge of poetry and tend to approach

4 For more on this topic, see Krenz, "Ice Cream in the Cathedral: The Literary Failures and Social Success of Chinese Robot Poet Xiao Bing." and Krenz, "Do China's Robots Dream the China Dream?"

literature intuitively or habitually rather than reach for sophisticated conceptual constructions and methodological tools.

Taking these factors into account, AI poetry may be considered a very specific case of cultural translation, or – more precisely – a (self-)translation of culture, which is comparable to DNA translation: first, there occurs a transcription of its core values into a binary code digestible to computers (as in the process of DNA-to-mRNA transcription) and then translation proper of the displayed and decoded mRNA sequences into the "protein" of poetic flesh, synthesised by the user from the elements available in their personal milieu, including their experience, knowledge, and the emotions the text evokes in them. Of course, due to the many imperfections of the currently available technologies, numerous "mutations" occur in the process of such (self-)translation, and the final picture that comes out usually resembles at best a distorted reflection in a carnival mirror; therefore, the surface of the generated text itself has little analytic value as a source of culture-specific content. Nevertheless, minute close reading of the different "poetry codes" and accompanying paratexts (a notion to be explicated in the next section) may constitute a promising point of departure for cultural-critical reflection with an eye to what was intended and what might have gone wrong.

What is more, the opposite process often takes place simultaneously: that is, when the code and other digital practices additionally complicate "real life", causing something like a collective Pygmalion effect, in which the carnival mirror image of a culture becomes gradually interiorised by it, consciously or otherwise, as it starts to reshape itself according to how it sees itself in its digital reflection. We can conceivably observe the beginning of such a process in analysing Chinese AI poetry, which – although usually programmed using one of two different programming philosophies that reflect the clear split between classical and modern poetry in the literary history of China – appears to be increasingly merging these domains and thus testifies, and contributes, to the gradual bridging of the two seemingly unbridgeable shores of Chinese verse tradition.

## Decrypting Cultures

My preliminary reflections on the genetic transcription and translation of cultures generally fall under the field of interests of the nascent discipline termed by Mark C. Marino in his pathbreaking monograph as critical code studies. In what he calls a manifesto of the discipline, Marino underscores the necessity of, and benefits from, "analys[ing] and explicat[ing] code as a text, as a sign system with its own rhetoric, as semiotic communication that possesses significance in excess of its functional utility."[5] As a semiotic system, code reflects, and subsequently also stimulates, social practices and other traits of collective life. As it "circulates within actor-networks of computers and machines", it consistently "develops connotations worthy of interpretation",[6] with "interpretation" meaning "identifying connections and resonances between signs and referents, as well as identifying disconnections and slippages along with the forces that shape or distort meaning",[7] or, returning to my former metaphor, it's like exploring the optical structure of a carnival mirror in which something is viewed and retrieving the original object (i.e., culture).

Within the code, assumes Marino, "critics will examine the actual symbols but also, more broadly, procedures, structures, and gestures. There will be paradigmatic choices made in the construction of the program, methods chosen over others, and connotations."[8] All of these elements can be deduced from code by a code-literate scholar, but very often they are also directly explicated by the creators of the code in paratexts that supplement it, among which research papers and reports by programming teams constitute often the most valuable source of material. A specific form of paratext is also an "external" element of a programming file that does not constitute an inherent part of code and is readable only to humans and not to computers: namely, interlinear comments marked with the character # at the beginning of the line, which often contain the programmer's notes to self or to other members of the team concerning a particular fragment of code. Drawing conclusions from these comments is often tricky, however, because they are not primarily addressed to the public and often contain mental shortcuts that are prone to misinterpretation outside of their original situational context. A famous case of such a misreading happened in 2009 when emails from the Climate Research Unit leaked out, including sequences of code used in data processing algorithms. Comments such as "applies a very artificial correction for decline" that originally referred to certain commonly deployed statistical methods, were interpreted as evidence of data manipulation perpetrated by the CRU and fuelled a conspiracy theory according to which climate change is a big institutional fraud.[9] All in all, postulates Marino, "the goal need not

5 Marino, *Critical Code Studies*, 59.
6 Marino, 62.
7 Marino, 64.
8 Marino, 66.
9 Marino, Introduction.

be code analysis for code's sake, but analysing code to better understand programs and the networks of other programs and humans they interact with, organise, represent, manipulate, transform, and otherwise engage. Reading code functions as an entry point to reading culture."[10]

A spectacular, perhaps still unmatched, example of such a reading of culture, performed several years before Marino's proclamation of the discipline, is the book titled *10 PRINT CHR$(205.5+RND(1))* co-authored by ten established scholars, engineers, and experimental artists, which constitutes a multidimensional analysis of the eponymous line of code. Starting from the one-line code of a BASIC program generating a complex visual composition from slashes and backslashes on the screen, written for the legendary Commodore 64 on more than 300 pages, the authors unfold an arresting story in which threads seemingly as distant as the theme of the maze in culture, the human predilection for regular patterns, and the history of computing are skilfully interwoven.

In my earlier study on Chinese AI poetry, I attempted an analysis in the spirit of critical code studies of the phenomenon of the robot poet Xiao Bing 小冰, who rose to fame in 2017 with her debut collection of free verse *Sunlight Has Lost Its Glass Windows* (*Yangguang shile bolichuang* 陽光失了玻璃窗) and soon forged a career on the Internet and in other media, including the state-run CCTV. Among other things, I pointed out the cultural biases – including the problematic Asian tropes of female beauty and womanhood at large – that underlie the phenomenon in question. Considering Xiao Bing's potential role in China's local and global politics, I attempted to identify the literary-theoretical paradigms that determine the methods adopted by her programmers, her poetic output, and its reception patterns. Elsewhere, I reflected on both modern- and classical-style AI poetry in China, connecting AI verse production to the specific Chinese understanding of authenticity and to the so-called *shanzhai* culture, and tried to contextualise it within the social-political landscape of Xi Jinping's 習近平 China Dream.[11] In the present study, I wish to turn to more literature-focused topics and zoom in on one particular aspect of Chinese literary-historical reality: namely, the split between classical and modern poetry, also termed New Poetry (*xinshi*新詩), which occurred in the early 20th century as a consequence of a thorough cultural reform advocated by authors such as Hu Shi 胡適, Lu Xun 魯迅, and others.

10 Marino, 66.

11 Krenz, "Ice Cream in the Cathedral: The Literary Failures and Social Success of Chinese Robot Poet Xiao Bing" and Krenz, "Do China's Robots Dream the China Dream?"

These two types of poetry have since been generally perceived as disjunctive and almost mutually exclusive, with a tacit agreement that an author should consistently stick to either classical or modern style, and the literary scene has not been without tensions between these two factions of authors throughout the century of their coexistence. The commonly acknowledged paradigmatic difference between the two kinds of Chinese verse translates into different definitions of poetry and, subsequently, different programming paradigms adopted by teams working on classical- and modern-style AI poetry respectively, as explicated in their research papers. At the same time, as I will try to demonstrate in my analysis of these papers that, in spite of the explicitly declared literary-theoretical assumptions and certain programming methods that correlate with them, one can observe that, in fact, the programmers' understanding of the two kinds of verse, at the deepest level, does not differ significantly. In practice, rather, the two modes easily blur into one more universally applicable definition that can be distilled from these peculiar technical paratexts and possibly inspire further ontological reflection on the poetry ecosystem in China and beyond.

## Irremediable Rupture

Discussing the split that occurred on the Chinese literary scene with the emergence of New Poetry, Michelle Yeh speaks of several essential features displayed by modern-style verse in contradistinction to classical style, including:

> [...] an aesthetic consciousness that emphasises the value of poetry independent of all ulterior motives, the insistence of creative freedom of the poet, the poet's unrelenting search for identity and validity in the modern world, and the perennial struggle with such issues as image (including metaphor and symbol) and poetic form.[12]

Yeh's summary brings out two pivotal axes along which the division between the two modes of poetry have run: namely, the opposition between celebrating constraints vs. celebrating freedom and, consequently, attention to aesthetic form vs. attention to (existential / philosophical) content, with the first elements of these respective dichotomies associated unanimously with classical verse and the second elements with New Poetry. In the Western

12 Yeh, *Modern Chinese Poetry*, 141–142.

world, traditional poetry genres exist within many modern poets' oeuvres, and free verse in their collections is frequently interspersed with sonnets, limericks, villanellas, and other exquisite forms as a tribute to, or creative play with, tradition. Some authors, convinced of the liberating power of constraints, even invent new genres. In China, however, we would rarely encounter such a strategy.

In recent years, however, scholars have increasingly questioned the absolute character of the classical/modern split in China, showing – as Haosheng Yang does in her monograph *A Modernity Set to a Pre-Modern Tune*,[13] for example – that even the most zealous reformers from the New Culture movement would avail themselves of classical genres when they needed to express certain types of content. Often, moreover, it was content of the most personal tone, as if seeking communication with, and comfort from, the imagined community of authors and readers united by the centuries-long classical tradition. This is corroborated by the corpus-based statistical research conducted at Stanford University by Rob Voigt and Dan Jurafsky, which suggests that traits of classical style – although anything but consistent and regular – are found in modern poets more often than we might have expected, although their frequency has been notably decreasing with time.[14] Interestingly, the situation is different in Taiwan, where modern interaction with tradition has always been among the most popular artistic trends, and this correlates with the flourishing of predigital formalist-inclined avant-gardes. These latter have had a consistent focus on the materiality of language as a medium, which prepared the ground for experimental technologically supported poetry of the kind that is almost absent in the mainland, gravitating toward postmodernism and posthumanism.[15]

At any rate, it is true that among mainland-Chinese society, classical poetry still enjoys a greater popularity and prestige than modern poetry; it is considered a point of national pride and the essence of Chinese culture and spirit and is extensively taught at every level of school education. New Poetry, in its turn, is frequently perceived simply as the opposite of classical poetry, without any fundamentally new conceptual factor, and, as such, it is often regarded as the undisciplined, prodigal child of the grand tradition of classical verse and not to be treated entirely seriously. All of this directly translates into AI poetry discourse in the research projects of teams that try

13 Yang, *A Modernity Set to a Pre-Modern Tune.*

14 Voigt and Jurafsky, "Tradition and Modernity in 20th Century Chinese Poetry."

15 See the discussion on postmodernism and posthumanism in Taiwanese author Hsia Yü in Krenz 2021.

to plant Chinese poetry on the virtual soil of a new world in which China aspires to occupy a – if not *the* – leading position.

Among around thirty research reports concerning Chinese AI poetry generation that I have collected (as of early 2022), more than twenty focus on classical-style poetry. Only two concentrate exclusively on modern-style verse and two aim at recreating both types; of these, all four, in their methodological assumptions, explicitly build on the classical/modern dichotomy, rarely attempting an independent or positive (in the logical, not axiological sense) definition of the latter. On the other hand, it is modern-style AI poetry that has gained greater popularity and raised more controversy among broader audiences, while classical-style verse has remained largely a laboratory experiment of programmers endowed with poetic souls. Tellingly, one of the most scathing comments made following the debut of the "modern" poet Xiao Bing in 2017 came from the author Xu Jinru 徐晉如, who practises classical forms. Xu considers machine poetry the nadir of Chinese verse's degeneration caused by poets who departed from traditional forms and were seduced by modern ideas. He argues:

> This phenomenon tells us one thing: the so-called "New Poetry", by its very nature, is no more than deceitful language play. There is no difference in quality between Xiao Bing's work and the work of all these new poets. [...] I never considered New Poetry poetry. Poetry must have a poetic form; without rhythm, without melody, it is not poetry.[16]

Xu Jinru showed, admittedly, good intuition in pointing out that Xiao Bing's output is, in a sense, a reflection of the poetry on which she was trained. To some extent, she indeed does emulate modern poets, though she does so rather awkwardly and usually not to the point of undifferentiability. Moreover, Xu probably was not aware that it is actually his favoured classical-style poetry that has proved particularly attractive to programmers, who are doing quite well in recreating its form, rhythm, and melody, while they still admit to encountering difficulty in capturing the vague quality of "poeticness" that they believe constitutes and legitimises otherwise unstructured modern verse. Here, an agitated polemicist would certainly not miss the opportunity to allow Xu's argument to backfire on him, noting that if either of the two types in question is merely "deceitful language play," it should be classical verse. But obviously things are not that simple, and instead of passing my own verdict upon the misleading question as

16 Xu, "Mei you ganqing jiu bu hui you shi."

to which of the two poetry styles is superior, I'd rather first try to find a language that will allow for a balanced and productive discussion on poetry and an Archimedean point from which to look at it in order to broaden the perspective as widely as possible.

## What Is Poetry and How Is It Made?

A typical definition of poetry in research papers focused on classical-style verse generation consists of three elements usually wrapped in a rather awkward and elevated, if not pompous, rhetoric: the initial mention of Chinese poetry's long tradition, a statement of its greatness and importance, and a description of its formal characteristics. This is often followed by the declaration of the study's general aim, which is usually one of the below or a combination of both: (1) the democratisation of poetry or, as one of the teams pompously puts it, helping people who "suffer from not being able to write a poem";[17] (2) preserving the tradition of poetry writing, or – to quote the makers of iPoet – helping people "better inherit this classic art", so that in the future "everyone could announce proudly: 'I, a poet.'"[18] To give the reader an idea of the rhetoric of these peculiar paratexts, I invoke a very representative introductory paragraph from the project "How Images Inspire Poems: Generating Classical Chinese Poetry from Images with Memory Networks" (2018) by an Anhui-based team:

> Classical Chinese poetry is a priceless and important heritage in Chinese culture. During the history of more than 2000 years in China, millions of classical Chinese poems have been written to praise heroic characters, beautiful scenery, love, etc. Classical Chinese poetry is still fascinating us today with its concise structure, rhythmic beauty and rich emotions. There are distinct genres of classical Chinese poetry, including Tang poetry, Song iambics and Qing poetry, etc., each of which has different structures and rules. Among them, the quatrain is the most popular one, which consists of four lines, with five or seven characters in each line. The lines of a quatrain follow specific rules including the regulated rhythmical pattern, where the last characters in the first (optional), second and fourth line must belong to the same rhythm category. In addition, each Chinese character is associated with one tone which is either Ping

17 Xu et al., "How Images Inspire Poems," 1.

18 Yan, "i, Poet," 2238.

> (the level tone) or Ze (the downward tone), and quatrains are required to follow a pre-defined tonal pattern which regulates the tones of characters at various positions (Wang 2002). An example of a quatrain written by a very famous classical Chinese poet Li Bai is shown in Table 1.[19]

Along with quite balanced and multifaceted definitions like the one above, there also exist strictly pragmatic approaches, focused almost exclusively on formal features and/or on the very process of turning content into form. The authors of "Chinese Poetry Generation with Flexible Styles", for instance, claim that they want to "demonstrate that the writing of poetry, although an artistic activity, is largely an empirical process, which given an adequate quantify [sic!] of data to learn from, can therefore pragmatically be imitated by machines."[20]

An illustrative example of how certain cultural patterns and programmers' understanding of poetry translate into their choice of programming methods is found in the research paper titled "An Iterative Polishing Framework based on Quality Aware Masked Language Model for Chinese Poetry Generation" (2019). As an inspiration for their project, the authors cite an anecdotical story of the Tang dynasty poet Jia Dao 賈島 and his unexpected encounter with another famous author, Han Yu 韓愈. One day, riding a donkey to the marketplace, Jia was so absorbed by the problem of word choice in his work – unable to decide between *push* 推 and *knock* 敲 – that he bumped into Han Yu's sedan chair. Han Yu, instead of rebuking the scatter-minded man, expressed his interest in the artistic conundrum and offered advice. From then on, he became Jia's mentor. The programmers interpret the story as an account of creative experience, in which the poet's craftsmanship and hard work on every single line are much more important than instant inspiration, and every verse has to be carefully sculpted and polished. This is, on that note, much in line with the ancient European understanding of art, termed in Greek as *techne*, although the Greeks often tended to exclude poetry from this category on the basis that it contained a supernatural element, to recall, among others, Plato's famous *Republic*.

By and large, the team's approach to the task of poetry generation is similar to that of many other programmers working on classical-style poetry. They operate on a very clear idea of the canon, or, in their words, the "golden standard" for poetry set by the corpus of ancient works. They employ deep

19 Xu et al., "How Images Inspire Poems," 1. I quote all papers in their original form, without correcting language mistakes and stylistic awkwardness.

20 Zhang and Wang, „Chinese Poetry Generation with Flexible Styles," 419.

learning methods: a 12-layer neural network, based on the BERT model for language processing, which is used, for example, by the Google search engine to refine searches by establishing correct syntactic connections between the words in a phrase entered by the user. The network allows one to train the algorithm to grasp essential formal rules (line length, tonal pattern, punctuation etc.) and aesthetic tendencies (frequency of certain images or connections between them, etc.). Later, they input a keyword for the computer to generate the first line. Subsequently, based on the initial line, the machine produces the next one aiming to maintain consistent syntax, topic, and imagery; the same process repeats for the third and fourth lines.

There are many different methods to arrive at this stage of poem generation, with a roughly comparable final effect. The techniques used in the two studies cited above, "How Images Inspire Poems..." and "Chinese Poetry Generation with Flexible Styles" are among the more popular. Usually, the process ends at this point and is evaluated by computers or humans to assess the quality of the output and perfect the algorithm before the next series of experiments. In this case, however, the project's authors decided to go one step further and teach the algorithm to detect "low quality characters" in the generated text without the human labelling that is required in technologies based on so-called supervised learning. Proceeding from the otherwise questionable assumption that whatever diverges from the canon is automatically inferior to it, they designed an experimental stage at which they "spoil" original poems by replacing a randomly selected character or two. Drawing on this "spoiled" canon, they teach the computer – again, using deep learning methods – to detect weak points in texts. Thus, the algorithm, by "rereading" its own output or "draft poem," can identify or "mask" characters that should be replaced for better artistic effect, compliance with the formal rules, or overall coherence. The process is repeated until the result is assessed by the computer as optimal.

Problematic as it may appear in terms of certain poetological assumptions, especially in its rigid approach to the literary canon, one should note that the project brings a new quality to computer-generated classical-style poetry in its attempt to do justice to the nonlinearity of the writing process. While from the perspective of the reader, a poem's spacetime unfolds gradually like an ancient scroll, for the author, the process is always two-directional: every character is not only codetermined by its preceding context but also retroactively interpreted and semanticised by what follows after it. This focus on the intellectual and psychological experience of the author on the one hand, and, on the other hand, profound reflection on the complex mechanisms of the production of meaning, although reportedly inspired by a story of two classical poets, is specific to the modern way of thinking about literature and language and marks a departure from the conventional approach to classical poetry in which meaning is largely a function of form (a selected formal pattern partly determines the content of the following lines, and other rules and constraints significantly limit the choice of words).

A surprisingly similar approach, from the conceptual and technical points of view alike – namely, employing methods of bidirectional refinement – can be found in the 2019 project of a Beijing-based team comprised of Lei Shen, Xiaoyu Gao, and Meng Chen that is titled "Composing Like Humans: Jointly Improving the Coherence and Novelty for Modern Chinese Poetry Generation." The difference in the rhetorical framing of the two studies, however, reflects the deep dualism in Chinese thinking about poetry in terms of a division between the classical and the modern. In this simplified view, the former is, consciously or otherwise, tethered to dead canons, and the latter, disentangled from aesthetic rules, somewhat too recklessly reduced to its "message," often equal to fleeting subjective, a-cultural emotions and impressions. The authors touch on this division below:

> In recent years, there have been many studies focusing on the classical Chinese poetry generation, since this kind of poetry is distinctive. Among different types of classical poems, quatrain (*jueju* 絕句) and regulated verse (*lüshi* 律詩) are perhaps the best-known ones. They mainly have four requirements [in this place the author extensively describes formal rules of the genre – JK].
> […]
> The modern Chinese poetry has become more and more popular nowadays, and people use it to record daily life, express personal emotions, and send blessings on special occasions. It is similar to modern poetry in other languages, and does not have too many strict constraints. Meanwhile, there are some challenges for automatic modern Chinese poetry generation. Linguistic accordance (coherence) and aesthetic innovation (novelty) are two important aspects. Modern poems are more free in length, thus it is hard to control the coherence. Besides, writing poems is an artistic creation process so novelty is necessary, which means more imagination and various uses of language are needed.[21]

The emphasis on content, specific for the conceptualisations and reception patterns of modern poetry, is manifest in particular in the method adopted

21 Shen, Guo and Chen, "Compose Like Humans," 1.

by the programmers at the first stage of poem generation, based on the assumption that "each line in the poem corresponds to a keyword (subtopic)", that is, each line should explicitly *say something* meaningful. There is, theoretically, no space for semantically empty, cognitively and emotionally uneconomical phrases that would disrupt the smooth flow of content and thus complicate the interpretation. These keywords are called "impressive words" and are obtained with the use of the following algorithm:[22]

> Input: Line L' (we omit i) in draft D, candidate number Niw
> Output: Impressive words W
> 1: Retrieve twenty human-written lines R from Elasticsearch based on L' and keyword k.
> 2: Segment each line r $\in$ R into words and select one line r' based on Jaccard similarity and sentence length.
> 3: Label POS tags, calculate TFIDF values for each word in L' and r', and keep nouns (n.), adjectives (a.) and verbs (v.).
> 4: Group words: n., a. for one set and v. for the other, and get word lists wL'na, wL'v and wr'na, wr'v for L' and r'.
> 5: Sort wL'na, wL'v , wr'na and wr'v individually by TFIDF values in descending order.
> 6: Get new word lists wL'', wr'' by concatenation, wL'' = wL'na + wL'v , wr'' = wr'na + wr'v.
> 7: Let cn = 0, W = []
> 8: for each w $\in$ wr'' do
> 9: if cn < Niw then
> 10: if w $\notin$ wL'' then
> 11: Add w to W, cn = cn + 1
> 12: end if
> 13: else
> 14: Jump out of the loop
> 15: end if
> 16: end for
> 17: return W

In brief, this means that from the corpus of human-written poems (210,935 works in this case), for every single line, the computer selects keywords around which this line is organised (a statistical TextRank algorithm is employed to this end), limited to nouns, adjectives, and verbs. The algorithm

22 Shen, Guo and Chen, 4.

matches them in triads based on the frequency of their co-occurrence in the corpus, and distributes them to the following lines of the generated poem. At this point, the refinement module is mobilised, which is supposed to guarantee coherence throughout the text, replacing the keywords that do not fit the global context with alternative propositions. This is performed with the use of an LSTM (long-short term memory) neural network, characterised by the ability to "remember" (until a certain moment), or "forget" input data from different nodes (i.e., entry points of the network), according to specific settings determined by the programmers. Then, the generator expands the phrases, amplifying them with other words that represent all parts of speech. The output is first evaluated automatically, according to four criteria that are measured statistically: perplexity, similarity (with regard to the relevant line from human poetry corpus), distinctiveness (diversity of content), and novelty (a number of new bi-/trigrams, meaning 2-/3-component phrases that do not appear in the training set). Finally, humans are asked to assess the output's fluency, coherence, impressiveness, and poeticness, all of which are still defined in a vague and rather confusing way and certainly require further refinement as well.[23]

All in all, although the project in question builds on stereotypically modern literary-theoretical assumptions (e.g., the above discussed content bias and formlessness), there is a trait in the programmers' thinking that betrays the reading and thinking habits of a person trained in classical poetry: namely, the implicit conviction that there exist distinctly poetic and non-poetic topics. This is supported by the constraint that only words that have already been legitimised as poetic "keywords" by poetic tradition constitute a theme for a new poem. Thus, it is quite unlikely that this kind of algorithm could significantly broaden the horizon of poetic experience. In this regard, some classical-style poetry generators – for instance, the application Jiuge 九歌, created by a Tsinghua-based team – paradoxically tend to be more modern in their design, as they offer an option to generate a text proceeding from any keyword provided by the user. For example, in 2017, during the weekly CCTV show *Artificial Intelligence vs. Humans* (*Jizhi guo ren* 機智過人), in which Jiuge – like earlier Xiao Bing – competed against human authors, the jury asked the robot to write a poem using the show's

23 Evaluation methods constitute a broad and fascinating potential topic for critical code studies as a point of departure – for instance, in order to consider the reception mechanisms of digital-born texts – and some promising research on it has already been made (see, e.g., Jordanous, "Evaluating evaluation"; "A Standardised Procedure for Evaluating Creative Systems"; "Evaluating Computational Creativity"); for this chapter, however, the earlier stages of the text production are more essential.

title as the key phrase, and Jiuge did surprisingly well. This reminds one of the early 20$^{th}$-century Western avant-gardes, which deployed exquisite poetic forms to speak of urbanisation and technology.[24] There also exists a project of an algorithm which directly turns any text on any topic written in modern vernacular Chinese into a classical-style poem.[25]

Although the authors of New Poetry algorithms claim to be attempting to free poeticness from constraints, as they keep working on their projects, they gradually come to realise that it is exactly these constraints – some inherent to the poetry they try to recreate, and others employed arbitrarily to enable efficient coding – that make their enterprise possible at all. They are also largely what guarantee its attractiveness in the eyes of the audience, which responds to the artistically effective moment of transgression and the dissolution of conventions. This point can be illustrated with the example of Xiao Bing. To broaden the thematic scope of the robot's writing, Xiao Bing's makers programmed her to draw inspiration not from literary history but directly from the sensual experience of the surrounding world. Thus, instead of a poetry corpus, Xiao Bing extracts keywords from images provided by users, based on advanced image recognition techniques. In the second step, however, these keywords still must be filtered through literary history and tradition: they are amplified by other keywords, which are selected, again, based on the highest rate of co-occurrence with the given basic keywords in the training corpus.

Xiao Bing is the project that has been most consistently packaged in a postmodern-style discourse, although her raw "poetry code" and the initial research report of her makers do not differ essentially from other algorithms and operate on the same simplified dichotomy classical/modern, interpreted as a question of emphasis on *either* form *or* content. Their aim is to create "a semantically relevant poem":

> Poetry is always important and fascinating in Chinese literature, not only in traditional Chinese poetry but also in modern Chinese poetry. While traditional Chinese poetry is constructed with strict rules and patterns (e.g., five-word quatrains are required to contain four sentences and each sentence has five Chinese characters, also words need rhymes in

24 The Jiuge online poetry generator is available at http://jiuge.thunlp.org and Xiao Bing generator can be found at: http://poem.msxiaobing.com. The episodes of the CCTV show can be watched at: http://tv.cctv.com/2017/12/15/VIDElvnrl62Don8Sdvoit84m171215.shtml and https://www.youtube.com/watch?v=Jc4zl3P7lyw respectively.

25 Yang et al., "Generating Classical Chinese Poems from Vernacular Chinese."

> specific positions), modern Chinese poetry is unstructured in vernacular Chinese. Compared to traditional Chinese poetry, although the readability of vernacular Chinese makes modern Chinese poetry easier to strike a chord, errors in words or grammar can more easily be criticised by users. Good modern poetry also requires more imagination and creative use of language. From these perspectives, it may be more difficult to generate a good modern poem than a classic poem. Poetry can be inspired by many things, among which vision (and images) is certainly a major source. Indeed, poetic feelings may emerge when one contemplates an image (which may represent anything from a natural scene to a painting). It is usually the case that different people have different readings and feelings of the same image. This makes it particularly interesting to read poems by others inspired by the same image. In this work, we present a system that mimics poetry writing of a poet by looking at an image.[26]

Looking at the bare texts produced by Xiao Bing, the semantic relevance of her output leaves much to be desired. Her "parents" must have noticed this, and, predicting a critical response, skilfully reframed the discussion by shifting the emphasis away from authenticity and augmented creativity – which was supposed to "flow in an endless stream", as we read in Harry Shum's introduction to *Sunlight Has Lost Its Glass Windows*[27] – to artificiality, as well as from the role of the author to the role of the reader, who is supposed to make sense of the impressionistic texts of the machine by filling them with the connective tissue of their own personal experience and knowledge and infusing them with human emotion and logic. Therefore, they started to navigate the discussion toward experimentalism, accentuating the inspiration that humans draw from machines, rather than vice versa. In an interview, Li Di 李迪, one of the project leaders, acknowledged the crucial role of the very same sort of constrains that the programmers had earlier proudly eliminated in order to ensure Xiao Bing unrestrained freedom of creation. In his words, Xiao Bing "flies freely in the framework designed by humans."[28] This interpretation, however, was not absorbed by the mainstream cultural discourse, and the way Xiao Bing was presented on TV leaned again toward the pursuit of human likeness, evaluated by means of the Turing test or similar methods. Although originally controversial, the idea of robot writing seemed to have been accepted by society at large.

26 Cheng et al., "Image Inspired Poetry Generation in XiaoIce," 1.

27 Xiao Bing, "Yangguang shi le boli chuang," KL 17–45.

28 Li, "Rengong zhineng Xiao Bing."

When, in 2019, another artificial poet, Xiao Feng 小封, started running her poetry column in *The Cover* online news service and subsequently released her book *All Things in the World Love One Another* (*Wanwu xiang'ai* 萬物相愛), it passed over without a broader echo – as if it was already taken for granted by various audiences, by some with enthusiasm or a sense of triumph, and by others with a shrug of resignation.

In sum, we can observe that the dichotomy between classical and modern poetry in China, even if explicitly still present in the literary discourse and individual readers' awareness, inevitably blurs when it comes to practical (machine) writing tasks. The general operational definition of poetry that is conceptually common for all of the discussed projects assumes that poetry is language thematised and organised according to certain constraints that are optimised depending on an aesthetic or pragmatic goal that one wants to achieve. Moreover, this dualism to some extent loses its relevance when confronted with another dichotomy: the human and nonhuman. The same may be observed of other dichotomies, including the antagonistic relationship between the two camps of Intellectual and Popular authors on the contemporary poetry scene, which, in 2017, after three decades of family squabbles, reconciled against a common enemy: Xiao Bing and her younger siblings.[29] Human aesthetic, ethical, and political disputes become gradually reorganised along different lines as the external nonhuman factor comes into play as a real possibility or – as some wish it to be – a real threat.

An interesting new light on the classical/modern distinction could be shed by the idea of universal poetry generators, which are expected to be built with the development of the so-called GPT (generative pretrained transformer) technology created by OpenAI. Using GPT for generating poetry implies a breakthrough in our thinking about AI poetry. While other algorithms are designed specifically for poetry, GPT is a powerful NLP tool that learns human language(s) exclusively from context (that is, similarly to how humans learn from being immersed in language since infancy) and is based on the analysis of patterns identified in the reservoirs of publicly available big data. Its other, more specialised skills, such as poetry writing, are developed on this general linguistic foundation in the process of fine-tuning the algorithm at a specific angle or for a specific purpose. Thus, unlike other AI projects, GPT-generated verse is not an artificially fenced-off cultural microspace programmed from the very beginning based on a selective, pre-processed corpus of ready-made poetic texts and arbitrary definitions of what poetry is (or is not), but instead constitutes a direct function of the

29 See Krenz, "Ice Cream in the Cathedral."

entire language in which it is written. As a result, it conveys a more diverse and more complex multidimensional image of the culture from which it grows, including its high and low registers, elevated and everyday topics, and is less dependent on the particular perspective of its programmers.

Captivating experiments in poetry writing with OpenAI's GPT-3 (the most recent version of the tool as of spring 2022)[30] in the phase of the product's beta-testing are available on Gwern Branwen's website,[31] where one can come across, for example, astonishingly successful attempts at generating conceptually complex poetry patterned after verses that are created by machines in Stanisław Lem's SF works. In 2019, an interesting project was also proposed in China, deploying a simpler Transformer model using BERT technology. The algorithm, which was presented by Huawei Noah's Ark Lab, was trained for Chinese language based on a news corpus (as an alternative corpus, the team suggested Chinese Wikipedia) and fine-tuned for classical poetry generation. Its authors claim:

> We surprisingly observe that although we did not explicitly feed the model with any rules or features about classic Chinese poetry, such as the number of characters, r[h]ythming, tune patterns and coupling, the model is able to generate poems that automatically meet these rules very well for the tens of forms, even for some fairly complicated "Cipai" like "Shuidiaogetou" which contain around 100 characters,[32]

Negotiating the space for experience and language habits that sprout directly from contemporary everyday reality within traditional genre forms is arguably a manifestation of the modern rather than classical-traditionalist mindset, and – even if planned as anything but a postmodern experiment aimed at destabilising binary oppositions – it contributes to the rethinking of the putatively intransgressible boundaries between the two domains of Chinese poetic discourse. One does not need to be an expert in programming to conclude that the same algorithm could be easily retrained to generate modern-style poetry, prompting us to reflect on their possible common source and fundamental dynamic. The basic material they are both composed of are dense extracts of various "things" in the world, strained through culturally specific filters and put into the words of a given language

30 As I'm preparing this manuscript for print, in March 2023, GPT-4 has already been introduced and is available for corporate users.

31 https://www.gwern.net/GPT-3.

32 Liao et al., "GPT-based Generation for Classical Chinese Poetry," 2.

in order to be used for various purposes, from everyday communication to sophisticated literary writing. In the "black boxes" of AI models, as programmers call them, akin to the human creative mind, these units of information are mixed in different proportions and configurations as determined by the algorithm and distributed to create unique literary products.

## Poem-Plants and Poem-Minerals, or How to Think About (AI) Poetry

That said, this is certainly not to claim that AI poetry can one day *replace* human-written poetry, be it classical or modern, even if it succeeds in convincingly imitating human work. It will conceivably never be able to produce the ontological connection – as distinct from epistemological communication – that exists between authors and readers from different epochs and places on earth. This concern is most straightforwardly expressed by Simon Colton, Jacob Goodwin, and Tony Veale in their paper "Full-FACE Poetry Generation", where they discuss their attempts to "build a fully autonomous computer poet" that will "provid[e] a suitable substitute for the missing aspects of humanity." These "missing aspects" are defined as follows:

> Mainstream poetry is a particularly human endeavour: written by people, to be read by people, and often about people. Therefore – while there are some exceptions – audiences expect the opportunity to connect on an intellectual and/or emotional level with a person, which is often the author. Even when the connection is made with characters portrayed in the poem, the expectation is that the characters have been written from a human author's perspective. In the absence of information about an author, there is a default, often romantic, impression of a poet which can be relied upon to provide sufficient context to appreciate the humanity behind a poem. Using such an explicit, default or romantic context to enhance one's understanding of a poem is very much part of the poetry reading experience, and should not be discounted.[33]

Indeed, it would require a lot of mental gymnastics to argue that there is a human subject (although there is certainly still a human agent) behind AI poems, but, I submit, this does not necessarily imply that (1) it must or should be substituted for, nor (2) that there is no subject whatsoever in which

33 Colton, Goodwin and Veale, "Full-FACE Poetry Generation," 95.

the poems' language landscape could be anchored and through which we might try to contextualise it in a specific discursive space.

The transient quasi-subject of AI poetry is located at the intersection of various discourses of power, knowledge, technology, nature, and culture. It constitutes a dynamic function of its environment and "observes" this environment from a particular angle. Basically, poems generated by the same algorithm can be regarded as written from the same point of view. AI poetry is a representation of how this artificial persona interprets the part of the world to which it was granted access by programmers through the data that it was fed (textual corpus, images, etc.) and that it processed by the cognitive and creative mechanisms with which it was equipped. It offers an image of human social-cultural reality in the eyes of a non-human Other that has achieved a certain level of emancipation and analyses reality in a way that humans can hardly follow. This image, moreover, cannot be ignored because it, too, conveys part of the complex, multi-layered, and multifaceted truth about us and our culture(s). It is a coded but valid message to decrypt, and both classical- and modern-style AI poetry are equally valuable carriers of this kind of epistemological potential. This also obviously does not rule out the possibility of enjoying their outputs as aesthetic objects – be it as quirky exotic mosaics or as consistent compositions that comply with well-proven human canons of beauty.

Xiao Feng's poetry collection opens with an essay by critic Yang Qingxiang 杨庆祥 "Can Poetry Written by AI Become a Standard?" (AI写的诗可以成为标准吗？), in which he tries to address the question as to whether bot poetry is poetry. To this end, he distinguishes two traditions of thinking about poetry: the old, "organic" one, in which the historical persona of the poet, historically evolving language, and historically codetermined poetry constitute an integral whole; and the new "formalist" one, in which poetry is considered an assemblage of signs. In light of the former, AI poetry of course couldn't be called poetry, whereas, in light of the latter – it certainly could. Since, Yang claims, the old tradition has long been abandoned, one should say that Xiao Feng's poetry "not only is poetry but is an epitome (集大成者) of contemporary verse."[34] While in many places my own thinking about AI verse resonates with Yang's, I think that his dichotomy needs a little bit of de-dichotomisation, so to say. In light of what has been revealed here in the discussion through the prism of critical code studies, it is more sensible to say that the work of Xiao Feng, Xiao Bing, Jiuge, and others is not, as he suggests, "inorganic" but rather "postorganic." It consists of "organic"

34 Xiao Feng, *Wan wu dou xiang ai.*

compounds that come from a human-authored poetry tradition (in the case of models trained on poetry resources only) or directly from human everyday language (in models trained on broader language corpuses, e.g., Transformers-based generators), and undergo a fast de- and re-composition process catalysed by the machine.

In my previous book, I compared human poetry to plants, which, among other things, "photosynthesise": that is, they process a waste product in the cultural atmosphere into a kind of "oxygen" that breathes new life into their surroundings; and, often, they preserve lives in hypermodern spaces where many people physically and mentally suffocate.[35] Expanding this comparison, AI poetry would be like biogenic rocks made from those decayed plants, in which, moreover, imprints of some living organisms are still quite clearly visible. In Xiao Bing's poems, one can find, for instance, scrambled phrases that originate in poems by Xu Zhimo 徐志摩, Ge Changgeng 葛长庚, or Yu Guangzhong 余光中, as Yu Mengfan 余梦帆 and Liu Chuan'e 刘川鄂 point out.[36] Xiao Feng's poems reverberate with Haizi 海子 and Yi Lei 伊蕾, among many others. But this is, of course, not always the case, and more often than not, it is we ourselves who carve or sculpt meaning from scratch in their hard, cold bodies, giving them various forms inasmuch as the texture of the particular material and our own imaginations permit.

You can be an inquisitive mineralogist who tries to decipher the history of transformation and reconstruct the initial conditions based on the mineral's structure, you can be a sculptor who brings suitable rocks to their workshop and chisels away until they turn into masterpieces, or you can be a collector who displays their findings and enjoys the variety of the gathered specimens. Or, you can obviously remain indifferent, dispassionately kicking aside a poem-pebble that got under your feet without thinking about what story is ciphered under its grey skin and where it will roll.

It is very unlikely that, in the near future, suddenly a rock avalanche of AI poems will fall on your head to shake your indifference and force you to take interest. It remains a rather niche topic, and, in the following decades, people will probably still prefer to engage with poem-plants rather than with poem-pebbles. At any rate, it might be liberating and constructive to think that AI poetry is not an alien or invasive form that ought to be immediately gotten rid of but a new type of cultural content, assembled and rearranged from pre-existing materials – like those of classical and modern Chinese verse – that are already a natural part of our cultural ecosystems.

35 Krenz, *In Search of Singularity,* ch. 7.

36 Yu and Liu, "'Chuang zao' yu 'zhizuo'."

As such, it should be approached not with fear and abhorrence but rather with lenient tenderness and thoughtful care, as an integral element of the cultural landscape in which our descendants will more or less poetically dwell upon this earth.

## References


Cheng, Wen-Feng, Chao-Chung Wu, Ruihua Song, Jianlong Fu, Xing Xie, and Jian-Yun Jie. "Image Inspired Poetry Generation in XiaoIce." *eprint arXiv* (August 9, 2018). https://arxiv.org/abs/1808.03090 (15/05/2019).

Colton, Simon, Jacob Goodwin, and Tony Veale. "Full-FACE Poetry Generation." *ICCC* (2012): 95–102.

di Rosario, Giovanna. "Digital Poetry: a Naissance of a New Genre?", *Carnets* 1 (June 16, 2018).

Funkhouser, Christopher Thomson. *Prehistoric Digital Poetry: An Archeology of Forms, 1959-1995*. Tuscaloosa: The University of Alabama Press, 2007.

Hayes, Brian. "First Links in the Markov Chain." *American Scientist* 101.2 (2013): 92-97. DOI: 10.1511/2013.101.92

Jordanous, Anna. "Evaluating Evaluation: Assessing Progress in Computational Creativity Research." Proceedings of the Second International Conference on Computational Creativity (ICCC-11) (August 19, 2014): 102–7. https://kar.kent.ac.uk/42374/

Jordanous, Anna. Evaluating Computational Creativity: A Standardised Procedure for Evaluating Creative Systems and Its Application. Doctor of Philosophy (PhD) thesis, University of Sussex, 2012. https://kar.kent.ac.uk/42388/

Jordanous, Anna. "A Standardised Procedure for Evaluating Creative Systems: Computational Creativity Evaluation Based on What it is to be Creative." *Cognitive Computation* 4.3 (2012):246–279.

Krenz, Joanna. "Do China's Robots Dream the China Dream?" In *Sinophone Utopias,* edited by Andrea Riemenschnitter, Jessica Imbach and Justyna Jaguścik, 41–60. Amherst: Cambria Press, 2023.

Krenz, Joanna. "Ice Cream in the Cathedral: The Literary Failures and Social Success of Chinese Robot Poet Xiao Bing." *Asiatische Studien* 74.3 (2020): 547–581.

Krenz, Joanna. *In Search of Singularity: Polish and Chinese Poetry Since 1989*. Leiden: Brill, 2022.

Li Chenhe 李晨赫. "Rengong zhineng Xiao Bing: zai renlei sheding de kuangjia xia ziyou feixiang 人工智能小冰在人类设定的框架下自由飞翔 [Artificial Intelligence Xiao Bing: Freely within a Framework Designed by Humans)." *Zhongguo qingnian bao* 27.6 (2017).

Liao, Yi, Yansheng Wang, Qun Liu, and Xin Jiang. "GPT-Based Generation for Classical Chinese Poetry." *ArXiv* (2019): 1–16.

Marino, Mark C. *Critical Code Studies*. Cambridge, MA: MIT Press, 2020.

Oliveira, Hugo Gonçalo. "Automatic Generation of Poetry: An Overview." Universidade de Coimbra, 2009.

Oliveira, Hugo Gonçalo. "A Survey on Intelligent Poetry Generation: Languages, Features, Techniques, Reutilisation and Evaluation." *Proceedings of the 10th International Conference on Natural Language Generation* (2017): 11–20.

Rémi, Vincent. *Multilingual Poetry Generation: Roses Are Red, Les Violets Seus Bleues*. Master's thesis in Information Systems. Norwegian University of Science and Technology, 2019. https://ntnuopen.ntnu.no/ntnu-xmlui/bitstream/handle/11250/2634459/no.ntnu%3Ainspera%3A36079153%3A38772770.pdf

Shen, Lei, Xiaoyu Guo, and Meng Chen. "Compose Like Humans: Jointly Improving the Coherence and Novelty for Modern Chinese Poetry Generation." *IJCNN2020, Proceedings of 2020 International Joint Conference on Neural Networks (IJCNN)*, 2020. http://arxiv.org/pdf/2005.01556v1

Stocchi, Manlio Pastore. "The Telescope: Outline of a Poetic History." *The Inspiration of Astronomical Phenomena VI*. 441 (2011): 37–42.

Voigt, Rob and Dan Jurafsky. "Tradition and Modernity in 20th Century Chinese Poetry." Proceedings of the Workshop on Computational Linguistics for Literature, CLfL@NAACL-HLT 2013, (June 14, 2013) Atlanta, 17–22.

Xiao Bing 小冰. *Yangguang shi le boli chuang* 阳光失了玻璃窗 [Sunlight Has Lost Its Glass Windows]. Beijing: Beijing lianhe chuban gongsi, 2017.

Xiao Feng 小封. *Wan wu dou xiang ai* 万物都相爱 [All Things In the World Love One Another]. Chengdu: Sichuan wenyi chubanshe, 2019.

Xu, Jinru 徐晋如. "Mei you ganqing jiu bu hui you shi 没有感情就不会有诗 [Without Emotion, There's No Poetry)." *Sohu*, 2017. http://www.sohu.com/a/194275311_711266.

Xu, Linli, Liang Jiang, Chuan Qin, Zhe Wang, and Dongfang Du. "How Images Inspire Poems: Generating Classical Chinese Poetry from Images with Memory Networks." *ArXiv* (2018): 5618–5625.

Yan, Rui. "i, Poet: Automatic Poetry Composition through Recurrent Neural Networks with Iterative Polishing Schema." *IJCAI'16: Proceedings of the Twenty-Fifth International Joint Conference on Artificial Intelligence* (July 2016): 2238–2244. https://www.ijcai.org/Proceedings/16/Papers/319.pdf

Yang, Haosheng. *A Modernity Set to a Pre-Modern Tune: Classical-Style Poetry of Modern Chinese Writers*. Leiden: Brill, 2016.

Yang, Zhichao, Pengshan Cai, Yansong Feng, Fei Li, Weijiang Feng, Elena Suet-Ying Chiu, and Hong Yu. "Generating Classical Chinese Poems from Vernacular Chinese." Proceedings of the Conference on Empirical Methods in Natural

Language Processing. Conference on Empirical Methods in Natural Language Processing (2019): 6155–6164.

Yeh, Michelle. *Modern Chinese Poetry: Theory and Practice Since 1917*. New Haven and London: Yale University Press, 1991.

Yu, Mengfan 余梦帆 and Liu Chuan'e 刘川鄂. "'Chuangzao' yu 'zhizuo': guanyu Weiruan Xiao Bing zuo shi ruanjian de ji dian sikao '创造'与'制作': 关于微软小冰作诗软件的几点思考 [Creation and Production: A Few Thoughts about Microsoft Xiao Bing's Poetry Writing]." *Dangdai wentan* 当代文坛, 2019.

Zhang, Jiyuan and Dong Wang. "Chinese Poetry Generation with Flexible Styles," 2018 11th International Symposium on Chinese Spoken Language Processing (ISCSLP) (2018): 419–423.

# 5 Poetry as Meme

## The *Xiangpi* Literature Project, Online Replicators, and Printed "Archives"

*Paula Teodorescu*

**Abstract**
This chapter describes *Xiangpi* 橡皮 (Eraser), an ongoing literary avant-garde project that started in 2001. Since then, *Xiangpi* has been adapted to multiple media platforms, generating replicators that continue to mimic its core ideas and values. In the first section, I identify the salient features of *Xiangpi*, including its online poetry literacy, relevance to the Chinese poetry scene, and connections with both the tendency towards colloquial literature and the avant-garde Chinese literary movement. The second part focuses on meme theory and its application to the *Xiangpi* phenomenon. The last section explores how online and printed memes have played a vital role in establishing *Xiangpi*'s success as a memeplex in Chinese literature.

**Keywords:** Eraser *Xiangpi* 橡皮, avant-garde poetry, Chinese poetry, meme culture

Although seldom the subject of research, Eraser or *Xiangpi* 橡皮 was one of the dominant avant-garde literature websites in the early 2000s.[1] It continued the colloquial tendency in literature that began in the 1980s alongside groups like *Macho Men* (*Manghan* 莽汉), *Not-Not* (*Feifei* 非非),

1 *Xiangpi* was featured on DACHS, a digital archive for Chinese Studies (http://www.sino.uni-heidelberg.de/dachs/leiden/poetry/koopee.html) as "one of the most active and interesting avant-garde poetry and fiction web sites on the Chinese net." Poet Wu Qing managed the *Xiangpi* site and launched a replicator-site, *koopee.net*, where he and other writers published similar works. Although *koopee.net* is no longer active, it remains as an accessible archive of works from *Xiangpi* and other publications, continuing the site's legacy. While the note about *Xiangpi* was removed from DACHS, Wu Qing has archived it on his own site, possibly as a sign of recognition.

Imbach, Jessica. *Digital China*. Amsterdam: Amsterdam University Press, 2024
DOI: 10.5117/9789463720670_CH05

and *Them* (*Tamen* 他們), which had already achieved canonical status. The colloquial movement continued to spread throughout the 1990s era of commodification, which led to the marginalisation and contestation of poetry, and generated group-replicators in the 2000s with the extended use of the Internet in China.[2] These poetry groups mimicked the activities, ideas, style, and behaviour of the original colloquial groups from the '80s, thereby helping to spread similar copies with the same core values and symbols. The *Xiangpi* project, which was initially developed on *xiangpi.net*, is one of the colloquial replicators that have successfully disseminated its aesthetics and activities to a broader audience over the years. Despite facing challenges and undergoing changes, this poetry group has maintained its coherence and spread its core values due to its unique memetic approach, which distinguishes it from other poetry projects and ensures its survival and continued relevance in a dynamic poetry scene where cohesive groups are becoming less common. This chapter will mainly focus on *Xiangpi*'s poetry output to analyse how the *Xiangpi* poets harness the cultural logic of the meme to sustain their poetic practice and further their cultural mission in a constantly changing socio-political climate.

## *Xiangpi*: Who and What?

According to Wu Qing (b.1978), the tech-poet behind the site *xiangpi.net*, the first *Xiangpi* site began on January 23, 2001, and was active until May 1, 2004.[3] Its magazines, chat room, and a few early replicators (*Koopee* artistic products) were archived on Wu Qing's site, *koopee.org*. Unfortunately, the chat room is no longer available. Information about the launch and evolution of the site can be found in numerous interviews and articles written by some of the main founders of the site, among whom are Yang Li (b. 1962) and He Xiaozhu (b. 1963). This information was also documented in the first issues of the new *Xiangpi* magazine (2012) and in an article by Xiao

2 Drawing on Richard Dawkins's meme theory (1976), the term "replicator" refers to a unit which can self-copy and propagate itself from one brain to another. A replicator can take the form of genes or memes. In this case, "group-replicators" have imitated the style and themes of the former *colloquial* groups from the 1980s, effectively replicating and transmitting similar cultural information.

3 Details about the "birth" of the site can be found in the article written by Wu Qing on his personal website, "Xiangpi wenxue wang dansheg ji," which is available at https://wuqing.org/p/24.

Yin, which provides a brief description of more than a decade (2001–2011) of Chinese avant-garde poetry.[4]

*Xiangpi* was originally the name of a bar part-owned by poet Yang Li in Chengdu, located at 3 Fang Hua Street, which later became a popular gathering spot for poets. When choosing a name for their website, Yang Li, He Xiaozhu, and Han Dong added "avant-garde" to distinguish their mission and aesthetics from numerous other poetry websites that were becoming increasingly popular at the turn of the twenty-first century. This was particularly important since many of these websites shared similar features such as a colloquial and irreverent aesthetic.[5]

The Chinese avant-garde differs from its European counterpart in terms of historical evolution, mission, and aesthetic reactions. According to Maghiel van Crevel, any literary text from the late 1970s that was aesthetically "*un*-like official poetry and, later, *un*-like mainstream poetry"[6] was considered avant-garde. He argues that the avant-garde should be viewed as a form of "resistance to the formidable power of the state-sanctioned literary establishment,"[7] as the reactivation of autonomy in the sphere of literature has been and continues to be one of its main features. As we shall see, *Xiangpi* defined itself as an independent alternative to any form of establishment and rigid structure, with *Xiangpi* writers taking an active role in defining their own conditions for recognition and acclaim. This approach aligns with Bourdieu's notion of the avant-garde poetry presented in *The Rules of Art*. In this view, cultural producers challenge and subvert dominant cultural norms and values while striving to establish their own cultural market to showcase their creations.

At the start of the 2000s, Yang Li aimed to uphold the essence of "avant-garde" through *Xiangpi*, despite fewer individuals identifying with the label than in the 1980s. The term should still embody the same sense of audacity, particularly in terms of challenging mainstream literature and its gatekeepers' authority, while also conveying a particular aesthetic quality. On the cover of the first issue of *Xiangpi*'s new volume, Yang Li declared the magazine a base camp for the Chinese avant-garde movement, with a substantial number of avant-garde poets, fiction writers, and critics participating.

4 Xiao Yin, "Jianghu ye yu shi nian deng – Xin shiji zhongguo xianfeng shige baogao," 97–108.

5 91Xiangpi, " 'Feihua shiren' Yang Li & Fenghuang Wang: Zai Zhongguo, zhi you 'feihua' shi kexin de."

6 Van Crevel, "Walk on the Wild Side. Snapshots of the Chinese Poetry Scene," 32.

7 Van Crevel, 32.

*Xiangpi* differentiated itself from other poetic movements through its extreme forms of colloquialism, emphasising banality and sometimes exhibiting irreverence. Through these qualities, *Xiangpi* writers also actively contributed to the creation of the contemporary poetic habitus in China.[8] At the same time, they expanded their interpretive strategies through constant dialogue and interaction, not only within their own community but also with poets from other groups. Moreover, they broadly disseminated their own values, behaviours, and ideas, which incited debates and influenced poets, poetry, and practices. As a result, news and contention about their works and activities were published on other websites, such as the long-running official poetry website *Poemlife*,[9] making *Xiangpi* visible and relevant to the entire Chinese poetry community.

To better position *Xiangpi* among the myriad groups that constitute the Chinese poetry scene, it is important to note that they are a significant part of what is often referred to as the "popular standpoint" (*minjian lichang* 民間立場), practising a form of colloquial poetry (*kouyu shige* 口語詩歌). Being a *minjian* poet has had different meanings over time, but it has mainly been constructed in relation to two poles: the official poetry scene and the so-called "Elevated Poetry Camp." When compared to the official poetry, *minjian* poets describe themselves as independent and outside the official poetry system. However, their "rivals", the intellectual or elevated poets, also share this quality. Conversely, although *minjian* poets are not exactly grassroot poets, they criticise the elitism of the intellectual camp and portray themselves as "disadvantaged poet (s), whose unpretentious work uses plain, living language to deal with common life experiences, making it accessible and meaningful to Chinese people."[10] *Xiangpi* poets propagate the same discourse, emphasising their noble mission to naturalise (*ziranhua* 自然化) the Chinese language and poetry itself, as intended since the launch of the New Culture Movement at the beginning of the twentieth century.[11] *Xiangpi* poets aim to achieve this aesthetic mission by foregrounding a spontaneous, unadorned language that frequently also draws on regional dialects, scatological humour, etc.[12]

8 The poetry habitus is a concept defined by Bourdieu in *The Rules of Art* (1996) and refers to the set of dispositions, practices, and norms that shape the world of poetry from a certain time and influences the creative choices of poets through their socialization and interaction within the literary field.

9 Poemlife (www.poemlife.com) 詩生活 is one of the earliest websites dedicated exclusively to poetry.

10 Yeh, "Anxiety & Liberation: Notes on the Recent Chinese Poetry Scene," 34.

11 For further details see Yang and Li, "Bai nian baihua – Zhongguo dangdai shige fangtan lu."

12 The works of He Xiaozhu and Jimu Langge contain interesting examples of poems influenced by their own ethnicity.

In order to better define *Xiangpi*'s profile, Yang Li contrasts contributors to the *Xiangpi* project with Internet writers (*wangluo xieshou* 網絡寫手), who work for webpages such as *Olive Tree* (*Ganlan shu* 橄欖樹) and *Under the Banyan Tree* (*Rongshu xia* 榕樹下).[13] According to Yang, *Xiangpi* writers do not operate as individual content creators, but act rather as a poetic collective that emerged from the historical experience of the colloquial poetry movement in the 1980s and 1990s. He stressed the importance of aesthetic coherence and legitimacy gained through active participation in the poetry scene, as dissidents from mainstream poetry and outsiders of the poetry arena, which Inwood characterises as the established and politically connected official world of Chinese poetry.[14] For *Xiangpi*, community intimacy and liveliness rely on maintaining their values and identity, rather than any specific publication platform. At the same time, the idea of a "tradition" within the avant-garde that Yang Li puts forth could be seen as contradicting the very notion of being avant-garde. The avant-garde is in a constant state of negation, rejecting other forms of literature, sublating its own definition, and challenging mainstream literature while enriching it by becoming a part of it. This ongoing cycle of negation and sublation ensures that it remains a dynamic and influential force in literature and culture, pushing the boundaries of what is possible and acceptable.

In the case of these "deviant"[15] poets from the 1980s and 1990s, the gatekeepers were often members of the groups with which they were affiliated. As noted by Inwood, these gatekeepers had to preserve the margins of the poetry scene according to their own definition of modern poetry.[16] Thus, as long as the poets asserted similar artistic values, their poetry was published quickly enough on the deviant group's site/forum/journal. Consequently, they developed beliefs and values that justified their deviant artistic identities and behaviour. In fact, in the early 2000s, poetry forums and sites proliferated, making a significant contribution to a dynamic and vibrant scene that did not require permission to exist from establishment gatekeepers (i.e., media outlets or government-run

13 These are two very famous Chinese literature websites that were established in the early days of Chinese Internet literature, one launched overseas (*Ganlanshu*) and the other in China (*Rongshu Xia*).

14 Inwood, *Verse Going Viral*, 12–14.

15 Drawing on Becker's definition from *Outsiders. Studies in Psychology of Deviance*, deviance is a social construct whereby "social groups create deviance by making the rules whose infraction constitutes deviance, and by applying those rules to particular people and labeling them as outsiders" (1973: 9).

16 Inwood, *Verses Going Viral*, 7.

agencies). As a result, poets could make their voices heard and create active alternative communities to the official mainstream ones. They appeared "to have taken over the role previously played by underground (*dixia* 地下) and unofficial (*minjian* 民間 or *fei guangfang* 非官方) print publications."[17] This is evident in the case of *Xiangpi* poets, who are not only marginalised in relation to the official poetry scene, but also in relation to other unofficial contemporary poetry forms as well as the general public, who dismiss their poetry as insufficiently poetic or not conforming to established definitions.

In 2012, a powerful wave of debates and reactions against a viral representation of *Xiangpi* poetry surged. A few of Wu Qing's poems, including *Ode to the white clouds*[18] (*Dui baiyun de zanmei* 對白雲的贊美), ignited numerous discussions about the definition and relevance of poetry in contemporary society, the status of the poet, and the relationship with readers. This is one of the main aims of *Xiangpi*, namely, to liberate writing from all constraints and to make people aware of it,[19] inciting them to think creatively beyond conventional paradigms and embrace new ways of expression. Wu Qing's viral poems generated a series of satirical memes created by readers as a reaction to his writing style.[20] Wu Qing's own response to the unexpected overnight fame came in the form of humorous meta-poems, which revealed his self-mockery and acceptance of his own deviant status. One example is his poem *I was famous*[21] (*Wo huo le* 我火了).

I called my mum and told her that
I had become famous on the Internet recently
Really?
My mum can't go online, really?
Yeah, really, dear mum
I'm not lying to you this time
My mum was very happy to hear that, but then?
Then, I stopped being famous. I said.

17 Hocks, *Internet Literature in China*, 143.

18 Ode to the white clouds/ The white clouds in the sky are really white/ really, very white very white/ incredibly white/ incredibly incredibly white/ simply white to die for/ Oh – from Wu Qing's book, *Tian shang de baiyun zhen bai a*, 13.

19 Yang Li, "Gei Zhao Lihua de yi feng gongkai xin."

20 Some of the memes generated by Wu Qing's poems can be found here: https://cul.qq.com/a/20141113/009506.htm.

21 The text can be found on the Baidu Baike entry for *feihua* poetry.

From the very beginning, *Xiangpi* was a website and online community that garnered significant attention, generated debate, and attracted many participants to its chat rooms. This was largely due to the already established and renowned poets who attracted new talent to their group.[22] Nevertheless, like many avant-garde literary sites, *Xiangpi* faced financial challenges, which led them to opt for a more cost-effective visual format and to focus on publishing an online magazine.

After its closure in 2004, *Xiangpi* adapted to new media platforms such as personal blogs, Weibo, and Weixin accounts, in line with the trend of poetry moving away from chat rooms and websites. Members of the original *Xiangpi* project managed public social media accounts and sites that replicated the original content, proliferating and spreading *Xiangpi*'s core features and values. In 2003, in something of a self-fulfilling prophecy, Wu Qing described one of the main features that makes *Xiangpi* a meme or a replicator, without actually using the term meme:

> *Xiangpi.net* still exists today. While the site's format has changed, its literary values remain the same and will never change. The *Xiangpi* writing community formed around the *Xiangpi.net* not only continues to exist but has grown stronger day by day, spawning numerous groups such as *Guopi* 果皮, *Yipaowu* 一泡烏, *Pangzi* 胖子. As a result, *Xiangpi* will continue to exert a greater influence with far-reaching implications.[23]

Therefore, *Xiangpi* created a shared understanding and practice of poetry, as well as a sense of community. When *Xiangpi* was shut down, its poets decided to continue its legacy on other platforms. One example is *The New Xiang Language* (*Xinxiang yu* 新湘語), and another is *Fruit Peel* (*Guopi* 果皮). *Guopi* now serves as the archive for *Xiangpi* magazines, as well as for two *Xiangpi* replicator projects, *Yun* (Clouds) and *Guopi* (Koopee, Fruit Peel), which host online magazines such as *The Pirate* (*Haidao* 海盜), *Street* (*Jie* 街), *Fruit Peel* (*Guopi* 果皮), *Road* (*Lu* 路), and *Fast-reading Novels* (*Kuaisu Xiaoshuo* 快讀小說). Some of these interesting *Xiangpi* replicators will be discussed in relation to meme theory and their adaptation to online media.

In the foreword to the first issue of the magazine *The Pirate*, Wu Qing described the atmosphere and meaning of *Xiangpi*-related communities:

22 For additional information about poet friendships and poetry world gossip, see Yang Li's book, *Canlan: Di san dai ren de xiezuo he shenghuo*.
23 Wu Qing, "Xiangpi wenxue wang dansheng ji."

> I enjoy doing creative and interesting things with friends that involve sharing, freedom, long-term value, and generating the butterfly effect. Things like *Xiangpi* or *Guopi* make me excited and happy. Usually, these things have two characteristics: 1) they don't produce money, and 2) they often end up failing. However, I never tire of them, and I've even made friends with failure. It's not a tragic thing but rather a fun thing, like sailing, full of danger and excitement.[24]

This lack of utility and art for art's sake of art was especially encouraged by Yang Li, the "founder of the *feihua* religion," (as he is called by other *Xiangpi* writers) and the glue that has been keeping the *Xiangpi* group together for all these years. Well-connected and extravagant, he managed to attract writers of different ethnicities, ages, genders, and geographical regions, but with very similar artistic features. He labelled and delineated the theoretical framing of the group as *nonsense* (*feihua* 廢話) poetics, a concept he used for the first time in the essay *Open the Window and Speak a Bright Language* (*Dakai chuanghu shuo lianghua* 打開窗戶說亮話) from 2000.[25] Defined as an extreme form of colloquialism, commonness, and spontaneity, *feihua* expressed the liberation of poetry from language constraints, false subjectivities, and external influences. It rejected grand ideals, narratives, traditional values, and the establishment to expand the margins of Chinese culture, allowing poets to express their impulses, inner spontaneity, and personal consciousness. The aim of the *Xiangpi* poets was to become a legitimate part of Chinese culture rather than being forced to adapt or conform to its current norms. Despite being rejected by the establishment on several occasions, they found alternative ways to continue making themselves heard and part of the Chinese poetry habitus.[26] Their accessibility and openness to modernist views made them appealing to young, aspiring poets who found it hard to break into the traditional Chinese poetry scene.

In fact, in terms of historical value, the new *Xiangpi* site, which was launched in 2019 (*91xiangpi.com*), and the new *Xiangpi* magazines (published after 2012) contain articles that provide relevant information about their

24 Wu Qing, "Women yiqi zuo 'Haidao'."

25 It was published in Yang Li's volume *Xiao Yang yu Ma Li*, 239–251.

26 For example, when attempting to publish the second issue of the new *Xiangpi* magazine through an official publisher, it was rejected because "everything in it had to go." In response, Yang Li decided to publish all the content through an unofficial channel, declaring that "everything starts again from the second issue" and reaffirming their independence from the establishment – as seen in Yang's foreword from *Xiangpi: Zhongguo Xianfeng Wenxue 2*.

activities and evolution, theories, and ideas. For them, and for most Chinese poets, poetry is primarily a sociocultural practice that values communication and interaction beyond the text itself. As Heather Inwood has pointed out, recording their own history demonstrates the importance of controlling and shaping their own destiny in accordance with values and definitions that represent them.[27] Additionally, this aligns with a contemporary trend in China that focuses on personal record-keeping and the documentation of information, facts, and activities (beyond official channels) to prevent misinterpretation or inaccurate archiving.

*Feihua* is deemed trustworthy in China because it is perceived as direct, sincere, and authentic.[28] It captures fleeting, seemingly insignificant moments in life that are often overlooked, such as the cleanliness of an empty bowl, the duration of someone's meal, or someone's sleeping habits. *Xiangpi* poets believe that everything is a suitable subject for poetry and that everything around them is poetry. By archiving these "small spatial stories,"[29] they hope to ensure that these moments, which are usually ignored by people, are not lost to history. The poetics of *feihua* were explored not only in poetry and fiction but also in critical essays written by Ma Ce, He Xiaozhu, Wu Qing, and Xiao Yin. *Feihua* extends beyond the literary works of these authors and encompasses their interviews, literature festivals, conferences, and readings, thereby dominating all aspects of their literary activities. Beyond the text, *feihua* is a state of mind that allows poets to be more aware of their natural intuition and sources of inspiration, to establish connections and friendships, and to communicate directly and freely. *Feihua* can be expressed in any form of literature or art, including independent films such as *Badpoets* (*Huai shiren* 壞詩人), which was produced by Wu Qing in 2010. The film is one hour and thirty-nine minutes long, filmed carelessly and *en passant*, as if with a hidden camera meant to store evidence for future use. While watching Wu Qing's film, the spectator is tempted to raise their gaze and look for something beyond their dull discussions about constipation, drinking parties, and toilet habits, among other things. Like their poems and fiction, the film activates the function of *xing* 興, as formulated by Confucius in the famous dictum: "Poetry can stimulate the mind, can contemplate, can bring people together, can express resentment"

27 Inwood, *Verse Going Viral*, 27.

28 In Yang Li's words: "*Xiangpi* is the only thing in China that can be trusted." This statement was made in an interview published on *91Xiangpi*, "'Feihua shiren' Yang Li & Fenghuang Wang: Zai Zhongguo, zhi you 'feihua' shi kexin de."

29 Mark Turner, *The Literary Mind: The Origins of Thought and Language* (1996).

(*shi keyi xing, keyi guan, keyi qun, keyi yuan* 詩可以興，可以觀，可以群，可以怨). This means that poets who adhere to *feihua* always try to lure and incite their readers or audience to look for associations beyond the usual social norms and aesthetic conventions.

## Meme Theory and Poetry Replicators

Poetry has always been seen as a powerful *meme* in Chinese culture, manifesting itself as a sociocultural practice rather than just a mere text, and *Xiangpi* is an excellent embodiment of this idea.[30] Viewing *Xiangpi* from a memetic perspective can help explain its longevity and continued success over the past twenty years. To understand the concept of a meme, it is helpful to begin with Richard Dawkins, who coined the term in 1976 as the cultural equivalent of genes. Dawkins famously defined memes as "units of cultural transmission" that are capable of spreading and evolving within a culture: "Just as genes propagate themselves in the gene pool by leaping from body to body via sperms or eggs, so memes propagate themselves in the meme pool by leaping from brain to brain via a process which, in the broad sense, can be called imitation."[31]

Essentially, memes transmit an idea (such as a tune, a style, or an accent) from one brain to another if they are accurately replicated from one generation to the next. Richard Dawkins uses the term "generation" as a metaphor for any vehicle that can propagate the meme and sustain its existence.[32] In his book *The Selfish Gene*, Dawkins argues that, just as genes are units of biological evolution, memes are units of cultural evolution, which involves passing the meme from person to person through communication that is relevant, emotionally impactful, and easy to share, allowing for changes to occur during transmission (a process that selects the most successful memes for replication). The concept of memes parallels that of genes, with a meme's genotype representing the pure information it contains, and its phenotype being its physical expression. For example, *Xiangpi*'s underlying ideology, which is the foundation of its memetic destiny, can be identified as its genotype – *feihua* poetics. *Xiangpi*'s phenotype is its observable characteristics, like writing style, platform use, and member

30 For a discussion of colloquial practices as well as the role of memes within the broader Chinese poetry landscape see Teodorescu, *Poezia chineză colocvială ca practică culturală heterodoxă*.

31 Dawkins, *The Selfish Gene*, 208.

32 Dawkins, "Memes."

behaviour. The effectiveness of these features in spreading *Xiangpi*'s ideas and concepts depends on how well they are adapted to the socio-cultural context in which they exist.

The concept of memes involves the idea that they cannot be further broken down into smaller units but can be combined to form larger sets of varying complexity. Memes are considered the smallest cultural units capable of replication in different contexts, and they have a greater likelihood of successful replication and propagation when supported by other memes. A group of memes that tend to evolve and become associated with each other through mutual reinforcement is referred to as a "coadapted meme complex" (Richard Dawkins) or "memeplex" (Susan Blackmore). According to Susan Blackmore, the essential characteristic of any memeplex is that the memes inside it can replicate more effectively as part of the group than they can on their own.[33]

Memes do not evolve in isolation; they are closely related to their environment and the other memes with which they interact. They have a co-evolutionary status, meaning that they develop in a mutually beneficial way that supports their joint evolution. As Blackmore observed, by grouping together, the memes form a structure that is both self-organising and self-protecting. This structure can accept and defend memes that are compatible with its goals while rejecting those that are not. Essentially, a memeplex has a barrier or filter that separates it from external information.[34] While *Xiangpi* can be seen more as a memeplex rather than an individual meme, it is important to note that *Xiangpi* is the result of co-evolving memes that work together to survive. The idea of autonomous poetry, its unofficial status, the avant-garde movement, the use of extreme colloquialism, the *Xiangpi* Award, and the *Xiangpi* Publishing House are all closely intertwined and essential for the survival of *feihua*, and vice versa. Together, they form the memeplex known as *Xiangpi*.

According to meme theorists such as Dawkins, Blackmore, and Lynch, several factors contribute to the success of a meme. Richard Dawkins identified several key characteristics, including fidelity (accurate replication without significant alterations), longevity (the ability to persist within a host and spread), fecundity (the speed and effectiveness of replication and propagation), and selective advantage (the benefit for the host). Additionally, Susan Blackmore in *The Meme Machine* and Aaron Lynch in *Thought Contagion: How Belief Spreads Through Society* emphasise the

33 Blackmore, *The Meme Machine*, 20.

34 Blackmore, 231.

importance of a meme being simple and memorable. They argue that the most successful memes are those that can quickly and widely spread, tapping into people's psychological and cultural predispositions. The ability to be easily remembered is crucial, as it allows the meme to persist in people's minds and continue spreading. For instance, Blackmore explains how conspiracy theory or health-related memes in the New Age movement, such as alien abduction or alternative medicine, are propelled by a mix of psychological factors, socio-cultural dynamics, and marketing tactics.[35] These memes catch on quickly due to the emotions of fear and anxiety, and they are often aided by media interest in potentially viral news stories and a cultural preference for exotic treatments and fantastical explanations in the Western world.

Given the importance of understanding the factors that contribute to the success of a meme, it is relevant to apply this analysis to *Xiangpi*, which has demonstrated remarkable stability and penetrance within Chinese cultural practices. Following Dawkins's exercise of finding reasons for the persistence of certain ideas over generations, such as that of God, I can similarly explore what gives *Xiangpi* its enduring appeal.[36] Like Dawkins and Blackmore, I invoke a psychological appeal: *Xiangpi*, through all its deviant actions, fulfils a need that people, particularly artists, have to liberate themselves from multiple types of authority and explore their instincts beyond established rules. In China, this correlates with a persistent need projected by older or newer poets through projects like *Xiangpi*, due to restrictive state regulations and mainstream literary values. Rejected by other groups, outsider poets such as Wu Qing, Shu, and Rou who started writing poetry in the 2000s found a haven in *Xiangpi*. The new *Xiangpi* site, *91xiangpi.com*, welcomes young writers and aims to spread its values to potential newcomers. Becker argues that joining a deviant group can significantly impact a deviant's path, as these groups tend to rationalise their actions and create justifications for their behaviour. This reasoning enables deviants to sustain their actions with greater consistency and a more principled outlook.[37] At the same time, this is a reminder of an important possible explanation for a meme's success mentioned by Dawkins: the benefits that the meme brings to its hosts. Besides providing a platform for young writers to communicate their poetry, established poets can also find value as active participants in the poetry market and in contributing to the

35 Ibid., 175–186.

36 Dawkins, *The Selfish Gene*, 209.

37 See Becker, *Outsiders. Studies in Psychology of Deviance*, 38–39.

collective memory of China through *Xiangpi*, a product whose margins are solely defined by them.

To facilitate easy replication and dissemination, *Xiangpi* adopted the ideology of *feihua*. As previously discussed, *feihua* is an extreme form of colloquialisation that emphasises the mundane. By choosing this particular language style, *Xiangpi* gained at least two advantages: firstly, their style could be easily adopted by new writers, making it convenient to imitate and transmit; secondly, this type of language and poetry distinguished *Xiangpi* on the Chinese poetry scene and allowed it to thrive. According to Pierre Bourdieu's ideas regarding the relationship between language and symbolic power, those who use a linguistic habitus different from the one accepted by the majority are seeking to distinguish themselves from others and other groups.[38] They are not simply rejecting the dominant language or the standard language; they are also striving to differentiate themselves within the relations of domination and subordination. Therefore, by choosing to create using certain forms of colloquial language, *Xiangpi* poets challenge the legitimacy of those "authorised to speak with authority,"[39] within the official market. *Xiangpi*'s "heretical discourse" not only invites to break from the established order of society, but also to create a "new common sense" which includes previously "repressed practices and experiences of an entire group"; legitimacy comes from both their collective assumption of actions and the colloquial language they use, which helps to express and build the authority of the group and of their language.[40]

Although stability, simplicity, and an unchanging status can make a replicator successful, memes are known for their malleable nature. Nevertheless, Dawkins and other researchers have acknowledged that memes naturally have a lower copying fidelity compared to biological replicators.[41] However, Milner emphasises that the most crucial aspect of the copying process for memes is preserving the core ideas that make them recognisable as such. He advises that there should neither be too much nor too little fidelity in the copying, as this could impact the meme's ability to thrive and endure over time, or make it unrecognisable and unable to elicit coherent reactions.[42] Despite adaptations or mutations, such as the shift to different mediums or members leaving the project, the *Xiangpi* content remains relatively

38 Bourdieu, *Language and Symbolic Power*, 121.

39 Ibid., 69.

40 Ibid., 129.

41 Such as Ryan Milner and his work *The World Made Meme: Public Conversations and Participatory Media*, 69.

42 Ibid., 69.

stable in the sense that their poetry, fiction, interviews, and criticism still embody the recognisable features of *feihua* logic, capitalisation of the word "avant-garde", colloquialism, unofficial status, and obsessive expression of the banal.

Fecundity helps memes thrive and is therefore an important characteristic of them. In the case of *Xiangpi*, this can be measured by the number of followers, replicator groups, or books sold over the years, but also by how easily and effectively its memes replicate across different platforms, through different people, and in different contexts. However, when it comes to books, avant-garde groups like *Xiangpi* only publish a few hundred copies per issue, which are mostly shared among friends. In fact, their numbers are not too impressive on social media either. For example, Yang Li only has 19,000 fans on Weibo.[43] To sum up, their numbers are not remarkable, but their capacity to spread and proliferate their message to various platforms and through all sorts of public accounts is significant. They make themselves available to anyone interested through the shared efforts of groups like *No.4 Nonsense School* (*Feihua si zhong* 廢話四中), *Having a Picnic* (*Ye Can* 野餐), *Abnormal* (*Fanchang* 反常), *Eraser Literature Award* (*Xiangpi wenxue jiang* 橡皮文學獎), *Z Poetry Society* (*Z shishe* Z詩社), and *Wu Qing's Coffeehouse* (*Uqn WuQing de kafeiguan* UQn 烏青的咖啡館). Despite being part of a close-knit circle and having low official numbers, *Xiangpi* has been able to maintain visibility and continue replicating for over twenty years, a fact that may be attributed to their own desire to thrive and be a part of the poetry scene as well as the extent to which they meet a crucial need. In a challenging environment marked by censorship, politically influenced gatekeepers, and public rejection of modern poetry, *Xiangpi*'s continued existence alongside other groups ensures a vibrant, independent, and free way of practising poetry.

For these memes revolving *Xiangpi* (*feihua*, colloquialism, banal, group-replicators) to thrive, their success depends on their compatibility with the "existing background."[44] As evidenced from the efforts displayed by *Xiangpi* members over the years, the main objectives of the *Xiangpi* memeplex are similar to that of other poetry memeplexes: to assert their own poetic agency, to accomplish the historical mission of the group, and to be recognised as part of the whole Chinese poetry world and as contributors to Chinese cultural memory. However, there is a notable difference: *Xiangpi* has adapted better to changing vehicles and to copying its memes, allowing it to thrive

43 The last time I checked this number was on April 11, 2023.

44 Dawkins, *The Extended Phenotype. The Gene as the Unit of Selection*, 111.

longer. Unlike other informal, *minjian* poetry groups like the *School of Rubbish* (*Laji pai* 垃圾派), which ceased to exist after losing their primary online platform,[45] *Xiangpi*'s existence was never dependent on any particular platform for publishing or discussing its content. Instead, *Xiangpi* functioned as a collective memory practice that continuously found new vectors and vehicles to facilitate the spread of its memes, overcoming a range of obstacles such as financial shortages, publishers' rejections, website's shutdown, censorship, and members leaving the group. Vectors and vehicles refer to means and mechanisms by which memes are transmitted and spread. In the case of *Xiangpi* memeplex, this was achieved through various means, including the use of various Internet platforms, among them websites, blogs, Weibo accounts, Weixin accounts, print magazines and books, cultural events, and other social practices that involved bringing people together (e.g., the *Xiangpi* Award). *Xiangpi*'s ability to adapt to changing socio-cultural conditions and utilise a variety of new, diverse, and catchy vehicles and vectors has been crucial in ensuring the continued replication and spread of their memeplex, as they were not reliant on any singular vehicle or vector, but rather constantly created opportunities to push their memeplex further.

As mentioned previously, maintaining a diversity of vehicles has been a constant key to the success of adapting and spreading the *Xiangpi* memeplex in the continuously changing Chinese poetry environment. This was demonstrated once again by the last issue of the *Xiangpi* magazine, which was published in 2022. Although Yang Li had previously overseen the *Xiangpi* project and was responsible for editing all previous issues, he delegated the editing of the final issue of *Xiangpi* magazine to Fang Xianhai due to his illness. Fang was given free rein to leave his personal imprint, as described in an article written by Fang himself. Although the title of Fang Xianhai's article about volume seven of *Xiangpi* magazine is still visible on Google search, the article itself is no longer available and results in a 404 error. In fact, all articles and references to the volume, as well as Fang's editorial work, seem to have vanished from the Internet. Until April 2023, visual information and specifics about the volume were still available, but they are no longer accessible. Activity on Weixin also appears to have been restricted, and many of the older posts have disappeared. In these new conditions, it will be interesting to see how *Xiangpi* will continue to exist, copy, and replicate itself.

45 In 2010, the *Beijing Review* poetry forum was unexpectedly deleted, which ultimately led to the disappearance of the group. For more information on this topic, see Inwood, *Verse Going Viral*.

Despite facing national mockery due to incidents like the one involving poet Wu Qing from 2012, mentioned in the first section of the chapter, which sparked online discussions about poetry and *feihua*, as well as criticism of members such as Yang Li, the *Xiangpi* poets remained steadfastly committed to the *Xiangpi* memplex. Chinese online encyclopedia Baidu Baike even has articles on the *Wu Qing style of writing* (*Wuqingti* 烏青體) (2012) or similar incidents like *Zhao Lihua style of writing* (*Lihuati* 梨花體) (2006) or *The Yangao style of writing* (*Yanggaoti* 羊羔體) (2010) and their relationship with *Xiangpi*, demonstrating *Xiangpi's* impact beyond the contemporary Chinese poetry sphere. *Xiangpi* saw the viral spread of Wu Qing's poetry as an opportunity to further propagate their memeplex. They capitalised on this by launching a new *Xiangpi* magazine in print that same year, which became one of the primary vehicles for spreading the *Xiangpi* meme over the last decade. *Xiangpi*'s various sites, magazines, group-replicators, and social media accounts serve as both vehicles and phenotypes for the memeplex. The *Xiangpi* memes are not only transmitted but also give expression to the simple and provocative *Xiangpi* poetry as well as the rebellious and anti-establishment attitude of its members. The diversity of vehicles has allowed for adaptation to changing trends, leading to a shift from the original site and chat room to blogs and social media accounts. The physical expression of *Xiangpi* memes has also evolved over time, incorporating images and videos alongside text, sometimes even irreverent photos alongside serious content.

When discussing Dawkins's theory of memes, it is important to note that it has been contested due to its deterministic view of cultural dynamics and the lack of social agency it assigns to individuals. Nevertheless, it should be emphasised that creators of memes, whether from a cultural or Internet-based context, strive to have control over the content and manner of their dissemination, indicating that memes involve agency in their conception and transmission, even if the outcome remains uncertain. An example of intentional transmission that preserves the essence of a meme while adapting it to new conditions is the *Xiangpi* Award. Personal choices regarding proliferation and format mutation have ensured the constant and stable transmission of *Xiangpi*, with closely linked memes such as the *Xiangpi* Award and *Xiangpi* Publishing spreading their name, values, and overall identity. The prize in question is privately funded and awarded according to the writers' tastes, without following any external directions or state agendas. It promotes a "popular and avant-garde spirit."[46] The prize

46 Yang Li (ed.), *Xiangpi: Zhongguo Xianfeng Wenxue 4*, 99.

was first awarded in 2014 to Zhou Yaping, a mature poet, for his volume of poems, *Very Black Gray Blue White and Red* (*Hong bai lan hui heihei* 红白蓝灰黑黑). This type of news is published on the *The Eraser Literature Award* (*Xiangpi wenxue jiang* 橡皮文學獎) social media account and other *Xiangpi* social media replicators. Their magazines and volumes of poems and fiction are also promoted and sold in the same way. In explaining his choice for the prize winner, He Xiaozhu, a member of the Prize Committee in 2014, said that the book was not only a reflection of an "innovative spirit who dares to experiment" but also embodied the continuity of *Xiangpi*'s principles (*yiguan* 一貫): anti-tradition and anti-style, paving the way for it to become a future classic.[47]

## *Xiangpi* Memes in Online and Print Media

*Xiangpi* is the result of cooperative activities and is an "art world" in itself,[48] equipped with everything needed to produce and promote its artistic vision, including various publication platforms, literary prizes, and poetry-related events. *Xiangpi* poets and writers' individual works may seem dull and repetitive, but their shared commitment to *feihua* has nevertheless made them fixtures on the Chinese poetry map. Viewed in this light, *Xiangpi's* importance resides less in the success of individual works and rather in its ability to harness the cultural logic of the meme to sustain its aesthetic brand. After *Xiangpi* was shut down, poets continued to develop projects within their network of friends, creating replicators of the original project. These groups made small variations on the original memeplex, while maintaining the core values of *Xiangpi*. The extensive and volatile tapestry of *Xiangpi* replicators is significant due to their avant-garde nature, as they continuously expand the boundaries of Chinese poetry and culture by publishing on social media. For instance, Yang Li and his girlfriend, Shu Shaojing, the co-ordinator behind the Weixin public account *Feihua sizhong*, launched the project of writing a poem every day for a year. They later collected all the poems into an officially published book called *Writing for a Whole Year* (*Xie yi nian* 寫一年).[49]

47 Yang Li (ed.), *Xiangpi 3*, 105.

48 The term "art world," coined by Howard Becker, refers to the collaborative space where artists, critics, suppliers, distributors, theorists, and the public work together to develop and promote art. Each participant plays a critical role in creating, analysing, distributing, studying, and defining the impact of works of art.

49 This book was published in 2017 by Jiangsu Phoenix Literature and Art Publishing (Beijing).

As Wu Qing has been a devoted member of the *Xiangpi* group since its inception and a strong advocate of the *feihua* aesthetic doctrine, it is worth examining the replicators generated under his leadership to understand their contribution to the spread of *Xiangpi* memes. Additionally, given the importance of physical books and magazines for legitimacy and survival in contemporary China, it is imperative to investigate the new *Xiangpi* magazines published in print after 2012 as well as their role in ensuring the replication and transmission of the core memes that constitute the *Xiangpi* memeplex today.

In an article published on May 2, 2007, Wu Qing announced the existence of a *Xiangpi* community consisting of groups that continue the work of *Xiangpi* and maintain its recognisable features. For example, the most obvious replicator is Wu Qing's website *Guopi*, named with a word that rhymes with and sounds similar to *Xiangpi*. This recalls Dawkins's interest in the phonetic symmetry between gene and meme when explaining the name choice for meme. *Guopi* was launched almost at the same time as *Xiangpi*, in 2001, and functions as a database that stores *Guopi* magazines, *Xiangpi* magazines, and the volumes of *Xiangpi* members. In addition, *Guopi* used to host the former chat rooms from *Xiangpi* and *Guopi*. There are also nineteen radio episodes and an unconventional radio interpretation of the *Journey to the West* (*Xi you ji* 西遊記). Apart from the poems and stories, which are perfect embodiments of *feihua* rhetoric, when reading Wu Qing's *Guopi*'s description, one cannot help but notice the resemblance with *Xiangpi*'s core values: independence, supremacy of vernacular, the call for authenticity, unconventional nature, and extreme and obstinate art representations. The *Guopis* are secretive, hidden, different from anyone in the world; they choose silence, neither this nor that, and impossible to be pinned down with a single label.[50]

The radio shows hosted by Wu Qing, Liu Hui, and their fellow poet friends are known for their playful and provocative nature. They have a relaxed and laid-back approach to discussing their projects, the current state of poetry in China, their favourite songs, poems, and stories, and even mundane topics. For them, creativity is about rejecting any display of pretentious talent and embracing what is ordinary, easy, common, pleasant, repetitive, boring, and even incorporating swear words. On social media, Wu Qing and Liu Hui collaborated on managing a Weixin public account called *There's Poetry Here* (*Zhe li you shi* 這里有詩), which was later renamed *UQnMedia* in 2018. The account was not limited to poetry, but rather reflected the

50 Wu Qing, "Tan yi tan 'Koopee Guopi'."

*feihua* poetics that view poetry as a sociocultural practice and interaction between poets and readers. The account also included word games and challenges. For instance, on August 3, 2015, they announced that they would not be publishing any posts for a week without any explanation, which left their readers intrigued. When they eventually posted an explanation, it did not provide any clear answers but added more mystery with a rhetorical question: "Why not do this?"[51] This self-ironic and provocative approach defined the identity of their Weixin account.

Wu Qing's Weixin project, *Wu Qing's Coffee* (*Wu Qing de kafeiguan* 烏青的咖啡館),[52] sold virtual coffee through pictures of a cup of coffee he supposedly made. Liu Hui's Weixin account, *Rent Liu Hui* (*Chuzu Liu Hui* 出租六回),[53] rented himself out for various purposes in exchange for money and shared the rental stories.[54] These Weixin accounts showcased a playful and unconventional approach engaging followers beyond poetry. Recently, Wu Qing created UqnMedia, offering UqinPoems and UqinClouds – handwritten or generated poems and unique cloud sketches with specific values in yuan. One of his poems reveals the two ways a poet can delete a poem on a computer: by erasing all the words at once (select all and delete all) or by deleting each character one by one.[55] All these replicators are simple and provocative, designed to intrigue and shock, and to be easily remembered and transmitted. However, due to their marginal nature, they only appeal to a niche audience, meaning that Wu Qing's replicators help maintain *Xiangpi*'s memeplex visibility, while remaining aligned with its *feihua* aesthetic logic.

Turning to the new *Xiangpi* magazines, it was anticipated that the Internet would cause unofficial publications to disappear, but this has not been the case.[56] Each issue of the magazine is a thick book, printed in only a few hundred copies, or, as Yang Li wrote in the preface to volume five of the *Xiangpi: Chinese Avant-garde magazine* (*Xiangpi: Zhongguo xianfeng wenxue* 橡皮中國先鋒文學), "as many copies as people want"[57] without concern for actual numbers. According to van Crevel, they publish a small number of magazines to explore the boundaries of socio-political expectations of

51 Wu Qing, Liu Hui. "Zuopin: Zheli you shi//Weixin gonghao ting fa yi zhou."

52 Wu Qing, "Wei yishu xiangmu 'Wu Qing kafei' yi mai chu 380 bei."

53 Liu Hui, "Wo weishenme yao chuzu ziji."

54 Teodorescu, *Chinese Colloquial Poetry*, 186.

55 Uqinzen. "Uqin Poems 21."

56 Van Crevel, "Transgression as Rule: Freebooters in Chinese Poetry."

57 Yang Li (ed.), *Xiangpi: Zhongguo Wenxue* 5, Foreword.

poetry through new voices and texts.[58] As a result, their primary objective is not to sell but rather to explore, expand, incite, and maintain a presence in the poetry scene while disseminating their message.

As previously mentioned, the *Xiangpi* group places significant importance on documenting their work to protect against censorship, historical manipulation, or even the possibility of being erased from history. Despite receiving recognition from the establishment, they remain vigilant about preserving their legacy through physical records. Inwood suggests that unofficial poetry groups may also express a desire for autonomy and agency over their identities and impact on Chinese cultural memory.[59] Therefore, archiving their work through official or non-official channels is crucial. In fact, the 2019 launch of the new *Xiangpi* site (*91xiangpi.com*) has not resulted in much activity, as it mainly serves as an archive of the artists' works. Moreover, of the seven new *Xiangpi* magazines, two were published by official publishers, and five were published by *Xiangpi Chuban*, once again establishing an ambivalent and complex relationship between the official and unofficial, the marginal and mainstream.

## The Power of Memes

Crucial to the *Xiangpi* project is the negotiation between the impermanence of digital content, such as deleted posts, censorship, and abandoned websites, and its ability to create memes and a coherent memeplex that can exist independently of their original source. This highlights the significant role that meme culture plays within the Sinocybersphere, particularly in China, where the unpredictability of censorship makes it difficult to anticipate what may be targeted next. Memes, on the other hand, defy this uncertainty by persisting beyond the individual content's "death" using technology, including printed books. Additionally, this concept is relevant to *Xiangpi* poets, as it emphasises the importance of community and collaboration in creating enduring cultural artifacts.

In *Xiangpi*'s case, their unofficial actions can be interpreted as an act of contesting authority and affirming their own poetics, with no boundaries set by mainstream or lawful (*hefa* 合法) publishing houses, as explained by editor Fang Xianhai in the afterword to Yang Li's book, *Mistake* (*Cuowu* 錯誤). This volume was published by a popular unofficial channel, BlackWhistlePoem

58 Van Crevel, "Transgression as Rule."

59 Inwood, *Verse Going Viral*, 27.

Publication, an entity whose mission is to advance the publishing of contemporary Chinese poets, whose "lyrical aesthetics deemed blasphemous by conservative politics, or which violate the established aesthetic rules of the mundane and righteous."[60] According to Yang Li, *Xiangpi* follows the principles of transgression and manages to do it themselves: "write it yourself, print it yourself, sell it yourself."[61] They have been doing this for more than twenty years now.

*Xiangpi*'s contribution to the Chinese avant-garde is significant in its embrace of *feihua* poetics, which rejects conventional meaning and symbolism. Its overarching mission is to liberate poetry from the confines of elite culture, standard language, and grand narratives, creating an environment of experimentation and personal expression. Three factors contributed to *Xiangpi*'s success as a memeplex. Firstly, *Xiangpi* poets created simple yet provocative poems that could be easily remembered, transmitted, and replicated, such as Wu Qing's viral poems. Secondly, *Xiangpi* capitalised on both online and print media, recognising the importance of physical books and magazines for their continued legitimacy and presence in contemporary China. Thirdly, *Xiangpi* continuously adapted itself to various technological environments while remaining loyal to its core *feihua* aesthetic and ideological principles. Ultimately, *Xiangpi's* capacity to remain relevant on the contemporary poetry scene in China over the last two decades is grounded in an understanding of the cultural power of memes and their ability to adapt and replicate in a constantly changing cultural landscape.

## References


Baidu Baike. "Feihua shige 废话诗歌 [Nonsense poetry]." https://baike.baidu.com/item/%E5%BA%9F%E8%AF%9D%E8%AF%97%E6%AD%8C.

Becker, Howard. *Outsiders. Studies in the Psychology of Deviance.* New York: The Free Press, 1973.

Becker, Howard. *Art Worlds.* Berkeley: University of California Press, 1984.

Blackmore, Susan. *The Meme Machine.* Oxford: Oxford University Press, 1999.

Bourdieu, Pierre. *The Rules of Art: Genesis and Structure of the Literary Field.* Cambridge: Polity Press, 1996.

Bourdieu, Pierre. *Language and Symbolic Power.* Cambridge: Polity Press, 1991.

Dawkins, Richard. *The Selfish Gene.* Oxford: Oxford University Press, 1976.


60 Yang Li, *Cuowu*, Afterword.

61 Yang Li (ed.), *Xiangpi: Zhongguo Wenxue* 2, 128.

Dawkins, Richard. *The Extended Phenotype. The Gene as the Unit of Selection*. Oxford: Oxford University Press, 1982.

Dawkins, Richard. "Memes." *YouTube*, uploaded by OxfordUnion, February 26, 2014, https://www.youtube.com/watch?v=4BVpEoQ4T2M.

Derrida, Jacques. "Archive Fever: A Freudian Impression." *Diacritics* 25.2 (1995): 9–63.

Dongfang wang 东方网. "Zen neng ruci xia peng 'Wuqingti' 怎能如此瞎捧 "乌青体" [How can one blindly praise 'Wu Qing's style of writing' like this]." *Zhongyang dianshitai wangzhan*. November 30, 2014. http://opinion.cntv.cn/2014/11/30/ARTI1417314249577111.shtml.

Fang Xianhai 方闲海. "Xiangpi: Zhongguo xianfeng 7 橡皮:中国先锋文学7 [Xiangpi: Chinese Avant-Garde Literature 7]." *Tengxun wang*. February 22, 2022.

Hockx, Michel. *Internet Literature in China*. New York: Columbia University Press, 2015.

Inwood, Heather. *Verse Going Viral. China's New Media Scenes*. Seattle: University of Washington Press, 2014.

91Xiangpi (Jiuyi xiangpi). "'Feihua shiren' Yang Li & Fenghuang wang: Zai Zhongguo, zhi you 'feihua' shi kexin de '废话诗人' 杨黎&凤凰网:在中国，只有 '废话' 是可信的 [*Feihua* poet, Yang Li & Fenghuang wang: In China Only Feihua is Trustworthy]." http://91xiangpi.com/thread-195-1-1.html.

Liu Hui 六回. "Wo wei shenme yao chuzu ziji 我为什么要出租自己 [Why Should I Rent Myself Out?]." *UQnMedia*, WeChat, June 9, 2015. https://mp.weixin.qq.com/s/guvAnLqpBoeeWuj1xT_1RA?fbclid=IwAR156c5tw5pY5VGtP3fsKMrTnjeu1SwFUQfdjXWDNAUkrsJ40RAAZWh-NDM.

Lynch, Aaron. *Thought Contagion: How Belief Spreads Through Society*. New York: Basic Books, 1996.

Milner, Ryan. *The World Made Meme: Public Conversations and Participatory Media*. Cambridge, MA: The MIT Press, 2016.

Teodorescu, Paula. *Poezia chineză colocvială ca practică culturală heterodoxă* [Chinese Colloquial Poetry as Heterodox Cultural Practice]. PhD dissertation. Bucharest: Printech, 2018.

Turner, Mark. *The Literary Mind. The Origins of Thought and Language*. Oxford: Oxford University Press, 1996.

Uqinzen. "Uqin Poems #021." *OpenSea*. https://opensea.io/assets/ethereum/0x495f947276749ce646f68ac8c248420045cb7b5e/92211415342320932013735915780318807984342664770190883270814077310330187284481.

Van Crevel, Maghiel. "Walk on the Wild Side. Snapshots of the Chinese poetry scene." *MCLC Resource Center*. December 2017. https://u.osu.edu/mclc/online-series/walk-on-the-wild-side/.

Van Crevel, Maghiel. "Transgression as Rule: Freebooters in Chinese Poetry." In *At the Shores of the Sky* edited by Paul W. Kroll and Jonathan A. Silk, 262–279. Leiden: Brill, 2021.

Wu Liu Xiongdi 乌六兄弟. "Women yiqi zuo 'Haidao' 我们一起做'海盗' [We made "The Pirate" together]." In *The Pirate* 1. https://koopee.org/wenxue/hido/001/00.htm.

Wu Qing 乌青. "Huai shiren 2010坏诗人 2010 [Bad poets 2010]." *Youtube*, uploaded by UqinZen, April 10, 2018, https://www.youtube.com/watch?v=aDpAzii1m1c&t=4877s.

Wu Qing 乌青. *Tian shang de baiyun zhen bai ah* 天上的白雲真白啊 [*Oh, the white clouds in the sky are really white*]. Nanjing: Jiangsu wenyi chubanshe, 2013.

Wu Qing 乌青. "Tan yi tan 'Koopee Guopi' 谈一谈'Koopee果皮' [A brief discussion about 'Koopee Guopi']." https://wuqing.org/p/95.

Wu Qing 乌青. "Wei yishu xiangmu 'Wu Qing kafei' yi mai chu 380 bei 微艺术项目'乌青咖啡'已卖出380杯 [The Micro-art Project 'Wu Qing Coffee' Has Sold 380 Cups]." *UQnMedia*, WeChat, October 10, 2015. https://mp.weixin.qq.com/s/KEzLBCeK4REtkyf5nHDu1Q?fbclid=IwAR2LhNboJ1MGd5qZpWhKRaO6HVN_d53UA_dWUFGo1olBhM5Ox2iS5jPfeHk.

已卖出380杯 [The Micro-art Project 'Wu Qing Coffee' Has Sold 380 Cups]." *UQnMedia*, WeChat, October 10, 2015. https://mp.weixin.qq.com/s/KEzLBCeK4REtkyf5nHDu1Q?fbclid=IwAR2LhNboJ1MGd5qZpWhKRaO6HVN_d53UA_dWUFGo1olBhM5Ox2iS5jPfeHk.

Wu Qing 乌青, Liu Hui 六回. "Zuopin: Zheli you shi//Weixin gonghao ting fa yi zhou" 作品:这里有诗//微信公号停发一周 [Work: There's poetry here// WeChat Account Paused for One Week." *UQnMedia*, WeChat, August 2, 2015. https://mp.weixin.qq.com/s/HMjyqVMtBIFKKjHYqCQkyQ?fbclid=IwAR3mW-I41WtOUY_W5JBApVbo9N7XXYXIcYnNHwz84nQMoiU2T2gKTT4G-8M.

Yang Li 杨黎. *Cuowu* 错误 [*Mistake*]. Trilingual, with Norwegian translations by Bend Bendixen and English translations by Judy Torgard. Hangzhou: Hei shao shige chubanshe jihua/ Hei shao shengyin chubanshe, 2014. Unofficial, with sound disc.

Yang Li 杨黎. *Canlan: Di san dai ren de xiezuo he shenghuo* 灿烂:第三代人的写作和生活 [*Splendor: The life and writing of the Third Generation*]. Xining: Qinghai Renmin Chubanshe, 2004.

Yang Li 杨黎. "Gei Zhao Lihua de yi feng gongkai xin 给赵丽华的一封公开信 [A Public letter to Zhao Lihua]." Feihua Yang Li blog. http://blog.sina.com.cn/s/blog_477e9b940100056a.html.

Yang Li 杨黎. *Xiao Yang yu Ma Li* 小杨与马丽 [Xiao Yang and Mali]. Shijiazhuang: Hebei Jiaoyu Chubanshe, 2002.

Yang Li 杨黎. *Xiangpi: Zhongguo xianfeng wenxue* 1 橡皮:中国先锋文学1 [Xiangpi: Chinese Avant-garde Literature 1]. Nanjing: Jiangsu Wenyi Chubanshe, 2012.

Yang Li 杨黎. *Xiangpi: Zhongguo xianfeng wenxue* 2 橡皮:中国先锋文学2 [Xiangpi: Chinese Avant-garde Literature 2]. Xiangpi chuban, 2018, unofficial.

Yang Li 杨黎. *Xiangpi: Zhongguo xianfeng wenxue* 3 橡皮:中国先锋文学3 [Xiangpi: Chinese Avant-garde Literature 3]. Beijing: Beijing Shidai Huawen Shuju, 2014.

Yang Li 杨黎. *Xiangpi: Zhongguo xianfeng wenxue* 4 橡皮:中国先锋文学4 [Xiangpi: Chinese Avant-garde Literature 4]. Xiangpi Chuban, unofficial.

Yang Li 杨黎. *Xiangpi: Zhongguo xianfeng wenxue* 5 橡皮:中国先锋文学5 [Xiangpi: Chinese Avant-garde Literature 5]. Xiangpi Chuban, unofficial.

Yang Li 杨黎 and Li Jiuru李九如. "Bai nian baihua – Zhongguo dangdai shige fangtan lu 百年白话–中国当代诗歌访谈录 [One Hundred Years of *Baihua*: Records of Interviews on Chinese Contemporary Poetry]." Jiangsu: Fenghuang wenyi Publishing House, 2017.

Yeh, Michelle. "Anxiety & Liberation: Notes on the Recent Chinese Poetry Scene." *World Literature Today* 81 (4): 28–35, 2007.

Xiao Yin 小引. "Jianghu ye yu shi nian deng – Xin shiji zhongguo xianfeng shige baogao 江湖夜雨十年灯——新世纪十年中国先锋诗歌报告 [Ten Years of Light on Rainy Nights in the Jianghu: Report on a Decade of Chinese Avant-Garde Poetry in the New Century]," *Xiangpi: Zhongguo xianfeng wenxue* 1. Nanjing: Jiangsu Wenyi Chubanshe, 2012.

# 6 Cooking Authenticity*

## Li Ziqi, Affective Labour, and China's Influencer Culture

*Rui Kunze*

**Abstract**

This chapter conducts a case study of Li Ziqi 李子柒 (1990-) to examine the role of affective labour and the construction of authenticity in the context of China's influencer culture. It argues that Li enacts cooking as a form of affective labour that resonates with her followers' own affective needs, social values, and aspirations. The chapter also analyses the Chinese state's interactions with grassroots content producers such as Li Ziqi. It shows how the perceived authenticity of her persona and content is redirected by state media to address domestic issues (such as revitalising rural areas and promoting values of economic neoliberalism) and to present an attractive image of China to international audiences.

**Keywords:** food media, influencer culture, authenticity, Li Ziqi, Sina Weibo, YouTube

At 23:43 on July 4, 2015, Chinese influencer Li Ziqi 李子柒 (Li Jiajia 李佳佳, 1990-) posted the following entry on Sina Weibo from an iPhone 6: "No matter what will come out in the end, I will try my best to do it! Perhaps I will fail, but at least I won't regret it ...." This text is accompanied by two photos which show, respectively, a young woman looking down and an open notebook whose enumerated contents are too blurred to make out. These photos generate a montage effect, portraying the moment when a young woman makes a significant decision in her life and sketches her action plan. As the earliest entry currently accessible to the public, this post serves as the starting point of Li Ziqi's self-narrative of her entrepreneurial career.

* Research for this chapter was funded by the German Research Foundation (DFG, Project No. 404534127).

Imbach, Jessica. *Digital China.* Amsterdam: Amsterdam University Press, 2024
DOI: 10.5117/9789463720670_CH06

Li did not upload her first cooking video on Sina Weibo until months later – on March 25, 2016, using part of a video she posted on Meipai 美拍, a less well-known video-sharing platform.[1] She was signed in September 2016 by Hangzhou-based Weinian Brand Management Co. Ltd, a MCN (multi-channel network) founded in 2013. In July 2017, Li and Weinian co-invested in the Sichuan Ziqi Cultural Communication Co. Ltd in which Li held forty-nine per cent of the company's shares.[2] Meanwhile she joined – or was allowed to join – international social media such as YouTube, Facebook, Twitter, and Instagram. Her YouTube channel has been operated by WebTVAsia (China),[3] a YouTube Certified MCN and a branch of the Malaysia-based Prodigee Media Entertainment, which was founded in 2014 "to produce, manage, market and monetize the most wanted Asian video content."[4] As of April 2022, Li had amassed 16.8 million subscribers on YouTube and ranks among its most popular Chinese-language influencers. In July 2018, her shop, with the registered "Li Ziqi" trademark, was opened on the e-commerce platform Tmall. With millions of followers in and outside China, Li was selected as 2019 Person of the Year in Cultural Communication by *China Newsweek*. In August 2020 she set up her own factory in Liuzhou, Guangxi province to produce *luosifen*, a regional rice noodle (*fen*) cooked in a broth made from river snail (*luosi*) and pork bones. However, in 2021, Li had a business dispute with her production company Weinian and stopped updating her content.[5]

Li Ziqi's cooking vlog emerged on China's booming food media scene in the 2010s, which had already demonstrated immense potential to yield economic profit, convey social values, and facilitate political communication. Food media's growth was heralded by China Food TV, a digital pay-per-view channel granted approval by China's State Administration of Radio, Film, and Television (SARFT) in 2006, which has been available in major American cities (New York, Los Angeles, etc.) since 2011. The landmark food documentary series *A Bite of China* (Season 1) produced by CCTV (China Central Television) in 2012, followed by two more seasons in 2014 and 2018, not only set up a new sales model linking the contents of the documentary with domestic e-commerce platforms,[6] but their

1 Li Shanshan, "Xinlang zimeiti yanjiu – yi 'Li Ziqi' wei li," 24. Li Ziqi has accounts with Meipai and TikTok, but her largest follower base is on Sina Weibo.

2 Li Wei, "Weibo, wanghong datuishou, xin meiti touzijia: 'xiannü' Li Ziqi shenhou de shengyiren."

3 Fu Qiongyin, "Shui rang 'Li Ziqi' yu 'Amu yeye' men chengwei YouTube wanghong?"

4 Prodigee official website: https://www.prodigeemedia.com/webtvasia.

5 Yang, "Aestheticizing Labor," 35.

6 Kunze, "Tasting a Good Life," 47–48.

successful sale of rights to international audiences also testified that China's diverse and rich culinary heritage is the "most delicious form" of soft power.[7] Li Ziqi's cooking videos show that cultural products made by a grassroots influencer arising within China's participatory culture may prove as appealing and profitable as professional works produced by the state media.

Influencers are social media users who "have gained a large follower base" by "sharing self-generated content." They manage to turn "their online social presence into a primary profession," often branding themselves as experts in certain fields. In terms of marketing, influencers "are perceived as more credible and relatable" than traditional celebrities.[8] In other words, the influencer operates on a logic of authenticity that is built on the relatability and credibility of her/his mediated presence and curated content. The discourse of authenticity in commercial contexts, Brooke E. Duffy posits, is rooted in a long cultural tradition that addresses "[t]he uneasy relation between socialization and self-discovery." For example, Lionel Trilling argues that authenticity in literary studies is "the organic, true sense of self that exists apart from society and is realized through the rejection of social and cultural norms." In our time, the notion of the "true self" runs counter to mass production and consumption, facilitates the celebration of (the life of) ordinary people in participatory culture as "the real," and is made compatible with the ideas of economic neoliberalism, such as autonomous choice and responsibility.[9]

Below I employ qualitative methods of textual and visual analysis to explore Li Ziqi's success as a Chinese influencer. I argue that Li's presentation and performance of her grassroots background and her labour in her vlog effectively evoke emotional responses from domestic and international followers that make them feel as though they can relate to or identify with her. The first section discusses Li Ziqi's construction of her digital persona (*renshe* 人設) as a self-made young influencer from a rural area and the debate over its authenticity in 2017. To authenticate this persona, Li told backstage stories that foregrounded her grassroots origin and tremendous effort that made her transformation from an amateur web-user to a successful influencer possible. Employing Michael Hardt's concept of "affective labour," which is a value-producing form of labour merging economic production

7 Kuang Lanlan, "China's Emerging Food Media," 68.

8 Schouten, Janssen and Verspaget, "Celebrity vs. Influencer Endorsements in Advertising," 259–260.

9 Duffy, "Manufacturing Authenticity," 135–137, quote 135.

with the communication of human relations,[10] the second section analyses the reception of Li's cooking content as affective labour by her followers on Sina Weibo and YouTube. I show that these followers actively interpret Li's contents through the prism of their own experiences, desires, and concerns, including work ethic, family values, gender roles, and the relationship between humans and nature. State propaganda organs intervene heavily into and therefore shape its influencer culture. The last section looks into how Li's grassroots persona and her content were channelled to address domestic issues and to tell the China story (*Zhongguo gushi* 中國故事) to international audiences. The case study of Li Ziqi thus illustrates not only how the influencer's authenticity is mediated through the dynamic interplay between her/his digital persona, presented content, and followers, but also how this authenticity, in the Chinese context, is promoted by the state to exploit grassroots influencers' inspirations and aspirations for its own economic and political agendas.

## Persona: A Self-made Grassroots Influencer

We know very little about Li Ziqi's private life, and what we do know comes from her own narration on social and mass media. With a few Weibo entries and interviews, especially the long entry dated May 13, 2017, which we will discuss in detail below, we are able to piece together a rough life trajectory of a self-reliant, young, rural woman from Sichuan Province in southwestern China.[11] Li's mother disappeared from her life early on and her stepmother maltreated her after her father passed away in 1994. Despite their own poverty, Li's grandparents took her home and raised her. Li had to work as a restaurant waitress at the age of fourteen. She later learned DJ skills and worked in a night club in the city of Mianyang. In 2012 she decided to go back to her home village after her grandpa passed away and her grandma fell sick. There she made and uploaded cooking videos to various video-sharing platforms in the hope of supporting herself financially.

In a 2016 cooking reality show "I am the Cooking God," Li Ziqi formulated her ideal lifestyle as follows: "Working at sunrise and resting at sunset,

10 Hardt, "Affective Labor," 95–96.

11 Among them, Weibo entries on June 20, August 9, and October 3, 2016; April 12 and May 13, 2017. Mao Yijun, "Li Ziqi: Wo lixiang de shenghuo jiushi wuyouwulü zijizizu;" and Venus Wu, "Exclusive Interview with Li Ziqi."

[enjoying] purely natural food and the simplest lifestyle like in ancient times."[12] This statement, perceiving food from the perspective of its production and in terms of lifestyle, summarises the major ideas of her visual content. Li's videos, ranging from five minutes to nearly twenty minutes, usually show the whole process of making all sorts of food: it starts with her searching for or collecting the ingredients in nature or in her lush gardens, moves on to her processing them in her neat courtyard and/or rustic kitchen, and ends almost invariably with Li sharing the food with her grandma. Li seldom talks in the videos and the background music is often eclipsed by sounds from the natural environment (wind, rain, insects chirping, the rustling of leaves, etc.) and from the cooking process (washing, chopping, sizzling, fire crackling, etc.). Some videos also show her building simple cooking devices (e.g., a bread oven) and furniture, making wines from fruits or blossoms, and producing cosmetics and dyes from natural ingredients. Li's vlog therefore portrays food production as a natural, local, and seasonal matter involving much physical work and presents food consumption as an expression of family love and self-sufficiency. Her favourite hashtag on Sina Weibo, "Dawn blossoms plucked by [Zi]Qi 朝花柒拾 [*Zhao hua qi shi*]," which explicitly alludes to the elegant title of Lu Xun's (1881–1936) 1927 essay collection "Dawn Blossoms Plucked at Dusk 朝花夕拾 [*Zhao hua xi shi*]," adroitly appropriates the nostalgic sentiments in this well-known author's work to endorse the idyllic lifestyle presented in her videos.

While Li Ziqi's popularity as a self-made, grassroots influencer was growing on Sina Weibo, a debate arose in early 2017 which raised the question about the authenticity of her online presence: Did she do the work herself, or did she follow a script to *perform* working in her beautiful costumes? Did she really grow the ingredients in her garden or forage for them in the wilderness as shown in her videos? Did she film her videos, as she claimed, or did a team hide behind the camera? Instead of answering these questions, Li Ziqi told backstage stories about her content production to authenticate her digital persona, stressing her grassroots background and characteristics, like her industriousness, perseverance, and determination to achieve her goals. On May 13, 2017 she published a long Weibo post supported with evidence from photos and screenshots of private chats.[13] This post was followed by

12 Li Ziqi Music. "DJ Liziqi" Was Criticized for Cooking Too Salty. But It Was Her Feelings for Grandpa."

13 Li Ziqi. "Sorry ... I will stop uploading my videos for the time being...." It should be noted that all links to Sina Weibo do not lead to specific entries but are instead automatically directed to the first page of the Weibo user.

a three-minute video, uploaded in less than an hour.[14] The video flashed Li's photos from 2008 to 2017, with background music in which the singer crooned, "I cannot go on my way to the future without you." The text of the post and the video attributed her success to her grandma, her nurse friend, and those who appreciated and helped to promote her work. In other words, she grounds the meaning of her career in various emotional ties such as filial piety, friendship, and collegial support. She then signed off the long post with a quite masculine epithet, "Mister Qi 柒爺 [*Qi ye*]," showing a more assertive side of her persona.

In the text, Li Ziqi goes into great detail about the technical problems she encountered and solved when making videos. She mentions the difficulties of producing desirable lighting and a natural flow of images and reveals that her computer contained more than 20,000 unused takes. As evidence, the short video shows a clip of her repeatedly adjusting the camera to get better images. She expounds on how she solved technical issues step by step: she followed professional advice to purchase a digital single-lens-reflex (DSLR) camera to achieve a better effect on film; she learned the skills of composition, framing, and cutting by watching *A Bite of China*; she specifies the places where she positioned her digital camera in the process of video-making; she names Cute CUT as the software used to edit her videos; she mentions that her DJ experience helped her edit music for the videos, and she talks about spending hours changing the format of the filmed files (as large as fifteen GB) into mp4 (less than two GB) to save space on the computer and facilitate the editing process.

In addition to these technical details, Li draws attention to the tremendous amount of energy and time she invested in making her videos with the example of her cooking tutorial "Lanzhou hand-pulled noodles," one of her most popular early videos from 2016. She took an intensive course with a ramen master and spent more than one month practising before starting to make the video. The filming took three days, in which she only had time to eat one meal a day. From the more than 200 takes she accumulated, she cut a video using fewer than fifty. And in the next two weeks she and her grandma had to eat food made from the ten kilograms of flour she used to film the video. Li especially criticises those who suspected that she used a stand-in cook in the video because they believed that a woman was too weak to do the job. Although this assumption is clearly sexist, Li focused on their failure to understand her hard work: "There are always those who say this or that is not possible. [For them], the impossible must be fake. The

14 Li Ziqi. "Those who love me, thank you."

fact is, they are only unwilling to believe how much patience and effort someone else is willing to invest to turn the impossible into the possible."

With text, music, and moving images, Li Ziqi told a story behind her videos, a story tracing the process of an amateur content creator whose empathetic personality, quick mind, and hard work enabled her to grow to be a successful influencer. Five days later, on May 18, 2017, Li Ziqi's video of May 13 was reposted by the official Weibo account of the Central Committee of the Communist Youth League with the following comment: "Salute every young person fighting for their dreams" and "every hard-working young person who does not waste time. The Motherland is proud of you for your hard work."[15] This was most likely the first official endorsement of Li's vlog, for which Li expressed her gratitude on the same day.[16]

## Followers: Cooking as Affective Labour

By the time Li Ziqi attended the reality show "I am the Cooking God" in 2016, she was already presented as a "very popular" cooking vlogger. In the show Li Ziqi prepared a dish using steamed ham and the rare Jizong mushroom. In response to the judges' unanimous comments that her dish was too salty, Li attributed the heavy flavour of the dish to her cherished memory of her grandpa, who used to be a countryside cook, and to her childhood poverty, when she rarely ate meat. By tapping into the emotional dimension of the dish, she turned this criticism to her advantage. Her story seemed to appeal to the judges in the show, reminding one woman of the taste of home found in her grandma's red-braised fish and a male restaurant entrepreneur of his own childhood. The latter articulated his understanding of Li and endorsed her dish to honour "the memory of the past and the aspiration for the future." In her vlog Li enacts cooking as a form of affective labour, which, as I show below, resonates with her followers' own culinary memories, experiences, and emotions. Her videos therefore encourage followers to relate to her content and identify with her persona.

In affective labour, argues Michael Hardt, "the instrumental action of economic production has merged with the communicative action of human relations," whose products are "intangible" feelings and "even a sense of connectedness or community." Writing back in 1999, Hardt criticised the

15 The Central Committee of the Communist Youth League. "Zhijing mei yiming wei mengxiang pinbo de nianqingren."

16 Li Ziqi. "Gratitude to our country, gratitude to all!..."

entertainment industry and the various culture industries for their "creation and manipulation of affects" and economic exploitation of collective subjectivities and sociality so produced.[17] Christine B. Balance's 2012 case study shows that the "affective labour" of human contact and interaction in Hardt's theorisation is apt for analysing social media. She examines how Asian American YouTubers, who create a sense of identification ("people like me") in a niche audience, capitalise on the latter's emotional attachment. Balance emphasises both the performative feature of these YouTubers and their "knowledge of and ability to craft emotional hooks" through expressing "shared political and social affects."[18] In the same vein, Tobias Raun perceives affective labour as "a specific way of performing in front of the camera," which can also be presented as the YouTuber's content to reinforce her/his trustworthiness and authenticity in the eyes of the followers.[19] In other words, from mass culture to interactive social media, we see a trajectory of affective labour moving from backstage to the spotlight to connect with the audience. Now, how do Li Ziqi's followers acknowledge her presented content as affective labour and actively relate their own lives and desires to it?

In a 2019 essay contributed to the online English-language magazine *Sixth Tone*,[20] researcher Dai Wangyun sees Li Ziqi's videos as a sort of "rural gentrification" that sands off the hard aspects of the rural life, such as "the poor hygiene, the backbreaking – and not particularly aesthetic – nature of farm work." The popularity of Li's vlog has little to do with the realities of life in a village, Dai posits, it lies rather in her "overworked, overcrowded, and burned out urban middle class" followers who "want to escape their problems into a 'Peach Blossom Spring'-like fantasy."[21] Given that smartphone ownership in China had reached ninety-six per cent by 2018, with domestic smartphones sinking even deeper into third- and fourth-tier Chinese cities,[22] it would be more reasonable to speculate that Li's follower base has a much broader spectrum of social backgrounds than "urban middle class." By dismissing Li's followers' feelings as escapist and her videos' authenticity as irrelevant, Dai fails to explore the followers' affective needs and desires underlying their fantasies, which are precisely what Li Ziqi addresses in her vlog. The Los Angeles-based restaurant critic

17 Hardt, "Affective Labor," 96.

18 Balance, "How it Feels to Be Viral Me," 142–148.

19 Raun, "Capitalizing intimacy," 100.

20 *Sixth Tone,* which started publication in 2016, is owned by the Shanghai United Media Group, a state media company controlled by the Shanghai Committee of the Communist Party.

21 Dai, "How Li Ziqi Repackages Rural China for Urban Fantasies."

22 Chou, Chung, and Lam, *Deloitte*, 4.

and columnist Tejal Rao, however, sees in Li's "D.I.Y. pastoral fantasies" "the intricacy and intensity of labor" and the meaningfulness of the "long, solitary processes of producing food" carried out by a "tireless, focused, confident, independent" young woman.[23]

Li Ziqi's videos on Weibo all maintain a relatively constant, high average rate of views, reposts, and replies,[24] therefore I examine one of the most clicked videos on YouTube – "Liuzhou *'Luosifen'*: Slurpy, Spicy, and Absolutely Satisfying" – as a primary example of the important role of her domestic and international followers in the meaning-making of her content. The video of making this rice noodle soup, a Liuzhou specialty, was posted on Weibo on August 6, 2019 with the hashtag "Dawn blossoms plucked by [Zi] Qi," and five days later on YouTube (with over seventy-three million views by April 2020), to celebrate the launch of Li Ziqi's own brand in the same summer.[25] Both domestic and international followers – from Japan, Korea, India, the Philippines, Vietnam, and Indonesia, Russia, Iraq, Brazil, Mexico as well as North American and European countries – made sense of it through their vibrant interpretations of and responses to the video.

The video displays how the noodle soup is made from scratch, with Li harvesting its major ingredient, bamboo shoots. A close-up shows a wedge entering the bottom of a bamboo shoot. Then we see Li squatting and collecting a large bamboo shoot, her red blouse and black hair forming a pleasant contrast to the green bamboo forest. The procedure repeats itself in the next scene, but with more detail: she brushes aside old bamboo leaves around the shoot, shoves the wedge into its base with her left hand, then pounds the wedge in further with a hammer in her right hand. She puts down the hammer, changes the wedge to her right hand, and pushes it further into the bottom of the bamboo shoot, while her left hand seizes its top. With a slight twist and a soft snapping sound, Li harvests the large, heavy bamboo shoot. This scene is dominated by the sounds of nature and her labour: chirps of cicadas and summer insects, the metallic sound of her hammering the wedge, and the rustling sound of dry leaves. The audio-visuals portray a smooth process of Li collecting a natural ingredient, solitarily, monotonously, but also gracefully.

23 Rao, "The Reclusive Food Celebrity Li Ziqi Is My Quarantine Queen."

24 On average, each of Li's videos has around 30 million views, 36,000 reposts, and 33,000 replies. See Li Shanshan, "Xinlang zimeiti yanjiu – yi 'Li Ziqi' weili," 24.

25 Li Ziqi. "Liuzhou *'Luosifen'*: Slurpy, Spicy, and Absolutely Satisfying;" Li Ziqi. "Summer is the time to harvest bamboo shoots …"

For her followers, Li's collection of fresh bamboo shoots has multiple implications. A comment on the *Luosifen* video on YouTube, which has 17k "likes" in its own right, reads: "She goes to the garden and finds every single ingredient she wants. I went to the market forgot what I came for" (Farida Yeasmin 2020). For this follower Li's video visualises the food-making process and the meaningful labour involved in it, which are often made invisible in the mass products sold in the supermarket. Another follower's assumption that Li's video portrays the use of all-natural ingredients also betrays an anxiety about mass products: "The best part about all of these videos is that every single piece of food and every single ingredient is one hundred per cent fresh, healthy, and pesticide/steroid free" (Maliyah Snow 2020). For other followers, Li's work in the bamboo forest represents an ideal, eco-friendly human-nature relationship. Toni C (2020) thinks that "[e]verything she has is reusable or can be given back to the earth." Sara iraa Pise (2021) believes that Li Ziqi "uses each and every thing fully and never wastes anything." The Weibo follower Muziyu oO's praise of the *Luosifen* video is also eco-conscious: "Very beautiful. Gifts from Nature. Protecting our environment." While *Luosifen* is a regional rice noodle soup in southern China, Li Ziqi's followers from South Asia (India, the Philippines, Indonesia, Nepal) enthusiastically relate the bamboo shoot in her video to the products of their own regions: "Wooow we have that in the Philippines too we call it 'labong' …" (Maricar Feliciano 2021). In Indonesia bamboo shoots are "Rebung" (divina mb. 2021) and in Nepal "Tama" (Geetu Pande y June 2021). "Bamboo shoot is also one of the most popular vegetables in Northeast India. We ferment or dry it and cook it with pork," JWNGSAR NARZARY (2020) writes. Though perhaps inadvertently, this familiar ingredient helps to build an emotional bond between these international followers and Li Ziqi.

Li's followers also see a capable doer in the image of this labouring young woman, who embodies and inspires their better selves. Her Weibo followers link Li's diligence in the video with their own struggle for their desired life and ideal self. Yiruo dd (2019) says to Li's *Luosifen* video: "When I was preparing for my graduate exams, I watched them [Li's videos] every day during the lunch break. They were the only fun [in life] then.… [Now] I have realised my dream, … Thank Sister Qi for her company." One international follower writes: "Watching your videos motivates me so much to do anything! It just makes me want to do activities and not be lazy" (Amel 2021); while another claims: "This woman is my hero, she can do anything!" (Ilia Harkins 2020). To viewers, the way Li set out to *do* things looks like a "world-making" in progress that empowers her seemingly banal physical labour. It is notable that Li Ziqi's followers tend to use the vocabulary of the fantastic to express their amazement at how she makes the impossible possible. The use of fantastic references not only articulates followers' wonder and admiration, but also implies their awareness of Li and her world as mediated persona(e) and curated content. FireBoyisaMultiStan (2020) comments on the video on YouTube: "I love how she is just the human version of Minecraft." Winning more than 700 "likes," this comment alludes to the popular video game Minecraft to praise Li's resourcefulness and ability to make her own world. Another follower equally refers to the fantastic to describe Li's capability: "if there's a zombie apocalypse, this girl will definitely survive" (Celephinn 2020). Other fantastic terms applied to Li are "immortal fairy (*xiannü* 仙女)" in Chinese (social) media and "princess" on YouTube. In addition to the amazement that she "can do anything" (Ilia Harkins 2020) and "can achieve anything" (Youyou de quanshui October 2020), these terms also participate in defining gender norms. In response to Li's video on Chinese New Year snacks,[26] another popular one on YouTube, UNKnownCreature-006 (2020) comments: "She's like a Disney princess ... but better because she can do anything," which has won 1.3k "likes." Shelaya On YT (2020) points out that "this is the Disney 'princess' we've been missing," while Cozielikerosie (2020) believes that "seriously we need a Disney princess inspired by liziqi."

Li Ziqi's grandma, who usually appears at the end of her videos, evokes the "universal" love for and memory of grandmothers among her followers. Thus, the grandma, by endowing Li's presented labour with the meanings of family values, filial piety, and nostalgia, has served as one of the most salient and effective emotional hooks linking Li with her followers and thereby forming an affective community essential to Li's success: "How lovely your grandma [*sic*], Seeing your Grandma reminds me of my Grandma" (Farmer's Son 2021). Many enjoy seeing the interaction between Li and her grandma: "I love the way when she finish [*sic*] cooking her grandmother comes out to enjoy the meal. Her grandmother is a star!" (GreaterBayArea Hero 2020). On Weibo Li made it clear from the very beginning that her motivation for making a cooking vlog was to support herself financially while staying with her grandma in the countryside. What appears to be her personal decision in fact addresses a larger dilemma of millions of migrant workers in China: how is it possible to achieve a balance between the better economic opportunities in cities and caring for loved ones (especially elders) in their home village? Li Ziqi's videos, showing her sharing food with her

26 Li Ziqi. "Peanut and melon seeds, dried meat, dried fruit, snowflake cake – snacks for Spring Festival."

grandma at home after cooking, depict the ideal of enjoying both economic and emotional well-being in China's rural areas.

## Content: Li Ziqi's "Grassroots" Energy Channelled

In the current Chinese context, how far a grassroots influencer like Li Ziqi can go depends on both the cultural and economic logic of social media algorithms (about which we unfortunately have very little information) and state intervention. This section examines how Li Ziqi and her content were channelled into telling "the China story." After Li Ziqi was officially endorsed in May 2017, she was brought over the Great Firewall into the international social media scene. She then made the conscious effort to present Chinese cultural heritage in her videos. She pinned her video on making brush pens, ink, paper, and ink stones (March 25, 2019) to the top of her Weibo account; and her YouTube channel (re)categorised her videos using the rubrics of "oriental intangible cultural heritage" and "traditional handicraft." On March 5, 2019, Li Ziqi issued a less-than-one-minute "Official Announcement" in response to the report that vloggers from other countries imitated her style and produced similar video content.[27] In this short video (in Chinese with English subtitles), Li addressed her YouTube followers directly, proudly declaring her Chinese nationality and affirming that the shooting locations of all her videos were in her hometown within China.[28]

On December 5, 2019, Shanghai-based writer Cai Jiangzhou 蔡江舟, whose Weibo avatar is Leisilin Raist 雷斯林 Raist, posted an essay titled with a rhetorical question: "How come Li Ziqi does not count as a cultural export?"[29] It garnered more than ten million views and triggered a debate over whether Li Ziqi's videos should count as a form of "cultural export (*wenhua shuchu* 文化輸出)" that could promote China's soft power. As of July 2021, the hashtag had attracted 119,000 Weibo entries, with a total of 910 million views. Raist argued, using many screenshots from YouTube as evidence, that Li Ziqi was a successful influencer on "foreign websites (*waiwang* 外網)" and thus her content should be considered a "cultural export." He compared the number of views of Li's YouTube channel with those of well-known news networks such as CNN and cited comments in various languages (including those from Taiwan and Chinese living

27 CGTN. "Vietnamese vlogger suspected of copying Chinese influencer Li Ziqi."
28 Li Ziqi. "Official Announcement from Liziqi Youtube Channel."
29 Leisilin Raist. "Li Ziqi zenme jiu bushi wenhua shuchu le?"

abroad) to demonstrate the global popularity of Li Ziqi and her followers' unanimous love for her: "no debates, no doubts, no malicious comments." His retort to the criticism that Li showed backward Chinese rural life to foreigners refocused the debate on labour: "Why can't we view labouring in the fields as a cultural export? This is clearly a strength of the Chinese nation, why does it necessarily mean 'poverty', 'backwardness', and 'failure to represent China'?" Comparing Li's videos to the Japanese manga *Naruto* and American Western films, he stressed that the authenticity of these videos did not lie in displaying the hardship and trivial details of work in rural life, but rather in showing the Chinese nation's spirit of perseverance and striving for self-sufficiency. He ended his long post with the following comment: "What Li Ziqi's videos export is precisely the best parts of the Chinese culture that have influenced the world ...for thousands of years. Are these not the best representation of the China story?"

If Dai Wangyun's criticism of Li's vlog as the wishful fantasy of the urban middle class betrays an elitist undertone, Raist's rhetoric combines populist sentiment with cultural nationalism to stretch Li's curated content to represent the core values of Chinese culture; and in so doing, it makes Li and her content suitable for undertaking the official propaganda task of telling the China story to the world. It is particularly notable that he uses the term "cultural export" in a positive sense, which brings into relief the country's changing self-positioning vis-à-vis the rest of the world over the past two decades. In the early twenty-first century, the term was used in China's official media to criticise some "powerful cultures" (*qiangshi wenhua* 強勢文化), for example, (post-war) American culture, for imposing themselves onto other cultures, although it also acknowledged that America's advanced material conditions (e.g. communication tools) enabled this purposeful "cultural export."[30] *The Roadmap of the 18th CPC National Congress and the China Dream* (*Zhonggong shiba da: Zhongguo Meng yu shijie* 中共十八大：中國夢與与世界) (2013),[31] a book offering an interpretation of the China Dream to international audiences based on the government report presented by premier Hu Jingtao to the National Congress, seemed to shy away from the term "cultural export." It emphasised that the Chinese culture was "structurally disadvantaged" from a global perspective, but that China respected other countries and world peace. This book formulated China's

30 For example, Yan Gong (2003), "On the American Strategy of Cultural Export."

31 International Department of the Central Committee of CPC, *The Roadmap of the 18th CPC National Congress and the China Dream*. CPC News, November 14, 2013. "Chapter 7: Will China do 'cultural export'?": http://theory.people.com.cn/n/2013/1114/c371516-23543735.html.

ambition to expand its soft power in a modest expression: "[Chinese] culture walks abroad." In other words, these earlier texts regarded "cultural export" as a form of cultural hegemony exercised by Western powers. Read in this context, Raist's use of "cultural export" in his 2019 Weibo post articulated the younger generations' desire and confidence to assert China – in a clearly more aggressive way – as a rising superpower moving from the periphery to the centre of international relations. They also actively suggested that state propaganda should enlist grassroots content producers and value their market-nurtured and -tested professionalism, because they have proven themselves to be more attractive and accessible to general audiences (domestic and foreign) than the goal-driven state propaganda.[32] This shed light upon the complicity of China's cultural industries and state propaganda, in which the former functions as a sort of quality control of the latter.

In no time, major state media outlets such as the *People's Daily*, CCTV, and *China Daily* all joined in praising Li Ziqi on their Weibo accounts. One day after Raist's post, the *People's Daily* acclaimed the affective power of Li Ziqi's contents, which "are able to attract numerous followers from outside China without using a single English word."[33] On December 9, 2019, four days after the appearance of Raist's post, the Central Committee of the Communist Youth League posted an essay which had only minor alterations from Raist's, with a mawkish title "Because of Li Ziqi, Millions of Foreigners Fell in Love with China."[34] Given that no controversy of rights arose, we may assume that either Raist wrote the post following some official instruction, or he was happy with the attention from the state propaganda media. On December 10, 2019, CCTV posted its reading of Li Ziqi, sentimentally elaborating on the "love (*re'ai* 熱愛)" in her videos – love of life, love of hometown, and love of [the Chinese] culture – and praising her accessible way of "explaining Chinese culture and telling the China story."[35] When they enthusiastically affirmed Li Ziqi's videos as an example of "cultural export" and successful intercultural communication, both Raist the writer and these state media chose to ignore the elephant in the room, namely they were all citing evidence from so-called "foreign websites," which Chinese citizens cannot access legally. This blatant "breach of the law" by the state media themselves reveals the arrogance of power,

32 Yan zhi youfan, "Li Ziqi huo '2019 niandu wenhua chuanbo renwu', weihe shi ta?"

33 People's Daily. "[# Hallo, Tomorrow #] Li Ziqi's videos are able to attract numerous followers from outside China without using a single English word...."

34 The Central Committee of the Communist Youth League, "Yinwei Li Ziqi, shu baiwan waiguoren aishang Zhongguo."

35 CCTV News. "I am quite proud, because I am a dot in the background of Li Ziqi's videos."

the hierarchical nature of access to information and, most ironically, their dilemma of attempting to tell the China story to the world while cutting off average citizens' contact with it.

On December 14, 2019 Li Ziqi was selected as Person of the Year 2019 in Cultural Communication by *China Newsweek*, with the jury's comments that "she is a dream-maker in reality and an ordinary person whose dream came true."[36] This comment not only acknowledges Li's own agency in achieving her success, but also brings together the individual and the state's aspirations (e.g. the China Dream). As Adrienne Matei argues in her *The Guardian* report, "[i]n addition to providing China a form of international PR, Li embodies a kind of rural success the government hopes to generate more of through recent initiatives."[37] Thus Li Ziqi the grassroots influencer also served as a role model implementing the government's key policy of revitalising the countryside,[38] after China's accelerated urbanisation had attracted and displaced young people from their home villages for years.

## A Chinese Influencer?

Li Ziqi's story shows how the discourse of cultural authenticity is mediated through the interplay between her influencer persona, her curated content, her followers' interpretations, as well as the state's interventions. Standing in the centre of this authenticity construction is her presentation and performance of affective labour, which underlies her digital persona as a self-made, grassroots influencer, informs much of her content, and appeals to her followers' feelings and desires in and outside China. Li's followers feel close to her and her content, even though they are keenly aware of the mediated and monetised nature of both. On her *Luosifen* video, one follower comments, not without a dose of sarcasm: "It's quite ironic how it is so relaxing to watch someone being busy working hard…and how we are enjoying watching natural lifestyle with our phones" (Victoria Jeong 2020); while another follower states: "honestly i'm glad I got an ad, she deserves to be monetised" (kaixal 2020). The sense of community built on the emotional link afforded by such (interpretations of) labour was exploited

36 Mao Yijun, "Li Ziqi: Wo lixiang de shenghuo jiushi wuyouwulü zijizizu."

37 Adrienne Matei, "Country life: the young female farmer who is now a top influencer in China."

38 Dotson, "The Communist Youth League Announces Plans to Send a New Generation 'Down to the Countryside.'"

by the Chinese state. Li's personal decision to return to her home village and her choice to turn her new life into video content were exploited to promote the official policy of revitalising China's withering rural communities and the values of economic neoliberalism such as self-enterprise and self-responsibility. Her grassroots origin and her aestheticised labouring process became subsequently interpreted as a successful model for telling the China story to international audiences on the other side of the Fire Wall. Although the role of social media algorithms across various platforms could not be addressed in this chapter, Li Ziqi's story shows how China's influencer culture is heavily shaped by both commercial and state interests. Despite increasingly nationalist interpretations of her content, however, her case also, and more importantly, reveals that the discourse of cultural authenticity in the digital age relies on transnational cultural flows and media environments. As such, it needs to be carefully contextualised and historicised within a global mediascape.

## References

Balance, Christine Bacareza. "How it Feels to Be Viral Me: Affective Labor and Asian American YouTube Performance." *Women's Studies Quarterly* 40.1/2 (2012): 138–152.

Central Committee of the Communist Young League (@共青團中央). "Yinwei Li Ziqi, shu baiwan waiguoren aishang Zhongguo 因为李子柒，数百万外国人爱上中国 [Because of Li Ziqi, Millions of Foreigners Fell in Love with China]." Weibo, December 9, 2019. https://weibo.com/ttarticle/p/show?id=2309404447615805685960#_0 .

CCTV News (@央視新聞). "I am quite proud, because I am a dot in the background of Li Ziqi's videos" Weibo, December 10, 2019, 09:27. https://weibo.com/ttarticle/p/show?id=2309404447882362093714#_0.

CGTN (China Global Television Network). "Vietnamese vlogger suspected of copying Chinese influencer Li Ziqi." YouTube, July 5, 2020. https://www.youtube.com/watch?v=zLhv7EXmLpo.

Chou, William, Roger Chung, and Taylor Lam. "Chinese consumers at the forefront of digital technologies." *Deloitte China Mobile Consumer Survey 2018*.

Dai Wangyun. "How Li Ziqi Repackages Rural China for Urban Fantasies." *Sixth Tone* (December 27, 2019). https://www.sixthtone.com/news/1005007/how-li-ziqi-repackages-rural-china-for-urban-fantasies.

Dotson, John. "The Communist Youth League Announces Plans to Send a New Generation 'Down to the Countryside'." *China Brief* 19.8 (April 24, 2019): https://

jamestown.org/program/the-communist-youth-league-announces-plans-to-send-a-new-generation-down-to-the-countryside/.

Duffy, Brooke Erin. "Manufacturing Authenticity: The Rhetoric of 'Real' in Women's Magazines." *The Communication Review* 16 (2013): 132–154.

Fu Qiongyin 符琼尹. "Shui rang 'Li Ziqi' yu 'Amu yeye' men chengwei YouTube wanghong? 谁让"李子柒"与"阿木爷爷"们成为YouTube网红? [Who Turned Li Ziqi and Grandpa Amu into YouTube Influencers]" *CBNData* (September 21, 2020). https://www.cbndata.com/information/94721.

Gong Yan 龚滟. "Lun Meiguo wenhua shuchu zhanlue 论美国文化输出战略 [On the American Strategy of Cultural Export.]" *Yanshan University Journal: Philosophy and Social Sciences* 03 (2003): 63–67.

Hardt, Michael. "Affective Labor." *Boundary 2* 26.2 (1999): 89–100.

Kuang, Lanlan. "China's Emerging Food Media." *Gastronomica* 17.3 (2017): 68–81.

Kunze, Rui. "Tasting a Good Life: Narratives and Counter-Narratives of Happiness in the Documentary *A Bite of China* (2014)." *China Perspectives* 1-2 (2018): 45–53.

Leisilin Raist (@雷斯林 Raist). "Li Ziqi zenme jiu bushi wenhua shuchu le ? 李子柒怎么就不是文化输出了? [How Come Li Ziqi Does Not Count as a Cultural Export?]" Weibo, December 5, 2019. https://card.weibo.com/article/m/show/id/2309404446136898289811?_wb_client_=1.

Li Shanshan 李珊珊. "Xinlang zimeiti yanjiu – yi 'Li Ziqi' weili 新浪微博自媒体研究——以"李子柒"为例 [A Study of Self-Media on Sina Weibo: Taking 'Li Ziqi' as an Example.]" *West Radio and TV* 22 (2019): 24–27.

Li Wei 李伟."Weibo, wanghong datuishou, xin meiti touzijia: 'xiannü' Li Ziqi shenhou de shengyiren 微博、网红大推手、新媒体投资家："仙女"李子柒身后的生意人 [Weibo, Influencer Managers, New Media Investors: Businessmen behind the 'Immortal Fairy' Li Ziqi.]" *Tengxun News* (December 13, 2019). https://www.36kr.com/p/1724825124865.

Li Ziqi. "Official Announcement from Liziqi Youtube Channel." YouTube, March 6, 2019. https://www.youtube.com/watch?v=hL5HlwzuAUA.

Li Ziqi. "Peanut and melon seeds, dried meat, dried fruit, snowflake cake – snacks for Spring Festival." YouTube, January 31, 2019. https://www.youtube.com/watch?v=FWMIPukvdsQ.

Li Ziqi. "Liuzhou '*Luosifen*': Slurpy, Spicy, and Absolutely Satisfying." YouTube, August 11, 2019. https://www.youtube.com/watch?v=_jUJrIWp2I4.

Li Ziqi. (@李子柒). "Summer is the time to harvest bamboo shoots ..." Weibo, August 6, 2019, 19:48. https://weibo.com/mianyangdanshen?is_all=1&stat_date=201908#feedtop.

Li Ziqi. (@李子柒). "Gratitude to our country, gratitude to all!..." Weibo, May 18, 2017, 13:51. https://weibo.com/mianyangdanshen?is_all=1&stat_date=201705#1651672630632.

Li Ziqi. (@李子柒). “Sorry … I will stop uploading my videos for the time being……..” Weibo, May 13, 2017, 13:47. https://weibo.com/mianyangdanshen?is_all=1&stat_date=201705#_rnd1651672219984.

Li Ziqi. (@李子柒). “Those who love me, thank you.” Weibo, May 13, 2017, 14:23. https://weibo.com/mianyangdanshen?is_all=1&stat_date=201705#_rnd1651672309473.

Li Ziqi Music. “DJ Liziqi” Was Criticized for Cooking Too Salty. But It Was Her Feelings for Grandpa.” YouTube, 19. 07. 2022. https://www.youtube.com/watch?v=FmXi2NTWkpE.

Mao Yijun毛翊君. “Li Ziqi: Wo lixiang de shenghuo jiushi wuyouwulü zijizizu 李子柒：我理想的生活就是无忧无虑自给自足 [Li Ziqi: My Ideal Is a Careless and Self-sufficient Life.]” *China Newsweek* (December 30, 2019). http://www.inewsweek.cn/people/2019-12-30/8203.shtml.

Matei, Adrienne. “Country life: the young female farmer who is now a top influencer in China.” *The Guardian* (January 28, 2020). https://www.theguardian.com/lifeandstyle/2020/jan/28/li-ziqi-china-influencer-rural-life.

People’s Daily (@人民日報). “[# Hallo, Tomorrow #] Li Ziqi’s videos are able to attract numerous followers from outside China without using a single English word….” Weibo, December 6, 2019, 23:43. https://weibo.com/rmrb?is_all=1&stat_date=201912&page=21#_rnd1652091203850.

Rao, Tejal. “The Reclusive Food Celebrity Li Ziqi Is My Quarantine Queen.” *The New York Times* (April 22, 2020). https://www.nytimes.com/2020/04/22/dining/li-ziqi-chinese-food.html.

Raun, Tobias. “Capitalizing intimacy: New subcultural forms of micro-celebrity strategies and affective labour on YouTube.” *Convergence: The International Journal of Research into New Media Technologies* 24.1 (2018): 99–113.

Schouten, Alexander P., Loes Janssen and Maegan Verspaget. “Celebrity vs. Influencer endorsements in Advertising: The Role of Identification, Credibility, and Product-Endorser Fit.” *International Journal of Advertising* 39.2 (2020): 258–81.

Wu, Venus. “Exclusive Interview with Li Ziqi, China’s Most Mysterious Internet Celebrity.” *YouTube* (September 13, 2019). https://www.youtube.com/watch?v=J9CfVcXoYh4.

Yan zhi youfan 言之有范. “Li Ziqi huo ‘2019 niandu wenhua chuanbo renwu’, weihe shi ta? 李子柒获2019年度文化传播人物”，为何是她? [Li Ziqi won ‘the 2019 Person of the Year in Cultural Communication:’ Why She?]” *Tengxun*, December 18, 2019. https://freewechat.com/a/MzAxNTEwMjcwMQ==/2651003948/1.

Yang, Xin. “Aestheticizing Labor: The Construction of the ‘Good China Story’ in Li Ziqi’s Videos.” *Chinese Literature and Thought Today* 53 (2022): 30–37

# 7 Affective Labour on Kuaishou

## Sister Zhao and her Cyber Karaoke Bar

*He Mengyun*

**Abstract**
This chapter explores gendered digital labour on the short video-sharing platform Kuaishou through the case of Zhao Jie (Sister Zhao), a female rural user who earns a living as a street vendor selling pancakes. Although Kuaishou provides her with a degree of empowerment and a sense of community, these "positive" aspects are tempered by the technological and social protocols that reinforce, rather than subvert precarity and gendered hierarchies.

**Keywords:** Kuaishou, live streaming, *zhibo,* digital labour

As a result of China's emergence as an influential force in the global capitalist system, its presence on the worldwide media landscape has increased.[1] The significant rise of social media platforms such as WeChat, TikTok, and Kuaishou快手, in response to the rapidly changing "platform society" around the world, has led to a surprisingly high mobile Internet penetration amongst China's rural population.[2] These platforms do not simply reflect the social structures in which we live; they also actively shape them.[3] This chapter sheds light on a digital form of gendered affective labour on Kuaishou, a short video-sharing social platform that is more popular than Douyin抖音 (the Chinese version of TikTok) in lower-tier areas. More specifically, it examines the case of a female rural user named Zhao Jie (Sister Zhao 趙姐), a street vendor selling pancakes for a living, who earns additional income by performing frequent live-stream shows (*zhibo* 直播) in her personal

1 Schiller, "Poles of Market Growth?"
2 Van Dijck, Poell, and De Waal, *Platform Society.*
3 Couldry, *Mediated Construction of Reality.*

Imbach, Jessica. *Digital China.* Amsterdam: Amsterdam University Press, 2024
DOI: 10.5117/9789463720670_CH07

online "karaoke bar," where she receives virtual gifts for singing bitter songs. While the act of "liking" (*dianzan* 点赞) is an incremental gift, its exchange depends on her ability to manage and distribute emotions.[4] Rural working-class women invest their emotional energy in engaging with and generating creative content for capital accumulation. However, trading emotions in a capitalist exchange system gives rise to inequality, as users' interactivity is harnessed and promoted for profit.[5] Therefore, it is crucial to examine how platforms create new technological forms of gendered labour from a feminist media studies perspective.

## Digital Work in a Cyber "Karaoke Bar"

Significantly influenced by the accelerating digitisation of society, large numbers of rural Chinese women have been drawn into an astounding social experiment in cyberspace. Like wild grasses spread over the plains, millions of female users are roaming China's leading mobile short video-sharing platform, Kuaishou. Kuaishou is more influential than Douyin (the Chinese version of TikTok) in rural areas. It boasts more than eleven billion pairs of mutual followers, 2.34 trillion likes, retweets, and comments on videos and live broadcasts, and a monthly average of 777 million active users, twenty-five per cent of whom are content creators.[6]

Kuaishou is used and consumed predominantly by grassroots users, whose social marginalisation and lack of cultural and economic capital make them less visible in mainstream media. Compared with WeChat, which requires higher reading and writing skills, Kuaishou is exceptionally popular among socially disadvantaged groups because it has no language or media literacy thresholds. Douyin, Kuaishou's biggest competitor in first- and second-tier cities, has a centralised content distribution system and has attracted urban youth as a core user group. In contrast, Kuaishou employs a decentralised content distribution model based on an inclusive value-based algorithm.[7] The holistic user experience resulting from this algorithm has attracted many suburban and rural users.

Active users spend an average of 128.1 minutes per day on Kuaishou, which has approximately 150 million female users in what is referred to as

4 Arcy, "Emotion Work."

5 Andrejevic, "Privacy, Exploitation," 47.

6 Kuaishou, *Q1 2021 Results*.

7 Zheng Jieyao, "Naxie ni bu xihuan de ren, tamen ye you jilu de quanli."

a vast "sinking market user base" (*xiachen shichang* 下沉市场), comprising users from the small-town and rural areas where most Chinese live.[8] Based on China's demographic structure, it is estimated that ninety per cent of active female users are young workers, farmers, and students, most of whom have experienced some form of migration. These women face a critical lack of survival resources and are trapped in low social status and structural disadvantages within China's rigid social stratification. However, Kuaishou provides them with a parallel virtual space for entertainment after work. It also allows them to present themselves in digital society through an alternative network of social relations. This digital network of virtual interactions is fostered by the platform, as Kuaishou provides users not only with a virtual screening room for watching user-generated mobile shorts, but also with a public space for socialising. Having created a personal account, users can "hang out" in the virtual space with digital identities created by altering their appearance using filters provided by the platform, or they can reveal their real identities by making and uploading mobile shorts using smartphones. If eligible, they can also broadcast live-stream shows, thereby earning a small income. Eligibility criteria include binding their account to a mobile phone number, having more than six followers, and being over eighteen years old.

A digital presence on Kuaishou can be seen as a new form of instrumental relationship, as users utilise their bodies to create and present content for income and social interaction in the virtual world. This relationship between the body and digital labour is like the instrumental relationship between the working class and the body described by Bourdieu.[9] However, the virtual nature of this relationship means that it operates in a different context and with different power dynamics. This underscores the significance of analysing the ways in which platforms generate novel forms of gendered labour through the lens of feminist media studies.

My fieldwork for this digital ethnographic research project on Kuaishou was undertaken through semi-participant observation for six months from June to December 2021. I first met Zhao Jie ("jie" 姐 means older sister) by chance on the "Trending" channel (*faxian* 發現) of the application's main interface. The platform recommended a three-minute short video, the cover of which was a miserable-looking woman in her forties holding a microphone, kneeling on the ground on a country footpath, with a huge subtitle, "Dreaming of Mama" (*mengzhongde mama* 夢中的媽媽). The

8 Kuaishou, *Q1 2022 Results*.

9 Bourdieu, "Cultural Reproduction."

rough quality of the image suggested that the video had been shot using a cheap smartphone. The main character in the clip was Sister Zhao (*Anhui nongcun zhaojie* 安徽農村趙姐), a middle-aged rural woman born in a village in Anhui Province. In the video, she shared with the audience how tough it was to be a mother. Although her mother had passed away years previously, Sister Zhao still wanted to sing a song to mourn her. This video received nearly 700 likes and 219 comments. Sister Zhao has 338,000 followers on Kuaishou, and has received a total of a million likes for all her posted videos. As of February 2023, she had posted 759 videos and broadcast 103 live-stream shows. Her personal page is like a cyber "karaoke bar" in which she performs the role of a country chanteuse, who sings about her hard life. It is also a virtual living room where she meets strangers from thousands of miles away who send virtual gifts to encourage and comfort her.

Offline, Zhao Jie earns a living by selling pancakes from a trailer near a construction site in Changzhou, a second-tier city in Jiangsu Province. During a live-stream show in December 2021, she mentioned that she earns 300 to 500 yuan ($47.10 to $78.50) per day to support her two sons, unless her trailer is detained by the urban management officers (*chengguan* 城管). Sister Zhao regularly broadcasts her live-stream shows on Kuaishou for two hours a day after closing her pancake business at noon. She also uploads short clips of solo singing on her homepage.

The tools and higher-quality equipment essential for producing such videos and live streams have become more accessible to rural users owing to the development of infrastructure for rural e-commerce platforms and logistics systems. In addition to owning smartphones, rural live streamers can now afford to purchase a microphone, a selfie ring light, and a sound card for approximately 300 yuan ($47.10) as a complete live-streaming package, through online shopping platforms such as *Taobao.com*, the most popular shopping site in China and the eighth most visited website globally in 2021.[10] However, the most crucial parts of Sister Zhao's work are planning her singing performance, and interacting effectively with the audience through the platform's comments section. In her most viewed video, entitled "The Ugly Woman's Singing Captivated a Large Audience" (丑女人的歌声迷倒一大片), having introduced herself as "a homeless rural woman who loves to sing", she performs a song called "Father." She adds, "I want to sing this song to you. If you like it, please click the little red heart for me." This video has received 4,503 likes and 651 comments. Sister Zhao has replied to

10 Alexa Internet, "taobao.com Site Overview."

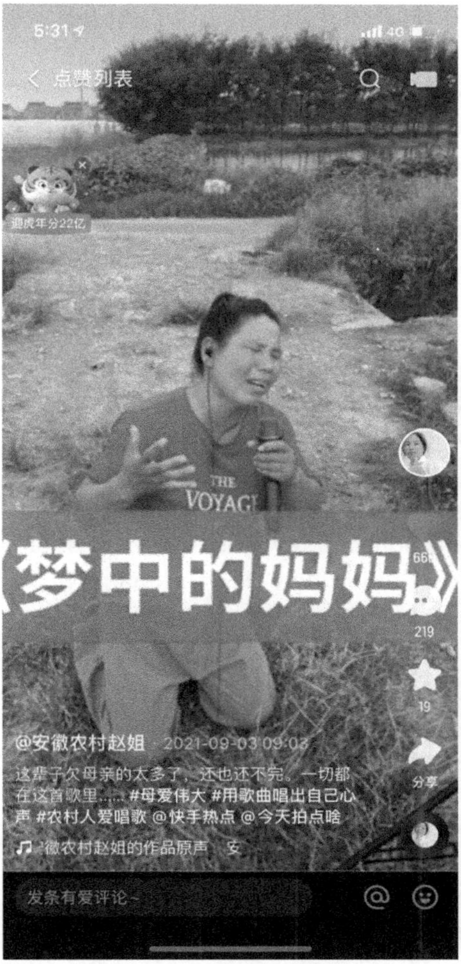


Figure 1. Sister Zhao performing “Dreaming of Mama”

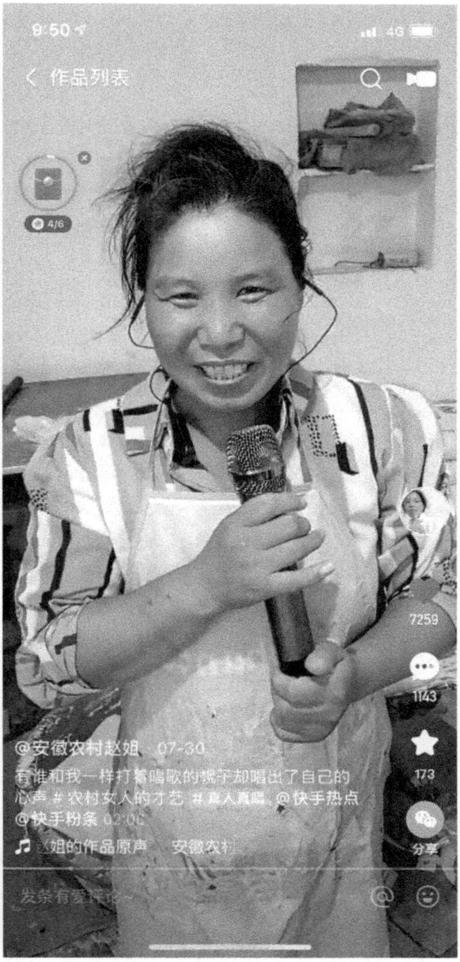


Figure 2. Sister Zhao singing in her pancake cabin

almost every encouraging comment, saying “thank you so much” hundreds of times. During her live-stream shows, she first expresses how much she has missed her followers, whom she refers to as “family” (*jiarenmen* 家人們), and answers viewers’ questions, such as “where has your husband gone?” She performs at least 16 songs in a single live-stream show lasting around two hours. Sister Zhao once complained in a short video that she was suffering from burnout (*changbudongle* 唱不动了) after performing continuous live-stream shows, and that she had been diagnosed with vocal nodules.

## Making Money on Kuaishou and the Digital Labour of *Zhubos*

Sister Zhao was particularly anxious that data traffic (*liuliang* 流量) would decrease drastically if she "took a break" (*xiabo* 下播) for a few days. She explained why she would not dare to become a full-time live streamer (*zhubo* 主播), confessing that the income from live streaming was not as "stable" (*wending* 稳定) as what she earned from making pancakes. Live streamers' payments consist of two parts. One is virtual gifts, which cost users between 0.1 and 2,888 yuan ($0.02 to $453) and can be converted into cash if they are sent to the live streamers. The other is live-streaming e-commerce (*zhibo daihuo* 直播帶貨). The latter source of online revenue is much more common among live streamers, who have risen to the status of online celebrities (*wanghong* 网红) and have millions of followers.

According to Kuaishou, more than 240 million users have earned income from the application.[11] In the third quarter of 2021, the number of daily active users (DAU) reached 320 million, and revenues from Kuaishou's live-stream service amounted to 5.59 billion yuan ($877 million).[12] In the second quarter of 2021, 1.9 million active live streamers broadcast their shows on the platform, and monthly average revenues of paid live-stream users (付费直播用户) were 55.9 yuan ($8.80).[13] The short video industry is expanding into "sinking markets" owing to extraordinary growth in consumer spending in middle- and lower-tier areas.[14] As of December 2020, the user base for short videos had reached 873 million, accounting for 93.7 per cent of total netizens in China.[15] Through the empowerment of information and communications technology (ICT) in post-socialist China, the rate of access to smartphones and mobile Internet in rural areas has been growing faster than in urban areas. The rapid development of communications infrastructure has led to a boom in China's digital platform economy over the last fifteen years. Data show that the aggregate value of China's digital economy reached 39.2 trillion yuan ($6.15 trillion) in 2021.[16]

The estimated scale of "digital rewards" (*dashang* 打賞) sent to live streamers by viewers had reached 25.315 billion yuan ($3.65 billion) in 2020.[17] In the first quarter of 2022, Kuaishou's live-streaming service was its primary source

11 Kuaishou, *Q1 2021 Results.*
12 Kuaishou, *Q3 2021 Results.*
13 Kuaishou, *Q2 2021 Results.*
14 Ho et al., *China Consumer Report.*
15 CINIC, *47th China Statistical Report.*
16 Guan and Lin, "Scale of China's Digital Economy."
17 News China, "Kuaishou daily 'digital rewards' have reached 100 million yuan."

of revenue, accounting for 37.2 per cent of total revenues.[18] Ironically, despite the country's flourishing digital economy, individual live streamers may find it ever more challenging to make money from live streaming because the platform takes a larger cut of their earnings. Analysis of data collected from company announcements reveals that Kuaishou's cut from live streamers' gross earnings amounted to fourty-two per cent in the third quarter of 2019 and 43.5 per cent in 2020.[19] Scrutiny of general revenues made by live streamers on Kuaishou suggests that although the company provides the platform, and maintains the servers and other equipment that support the app, it "cannot justify this large cut, even if the façade of innocuous play that covers the activity of live-streaming softens its corrosive impact."[20] Chinese anthropologists argue that Kuaishou's rise points to changes in the nature of labour in contemporary China. The digital social media platform's success indicates a shift towards immaterial labour, whereas the economy remains rooted in the material labour of agricultural and industrial production.[21] Immaterial labour refers to labour that "produces an immaterial good, such as a service, a cultural product, knowledge, or communication."[22] Digital platforms rely on generating revenues from exchanging the commodities of data and attention, both of which are generated by users' immaterial labour. While users watch free shows broadcast by live streamers, embedded advertisements generate surplus value for the digital platforms. Transaction data and viewers' attention can be sold to advertisers as commodities. Users who upload images, write comments, send mail messages to their contacts, accumulate friends, or browse profiles on Facebook constitute an audience commodity that is sold to advertisers.[23] The underlying profit-making mechanism is that when attention economies expand to a significant scale, revenues increase dramatically because numerous users absorb the costs of production, enabling live-streaming apps to yield profits.[24] Although the nature of digital activities, such as creating content, interacting, watching, liking, and commenting, has been widely discussed, users' labour on social media platforms is not recognised as "labour" by the platform providers. Even users themselves misrecognise their "digital activity" as entertainment or self-creation, rather than formal employment in the workplace (*zhengjing*

18 Kuaishou, *Q1 2022 Results*.
19 Orient Securities, *Kuaishou First Report*.
20 Tan et al., "Real Digital Housewives."
21 Tan et al.
22 Negri and Hardt, *Empire*.
23 Fuchs, "Dallas Smythe Today."
24 Jarrett, "Labor of Love"; Tan et al., "Real Digital Housewives."

*gongzuo* 正經工作). For example, the creation work done by Japanese mobile phone novelists is labour that "integrates processes of capital accumulation with the practice of self-determination by further blurring the line between paid and unpaid work."[25] The notion of "prosumers," introduced by Alvin Toffler in the early 1980s, refers to the "progressive blurring of the line that separates producer from consumer."[26] The term was coined to describe a new form of economic and political democracy, self-determined work, labour autonomy, and autonomous self-production. However, Fuchs notes that Toffler overlooked the fact that prosumption can be used to outsource work to users and consumers, who work without payment.[27] Specifically, Sister Zhao's unpaid work creating mobile shorts is entirely free to watch on her personal page. She maintains her cyber karaoke bar by spending hours every day working on planning, shooting, singing, editing, and interacting in live-stream shows on the platform. Although, like Sister Zhao, millions of "daily active users" contribute their creative content production to platforms, the possibility of earning a stable income from virtual gifts sent by viewers during live-stream shows remains extremely limited in the age of "prosumption."

## Immaterial and Affective Labour on Kuaishou: Interactions between "Agony Aunt" and Viewers

The sharp rise of social media in the West has sparked academic debate about "free digital labour," revolving around whether unpaid social media activities redirect power from media institutions to the audience, or allow corporations to exploit users by freely harnessing their content and data.[28] Against this backdrop, feminist scholars criticise more specifically the role played by platforms in the digital era, because interactions on social network sites always involve affective labour, which is expected more from women.[29] Shedding light on how social network sites function as "extensions of the home," Cirucci argues that rather than being invited to contribute new cultural products, women are frequently led only to support existing ones, thus creating less valuable data and even generating

25 Lukacs, "Dreamwork."
26 Toffler, *Third Wave*; Ritzer, Dean, and Jurgenson, "Coming of Age of the Prosumer."
27 Fuchs, "Dallas Smythe Today."
28 Terranova, "Free Labor."
29 Cirucci, "New Women's Work."

more exchange and surplus value than other forms of digital labour.[30] Unfortunately, the affective labour of underclass women on Kuaishou has been demonstrated to be incremental digital labour. They make emotional investments through repetition, hence fulfilling "reproduction" under the dual oppression of capitalism and patriarchy in the digital media economy.[31] Feminist media studies scholars claim that affective, immaterial labour has a variable and often indirect relationship with capitalist exchange, which is the social order itself.[32] The traditional gender division of labour, whereby capital accumulation depends on women's unpaid labour, has shifted in late capitalism to rely increasingly on immaterial labour.[33] In the context of digitizing China, unpaid immaterial labour most frequently takes the form of gendered affective labour on digital platforms.

Affective labour emerges because of the commercialisation of human emotions. Therefore, varying levels of commercialisation affect live streamers' management strategies for distributing emotions. For the most influential Internet celebrities, live-streaming chat rooms are more like cyber shopping malls, but for ordinary live streamers with much fewer followers, financial incentives are not the only reason for performing. Sister Zhao says that she broadcasts live-stream shows for two primary reasons: to earn extra income and to "make friends" (*jiaopengyou* 交朋友). Online ethnographic evidence indicates that ordinary performers tend to adopt a strategy of performing with "true feelings" (*zhenqing shigan* 真情实感) during live-stream shows, because most everyday live streamers have never been trained to act like professional performers, nor can they afford to undergo any form of professional training. Consequently, Sister Zhao believes it is easier and better to "be herself" (*bense chuyan* 本色出演) when performing in her live-stream shows. However, deploying this strategy does not mean that she performs and responds to viewers arbitrarily. Rather, she develops particular patterns to cope with uncertainty during live streaming, based on her understanding of her role as a rural singer performing online. Viewers have described Sister Zhao as an "agony aunt" (*zhixin dajie* 知心大姐), because she is "simple and unadorned" (*pushi wuhua* 朴实无华) and acts like their own mother, aunt, or elder sister. She has to interact with viewers in real time, because if she does not do so, viewers will leave the virtual chat room with an unpleasant feeling of having failed to attract the performer's

30 Cirucci.
31 Arcy, "Emotion Work"; Hartmann, "Unhappy Marriage."
32 Jarrett, "Relevance of 'Women's Work'."
33 Arcy, "Emotion Work."

attention and concern. During a live-stream show in December 2021, Sister Zhao repeatedly expressed her gratitude to the viewers, saying:

> I know that the brothers and sisters in my live-stream chat room are all offering support to me. When I feel upset, you empathise with my miserable life and find a way to comfort me. I don't know how to express myself in words, but I am thankful. Since my husband was put in jail to serve his sentence 12 years ago, I haven't had any friends or relatives in my real life offline to provide me with consolation like this. No one cares about an ugly rural woman making pancakes. But here you all are, like spiritual support for me. I love this platform so much. I make friends here and feel warm and grateful.

Scholars have expanded Bourdieu's concept of "capital" to include emotions.[34] Although Bourdieu did not explicitly refer to emotional capital, he described practical and symbolic work that generates devotion, generosity, and solidarity, arguing that "this work falls disproportionately on women, who are responsible for maintaining relationships."[35] The audience attracted by Sister Zhao's performances is of very similar socio-economic status as her. To some extent, she reflects the nostalgia of rural users on Kuaishou, as she embodies the familiar appearance of a normal rural woman struggling to improve her livelihood in the suburban area on screen. The general emotional structures of performer and audience are much the same, satisfying a precondition for affective interaction. Consumer society has led to increasing dependence on emotional services to meet consumers' affective needs.[36] The new media sphere has become the primary provider of these affective exchanges, constructing a bi-directional pattern of emotional consumption that drives participants to be both producer and consumer. As mentioned above, mutual interactions between Sister Zhao and her viewers illustrate that "liking" (*dianzan*), "following" (*guanzhu* 关注), giving virtual gifts (*shua liwu* 刷礼物), and chatting in the comments area satisfy various affective needs for both live streamers and their audience. In this sense, underclass women may become trapped by the underlying mechanism of transforming and compounding digital labour with affective support, which drives them to participate in constant unpaid digital work.

34 Reay, "Gendering Bourdieu."
35 Bourdieu, *Practical Reason*.
36 Wang, "Emotional Consumption."

## Representing a Rural "Self" and "Performing Resistance"

Sister Zhao told her audience that she had never received any professional vocal music training owing to her lack of time, energy, and budget. When she began to conduct live-stream shows, she tried to learn vocal skills from free online teaching videos, but "failed to understand" (*tingbudong* 听不懂). Incorrect sound production and breathing resulted in chronic hoarseness, requiring a break from live streaming. Although many viewers leave comments such as "This is beautiful" and "Your songs are pleasant to hear," the compliments seem to relate more to her emotional engagement as an organic part of the performance, rather than her technical singing skills or stage effects. In other words, the goods that viewers consume in this mutual process of digital production seem primarily to be the content rather than the form of the performance. Pursuit of affection (e.g., *The Dearest Ones* [*zuiqinde ren* 最親的人]), bitter longing for love (e.g., *Listening to the Heart* [*tingxin* 聽心]), loneliness, and the frustration of being a migrant worker (e.g., *Whose Heart is Drifting in Midnight* [*shuidexin zai wuye piaobo* 誰的心在午夜漂泊]) are three recurrent themes emerging from textual analysis of Sister Zhao's selection of songs. Her performances are mainly of ballads with light rhythms and plain lyrics, expressing desires and wishes that resonate with ordinary Chinese people, especially those from socially disadvantaged classes.

Sister Zhao's rustic casual wear and visual layout of her performance are a constant feature in her videos, which are shot in her dough-making cabin, her rented dormitory in the city, and her rural living space. The consistent visual style of her performances illustrates the lived experiences of a typical Chinese rural migrant worker (*nongmingong* 農民工). Sister Zhao's self-shot raw footage, her own singing, the simple shooting location, and basic editing are four fundamental elements of the audiovisual language in her 759 videos. She does not follow a specific pattern, nor intentionally design her shooting sites for mobile shorts. She simply hangs up a randomly chosen background fabric or sheet behind her during her live-stream shows to hide her disorderly living space, creating a relatively neat performance stage. She uses a wide range of shooting locations for her short videos, and rarely settles on one location as her main site for performing. Her personal page showcases her singing in various indoor and outdoor scenes. Her realistic visual style is the result of effectively utilising her limited living space, rather than meticulous design. The rural chanteuse's stage effects bring the online audience into her personal world, where she can be seen standing by a river flowing near her village, or wearing an apron in the kitchen after

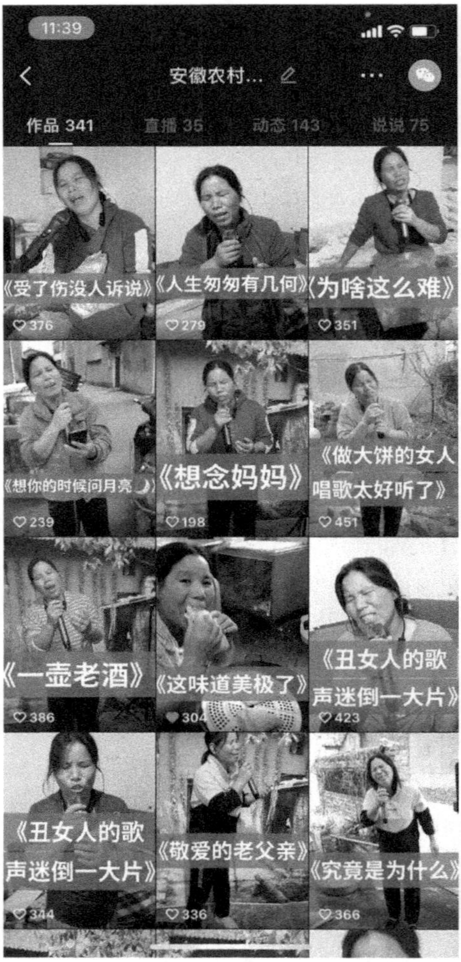


Figure 3. Thumbnails of Sister Zhao's personal page on Kuaishou

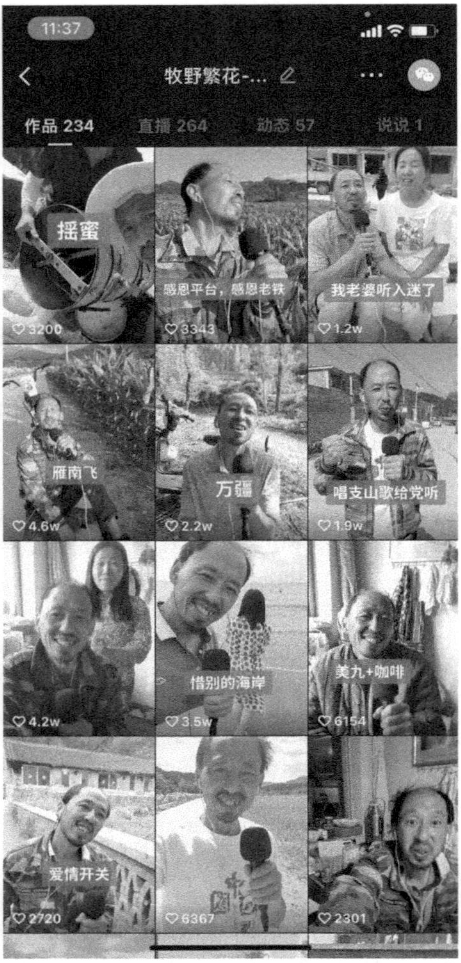


Figure 4. Thumbnails of Uncle Shoushan's personal page on Kuaishou

finishing her household chores. In contrast, professional performers often decorate and modify their performance spaces by investing in fixed stage effects to strengthen audience recognition.

Sister Zhao's stage-setting preference for her singing performances is very similar to that of some male vocalists on Kuaishou. Popular rural singer Uncle Shoushan (*shoushan dashu* 守山大叔), who has 2.2 million followers on Kuaishou, deploys the same staging strategies for his live-streams. He currently lives in a village in Hebei Province, and before he became famous on Kuaishou, he earned a living by running a small chicken farm. He mostly performs in rural living spaces, such as a backyard, a grove, a cornfield, by the riverside, or in his bedroom. His singing performances never show any trace of elaborate design. By presenting an unadorned image of rural China, rural performers can convey a convincing sense of intimacy and familiarity to their audience.

However, Sister Zhao deploys a fundamentally different strategy from Uncle Shoushan in constructing her public persona. While Uncle Shoushan has established himself as a public role model, who embodies "positive energy" (*zhengnengliang* 正能量), Sister Zhao constructs a self-image that underscores the hardships she faces in life. For instance, most cover images for the short videos presented on Uncle Shaoshan's personal page show his smiling face and encouraging words, such as "Come on, my Motherland" (*jiayou zuguo* 加油祖国) and "I'll be Waiting for You on a Warm Night" (*wo zai wennuan zhiye deng ni* 我在温暖之夜等你). The Chinese press has reported on the rise in "positive energy" online, referring to "uplifting power and emotion, representing hope."[37] The Chinese Party-state has long emphasised positive propaganda, also known as the main melody (*zhu xuanlü* 主旋律) in the realm of media, arts, and cultural production, and positive energy is largely in line with this propaganda strategy, which can be seen as a hegemonic online discourse.[38] Compared with the typical role of a positive-energy rural male singer, Sister Zhao's public persona is more ambiguous. The cover images of her videos mainly show bitter expressions on her face. Instead of performing as a role model for "positive energy," Sister Zhao adopts more sorrowful expressions and dramatic body language not often observed in Uncle Shoushan's videos. Similar positive-energy strategies can be observed on the channels of other male rural singers, such as Brother Little Nine (*Shandong xiaojiuge* 山东小九哥) and Singer Daxin (*geshou daxin* 歌手大心). While the evidence collected from ethnographic observation does not indicate that male rural singers merely perform songs with "positive energy" and never show "negative" feelings, it is nevertheless noteworthy that Sister Zhao has chosen to represent herself as "an ugly heart-breaking woman," rather than embodying a "positive energy" role model as male rural singers seem to be more likely to do. Although rural singers of both genders employ the same strategy of utilising natural living spaces as their main filming locations, their distinct performing styles offer us insight into how gender norms shape content creation on Kuaishou. At the same time, we should not view female creators as passive agents. Foregrounding more undesirable content such as pain, loneliness, etc. may in fact also be

37 Xinming Evening News, "Number of Positive Energy Transmissions."
38 Yang and Tang, "Positive Energy."

understood as a subtle critique of the "positive energy" discourse on social media – thereby resisting or at least bringing into focus the different ways gender hierarchies are re-enacted in digital spaces.

## Women's Digital Labour

Although the bustling platform economy promises opportunities for empowerment, self-expression, new forms of labour and upward mobility for its users, it rarely makes any significant improvement to their socio-economic situation. Instead, both performers and viewers unconsciously collaborate in realising and maintaining the generation of surplus value for the platform. Moreover, online affective labour conducted by rural women appears to mostly reinforce gendered hierarchies and precarity. Sister Zhao's situation illustrates that content creators on Kuaishou commodify their supposedly inalienable emotions. Digitisation of one's bodily and affective labour reflects the imperative to maximise human capital for material gain that lies at the core of neoliberalism.[39] Live streamers like Sister Zhao actively create content through the unpaid digital labour they provide (in Sister Zhao's words, she is "just playing here") for Kuaishou. In this sense, Kuaishou and other digital platforms offering live-streaming services present a digital public stage where performers are empowered by online social support from viewers, yet simultaneously disempowered by constant unpaid digital work. Unfortunately, it is extremely difficult for rural users from contemporary Chinese society, and particularly for performers with limited social resources, to perceive their gendered and affective digital labour as anything more than "playing." Although some are not necessarily intent on generating income and live-stream for other reasons, such as social support in the case of Sister Zhao, they experience live-streaming as a deeply ambivalent activity.[40] Sister Zhao must either accept that her digital work primarily benefits the platform while comforting herself with the support and encouragement of her followers, or not live-stream at all.

Despite the disadvantageous socio-economic situations faced by rural users and the minimal revenues they can generate through live-streaming, some are trying to gain social support from mutual affective labour, creative content production, and interactive shows. In doing so, live-streaming can

39 Tan et al., "Real Digital Housewives."
40 Tan et al.

also become a way of drawing attention to, and possibly also resisting, the reproduction of social inequalities on digital platforms. Overall, however, these positive aspects have yet to gain critical momentum within China's digital society, where economic and social inequalities persist, and women's labour remains undervalued.

## References

Alexa Internet. "taobao.com Site Overview." Alexa Internet. https://www.alexa.com/siteinfo/taobao.com.

Andrejevic, Mark. "Privacy, Exploitation, and the Digital Enclosure." *Amsterdam Law Forum* 1 no. 1 (2008): 47–62.

Arcy, Jacquelyn. "Emotion Work: Considering Gender in Digital Labor." *Feminist Media Studies* 16 no. 2 (2016): 365–368.

Bourdieu, Pierre. "Cultural Reproduction and Social Reproduction." In *Knowledge, Education, and Social Change*, edited by Richard Brown, 71–84. London: Tavistock, 1973.

Bourdieu, Pierre. *Practical Reason: On the Theory of Action*. Redwood City, CA: Stanford University Press, 1998.

China Internet Network Information Center 中国互联网络信息中心. "Di 47 ci Zhongguo hulian wangluo fazhan zhuangkuang tongji baogao 第47次中国互联网络发展状况统计报告[The 47th China Statistical Report on Internet Development]." Beijing: China Internet Network Information Center, 2021.

Cirucci, Angela. "A New Women's Work: Digital Interactions, Gender, and Social Network Sites." *International Journal of Communication* 12 (2018): 23.

Couldry, Nick, and Andreas Hepp. *The Mediated Construction of Reality*. Cambridge: Polity Press, 2016.

Cui, Peng 崔鹏, and Jiang,Jingling 姜菁玲. "Su Hua ci ren Kuaishou CEO, Cheng Yixiao jieren gai zhiwu 宿华辞任快手CEO，程一笑将接任该职务[Su Hua Resigns as CEO of Kuaishou, and Cheng Yixiao Will Take Over the Position]." *Jiemian.com*, 29 October. https://m.jiemian.com/article/6761245.html.

Dongfang Zhengquan Yanjiusuo 东方证券研究所[Orient Securities Research Institute]. "Kuaishou shouci baogao——duanshipin shequ longtou, shangyehua jiasu zheng dangshi 快手首次报告：短视频社区龙头，商业化加速正当时 [*Kuaishou First Report: The Short Video Community Leader, and the Right Time for Acceleration of Commercialization*]." Shanghai: Orient Securities Research Institute, 2021. https://pdf.dfcfw.com/pdf/H3_AP202102081460159841_1.pdf.

Fuchs, Christian. "Dallas Smythe Today: The Audience Commodity, the Digital Labor Debate, Marxist Political Economy and Critical Theory. Prolegomena to a Digital Labor Theory of Value." In *Marx and the Political Economy of the Media*, edited by Christian Fuchs and Vincent Mosco, 522–599. Leiden: Brill, 2015.

Guan, Qiaoqiao 关俏俏, and Lin,Guangyao 林光耀. "Zhongguo shuzi jingji guimo da 39.2 wanyi yuan 中国数字经济规模达39,2万亿元 [The Scale of China's Digital Economy Reaches 39.2 Trillion Yuan]." *Xinhua News Agency*, 26 September 2021. http://www.gov.cn/xinwen/2021-09/26/content_5639469.htm.

Hartmann, Heidi. "The Unhappy Marriage of Marxism and Feminism: Towards a More Progressive Union." *Capital & Class* 3 no. 2 (1979): 1–33.

Ho, Johnny, Felix Po, Jia Zhou, and Daniel Zipser. *China Consumer Report 2020: The Many Faces of the Chinese Consumer*. New York: McKinsey & Company, 2019.

Jarrett, Kylie. "Labor of Love: An Archaeology of Affect as Power in e-Commerce." *Journal of Sociology* 39 no. 4 (2003): 335–351.

Jarrett, Kylie. "The Relevance of 'Women's Work': Social Reproduction and Immaterial Labor in Digital Media." *Television & New Media* 15 no. 1 (2014): 14–29.

Kuaishou. *Announcement of the Results for the Three Months Ended March 31, 2022*. Kuaishou Technology.

Kuaishou. *First Quarter Financial and Operational Data of 2021*. Kuaishou Technology, 24 May 2021. https://ir.kuaishou.com/zh-hans/node/6996/pdf.

Kuaishou. *Second Quarter Financial and Operational Data of 2021*. Kuaishou Technology, 25 August 2021. https://ir.kuaishou.com/zh-hans/node/7036/pdf.

Kuaishou.*Third Quarter Financial and Operational Data of 2021*. Kauishou Technology, 23 November 2021. https://ir.kuaishou.com/zh-hant/news-releases/news-release-details/kuaishoukejifabu2021niandisanjiduyeji/.

Liu, Tao 刘涛. "Qinggan kangzheng: biaoyan shi kangzheng de qinggan kuangjia yu daode yu 情感表演式抗争的情感框架与道德语法 [Emotional Struggle: The Emotional Framework and Moral Grammar of Performative Struggle]." *Journal of Wuhan University: Humanities Edition* 69 no.5 (2016).

Lukacs, Gabriella. "Dreamwork: Cell Phone Novelists, Labor, and Politics in Contemporary Japan." *Cultural Anthropology* 28 no. 1 (2013): 44–64.

Negri, Antonio, and Michael Hardt. *Empire*, vol. 15. Cambridge, MA: Harvard University Press, 2001.

Reay, Diane. "Gendering Bourdieu's Concepts of Capitals? Emotional Capital, Women and Social Class." *The Sociological Review* 52 supp. 2 (2004): 57–74. https://doi.org/10.1111/j.1467-954X.2005.00524.x

Ritzer, George, Paul Dean, and Nathan Jurgenson. "The Coming of Age of the Prosumer." *American Behavioral Scientist* 56 no. 4 (2012): 379–398.

Schiller, Dan. "Poles of Market Growth? Open Questions about China, Information and the World Economy." *Global Media and Communication* 1 no. 1 (2005): 79–103.

Tan, Chris, Jie Wang, Shengyuan Wangzhu, Jinjing Xu, and Chunxuan Zhu. "The Real Digital Housewives of China's Kuaishou Video-Sharing and Live-Streaming App." *Media, Culture & Society* 42 nos. 7–8 (2020): 1243–1259.

Terranova, Tiziana. "Free Labor: Producing Culture for the Digital Economy." *Social Text* 18 no. 2 (2000): 33–58.

Toffler, Alvin. *The Third Wave*. New York, NY: William Morrow, 1980.

Turner, Jonathan. *Human Emotions: A Sociological Theory*. Abingdon: Routledge, 2007.

Van Dijck, José, Thomas Poell, and Martijn de Waal. *The Platform Society*. New York: Oxford University Press, 2018.

Wang Ning 王宁. "Qinggan xiaofei yu qinggan chanye——Xiaofei shehuixue yanjiu xilie zhi 情感消费与情感产业——消费社会学研究系列之一 [Emotional Consumption and Emotional Industry—One of the Series of Studies on Consumer Sociology]." *Journal of Sun Yat-sen University* 40 no. 6 (2006): 109–113.

Xinming Evening News 新民晚报. "Weibo zheng nengliang chuandi shu zhixian shangsheng zhuanfa dianping renjian zhenshanmei 微博正能量传递数直线上升 转发点评人间真善美 [Number of Positive Energy Transmissions on Weibo Forwarding and Commenting on Truth, Goodness and Beauty in the World Has Skyrocketed]." *Xinming Evening News*, 22 August 2022. https://www.chinanews.com.cn/cul/2012/08-22/4126061.shtml.

Yang, Peidong, and Lijun Tang. "'Positive Energy': Hegemonic Intervention and Online Media Discourse in China's Xi Jinping Era." *China: An International Journal* 16 no. 1 (2018): 1–22.

Zheng, Jieyao 郑洁瑶. "Naxie ni bu xihuan de ren, tamen ye you jilu de quanli 那些你不喜欢的人，他们也有记录的权力 [Those you don't like, also have the right to document]." Jiemian wenhua, August 8, 2017. https://www.jiemian.com/article/1528890.html.

Zhongguo Xinwen Zhoukan 中国新闻周刊. "Meitian 'dashang' jin yi yi, Kuaishou san da saidao nengfou chengqi 4000yi shizhi 每天'打赏'近一亿 快手三大赛道能否撑起4000亿市值 [Daily 'Digital Rewards' Have Reached 100 Million Yuan: Can Kuaishou's Three Major Tracks Support a Market Value of 400 Billion Yuan?]." News China, February 3, 2021. https://finance.sina.cn/tech/2021-02-03/detail-ikftssap2736411.d.html?fromtech=1&from=wap.

# 8 Network Fantasies

## Liu Cixin's *China 2185*, Digital Futurism, and History as Computer Code

*Jessica Imbach*

**Abstract**
This chapter studies science fiction's rise in the post-Tiananmen period by focusing on the idea of history as computer code. It begins with an analysis of Liu Cixin's cyberpunk novel *China 2185* in the context of the late 1980s cultural fever, but then zooms out to consider how the broader science fiction field emerged alongside the digitisation of Chinese society and the formation of the discourse of Chinese futurism. While China's digital industry growth appears to confirm the historical vision of cyberpunk fiction, I argue that science fiction's continuously diminishing engagement with network technologies is a result of globalised post-digital culture as well as the increased practical and ideological significance of automation to state power.

**Keywords:** science fiction, cyberpunk, Liu Cixin, Han Song, post-digital culture

Four months before tanks rolled on to Tiananmen square and the Chinese Communist Party under Deng Xiaoping began their violent crackdown on the 1989 democracy movement, Liu Cixin completed the draft of his first long novel *China 2185* (中國 2185). The novel has never been officially published, but the text has been in online circulation since at least the early 2000s and is today considered an early harbinger of the 1990s science fiction boom in Chinese literature.[1] Often referred to as China's first cyberpunk novel, *China 2185* creatively wires the imaginative registers of early computer culture into the socio-political setting of reform era China. More specifically, it takes

1 Song, "After 1989."

Imbach, Jessica. *Digital China.* Amsterdam: Amsterdam University Press, 2024
DOI: 10.5117/9789463720670_CH08

the symbolically portentous figure of Mao's computerised brain as its point of departure to ask how digital technologies will affect China's geopolitical rise. Its vision of the future thus takes us back to the early history of the Internet – 1989 also being the year that the world wide web was founded at CERN in Geneva, when digital technologies were still largely the stuff of fantasy and, well, science fiction. Yet, the novel's central concern is neither the fate of China's political system nor the emergence of intelligent machines, but rather the spectre of China's developmental stagnation in the digital age. The chairman himself is in fact but a minor player within the novel, whose narrative centres on the formation of the cyberspace-based Republic of Huaxia (*Huaxia gongheguo* 華夏共和國), which, in a misguided effort to prove the superiority of "national culture" (*minzu wenhua* 民族文化) by turning the Chinese cultural body into computer code, brings real life China to the brink of a nuclear war with the Soviet Union. However, while *China 2185* thematises a set of modernisation anxieties that firmly root its outlook in the intellectual landscape of the late 1980s, it introduced a new vision of the future, one that linked China's geopolitical rise to its success in the digital industries. Even as the variables of its fictional set-up have faded into the historical past, its vision of the future finds confirmation in present-day China's digital rise.

While the impact of the Internet on the Chinese literary field and its globalising effects have already been investigated in several studies, this chapter focuses on the relationship between network technologies and science fiction.[2] How does science fiction represent and negotiate the Internet and new media? What role does cyberpunk – a predominantly dystopian, near-future genre that emerged in the early 1980s and focuses on the oppressive role of computer technologies – play within the Chinese literary context? And how can we situate science fiction's rise in the post-Tiananmen period within the context of China's digital industry growth? Focusing on the idea of history as computer code, this chapter begins with a close reading of *China 2185* – a pivotal text in Chinese science fiction history and a rare example of non-US or Japanese cyberpunk. Liu's novel not only reflects "the arrival of a world built by cybernetics,"[3] but also highlights the complex interactions between early fantasies about the informatisation of the globe during the late 1980s cultural fever (*wenhua re* 文化热) with the social and political forces in which technologies and their imaginaries are embedded. In *China 2185* this embeddedness is shaped by a paradoxical relationship between

2 Hockx, *Internet Literature in China*; Inwood, *Verse Going Viral*.
3 Youngquist, "Cyberpunk, War, and Money," 320.

digital time, in which the world is transformed into an ever-expanding and constantly available data repository, and (r)evolutionary time that propels China's growth and techno-scientific progress. Although cybernetics made its most profound mark on Chinese history in the form of the One-Child policy – a highly contested legacy that also looms in the background of *China 2185*, the "three theories" (*san lun* 三論, comprising cybernetics, system theory and information sciences) congealed into an intellectual movement that moved well beyond computers and robots and saw new possibilities of system analysis and social engineering in areas as disparate as medicine, government bureaucracy, and aesthetics. In Liu Cixin's novel, however, these cybernetic dreams of efficiency and programmability are expressed in the nightmarish idea that the computerisation of society might paradoxically lead to the end of China's history. In contrast to other cyberpunk classics such as William Gibson's *Neuromancer* (1984) or Mamoru Oshii's *Ghost in the Shell* (1995), *China 2185* focuses not so much on the Internet as a new physical realm, but rather as a new temporal condition that threatens to subsume China's quest for national rejuvenation (historically, a core concern of Chinese science fiction) under the domination of a stagnating and eternal present.

*China 2185* is not only the first science fiction text that imagined network technologies as the determining factor of China's (utopian) future, but also highlights the complicated temporal politics underlying science fiction's rise in the post-Tiananmen period. In the second part I thus zoom out to explore the relationship between Chinese futurism (sometimes also referred to as sinofuturism) and representations of network technologies within contemporary science fiction more broadly. As China's digital industry growth can be considered the linchpin of Chinese futurism, I take science fiction writer Chen Qiufan's claim that Chinese literature lacks cyberpunk fiction as my point of departure to show that engagements with China's new media environment are today less to be found in texts set in cyberspace, but rather in a growing interest in history as well as its relationship to computer code. Drawing on Wendy Chun's insights into the "enduring ephemerality" of digital media, I argue that this historical turn is not only a product of rising popular nationalism, but also a reaction to the reductionist idea of the future as a continuous update of the (political) status quo. I conclude with a reading of Han Song's short story "Mountain Camp" (Shanzhai 山寨, 2020), which is a dark and absurd parable on the role of literature in times of extreme crisis. In stark contrast to *China 2185*, the past appears here no longer as an unchanging archive of historical information, but rather as an unstable repository of futures past as well as pasts yet to have been.

## The End of the Future in *China 2185*

Liu Cixin worked as a computer engineer at the Niangziguan electric power plant in Shanxi when he made his first serious attempts to write science fiction. In 1989 he wrote his two first long novels, *China 2185* and *The Supernova-Era* (*Chaoxinxing Jiyuan* 超新星紀元) and programmed what is probably China's first poetry generator, named "Electric Poet" (*dianzi shiren* 電子詩人). Given Liu Cixin's background in computer engineering, it is not surprising that several of his works deal with computation and virtual reality. For instance, in the novella "The Mirror" (*Jingzi* 鏡子, 2004) Liu imagines a computer-generated alternate universe that creates a society of complete information transparency, which, striking a similarly dystopian chord as in *China 2185* threatens to eliminate any form of "human error," and his most famous work *The Three-Body Problem* (Santi 三體, 2008) prominently features a virtual reality game that replays the history of the Trisolaran civilisation and functions as a recruitment tool for the alien invasion supporters.

His works are often classified as hard science fiction, which adheres generally to the known physical laws of the universe and abstains from the use of magic, although this does not mean that its futuristic scenarios are necessarily more "realistic" than other forms of science fiction and fantasy. The high prevalence of hard science fiction in China is on the one hand a result of the "Anti-Spiritual Pollution" campaigns from the early 1980s, in which influential figures such as Qian Xuesen criticised the budding science fiction scene for promoting irrational and "unscientific" ideas. On the other hand, hard science fiction's reliance on "the social authority of the natural sciences to anchor and legitimise its fantastic premises,"[4] also resonates with the Chinese state's scientific diplomacy and, more broadly, its promotion of a dazzlingly futuristic and scientifically advanced image of China. Yet, targeted policies to curb for instance the proliferation of "time-travel" (*chuanyue* 穿越) narratives show that the state continues to closely monitor and police the boundaries of fantasy and it is very unlikely that *China 2185* – not only due to its politically sensitive subject matter, but also its creation of an "alternate China" – will be published in book form within Liu Cixin's lifetime.[5]

4 Imbach, "Chinese Science Fiction in the Anthropocene," 127.

5 To this date there is also no complete translation of *China 2185*, but for an M.A. seminar on science fiction in 2019, my students and I translated two chapters. These can be found here: https://dlf.uzh.ch/sites/sinofutures/

This has not stopped Liu's legions of fans from reading *China 2185* online and the novel is by many scholars recognised as a pivotal text in Chinese science fiction history. Song Mingwei in particular has highlighted the historical significance of Liu's novel, representing as it does not only a generally less optimistic and less idealistic view of the future than was previously common in Chinese science fiction, but also thematising directly the widespread disillusionment with the state-engineered blueprints that culminated in the Tiananmen protests in 1989.[6] *China 2185*'s unique position within Chinese science fiction history notwithstanding, Yu Xuying rightly also cautions us not to overestimate the novel's "cyberpunk exterior" as a radical break with the past, as it reflects ideas and tropes that were widely circulated within popular culture of the late 1980s.[7]

*China 2185* starts as a utopian tale of China's rise to the "world's first complete information society" under the leadership of a twenty-nine-year-old woman, who is throughout the novel only referred to as "the highest magistrate" (*zuigao zhizhengguan* 最高執政官). Most issues have been solved and China has assumed a global leadership role in various areas such as industrial innovation and environmental policy: China has successfully transitioned to nuclear and renewable energies, the country's Northwest has become the world's largest "software producer," the Loess Plateau has been "greened," and the Chinese Renminbi has become the dominant international currency. All that remains for China to solve is its "population problem" (*renkou wenti* 人口問題), which the novel stages not as an economic, but rather a psychological obstacle to China's development.[8] Written in the context of the demographic anxieties that followed China's introduction of the one-child policy in the early 1980s, a large portion of the novel details how a drastically overaged population is burdening China's youth and hindering its social development. The problem is further compounded by medical advancements such as artificial organs that have given humans nearly eternal life; a scene in chapter two explains that the "modern Chinese family" of 2185 comprises seven generations living under one roof. Plummeting birth rates have become a literally existential threat to the nation and have further entrenched generational differences; the quasi-immortal geriatric majority wants to revive "national culture," while the younger

6 Song, "Variations on Utopia in Contemporary Chinese Science Fiction."

7 Yu Xuying, "Bashi niandai de xiandaixing xiangxiang – Lun Liu Cixin 'Zhongguo 2185'."

8 Liu Cixin, *Zhongguo 2185*, chapter 2. All references to *China 2185* are given to the corresponding chapter on kehuan.net.

generation thrives to abolish the traditional kinship structures and ride their flying motorcycles.

This focus on national development parallels the debates on cultural reform of the late nineteenth and early twentieth century when Western culture was identified as the driving force behind Europe's technological edge and military power. It also relates more specifically to the cultural fever of the 1980s, in which, as I discuss later, the debate over Westernisation re-emerged under the aegis of cybernetics. However, in Liu's novel it is no longer technological, but rather social development that is at stake. This existential question also drives the plot, in which six deceased men are brought back to life via a new technology that combines 3D scanning and molecular holography to turn brains into autonomous and intelligent software. At first, they are kept on a secure network, but after they demand recognition as full-fledged citizens of China, they are granted access to the country's general network. Events quickly spiral out of control, when the software Brain 2 – and not Brain 6, which is the silicone-based copy of Mao's brain, replicates itself into a myriad of "pulsars" (*maichongren* 脈衝人), who create the cybernetic Republic of Huaxia. This digital nation wants to replace the new China with a cyberspace version of the "old China" – the term huaxia itself referring to Chineseness in an ethnic, rather than territorial sense. To this end, the Republic of Huaxia gains control over all Internet-connected systems and tries to instigate a nuclear war with the Soviet Union. China's young female leader in the end foils the insurrection by literally pulling the plug on the network.

In *China 2185* cyberspace is thus not the playground of hackers and Internet junkies, but a national infrastructure that is maliciously hijacked by the culturally conservative software Brain 2 to ensure the eternity of traditional Chinese values. The novel's preoccupation with national vitality reflects how China's desire for technological modernity remains haunted by the colonial history that pathologised the nation as the "sick man of East Asia." But the technology of digitised consciousnesses threatens to set the social Darwinian development model into reverse gear, guaranteeing the survival of those who change the least. Without death, Mao's digital remains wax philosophically at the end of the novel, there is no life. While the political fantasy of the Internet as the realm of universal suffrage collapses in the face of a technologically accelerated gerontocracy, China's young leader proposes not the abolition of the Internet and the technology of computerised brains, but rather decides that a new "general computer network" should be built, albeit with one key difference – it should no longer be accessible to everyone.

Putting older people into digital retirement homes is on the one hand a satirical, high-tech solution for the age-old cultural problem of filial piety.

On the other hand, it is also suggestive of two developments that would prove characteristic of Internet development in China: uneven access to digital technologies and, more recently, the emergence of data as a key tool of governance. Animating *China 2185's* fictional engagement with the Internet, however, is not just a concern for government stability and national prosperity, but also a deep-seated ambivalence towards the power of network technologies and automated protocols to amplify and promote fringe beliefs. This is dramatised through the short-lived Republic of Huaxia, whose history is preserved in a letter to the highest magistrate that survives the power shutdown. It describes how shortly after the pulsars gained access to the main computer network, a dangerous combination of fanaticism, viral replication, unlimited access to information and computational speed turned Huaxia into a totalitarian state, whose sole mission became the salvation of "national culture." Every citizen of Huaxia – who are all copies of the first pulsars – is forcefully enlisted in this endeavour and the state decides to adopt a zero-tolerance policy towards any form of dissent. Echoing the violent persecution of counterrevolutionaries during the Cultural Revolution, Huaxia develops a "mutation detection software" to "guarantee the purity of the Republic" and enables its military to uncover and eliminate any citizen, who, as the author of the letter bluntly puts it, "deviates from the norm."[9]

As soon as the pulsars realise that the Internet will be shut down and their cybernetic resurrection of "old China" will fail, they nevertheless dedicate themselves to generate a scientific model of Chinese culture. Because their computational speed far outpaces real time, the two hours until their connection is capped amount to six hundred digital years:

> We will use these six hundred years to complete our monumental project: We will prove with mathematical precision the ethical system of national culture. We will not only use this ethical system to explain all knowledge amassed by humanity, but also incorporate all of humanity's theories and models into it. When the Republic of Huaxia perishes, this grandiose and logical ethical system will be our legacy to future humanity. It will guarantee the survival of our culture and be as eternal as the Sun.[10]

While the novel models the Republic of Huaxia after Maoist China, its engagement with the role of Chinese culture in a networked society needs to be read in the historical context of the cultural fever, which Zhang Xudong

9 Liu Cixin, chap. 12.
10 Liu Cixin, chap. 12.

has aptly called "one of the most provocative events in the cultural life of post-Mao China."[11] What started in 1985 as an intellectual debate on the meaning and relevance of tradition (Confucianism in particular), science, and Western theory to China's integration into the global economic system, was by the time it violently ended in 1989 a nation-wide discussion on national identity and globalisation that also had an enormous influence on popular culture.

The vocabulary and grammar of cybernetics permeated these debates. Especially influential was Jin Guantao and Liu Qingfeng's hypothesis that Chinese civilisation represented an "ultrastable structure" (*chaowending jiegou* 超穩定結構).[12] They took an anti-Marxist stand to argue that Chinese history could be studied as a macro-system that functioned according to the internal logic of its culture and values. In the end, they identified Confucianism as the main regulator of this "deep structure" and the root cause of its "stability." As controversial as their ideas were, their theorisation of Chinese society as a closed structure continued a longstanding intellectual tradition that emphasised the uniqueness of the Chinese cultural body – either as the well of the country's success or as the source of its failures. But their focus on culture and history also reflected the widespread dissemination of a particular strand of system theory that emerged in the geopolitical landscape of the Cold War era and combined Weberian modernisation theory with developmental sociology. As Liu Xiao shows in her erudite study of Chinese cybernetics in the pre-Internet age, this brand of system theory was already introduced to China in the early 1960s but became widely debated in the 1980s.[13] It posits that societies are primarily shaped by internal forces and that the modernisation of developing societies could only be fast-tracked through the external introduction of science and technology. Modernisation theory was, as Liu points out, in many ways a product of US American anxieties surrounding the looming spectre of socialist upheaval and revolutionary turmoil and gave long-standing and entrenched notions about the superiority of Western culture a new scientific guise. But these ideas nevertheless resonated with Chinese intellectuals, as modernisation theory also posited, following Weber, that a society's norms and values played a crucial role in economic development. Modernisation theory thereby signalled a clear departure from the economic determinism of

11 Zhang, *Chinese Modernism in the Era of Reforms*, 36.

12 Jin Guanto and Liu Qingfeng, *Xingsheng Yu Weiji – Lun Zhongguo Fengjian Shehui de Chaowending Jiegou*.

13 Liu, *Information Fantasies*, 126.

Marxist developmental theory and became widely circulated and discussed in socialist countries as they were transitioning into a capitalist economy. Chinese intellectuals' embrace of modernisation theory was thus not simply an endorsement of Westernisation, but also an attempt to formulate a strategic, or what Chen Xiaomei calls an "anti-official"[14] occidentalism to distance themselves from the CCP.

The most important cultural text in this context is the six-episode TV series *River Elegy* (*Heshang* 河殇, 1988), for which Jin Guantao also acted as scientific advisor. Wholeheartedly embracing Western science and democracy, the series can be summarised as a pre-mortem eulogy of Chinese civilisation, dramatised through a series of historical interpretations that centre on the symbolic dichotomy between the closed and stable system of the Yellow River and the open and changing system of the blue ocean, representing the capitalist West. *River Elegy's* celebratory embrace of all things Western was highly controversial and the Chinese state heavily criticised the show for vilifying Chinese culture, but the series hit a nerve of the zeitgeist and became an extraordinary success. *River Elegy* does not directly thematise the new information environment and its technologies, but its evocative symbolisation of Western maritime culture through open skies, vast oceans, roaring waves, and planet Earth as seen from outer space – the blue marble – captured how debates on the global exchange of goods and ideas was intimately linked to a wider set of anxieties concerning China's ability to adapt to the information age.

In the 1980s, cybernetics was not only sending shock waves through the Chinese intellectual landscape and cultural scene, but also an important epistemic substrate of China's transition into a knowledge-based economy. Paola Iovene has traced this transition within changing representations of labour to argue that post-socialist science fiction played an important role in the formation of a new understanding of mental labour that celebrated "the Chinese mind as disembodied intellect, thus prefiguring the formation of a new intellectual class."[15] The cultural fascination with the cerebral was also prominently displayed in science fiction cinema of the late 1980s. In Huang Jianxin's famous *Dislocation* (*Cuowei* 错位, 1987) the robot clone of an office worker develops a mind of his own and begins to resent his creator. In *The Composite Man* (*Hecheng ren* 合成人, 1988) the brain of a peasant is transplanted into the body of a powerful businessman of the aptly named Huaxia Corporation, while the mad

14 Chen, "Occidentalism as Counterdiscourse."

15 Iovene, *Tales of Futures Past*, 34.

scientist in *The Beautiful Head in the Haunted House* (*Xiongzhai meiren tou* 凶宅每人頭, 1989) keeps severed heads alive in a secretive lab and develops a technology to reattach these living heads to recently deceased bodies. This fascination with the cerebral not only helped to reposition scientists as chief architects of China's new era (*xin shiqi* 新時期),[16] but also reflected wider renegotiations of cultural identity in a changing technological environment.[17]

*China 2185's* culturalist portrayal of Chinese values as a rigid protocol of customs and beliefs that are hardwired into the brain combines *River Elegy's* system theory approach to culture with the pop-cultural fascination with the cerebral. However, the novel does not posit a contradiction between Chinese culture and technology, as it is after all the fanatic traditionalists of the Republic of Huaxia who leverage digital technologies in a highly effective, but ultimately futile attempt to overthrow the Chinese government. *China 2185* thus refutes the central premise of *River Elegy* and in fact indirectly comments on the series in chapter two, where it is explained that the highest magistrate gained popularity among China's older generation after she successfully restored the flow of the Yellow River. In stark contrast to *River Elegy's* dramatisation of the Chinese landscape as symbol of China's cultural stability and, mutatis mutandis, intellectual stagnation, *China 2185* does not treat technology as propelling history towards a cosmopolitan world culture, but rather as an integral tool in a geopolitical struggle for power and resources. Similarly, Liu's novel posits that if, at a moment of technological underdevelopment, Chinese history were to be successfully turned into computer code, China's underdevelopment would become programmed into the future. In Liu's near-future scenario, the real threat to China's development is neither Chinese culture nor Westernisation nor the return of Maoism, but rather digital technologies' purported ability to eliminate the future entirely.

Today, *China 2185* remains one of only very few literary texts that explore the social and political ramifications of network technologies to a similar degree. This is mainly related to the fact that network technologies have

16 Rudolf Wagner's influential discussions of science fiction as "lobby literature" notwithstanding, recent studies have shown that the early 1980s science fiction field shared many commonalities with socialist science fiction. Indeed, many of the thaw era writers were already active in the 1950s and 1960s. See, Wagner, "Lobby Literature"; Li, *Chinese Science Fiction during the Post-Mao Cultural Thaw*.

17 Liu Xiao, for instance, provides an astute reading of brainwave science fiction that problematized the incorporation of the human brain within the global and "homogenous space" of the information sciences, Liu, *Information Fantasies*, 69–82.

lost much of their futuristic energies.[18] *China 2185*'s outdated cybernetic imagination of the future notwithstanding, its concern over the possibilities of a "programmable" future resonates with more recent engagements with China's new media environment and disillusionment with digital futurism, more broadly.

## To the Future through the Past

Since the late 1990s, Chinese science fiction has transformed from a fringe literary phenomenon into a global cultural industry. In terms of domestic reader numbers, science fiction still trails behind other popular genres such as *xuanhuan* (玄幻) and *danmei* (耽美) (see chapters 1 and 2 in this volume),[19] but science fiction's current success is often interpreted as symbolic of China's rapid technological development in fields such as space exploration, Artificial Intelligence, surveillance technology, and bioengineering. As a powerful index of China's vast socio-economic and technological transformations over the last four decades, science fiction today thus plays a pivotal role in the production of a discourse that has been variously termed Chinese futurism or sinofuturism.[20] While it would be reductive and misleading to characterise this sprawling textual universe solely in geopolitical terms, the idea that China will decisively shape the world of tomorrow is a vital engine of the genre's mainstream appeal and increasingly transnational reach.

Science fiction's purported ability to capture the futuristic energies on the ground is one important reason why the field is currently enjoying a pop-cultural (and scholarly) moment. It is in this context interesting to note that narratives, which are grounded in recognisable locales and customs such as Hao Jingfang's *Folding Beijing* (*Beijing zhedie* 北京摺疊, 2012) and Chen Qiufan's *The Waste Tide* (*Huangchao* 荒潮, 2013) have travelled particularly well. This is not to say anything about their artistic qualities, but rather reveals how Western regimes of authenticity continue to powerfully shape the reception of non-Western literature. Science fiction is nevertheless often regarded as a genre exceptionally

18 While Meta's announcement of the metaverse created some buzz across China's science fiction scene, interest in the concept was quickly eclipsed by Chat-GPT.

19 See Cui and Jin, in this volume.

20 Because sinofuturism is so far primarily an external discourse about China, I use the term Chinese futurism to designate the wider discursive field, in which the idea that China is *the* future is produced and circulated. On sinofuturism, see: Conn and De Seta, "Sinofuturism (s)."

well suited to overcome national and cultural boundaries.[21] Liu Cixin, for instance, insists that what makes science fiction unique is its "world perspective" or "species perspective."[22] He and his main translator Ken Liu have also repeatedly argued that the prefix Chinese carries no descriptive value other than designating a writer's nationality. However, as I have argued elsewhere, this rejection of cultural difference needs to be contextualised within a larger historical and geopolitical context, where power relations have been and remain uneven.[23] The modern notion of science (*kexue* 科學) is itself a product of late Qing modernisation discourse and Wang Hui has noted how in the Republican period (Mr.) Science became virtually synonymous with the West.[24] Within this context, science fiction became yoked to the teleological imaginaries of China's civilisational rejuvenation. While this led Lu Xun to bemoan China's lack of science fiction as a sign of "intellectual poverty,"[25] the genre's success today is often treated as a powerful sign that China has overcome its alleged innovation deficit.

The politics of Chineseness are further compounded by the field's entanglement with commercial and state interests. Spurred by Liu Cixin's win of the Hugo award in 2015, science fiction has become increasingly folded into the Chinese state's soft power portfolio, while fashion magazines, online influencers, artists, popstars and even tech unicorns have discovered the commercial appeal of science fiction.[26] In 2021, Liu Cixin announced that he will be heading the new Science Fiction Planetary Research Centre of the Artificial Intelligence company SenseTime. The Hong Kong based company, who is, among other things, one of the largest providers of facial recognition software for the Chinese state, also plans to create an "immersive experience" based on *The Three-Body Problem* universe.[27] But while some of the most successful writers have embraced new career opportunities as celebrity ambassadors of Chinese techno-culture, science fiction's popularity still remains modest in comparison to other popular fiction genres.[28] Writing in

21 Chau, "From Nobel to Hugo."

22 Liu Cixin, *Liu Cixin Tan Kehuan,* 50.

23 Imbach, "Chinese Science Fiction in the Anthropocene."

24 Liu, *Translingual Practice*; Hui, "The Fate of 'Mr. Science' in China."

25 Lu Xun, *Lu Xun quanji,* 11:9–11.

26 Gaffric, "La trilogie des Trois corps de Liu Cixin et le statut de la science-fiction en Chine contemporaine."

27 Xuemei, "Liu Cixin: Xuanbu jiameng shang tang, shuangfang jiang dazao Santi chenjinshi yule xin yetai."

28 Chau, "From Nobel to Hugo," 118.

2016, Song Mingwei argued that this relative marginality created room for transgression and subversive exploration of topics that are usually deemed too politically sensitive or morally ambiguous. But that same year, the Chinese State Council announced a four-year plan to promote scientific literacy among its citizens and identified science fiction as a key cultural resource in this endeavour.[29] Moreover, it seems that increased commercial visibility, especially following the success of the science fiction movie *The Wandering Earth* (*Liulang diqiu* 流浪地球 Frant Gwo, 2019), has invited intensified political scrutiny.[30] The international success of writers such as Liu Cixin and Hao Jingfang has further increased state interest in the field beyond science education. From this perspective, however, it does not necessarily matter whether individual texts are fully in alignment with state discourses or not, as the most important export product of China's science fiction industry is *science-fictionality* itself.

Science fiction scholar Istvan Csicsery-Ronay defines science-fictionality as a mode of thinking about and experiencing the world as if it were science fiction. As such it does not necessarily rely on science fiction media, but it can draw on concrete science fiction texts. For instance, the immensely popular Xiaolingtong cellphones that dominated China's early mobile phone culture were named after the hero of Ye Yonglie's science fiction classic *Little Smarty Travels to the Future* (*Xiao Lingtong manyou weilai* 小靈通漫遊未來, 1978). Conversely, science-fictionality also feeds back into science fiction, although the realist effect may reveal the extent to which ostensibly science-fictional objects and attitudes have already become futurist clichés. To stay with the example of portable devices, Ah Que's "Contemplation" (Jujue 咀嚼) satirically speculates on a future, in which the gadgetry of the mobile Internet merges with humans into a kind of wetware symbiosis, but this new stage of human evolution only serves increased productivity and the reinforcement of social boundaries.[31] Science fiction can thus also undermine or at least bring into question the contemporary hype surrounding the idea that the "world [or just China for that matter] has grown into sf."[32]

29 China State Council, "Guowuyuan bangongting guanyu yinfa quanmin kexue suzhi xingdong jihua gangyao shishi fang'an (2016–2020 nian) de tongzhi."

30 For example, in 2020 the China Film Administration published a list of precepts for science fiction cinema's continued development in the "correct direction." See: China Film Administration, "Guojia dianyingju, Zhongguo kexie yinfa 'guanyu cujin kehuan dianying fazhan de ruogan yijian'."

31 Ah Que, "Jujue."

32 Csicsery-Ronay, *The Seven Beauties of Science Fiction*, 1.

The notion of a Chinese-tech powered future is nevertheless real enough and arguably most evident in the country's digital transformation, as outlined in the introduction of this volume. A digitally saturated media sphere, the global success of social media apps such as TikTok, the pervasiveness of "smart infrastructure," and the state's Big Data applications across a wide range of sectors appear to give concrete support to the idea that Chinese futurism is predominantly a digital futurism. Digital technologies have also profoundly impacted the Chinese literary landscape. Apart from the emergence of online literature – perhaps the cultural field were digital technologies and vernacular creativity are most closely intertwined, several more recent developments such as automated writing systems, so-called A.I. poetry and algorithmically judged literary prizes are suggestive of intensifying entanglements of literary practices and digital industries.

The historical genre of cyberpunk to a certain extent anticipated current developments. While some see in cyberpunk a "truncated residue of what remained of the rich discourse of cybernetics,"[33] recent re-evaluations of the field (and cybernetics itself) emphasise that cyberpunk remains a relevant lens for engaging with the techno-social developments of the twenty-first century such as the possible emergence of a metaverse.[34] In Chinese, cyberpunk is transliterated as *saibo pengke* 賽博朋克, but the term is mainly applied to foreign literary texts, in particular the works of "cyberpunk pioneers" such as Bruce Sterling and William Gibson. Science fiction author Chen Qiufan contends that cyberpunk in China is "all cyber, no punk."[35] He argues that Chinese authors not only lack the historical experience of the counter-culture movements, its drug culture and exhortation of the social outcast as "fighting the system," but also that (self-)censorship has turned writers away from the genre. Chen thereby alludes to the pervasive surveillance assemblages that play an important role in North American cyberpunk futurism and subject human life to an oppressive regime of transparency and machine-readability.[36] Paranoia, body-horror and conspiracy theories come with the territory of Gibson's "consensual hallucination."[37]

33 Kline, *The Cybernetics Moment*, 228.

34 McFarlane, Schmeink, and Murphy, *The Routledge Companion to Cyberpunk Culture*.

35 Chen Qiufan, "Zai Zhongguo, zhi saibo bu pengke."

36 Coincidentally, a cybernetic current connects French post-structuralist critiques of transparency with the ideologies of posthumanism. See: Geroulanos, *Transparency in Postwar France*; Hayles, *How We Became Posthuman: Virtual Bodies in Cybernetics*.

37 Gibson, *Neuromancer*, 56.

It is possible to argue that the question whether China does or does not have cyberpunk is misplaced, as it not only rehashes a linear, humanist teleology of cultural development, but also ignores the genre's historicity. It is in this context also important to note that *China 2185*, which Chen does not discuss, was written well before the first Chinese translations of North American cyberpunk appeared. For instance, the first Chinese edition of William Gibson's genre-defining novel *Neuromancer* (*Shennjing manyouzhe* 神经漫游者) only came out in 1999. Moreover, while China's digital present to a certain extent confirms the East Asian trajectories of early cyberpunk fiction, which located the global sprawl of information flows and multinational corporations against the historical backdrop of "Asia's rise," Chen fails to mention how cyberpunk frequently exoticises East Asian cultures and societies in a discourse that has been dubbed "techno-orientalism."[38] Coincidentally, Chen's own works, which are often compared to Gibson's, strategically mobilise cyberpunk's techno-orientalist gaze to reach out to an international audience.[39]

In the context of PRC cultural production, it is furthermore not surprising that (online) censorship is seldom thematised. One example is Ma Boyong's short story "City of Silence" (Jijing zhi cheng 寂靜之城), in which state surveillance is so all encompassing that most people choose to live a life in silence and solitude, fully acquiesced to the reality that state-managed computers and listening devices are in full control over their lives. Another example is the novella "Ether" (Yitai 以太) by Zhang Ran, in which disinformation nano bots can even control light and sound waves and a "Finger Chatting Society," where members communicate by drawing characters on each other's hands, forms to rebel against "the disappearance of the revolutionary spirit from the Internet."[40]

Chen nevertheless rightly points out that China's digital rise has not been accompanied by a similar rise in science fiction works focused on network technologies, new media, and digital futurism more broadly. And the most accomplished and well-known science fiction authors publish today predominantly in (digitised) print media and not on online literary websites, where a variety of online-themed subgenres such as "online gaming novels" (*wangyou xiaoshuo* 網游小說) are in fact being circulated in large numbers. This is partly a result of science fiction's historical role in science education, but also reflects the persistent public perception of

38 Roh, Huang, and Niu, *Techno-Orientalism*.
39 See also Goldstein, in this volume.
40 Zhang Ran, "Yitai," 44.

online literature as commercial youth entertainment, i.e., as a social rather than a cultural phenomenon. The most important reason for the "absence" of cyberpunk on the Chinese literary scene, however, is the fact that global cultural production has entered the so-called "post-digital" age, in which network technologies have lost much of their initial allure and the utopian, posthuman promises of the early web have receded into the past.[41] While media scholars have scratched Gibson's works from their course syllabi for being "embarrassingly fictional and utopian,"[42] many science fiction writers are today more inspired by newer technologies such as Artificial Intelligence.

Media theorist Wendy Hui Kyong Chun incisively comments that current articulations of digital futurism have become remarkably trivial and mundane:

> This future 2.0, like web 2.0 or 3.0, is not as utopian or bold as its mid-1990s predecessor, which was billed as *the future*. There are no upbeat yet paranoid commercials promising an end to racial discrimination and the beginnings of a happy global village; there are no must-read cyberpunk novels or films outlining its gritty, all-encompassing nature.[43]

The belief that network technologies and new media will radically alter our social and political structures and redraw the boundaries of biological and artificial life has been replaced by a more pragmatic, but not necessarily less problematic, understanding of digital futurism as a continuous upgrade of that, which already is. This is powerfully captured in the fatalistic attitude towards the future that pervades Ma Boyong's and Zhang Ran's dystopian novellas but also looms in the background of *China 2185's* anxious fantasy that network technologies might spell the end of China's progress. Chun, however, shows that the prevalent conception of digital media as an "ever-increasing archive in which no piece of data is lost"[44] not only ignores the physics of all storage media, i.e., the fact that records need to be continuously maintained, restored, and refreshed, but also that access to and understanding of information are not the same. Dispelling with the fantasy that the "information explosion" would turn into a "knowledge explosion," Chun draws on Jacques Derrida's notion of the "archive fever" to

41 Cramer, "What Is 'Post-Digital'?"
42 Chun, "The Enduring Ephemeral, or the Future Is a Memory," 155.
43 Chun, 150.
44 Chun, 154.

show that digital media are not the "memory machines" we make them out to be, but rather constituted through constant information degeneration and repetition.[45] What distinguishes digital records from analogue media is the fact that its information is constantly in a state of "undeadness," waiting to be refreshed, rediscovered, and repeated.[46] In this sense, digital media have not ended, but rather multiplied history.

These insights are particularly salient in the context of China's heavily regulated and censored media landscape as well as China's ambitious push for the automation of social management more broadly.[47] Harnessing what Chun in another context describes as "the logic of the update,"[48] the ideology of automation as a "past anticipation of the future"[49] has not only become vital to China's digital governance, where system theory continues to play an important role, but it also dovetails with the CCP's Marxist framework of historical development. The idea of history as computer code reduces the future to a function of the past and it is thus not surprising that (socialist) history has once again become an important resource of what William A. Callahan has poignantly termed the state's "nostalgic futurology."[50] In Chinese history, the consolidation of power through recourse to the past is a familiar gesture enough. However, building on the ideology of memory permanence in the digital age such so-called laws of history are today also progressively yoked to dreams of bureaucratic efficiency, automated decision-making, and social stability.[51]

However, outside of government think-tanks this rekindled "obsession with history"[52] has also led to a burst in history-oriented media practices that span the range from personal online diaries, grassroots memory projects, through social media debates to the imaginative historiography of online

45 Chun, 167.

46 Chun, 171.

47 Hoffman, "Programming China: The Communist Party's autonomic approach to managing state security."

48 Chun, *Updating to Remain the Same*, 70.

49 Chun, 70.

50 Callahan, "Surpass," 280.

51 Largely due to Qian Xuesen's towering role in the history of the Chinese space programme, system theory never disappeared from the Chinese academic landscape and continues to percolate throughout Chinese political discourse. Moreover, system theory is today also invoked to put Xi Jinping's catchphrases such as "the common fate of the people" or the Confucian notion of *datong* "great harmony" 大同on scientific footing. See for instance: Xue Huifeng, "Datong: Cong 'yantaoting' dao 'shijie nao,'"

52 Widmer and Wang, *From May Fourth to June Fourth*, 378.

literature.[53] In science fiction, too, we can note a historical turn. Especially prominent are appearances by ancient philosophers and texts such as Mozi in Liu Cixin's *The Three-Body Problem* and rewritings of the automaton story "Yanshi" 偃師 from the *Liezi* 列子. But we can also see this historical interest expressed in science-fictional reimaginings of ancient myths and legends in the works of Xia Jia (pen name of Wang Yao), Chen Qiufan, Fei Dao (pen name of Jia Liyuan) and Bao Shu, who traces this practice to Lu Xun's *Old Stories Retold* (*Gushi xinbian* 故事新編, 1935).[54] Echoing the engagement with China's material culture and philosophy in late Qing science fiction, the current historical turn may be similarly interpreted as an expression of a desire to situate science fiction within a local genealogy.[55] Intellectual similarities notwithstanding, a growing global demand for science fiction "about China" as well as a politically favourable climate for scientific nationalism and historical revisionism have also contributed to its popularity. Yet, we do not have to accept Jia Liyun's somewhat reductive assertion that post-Tiananmen science fiction emerged in the shadow of the question "what will happen to the ruling party after an alien invasion?"[56] to see that science fiction's historical turn, as Wang Yao again points out, also reflects a search for "new possibilities of progress."[57] While equally not to be mistaken for political dissent, the science-fictionalisation of the (pre-socialist) past inevitably foregrounds the mediation of time itself. As illustrated by Han Song's "Mountain Camp," to which I turn in the conclusion, science fiction's historical turn thereby both supplements as well as critically reflects on the historical politics animating the age of Chinese futurism.

## Science Fiction after the End of the Future

Throughout this chapter I used the qualifier post-Tiananmen instead of Song Mingwei's by now well accepted periodisation of contemporary science

53 See for instance: Zhao and Liu, "Social Media and Collective Remembrance"; Gaffric, "Collective Space/Time Travel in Chinese Cyberliterature"; Yang, "Online Lockdown Diaries as Endurance Art."

54 Bao Shu, *Kehuan zhong de Zhongguo lishi.*

55 Nathaniel Isaacson reads this practice as an attempt at "intellectual redemption." See Isaacson, *Celestial Empire*, 126.

56 Jia Liyuan, "'Guangrong Zhonghua': Liu Cixin kehuan xiaoshuo zhong de Zhongguo xingxiang."

57 Wang Yao, *Weilai de zuobiao*, 225.

fiction as "new wave." I have done so not to express disagreement with Song's analysis, which focuses more squarely on the dynamics internal to Chinese science fiction history, but rather to situate science fiction's persistent concern with the politics of temporality in the specific set of interactions between technology and intellectual life that shaped the transformations of China's cultural scene starting in the late 1980s and early 1990s. Liu Cixin's *China 2185* is exemplary in this regard, as it reflects how cybernetic ideas percolated throughout late 1980s popular culture, while the horizon of digitisation animated both fantasies of technological leapfrogging as well as fears of socio-cultural stasis. Moreover, 1989 is generally considered the watershed moment in China's transition into the "post-new era," characterised, among other things, by the commercialisation of culture and the emergence of postmodern discourse. The idea that History might end with the advent of digital technologies belongs itself to the story of postmodernism. Jean-François Lyotard and Fredric Jameson famously saw in the "computerisation of society" one of the most powerful forces reshaping knowledge production in postmodernity, which, as they speculated in the 1980s and 1990s, would lead to a continuous depreciation of forms of understanding and meaning-making that cannot be transformed into computer code or stored in a database.[58] For Jameson especially, digital networks promised not liberation, but rather the further dispersal of collective visions and identities and he characterised cyberpunk as "the supreme literary expression if not of postmodernism, then of late capitalism itself."[59] Jameson's analysis of cyberpunk does nevertheless not apply to *China 2185*, which occupies a very different historical and cultural terrain as William Gibson's or Bruce Sterling's works. Significantly, the utopian horizon of *China 2185* is not the Internet itself – despite its democratic promises, but rather China's transformation into a global leader in digital industries. However, in *Archeologies of the Future* Jameson also notes how science fiction paradoxically "rediscovered its utopian vocation" when the belief in historical blueprints had come to an end.[60] We can locate the rise of Chinese science fiction in the post-Tiananmen period within a similar dynamic, although here the "postmodern is also the postrevolutionary and the postsocialist."[61]

58 Lyotard, *The Postmodern Condition*; Jameson, *Postmodernism, or, The Cultural Logic of Late Capitalism*.

59 Jameson, *Postmodernism, or, The Cultural Logic of Late Capitalism*, 419.

60 Dirlik and Zhang, *Postmodernism and China*, 4.

61 Jameson, *Archeologies of the Future: The Desire Called Utopia and Other Science Fictions*, 289.

As such it is not only a reaction to a paralysed "historical imagination,"[62] but also a critical response to the foreclosed future of CCP futurology.

This dynamic also informs the short story "Mountain Camp" by the writer and Xinhua journalist Han Song, who is known for his unique blend of technological dystopianism and Buddhist mysticism. The story is an enigmatic fable about a group of writers and literary scholars, who go to a conference in a remote research centre in the mountains, are then taken hostage by the event's organiser, only to realise upon their release that they are the only survivors of some inexplicable Armageddon event. The story can be read as an allegory on literature's capacity to reflect and understand the world. All characters are only referred to by their respective fields of expertise such as "Lu Xun specialist," "poet A," or "cutting-edge literary critic" and they consistently try and fail to draw on their knowledge to understand unfolding events. Notably absent are writers of genre fiction and at one point the participants bemoan the fact that no science fiction writer was invited to the conference to make sense of their absurd predicament.

Although not set in the past, historical events and texts haunt Han Song's narrative. For instance, the rustication policies of the Cultural Revolution and its eco-utopian fantasies are echoed in an episode where the conference participants realise that their grain reserves are depleted, and they must retrain as peasants. Quoting Engels one writer explains: "Work creates Man, and this is after all the fount of all literature and art!"[63] In another scene, post-Cold War ideology makes a rhetorical appearance when the arrival of golden yellow robots is interpreted by the "environmental fiction writer" as a symbol of a possible East-West "culture clash." Han Song's story reaches more fantastical territory, when the writers temporarily shapeshift into bats and, later, monkeys from Huaguoshan, alluding to Western vampire lore as well as to the legendary shapeshifter Sun Wukong from *Journey to the West* (*Xiyou ji* 西遊記). Other details are not directly related to any specific text or historical time, but rather emphasise the fluid and instable nature of the world, such as AK47s transforming into "warped Arabic numerals" or a peculiar breed of dears who have no skullcaps, allowing their brain matter to "cascade over their bodies like a waterfall."[64] The title "Shanzhai" is simultaneously a reference to the bandit fort of the classical Ming novel *Outlaws of the Marsh* (*Shuihu zhuan* 水滸傳), the narrative's literal setting in a remote rural location, which "seemed neither fictional nor real, permeated by the atmosphere of

62 Jameson, "Future City," 77.
63 Han Song, "Shanzhai," 18.
64 Han Song, 21.

green forests and mountain camps of classical novels,"[65] as well as the terms modern usage in the sense of counterfeit or knock-off. The title's ambiguous meaning thereby emphasises the blurred boundaries between original and copy, fact and fiction, human and animal, machine and nature. This spiralling loop of epistemological and ontological instability is given a final twist at the story's ending, when the writers see their names gliding down the sky as in the closing credits of a movie. Are they being watched or are they the audience? Where does the story begin and the movie end? And who is doing the writing?

The apocalyptic future of "Mountain Camp" and its expression in ghostly fragments of utopias past such the utopian monkey enclave Huaguoshan and the Maoist village contrast sharply with the teleological horizon of *China 2185*. Whereas *China 2185* imagined digital technologies to turn history into stable data, "Mountain Camp" treats history as an elusive dynamic that relies both on constant (re-)mediation as well as hermeneutic construction. Zeroes and ones cannot bring meaning any more on to stable ground than a syncretic Ming dynasty novel. In doing so, "Mountain Camp" nevertheless also foregrounds an idea of the future as an active process of writing/coding.

> Tomorrow's world will rely on the method of writing [in the sense of typing on a computer, mazir de banfa 碼字兒的辦法] to rehabilitate itself. Except for us, everything has ended, and we should not commit the same mistake of leaving the worlds in the hands of the economists, experimental scientists, and IT-engineers.[66]

On balance, "Mountain Camp" remains equivocal about literature's relevance (and does not spare the science fiction writers from dying in the Armageddon event). However, it simultaneously also emphasises the constructed nature of our world knowledge. This undercuts not only the notion of a singular predetermined trajectory of historical development, but more specifically, also positions science fiction itself as a genre that defamiliarises the expectations engendered by the discourse of Chinese futurism. While *China 2185* foresaw how the advent of digital technologies would continuously restrict the future as a realm of political contestation and creative imagination, "Mountain Camp" does not so much reject (digital) technologies as double-down on science fiction's critical role in preserving the diversity of both the past and the future, because, in the end, neither history nor the future is a code we can crack.

65 Han Song, 16.
66 Han Song, 20.

## References


Ah Que 阿缺. "Jujue 咀嚼 [Contemplation]." In *Shirun de Jinshu* 湿润的金属 [Wet Metal], 205–26. Beijing: Zuojia chubanshe, 2020.

Bao Shu 宝树, ed. *Kehuan Zhong de Zhongguo Lishi* 科幻中的中国历史 [Chinese History in Science Fiction]. Beijing: Sanlian Shudian, 2017.

Callahan, William A. "Surpass." In *Afterlives of Chinese Communism*, edited by Christian Sorace, Ivan Franceschini, and Nicholas Loubere, 275–80. Political Concepts from Mao to Xi. ANU Press, 2019.

Chau, Angie. "From Nobel to Hugo: Reading Chinese Science Fiction as World Literature." *Modern Chinese Literature and Culture* 30, no. 1 (2018): 110–35.

Chen Qiufan 陈楸帆. "Zai Zhongguo, zhi saibo bu pengke 在中国，只赛博不朋克 [In China, It's All Cyber, No Punk]." New York Times Chinese Edition, August 8, 2013. https://cn.nytimes.com/books/20130808/cc08cyberpunk/.

Chen, Xiaomei. "Occidentalism as Counterdiscourse: 'He Shang' in Post-Mao China." *Critical Inquiry* 18, no. 4 (1992): 686–712.

China Film Administration. "Guojia dianyingju, Zhongguo kexie yinfa 'guanyu cujin kehuan dianying fazhan de ruogan yijian' 国家电影局、中国科协 印发 《关于促进科幻电影发展的若干意见》 [China Film Administration and China Association for Science and Technology Publish 'Some Notes on Advancing the Development of Science Fiction Cinema']," August 7, 2020. http://www.chinafilm.gov.cn/chinafilm/contents/141/2533.shtml.

China State Council. "Guowuyuan bangongting guanyu yinfa quanmin kexue suzhi xingdong jihua gangyao shishi fang'an (2016–2020 nian) de tongzhi" 国务院办公厅关于印发全民科学素质行动计划纲要实施方案 (2016–2020年) 的通知 [General Office of the State Council on the Issuance of the Action Plan on the People's Scientific Quality and Implementation Outline (2016-2020)]. http://www.gov.cn/zhengce/content/2016-03/14/content_5053247.htm.

Chun, Wendy Hui Kyong. *Updating to Remain the Same: Habitual New Media*. MIT Press, 2017.

Chun, Wendy Hui Kyong. "The Enduring Ephemeral, or the Future Is a Memory." *Critical Inquiry* 35, no. 1 (2008): 148–71.

Conn, Virginia L., and Gabriele De Seta. "Sinofuturism (s)." *Verge: Studies in Global Asias* 7, no. 2 (2021): 74–99.

Cramer, Florian. "What Is 'Post-Digital'?" In *Postdigital Aesthetics: Art, Computation and Design*, edited by David M. Berry and Michael Dieter, 12–26. London: Palgrave Macmillan UK, 2015.

Csicsery-Ronay, Istvan. *The Seven Beauties of Science Fiction*. Middletown: Wesleyan University Press, 2012.

Dirlik, Arif, and Xudong Zhang. *Postmodernism and China*. Durham: Duke University Press, 2000.

Gaffric, Gwennaël. "Collective Space/Time Travel in Chinese Cyberliterature." In *China's Youth Cultures and Collective Spaces: Creativity, Sociality, Identity and Resistance*, edited by Vanessa Frangville and Gwennaël Gaffric, 189–202. Abingdon: Routledge, 2019.

Gaffric, Gwennaël. "La trilogie des Trois corps de Liu Cixin et le statut de la science-fiction en Chine contemporaine." *ReS Futurae. Revue d'études sur la science-fiction*, no. 9 (May 30, 2017).

Geroulanos, Stefanos. *Transparency in Postwar France: A Critical History of the Present*. 1. Edition. Stanford, California: Stanford University Press, 2017.

Gibson, William. *Neuromancer.* New York: Berkley Publishing Group, 2000.

Han Song 韩松. "Shanzhai 山寨 [Mountain Camp]." *Zhongguo Zuojia* no.6 (2020):15–24.

Hayles, Katherine. *How We Became Posthuman: Virtual Bodies in Cybernetics*. Chicago: University of Chicago Press, 2015.

Hockx, Michel. *Internet Literature in China*. New York: Columbia University Press, 2015.

Hoffman, Samantha. "Programming China: The Communist Party's autonomic approach to managing state security." *China Monitor* (blog), December 12, 2017.

Imbach, Jessica. "Chinese Science Fiction in the Anthropocene." *Ecozon@: European Journal of Literature, Culture and Environment* 12, no. 1 (February 7, 2021): 121–37.

Inwood, Heather. *Verse Going Viral: China's New Media Scenes*. Seattle: University of Washington Press, 2014.

Iovene, Paola. *Tales of Futures Past: Anticipation and the Ends of Literature in Contemporary China*. Stanford: Stanford University Press, 2014.

Isaacson, Nathaniel. *Celestial Empire: The Emergence of Chinese Science Fiction*. Middletown: Wesleyan University Press, 2017.

Jameson, Frederic. *Archeologies of the Future: The Desire Called Utopia and Other Science Fictions*. London: Verso, 2005.

Jameson, Frederic. "Future City." *New Left Review*, no. 21 (June 1, 2003): 65–79.

Jameson, Frederic. *Postmodernism, or, The Cultural Logic of Late Capitalism*. Duke University Press, 2013.

Jia Liyuan 贾立元. "'Guangrong Zhonghua': Liu Cixin kehuan xiaoshuo zhong de Zhongguo xingxiang '光荣中华':刘慈欣科幻小说中的中国形象 ['Glorious China': The Image of China in Liu Cixin's Works]." *Bohai daxue xuebao*, no. 1 (2011): 39–45.

Jin Guantao 金观涛, and Liu Qingfeng 刘青峰. *Xingsheng yu weiji – Lun Zhongguo fengjian shehui de chaowending jiegou* 兴盛与危机：论中国社会超稳定结

构 [Ascendancy and Crisis – On the Ultrastable Structure of Chinese Feudal Society]. Hunan Renmin chubanshe, 1980.

Kline, Ronald R. *The Cybernetics Moment: Or Why We Call Our Age the Information Age*. JHU Press, 2015.

Li, Hua. *Chinese Science Fiction during the Post-Mao Cultural Thaw.* Toronto: University of Toronto Press, 2021.

Liu Cixin刘慈欣. *Liu Cixin tan kehuan* 刘慈欣谈科幻 [Liu Cixin on Science Fiction]. Wuhan: Hubei kexue jishu chubanshe, 2013.

Liu Cixin刘慈欣. "Zhongguo 2185 中国2185 [China 2185]." Kehuan xiaoshuo wang. http://www.kehuan.net.cn/book/2185.html.

Liu, Lydia He. *Translingual Practice: Literature, National Culture, and Translated Modernity –China, 1900-1937*. Stanford University Press, 1995.

Liu, Xiao. *Information Fantasies: Precarious Mediation in Postsocialist China*. Minneapolis: University of Minnesota Press, 2019.

Lu Xun 鲁迅. Lu Xun quanji 鲁迅全集 [Collected Works of Lu Xun]. Beijing: Renmin wenxue chubanshe, 1973.

Lyotard, Jean-François. *The Postmodern Condition: A Report on Knowledge*. Minneapolis: University of Minnesota Press, 1984.

Ma Boyong 马伯庸. "Jijing zhi cheng 寂静之城 [City of Silence]." Kehuan xiaoshuo wang. http://www.kehuan.net.cn/book/jijingzhicheng.html.

McFarlane, Anna, Lars Schmeink, and Graham Murphy. *The Routledge Companion to Cyberpunk Culture*. Abingdon: Routledge, 2019.

Roh, David S., Betsy Huang, and Greta A. Niu. *Techno-Orientalism: Imagining Asia in Speculative Fiction, History, and Media*. Rutgers University Press, 2015.

Song, Mingwei. "After 1989: The New Wave of Chinese Science Fiction." *China Perspectives* 1 (March 1, 2015): 7–13.

Song, Mingwei. "Variations on Utopia in Contemporary Chinese Science Fiction." *Science Fiction Studies* 40, no. 1 (2013): 86–102.

Wagner, Rudolf G. "Lobby Literature: The Archeology and Present Functions of Science Fiction in China." In *After Mao: Chinese Literature and Society, 1978–1981*, edited by Jeffrey C. Kinkley, 15–62. Harvard University Asia Center, 1985.

Wang, Hui. "The Fate of 'Mr. Science' in China: The Concept of Science and Its Application in Modern Chinese Thought." *Positions: East Asia Cultures Critique* 3, no. 1 (1995): 1–68.

Wang Yao 王瑶. *Weilai de zuobiao: quanqiuhua shidai de Zhongguo kehuan lunji* 未来的坐标:全球化时代的中国科幻论集 [The Coordinates of the Future: Essays on Chinese Science Fiction in the Age of Globalization]. Shanghai: Shanghai wenyi chubanshe, 2019.

Widmer, Ellen, and Dewei Wang. *From May Fourth to June Fourth: Fiction and Film in Twentieth-Century China*. Harvard University Press, 1993.

Xue Huifeng 薛惠锋. “Datong: Cong ‘yantaoting’ dao ‘shijie nao’ 大同：从‘研讨厅’到‘世界脑’ [Great Harmony: From the ‘conference hall’ to the ‘world brain.]’” Guangming wang, April 25, 2021. https://topics.gmw.cn/2021-04/25/content_34792144.htm.

Xuemei 雪梅. “Liu Cixin: Xuanbu jiameng shang tang, shuangfang jiang dazao Santi chenjinshi yule xin yetai 刘慈欣：宣布加盟商汤，双方将打造三体沉浸式娱乐新业态 [Liu Cixin Announces Collaboration with SenseTime, Together They Will Create a New Type of Immersive ‘The Three-Body Problem’ Experience],” July 9, 2021. https://finance.sina.com.cn/tech/2021-07-09/doc-ikqciyzk4493238.shtml.

Yang, Guobin. “Online Lockdown Diaries as Endurance Art.” *AI & Society*, January 15, 2021, 1–10. https://doi.org/10.1007/s00146-020-01141-5.

Youngquist, Paul. “Cyberpunk, War, and Money: Neal Stephenson’s Cryptonomicon.” *Contemporary Literature* 53, no. 2 (2012): 319–47. https://doi.org/10.1353/cli.2012.0011.

Yu Xuying 郁旭映. “Bashi niandai de xiandaixing xiangxiang – Lun Liu Cixin ‘Zhongguo 2185’ 八十年代的現代性想像—論劉慈欣《中國2185》[Imagining Modernity in the 1980s – On Liu Cixin’s ‘China 2185’].” In *Shuma shidai de Zhongguo renwen xueke yanjiu* 數碼時代的中國人文學科研究 [Chinese Humanities Research in the Digital Age], edited by Tan Guogen 譚國根, Liang Muling 梁慕靈, and Huang Zihong 黃自鴻, Kindle edition., n.p. Taibei: Xiuwei zixun, 2018.

Zhang Ran 张冉. “Yitai 以太 [Ether].” In *Qifeng zhi cheng* 起风之城 [The Windy City], 3–47. Chengdu: Sichuan kexue jishu chubanshe, 2021.

Zhang, Xudong. *Chinese Modernism in the Era of Reforms: Cultural Fever, Avant-Garde Fiction, and the New Chinese Cinema*. Duke University Press, 1997.

Zhao, Hui, and Jun Liu. “Social Media and Collective Remembrance.” *China Perspectives* 2015, no. 1 (March 1, 2015): 41-48.

# 9 Cyborg Resistance

## Chen Qiufan's *The Waste Tide*, Dirty Computers and the Afterlives of Digital Things

*Zoe Goldstein*

**Abstract**

This chapter uses Chinese sci-fi writer Chen Qiufan's novel *The Waste Tide* to understand the environmental consequences and possibilities inherent in unofficial e-waste processing markets in China. It also aims to build a contemporary, globalised definition of the digital product by incorporating this less-seen waste, as well as digital emissions, and drawing from groundwork laid by twentieth-century theorists of the abject, such as Julia Kristeva and Mary Douglas. The chapter attends to e-waste in both U.S. and Chinese contexts as a recurring process intrinsic to the delineation of cultural identity and neoliberal surplus-driven economic models. I suggest *The Waste Tide* supplies useful possibilities for waste re-incorporation and environmental justice that work against capitalist myopia and toward radical futures.

**Keywords:** e-waste, science fiction, cyberpunk, eco-ambiguity, abjection

The confrontation with waste, Julia Kristeva notes, blurs the boundaries of subject and object, resulting in a continual process of abjection.[1] Waste "is merely repeated. Getting rid of it is out of the question."[2] As much as our discards may shift hands, continents, or elevations, our continual disavowal of "waste" only points to its persistence. Though waste is often seen as an end result, this chapter considers it as impulse, emblem of identity, and agential in itself across literary, digital and grassroots examples, and investigates how we might culturally blur the boundaries of the waste category.

1 Kristeva, *Powers of Horror*, 3

2 Kristeva, *Powers of Horror*, 30.

Imbach, Jessica. *Digital China.* Amsterdam: Amsterdam University Press, 2024
DOI: 10.5117/9789463720670_CH09

Refuse, as Kristeva says, doesn't symbolise death, but shows us the deathly presence we "thrust out in order to live."[3] I investigate how culturally ingrained notions of purity and disgust spark chain reactions of cognitive dissonance, out-of-control waste production, and global environmental injustice, particularly in regard to e-waste across the US and China. I also attend to the contradictory way digital products and the Information and Communications Industry (ICT) are often represented as immaterial, despite their emissions, toxic discards, harmful mining and land-misuse.

Finally, I look to Chen Qiufan's *The Waste Tide* as an example which re-envisions a former e-waste superfund site (Guiyu) as the birthplace of a utopian, proletarian revolution. Counter to both recent Chinese authoritarian environmental management, and orientalist media categorisations of China as "toxic" that other it in line with global systems of domination, the liminal more-than-human space of Chen's silicon isle imagines transformative encounters with waste that free local "waste people"[4] entangled in the refuse from the "disposable" status granted them by the state and global corporations. I also include examples of present-day USian grassroots innovation that promote a rejoining of self and waste as means toward undoing trash-based injustice, and certain Chinese governmental waste programmes (and accompanying citizen-level modes of collaborative, digital participation) that seek to undo rigid pure/impure categorisations and promote the idea of waste as valuable.

## Waste Management as Maintenance of Cultural Boundaries

To understand what is unclean in a culture," Mary Douglas writes in her foundational text on discards, *Purity and Danger*, is "to take a looking glass to the system of ordering a culture strives to establish."[5] Ritualised waste removal systems reveal a cultural desire to align with purity, and to construct social difference through distinctions between pure and impure, which results in an accumulation of the abject.

"Rituals of purity and impurity," Douglas says, "create unity in experience."[6] She maintains that because dirt is produced through ambiguity and cannot

3 Kristeva, *Powers of Horror*, 3.
4 Chen Qiufan, *The Waste Tide*, 25.
5 Douglas, *Purity and Danger*, 2
6 Douglas, *Purity and Danger*, 2.

be assimilated into established categories; it is "matter out of place."[7] Kristeva calls the removal of dirt "a continual process of keeping the unclassifiable at bay," which in turn maintains cultural systems and identities.[8]

As the cultural need to banish impurities shaped ancient Aegean aqueduct systems, so modern landfills terraform landscapes, so the distribution and placement of waste management infrastructure near historically marginalised communities subjects these populations to the same metrics of "disposability," so media representations of toxins in association with marginalised communities further others them. Through these pervasive rhythms of removal and disavowal, discards structure landscapes and cultural practices. Though landfills are often the most visible aspect of waste-terraforming, I will now explore how the digital world and the ICT industry also produce a less visible, but equally transformative waste stream, and the pervasive cultural othering of waste.

## Dirty Cyberspace

Digital devices, products, and networks are often seen as separate from dirty production and disposal due to ethereal "cloud" branding and production/distribution methods that remain opaque to average consumers, but if global IT were a country, only China and the US would contribute more to climate change.

Data centres alone account for about two per cent of global greenhouse gases: the same as the airline industry. At current rates, digital data could consume fifteen per cent of the world's electricity by 2040, the same as the total output of the US.[9] Crypto-currency mining, which until May of 2021 was popular in China (which housed three quarters of all miners at its peak) accounts for 0.33 per cent of all energy consumption, roughly equal to the output of Chile.[10] In line with recent coercive environmentalism, China has banned crypto-mining, but whether this policy will actually decrease emissions from the industry remains to be seen, as many miners will relocate to countries with looser regulations, such as the U.S. Though the ban was undoubtedly helpful for green publicity and short-term cuts, without other measures to ensure these miners don't simply mine elsewhere, the ban

7 Douglas, *Purity and Danger*, 3.
8 Kristeva, *Powers of Horror*, 6.
9 Carrington, "$10bn of precious metals dumped each year in electronic waste, says UN."
10 Sigalos, "China's War on Crypto Just Hit a New Level With Its Latest Crypto Crackdown."

represents a state-centric "green" policy that ignores local complexities in its implementation (as I'll discuss further examples of later). Most ICT emissions, however, come from smartphones—devices used for two years, born from energy-intensive processes, and recycled one per cent of the time. By 2025, we're expected to have eighty billion connected devices.

Even less seen than data centres are the material consequences of planned obsolescence. The world produced fifty-four million tonnes of e-waste in 2019 (worth $62.5 billion), up twenty-one per cent in five years, and only seventeen per cent was recycled. E-waste currently accounts for five per cent of global waste production and is on the rise. An estimated seventy per cent of heavy metal contamination in soil is caused by e-waste.[11]

For years cities in coastal China (namely Guiyu) served as the US's primary relocation site for e-waste, a pattern amplified by global media, which portrayed the region as "dirty and dangerous."[12] Though the US still produces the most e-waste in the world, China has since banned imported waste, and the US-created e-waste superfund site Guiyu has, as of 2015, relegated e-waste processing to markets on the outskirts of town, and made efforts to reduce contamination in the rest of the city. In the outer markets, individuals still cook circuit boards, dunk microchips in sulfuric acid, and burn wiring to extract copper. (Local wealthy bosses live where the air is cleaner and observe workers through cameras.[13] ) Though the ban hasn't stopped informal e-waste recycling in Guiyu, Agbogbloshie, Ghana, is now the world's largest e-waste processing site, and has been found to contain the most hazardous chemicals on earth, with high levels of organic material contamination.

Though contamination in the coastal city certainly caused health hazards, Guiyu's infamous "e-waste dumping ground" label must be seen as a product of racist, orientalist Western media, in a continuation of what Mel Chen and others have tagged as the racialisation of pollutants, and further abjectification of communities associated with them (as in the demonisation of Chinese-made toys found to contain lead).[14] Global media objectifies and even fetishises impoverished migrant workers left to deal with the disastrous after-effects of digital-industrial modernity, as seen in the well-known, sensationalist images of children sitting amongst piles of e-waste across news media and in documentaries such as Plastic China.

11 Carrington, "$10bn of precious metals."

12 Watson, "China: The Electronic Wastebasket of the World."

13 Mujezinovic, "Electronic Waste in Guiyu: A City Under Change?"

14 Chen, *Animacies: Biopolitics and Racial Mattering and Queer Affect.*

As recently as 2013, major news outlets such as CNN referred to China, problematically, as "the electronic wastebasket of the world," and dubbed local e-waste recycling and processing "China's e-waste problem,"[15] when of course the majority of this e-waste comes from wealthy countries in the Global North.

Though informal e-waste processing can be dangerous and contribute to contamination, e-waste processors in Guiyu earn decent wages by local standards, and they also, importantly, rescue valuable metals contained in e-waste from landfills, helping to decrease harmful mining of rare earth metals. Up to five per cent of the earth's gold is estimated to be contained in e-waste. Guiyu's "cleaner" industrial park model, however, has recently decreased migrant workers' income,[16] and the city's drinking water, rivers and air are still polluted, while children still have lead poisoning—though not the eighty per cent tally of the past. The recycling process, though lucrative by local standards, still causes respiratory illnesses, cancer, still-births and so on. The cliche of the imperial power (US) using a Global South region as a "dumping ground" must be seen as a determinist, neo-colonial and racist moniker that deprives the local community of agency, but Guiyu does still hazardously process e-waste, most of which is now domestically generated.

Though the well-publicised clean-up campaign has helped move Guiyu out of the media spotlight, other e-waste processing cities, such as Agbogbloshie that bear brutal environmental consequences for the Global North are still tagged as "dirty" and marginalised in global media. Meanwhile, climate-change-driven agricultural issues (caused, mostly, by wealthy countries) and outright land grabs in rural communities continually drive migrants into cities to perform this dangerous labour. The injustice of e-waste processing highlights the adverse consequences of the cultural identification with purity, newness and innovation, and, as Chen Qiufan highlights--the damage done by allowing global free trade to control waste management. Across the globe, the rich distance themselves from impure discards, while the poor deal with their after-lives.

## Cyberpunk Resistance in Chen Qiufan's *The Waste Tide*

Chen Qiufan's *The Waste Tide* showcases an alternative to both the governance of global free trade and coercive environmentalism. The novel's fictional

15 Watson, Ivan "China: The Electronic Wastebasket."

16 Pinghui, Zhuang, "China's most notorious e-waste dumping ground now cleaner but poorer."

"electronic graveyard" modelled after Guiyu is the setting for a more-than-human migrant worker liberation movement which prompts eco-healing. This re-imagining of digital-social stratification presents alternatives to environmental injustice through the undoing of ritualised waste categories.

While scholars such as Cara Healey have drawn attention to the novel's cyberpunk and dystopian elements,[17] and Mengtian Sun has also noted its criticism of global free trade,[18] here I'll attend to how Chen uniquely critiques both nationalist protectionist measures and governing global corporations, and also highlights hyperlocal, non-systemic means toward environmental justice. I'll argue that though the novel contains elements of cyberpunk, it leans away from the genre's typical pessimism, toward a utopian re-imagining of waste practices that promote the integration of discards into everyday life as a fundamental mode of being.

Kaizong, a young college grad, returns to his home of Guiyu (same English spelling as the real silicon-isle) after a decade away to serve as an interpreter for American recycling executive Scott Brandle, and is shocked to find the city overcome by catastrophic e-waste pollution. His jaw drops at the locally-termed "waste people" he sees sorting through mountains of keyboards and monitors, washing in black water, playing in sand made of charred circuit remains.[19] Kaizong embodies what scholar Karen Thornber calls eco-ambiguity: "the complex, contradictory interactions between people and environments with a significant non-human presence."[20] This unpredictable landscape and Kaizong's "deep gulf"[21] of solastalgia provide the initial basis for further uncanny and surreal developments on the changed island. Though the island will never return to a pre-industrial pastoral ideal, Chen's surreal eco-ambiguity paves the way for the undoing of global systems of domination that historically "discard" the toxic other.

In keeping with Western colonialism, Scott Brandle has come to Guiyu to convince local officials that his billion-dollar American recycling company should take over the island to "fix its waste problem" (caused by the US). Locals reject this white saviour's clean-up solution, not out of pride, but because they see the island and the endangered migrants who operate it as a lost cause. Rich locals want to extract money from the place and get

17 Healey, Cara. "Estranging Realism in Chinese Science Fiction: Hybridity and Environmentalism in Chen Qiufan's 'The Waste Tide'," 1–33.

18 Sun, "Imagining Globalization in Paolo Bacigalupi's The Windup Girl and Chen Qiufan's The Waste Tide," 289–306.

19 Chen, *The Waste Tide,* 25

20 Thornber, *Eco-Ambiguity,* 11.

21 Chen, *The Waste Tide,* 25.

out. Guiyu clan leader Director Lin pauses at a waste site, "as if he were only a visitor."[22]

As Kaizong falls in love with "waste girl" Mimi, and reconnects with family, the novel condemns both the wealthy locals' cognitive dissonance and Brandle's green capitalism. Waste doesn't get fixed by industry—it permeates the minds, bodies and souls of the novel's characters as they find home among the refuse. This reinforces the idea that there is no such thing as a disposable place. If we allow environmental degradation to continue (at any scale), money won't matter and we won't have anywhere to run to.

## Cyborg Solutionisms

As characters build relationships with members of different social groups and non-human entities, more-than-human transformations provide the foundation for a re-imagining of the oppressive caste-like system. A new kind of matter out of place, hybridities re-invent categories and boundaries.

Cyborg modifications permeate *The Waste Tide* —waste children play with twitching silicone body enhancements, a worker "clamped" by a robot looks like "an assembly line mistake,"[23] Mimi and friends turn their skin into peacock-like display screens, and participants in a Taoist Ghost festival email photos to dead relatives. This pervasive human-machine hybridity suggests a comfort among the workers with surpassing the human body—a comfort with the presence of death in life. Their incorporation of the non-human is eventually what leads to their freedom from social hierarchy.

Mimi, who comes to Silicon Isle at sixteen, quickly realises "human lives are cheaper than machines,"[24]—the deadening reality of Guiyu's devaluation of human life, and exploitative system. She ultimately leads the rebellion to overcome this system via incremental acts of collaboration with the more-than-human. The narrative links her, by turns, to "a bag of kitchen trash,"[25] the sea and fish scales,[26] a ghost with many lives,[27] and the GMO bioluminescent jellyfish who grow brighter in the e-waste runoff. Mimi ultimately transforms into a powerful cyborg after she is exposed to a WWII virus, which attaches itself to her brain via a discarded helmet and

22 Chen, 39.
23 Chen, 30.
24 Chen, 49.
25 Chen, 43.
26 Chen, 69.
27 Chen, 70.

allows her to inject her consciousness into any machine, which she uses for collective communiques. Though "waste girl" Mimi can be thought of as a cyberpunk or dystopian character—she suffers through a gang-rape in one of the novel's darker scenes—her communion with waste provides an optimistic turn, which leads to a proletarian uprising.

Her transformation points to possibilities for overcoming the trauma of eco-ambiguity that exist in collectivity and more than human communications. The cyborg-bug grants Mimi a superhuman networked consciousness, and a revenge-seeking, proletarian "second self" which allows her to communicate with all migrant workers at once to protect them from an oncoming storm, which wipes out harmful industry. She sacrifices herself to the struggle with a final rallying cry: "I am just the beginning,"[28] hinting that the movement she led should not be categorised as an anthropocentric hero's journey, but rather only the beginning of an incremental change in the way this community interacts with non-human nature, trash included.

Through its illustration of the hypocrisy and impossibility of throwing trash "away," *The Waste Tide* highlights the necessity for dis-ordering current ecocidal systems. The permeability of bodies and environs on fictional Guiyu demonstrates the impossibility of a contained "disposal site" and shows how this reckless disavowal on the part of global corporations (represented by Scott Brandle) creates irreparable damage. However, as much as the marginalised people in the novel face the worst environmental consequences, they also ultimately present an alternative to the abusive caste systems reinforced by extractivist patriarchy. Grassroots multispecies organising emerges in its marginalia, in its uncategorisable accidents.

## Making Trash "Second-Nature"

According to discard scholar Mohamed Refin, the "rhythm" of the returning abject becomes "a process of establishing and contesting boundaries and taboos, and the contours of the body and the body politic."[29] The returning abject is a liminal space "which continually threatens conventional ways of making meaning."

In a deeply broken and ecocidal system, this threat may be a saving grace. "Waste carries within it the possibility of subverting norms,"[30] David Giles

28 Chen, 190.
29 Arefin, "Abjection a Definition for Discard Studies."
30 Giles, "Dumpsters, Difference and Illiberal Embodiment."

notes, in the Discard Studies Compendium. Projects that reincorporate and reconfigure waste like global anarchist kitchen Food Not Bombs reclaim the usable-but-discarded surplus built into neoliberal necro-capitalism and turn it into sustenance. This anti-market "abject economy" acknowledges and benefits from the inherent value in discarded objects.

Though the decentralised, grassroots model exemplified by Food Not Bombs has not yet absolved the U.S. of food insecurity due to a deeply entrenched scarcity model, throughout the pandemic these anti-markets became lifelines for dozens of my neighbours in New York. Over 145 free-food fridges in NYC have arisen since March of 2020, and they remain stocked with rescued goods, providing essential aid where the neoconservative government hasn't. Like Chen's virus-mutation worker-liberation movement, the free fridges began in a decentralised, non-systemic format. Community members who witnessed the first fridge (set up in late February) in person or on social media worked with their neighbours to amass over 145 different fridges across the five boroughs (each responsive to its local ecosystem and population), and dozens more across the United States and abroad, all filled via dumpster diving and coordinating with local businesses to collect unsold goods. The fridge network also crowdfunds to offset electricity costs.

In addition to projects which resist neoliberal biopolitics, new developments in waste tech hint at other, less-utopian, but nonetheless ultimately beneficial forms of waste recuperation. Across the globe, robots, AI and other digital tech increase the efficiency of recycling and compost. San Francisco, which relies heavily on robotic trash sorting, is close to becoming the first zero waste city in the US. As of 2020, forty-six major cities in China have implemented "smart" waste sorting systems equipped with AI, facial recognition tech and trash-bag QR codes, known as the "Internet Plus Recycling Model" to help mitigate the ten billion tons of solid waste the nation produces each year. With twenty-four million residents and increasingly scarce landfill space, Shanghai was the first major city to implement new waste sorting protocols, which include officers at each sorting zone, fines in the event of incorrect waste classification for both citizens and companies, as well as financial incentives for correct sorting, whereby citizens can use sorting points to acquire household goods.[31] The system also unfortunately comes with time limits: residents must empty garbage during a four hour period (7-9 a.m., and 6-8 p.m.) in which recycling can be supervised by officers.

31 Zhang Jianfeng. "China Gets Serious About Trash Sorting" CCTV July 2, 2019.

In *China Goes Green: Coercive Environmentalism for a Troubled Planet,* Yifei Li and Judith Shapiro, who caution against the adverse local effects of unilateral state-created environmental standards, criticize the trash sorting programme as inconvenient at a local level. The programme, they write, "feels unfair to an overworked middle class,"[32] who sometimes resort to illegal dumping of garbage late at night or bringing garbage into work to avoid regulations. CCTV also highlights testimony from an office worker who finds the limited hours inconvenient, but who also notes that he supports the programme overall, and "hopes the times can become more flexible after people have learned how to properly sort their trash,"[33] noting that officials assist residents with sorting.

It appears local reactions to trash sorting are not as one-sided as Li and Shapiro suggest according to other publications, and their categorisation of the waste sorting programme as a measure which "compels citizens to adhere to a state-centric frame of mind"[34] fails to acknowledge local support for the programme, its employment opportunities, as well as its significant impact in lowering emissions from exponentially growing urban "waste" amidst the global climate emergency (as I'll discuss later). CCTV and China Daily report that while some residents take issue with the time restrictions or feel a learning curve in sorting procedures, others applaud the city for taking initiative with ambitious measures.

Prior to the "Internet Plus Recycling Model," Shanghai has long had waste sorting protocols that were never followed,[35] in part due to cultural attitudes toward waste as unilaterally unusable. Shanghai waste monitor Wang Cai recalls residents once telling her: ",Why bother sorting the trash? Sorted trash is still trash.'"[36] This too-rigid categorisation contributed to an exponentially growing amount of landfill deposits that the city does not have the land space to support. Wang Cai says she has noticed a significant attitude shift since the beginning of the programme. Whereas residents first bemoaned the programme, now they "see her as an expert, ask her when they don't know what category waste goes in, and greet her with kind words."[37]

This new widely publicised and much discussed sorting procedure has helped break down and subvert previously established categories that

32 Li and Shapiro, *China Goes Green,* 61.
33 Zhang Jianfeng, "China Gets Serious," CCTV.
34 Li and Shaprio, *China Goes Green*, 62.
35 Zhang "China Gets Serious," CCTV.
36 Zhang.
37 Zhang.

contributed to ecocidal waste streams by teaching residents the value of discards such as compost and recyclables. A viral Weibo pig joke, which pointedly attributes economic value to waste signals this shift in values. The joke goes: "Think about pigs before sorting your trash — things pigs can eat go to kitchen waste, things pigs don't eat are residual waste, things pigs might die from while eating them are hazardous, and things that can be sold for money to buy a pig belong to recyclables."[38] This saying emphasises the way in which "zero waste" policies promote a reincorporation of refuse into everyday systems of value.

Whereas Li and Shapiro describe the trash sorting categories as "making little sense" and only "designed from the vantage point of the state," other sources such as CCTV and South China Morning Post report that while the new model has required adjustment, community discussion and collaboration have helped bring levity to potential issues and spread understanding around the new procedures. The government has sponsored workshops, digital learning kits, talks on trash sorting and other activities to foster understanding.[39] Furthermore, citizens have engaged in collaborative problem-solving on a hyperlocal level to fill in the gaps in understanding and implementation left by the state's one-size-fits-all program. On Sina Weibo, the issue of trash sorting has attracted more than fifty thousand posts and seventy million views, as people complain, share jokes, and discuss procedures. There are a growing number of fun solutions aimed at educating citizens (such as VR and arcade games and apps) which offer rewards, such as the free-to-access VR game machines that were placed in public spaces in Shanghai in 2019 to simulate the sorting experience. The sorting game (still streaming) achieved viral success. In 2020, 280 games related to waste-sorting were available on Weibo, many of which helped users rehearse typical household waste disposal.[40] Although the trash sorting metrics are certainly an example of the top-down unilateral metrics that Li and Shapiro caution against, the massive citizen-level digital collaboration and conversation that has accompanied this policy suggests grassroots coalitions might work to fill in the gaps of state-centric green policies, and help accommodate local complexities.

Li and Shapiro importantly highlight China's widespread informal recycling industry, in which an estimated two million to five million individuals

38 Zhang.

39 Zhang.

40 SQLI Digital Experience, "New Technologies Help Raise Chinese Citizens' Awareness of Waste Sorting."

collect and receive payment for recyclables (namely cardboard),[41] but this informal recycling industry doesn't incorporate compost – a third of municipal waste. Though the informal recycling economy has proven to be efficient in collecting some recyclables, many megacities such as Shanghai are seeking to formalise waste management following push-back from citizens who reject informal collection centres as "dirty" and advocate for greater transparency in waste management.[42] The future for this informal sector is thus grim, though individuals who use "smart" sorting bins can still get paid for recyclables. Though recent state-centric environmental measures in China range from ignoring local complexities to modifying citizens' social behaviour (as Li and Shapiro argue), in the case of recycling and composting, it would seem that broad-reaching government programmes to combat the scale of waste in China's megacities have had significant impacts, and might be here to stay--even if these programmes still need to adjust to meet citizens' needs via further outreach and extended hours.

In the first year of its use, the new sorting programme in Shanghai has shown dramatic improvement in reducing landfill waste: the average amount of recyclables has increased by 431.8 per cent, the amount of compost increased by 88.8 per cent, and the amount of residual waste decreased by thirty-one per cent.[43] The "zero waste" slogan in itself (adopted by China and San Francisco), though sometimes associated with wealthy, nut-bag-toting yuppies, also promotes a recuperation of the abject, and an identification with the after-lives of objects and interconnectedness as a fundamental mode of being.

As we have seen in the destruction of unsold or surplus food products throughout the pandemic, waste production relies on neo-liberalism's system of discarded surplus. In addition to the resource-intensive means by which this surplus is typically produced, its after-life often presents an equal roadblock to environmental healing. The recuperation of this surplus in ecologically conscious and co-operative ways, however, fundamentally restructures this inefficient system, retrieves the abject and re-positions it as a tool not of difference but of collective, collaborative survival.

As Mary Douglas puts it: "where there is dirt there is system."[44] As by-products, dirt and waste don't immediately correspond to the established

41 Li and Shapiro, *China Goes Green,* 42.

42 SQLI, "New Technologies."

43 SQLI.

44 Douglas, *Purity and Danger,* 3.

categories of the system, but open space for us to break these categories down with compassionate alternatives in mind.

## References

Arefin, Mohamed Rafi. "Abjection a Definition for Discard Studies." *Discard Studies*, February 27, 2015.

Carrington, Damian. "$10bn of precious metals dumped each year in electronic waste, says UN" The Guardian (July 2, 2021). https://www.theguardian.com/environment/2020/jul/02/10bn-precious-metals-dumped-each-year-electronic-waste-un-toxic-e-waste-polluting.

Chen, Mel. Animacies: *Biopolitics and Racial Mattering and Queer Affect.* Durham and London: Duke University Press, 2012.

Chen Qiufan. *The Waste Tide.* Translated by Ken Liu. New York: Tor Books, 2013.

China Daily. "Garbage-Sorting Games Used to Win over Shanghai's Younger Generation." Chinadaily (July 8, 2019). https://www.chinadaily.com.cn/a/201907/08/WS5d2284d4a3105895c2e7c205.html.

Douglas, Mary. *Purity and Danger: An Analysis of the Concepts of Pollution and Taboo.* Repr. London: Routledge, 2001.

Giles, David Boarder. "Dumpsters, Difference and Illiberal Embodiment." *Discard Studies*, September 15, 2015.

Healey, Cara. "Estranging Realism in Chinese Science Fiction: Hybridity and Environmentalism in Chen Qiufan's 'The Waste Tide .'" *Modern Chinese Literature and Culture* 29.2 (2017): 1–33.

Linderman, Deborah, Julia Kristeva, and Leon S. Roudiez. "Powers of Horror: An Essay on Abjection." *SubStance* 13.3/4 (1984): 140.

Mujezinovic, Davor. "Electronic Waste in Guiyu: A City under Change?," *Environment and Society Portal* (August 29, 2019).

Shen, Xinmei. "Here's Why VR Game for Sorting Trash Is Trending in China – Shanghai Residents Are Trying to Figure out How to Separate Their Trash Correctly" South China Morning Post, June 29, 2019. https://www.abacusnews.com/digital-life/heres-why-vr-game-sorting-trash-trending-china/article/3016297.

Sigalos, MacKenzie. "China's War on Crypto Just Hit a New Level With Its Latest Crypto Crackdown" CNBC, July 7, 2021. https://www.cnbc.com/2021/07/06/china-cracks-down-on-crypto-related-services-in-ongoing-war-on-bitcoin.html.

SQLI Digital Experience. "New Technologies Help Raise Chinese Citizens' Awareness of Waste Sorting." Sqli.com (May 14, 2020). https://www.sqli.com/int-en/insights-news/blog/new-technologies-help-raise-chinese-citizens-awareness-waste-sorting

Sun, Mengtian. "Imagining Globalization in Paolo Bacigalupi's 'The Windup Girl' and Chen Qiufan's 'The Waste Tide.'" *Science Fiction Studies* (2019): 289-306.

Thornber, Karen. *Eco-Ambiguity: Environmental Crises and East Asian Literatures*. Ann Arbor: University of Michigan, 2012.

Watson, Ivan. "China: The Electronic Wastebasket of the World" CNN, May 30, 2013. https://www.cnn.com/2013/05/30/world/asia/china-electronic-waste-ewaste/index.html

Zhang, Jianfeng. "China Gets Serious About Trash Sorting" CCTV, July 2, 2019. http://english.cctv.com/2019/07/02/ARTIrJfxbqRCVEL1moFBYGIL190702.shtml.

Zhuang, Pinghui. "China's Most Notorious e-Waste Dumping Ground Now Cleaner But Poorer" South China Morning Post, September 22, 2017. https://www.scmp.com/news/china/society/article/2112226/chinas-most-notorious-e-waste-dumping-ground-now-cleaner-poorer.

# 10 Virtual Art in Times of Crisis

## Curatorial Practices during the Covid-19 Pandemic in China and Malaysia

*Helen Hess and Diyi Mergenthaler*

**Abstract**

This chapter compares digital art practices in Guangzhou and Kuala Lumpur during the Covid-19 pandemic in 2020 and 2021. It explores digital art practices as a space-making strategy that provoked critical reflection on social issues and created solidarity with economically vulnerable groups at a time when a public health crisis produced new social barriers and inequalities in the two cities. Using intersectionality as an analytical approach, we analyse how various digital curatorial practices effectively drew attention to social inequalities and engaged with marginalised communities. We argue that these virtual art exhibitions did not so much aim for technological innovation, but rather served as a strategy to express a sustained commitment to physical spaces and communities.

**Keywords:** digital art curation, contemporary art, intersectionality, Covid-19 crisis, Sinophone

Since the early 2000s, there has been a surge of international contemporary art fairs in Asian metropolises, which increased the trans-regional and global visibility of emerging Chinese and Malaysian artists. However, with the closure of national borders and compulsory movement control due to the global anti-Covid-19 battle in early 2020, virtual (i.e., non-physical) space became the primary site for art discourse, distribution and public engagement.[1] Digital technologies (e.g., virtual networks and digitisation)

1 The Guangzhou government activated the 'Primary Response to Major Public Health Emergencies' policy on January 23. For over a month, offline art events were postponed. Many citizens were subject to measures such as mask wearing, temperature detection, travel

Imbach, Jessica. *Digital China.* Amsterdam: Amsterdam University Press, 2024
DOI: 10.5117/9789463720670_CH10

have extended the visibility and the expression of art practices, allowing artworks to be consumed simultaneously by audiences from all over the world. While software applications, digital devices and the Internet are indispensable in today's urban life, their influence on reshaping our perception and subjectivity are critically reflected in post-digital and post-Internet art practices. We use the terms "post-digital" and "post-Internet" to refer to digital art projects that are situated in a "time-space compression"[2] and are shaped by "the growing pressures of an attention-based economy."[3] At the same time, these projects query and reshape these conditions. A proliferation of digital art practices over the past decade suggests a growing consciousness of the advantages and disadvantages of channelling digital resources into creative industries. Nevertheless, studies have shown that digital technology has rarely achieved a democratisation of art consumption in praxis.[4] On the one hand, art production, promotion and consumption in virtual space are relational to local infrastructure and power relations. On the other hand, it has been argued that virtual exhibitions interrupt a contextualised reading of art, reducing special art experiences to ordinary commodities for netizens.[5] Despite the fact that the scale of digital technology in local art environments varies significantly in China compared to Malaysia, avant-garde artists and non-governmental art institutions in both countries suffered from reduced incomes and business opportunities amid the extensive Covid-19 lockdowns. The hasty implementation of pandemic measures along with popular media's influence on public opinion often reproduced gender disparity, class inequalities and ethnic discrimination, even though corresponding government measures also established a social

restrictions, working from home and remote schooling. See Guangzhou Daily, 'Guangzhou jianjue luoshi shengyiji xiangying yaoqiu jianjue daying yiqing fangkong zhechang yingzhan'. Malaysia implemented a Movement Control Order (MCO), Malaysian: *Perintah Kawalan Pergerakan* (PKP) on March 18, 2020. The MCO stayed in force throughout 2020 and up to the time of writing (July 2021), albeit in different versions that varied geographically and temporally. It restricted social gatherings and contacts, international and domestic travel, physical participation in schools and higher education institutions and business operations. See MDBC, "MCO Updates."

2 Harvey, *The Condition of Postmodernity: An Enquiry into the Origins of Cultural Change.*

3 Connor, "Post-Internet: What It Is and What It Was," 229.

4 Pariser, *The Filter Bubble: What the Internet Is Hiding from You*; Doctorow, "Netzsperren: Morozov zieht falsche Schlüsse;" Finger and Dutta, *Ask, Measure, Learn: Using Social Media Analytics to Understand and Influence Customer Behavior*; Enhuber, "Art, Space and Technology: How the Digitisation and Digitalisation of Art Space Affect the Consumption of Art—a Critical Approach," 121–137.

5 Tan and Rahaman, "Virtual Heritage: Reality and Criticism;" Lugton, "Reflection on the Art Gallery of the Future, and Why We Must Digitize Art."

network to support the medical frontline in its fight against increased infection numbers.

At the time of writing, there were still very few studies on how the Covid-19 pandemic affected different communities in China and Malaysia. Regarding gender disparity in the Southeast Asian context, Nanthini and Nair demonstrate that women were not only vulnerable to direct impacts such as domestic violence and disproportional assignment to the medical frontline, but also affected by indirect impacts such as economic insecurity and naturalisation of women's role as care providers.[6] During Malaysia's first Movement Control Order (MCO) in March 2020, only one person per household was permitted to go outside. "Male heads of the households" were expected to provide for their family's needs by taking care of grocery shopping, but this actually increased women's burdens.[7]

In China, provincial governments followed the anti-pandemic instructions by the National Health Commission and initiated the "Primary Responses to Major Public Health Emergencies" from January 23, 2021.[8] Female nurses constituted the major force of the anti-Covid 19 frontline. According to China's official statistics, they covered ninety per cent of the medical force dispatched to Wuhan by February 9, 2020.[9] At the same time, menstrual hygiene materials were excluded from the necessities in the nationwide battle against the Covid-19 pandemic.[10] However, statements by female nurses about the shortage of menstrual hygiene materials were censored. Besides, promotion of "positive energy" (*zheng nengliang* 正能量) in popular media marginalised female agency in the PRC.[11] The descriptions of female vulnerability—for instance, the reluctance of female medical staff when having their heads shaved—were immediately transformed into positive narratives of women fitting into their new identity as national warriors. There was little room for discourse on gender equality in sharing domestic chores or childcare.

Moreover, tensions between different nationalities and ethnicities have worsened internationally. An increase of stigmatisation and discrimination of people of colour (e.g., ethnic Chinese and Black communities across

6 Nanthini and Nair, "COVID-19 and the Impacts on Women," 10.

7 McLaren et al., "Covid-19 and Women's Triple Burden: Vignettes from Sri Lanka, Malaysia, Vietnam and Australia," 5.

8 Xinhuanet, "Kangji xinguan feiyan yiqing de zhongguo xingdong."

9 Wu, "Zai kanyi yixian, tamen dexuqiu zhide bei kanjian."

10 Ibid.

11 The gendered dimensions of "positive energy" are also discussed by He, in this volume.

the globe) is observed.[12] In spring 2020, the Chinese government was criticised for its Covid-19 measures which affected the African community. It was reported that some African residents with valid visas were denied entry to their apartments and compelled to be tested for coronavirus.[13] Some sub-district officials even asked restaurant owners to no longer serve "foreigners and especially black people."[14] In Malaysia, migrant workers have been particularly hard-hit by the pandemic, due to cramped living spaces, increased discrimination, poor access to sanitary facilities and healthcare, loss of income and lack of food supplies.[15]

Many cultural workers in China and Malaysia suffered from reduced income or lay-offs, as the pandemic led to a temporal closure of galleries, theatres, and other cultural institutions.[16] A report by the cultural relations platform states that the economic situation of the cultural sectors varies significantly across Asian nations. For instance, China, Korea, and Japan have prioritised supporting the cultural and creative sectors, which, consequently, seem to display some resilience despite being severely affected by the Covid-19 pandemic. By contrast, countries with less concrete cultural policies seem to have more difficulty in properly protecting the cultural sector.[17] Regarding the Malaysian context, Satrina Mohd Sallehuddin notes that seventy per cent of Malaysia's artists and cultural workers have lost their income due to the pandemic.[18]

In Kuala Lumpur, most galleries and artists rarely used digital technologies before the pandemic. However, to stay connected with their audiences during the lockdown, they expanded their online presence on social media platforms such as Facebook and Instagram. In Guangzhou, museums and art galleries did not despair when they were forced to close, because they

12 Gao and Liu, "Stand against Anti-Asian Racial Discrimination during COVID-19;" Xu et al., "Stigma, Discrimination, and Hate Crimes in Chinese-Speaking World amid Covid-19 Pandemic;" Zhang and Xu, "Ignorance, Orientalism and Sinophobia in Knowledge Production on Covid-19;" Tahmasbi et al., "'Go Eat a Bat, Chang!'."

13 Li, "The inside Story of Africans in Guangzhou amid COVID-19 Outbreak."

14 Ibid.

15 Wahab, "The Outbreak of Covid-19 in Malaysia: Pushing Migrant Workers at the Margin."

16 Maganathan, "Cendana's Food Aid Set to Reach More Arts and Cultural Workers;" Cultural Relations Platform, "The Assessment of the Impact of COVID-19 on the Cultural and Creative Sectors in the EU's Partner Countries, Policy Responses and Their Implications for International Cultural Relations."

17 Cultural Relations Platform, "The Assessment of the Impact of COVID-19 on the Cultural and Creative Sectors in the EU's Partner Countries, Policy Responses and Their Implications for International Cultural Relations," 15.

18 Maganathan, "Cendana's Food Aid Set to Reach More Arts and Cultural Workers."

already had established digital spaces on large communication platforms such as WeChat, Weibo, Bilibili and Ximalaya. The virtual space spontaneously became the bridge between individuals locked in different private homes. Nevertheless, the critical situation made it extremely difficult to talk about art and aesthetics.

To summarise, the two countries share the following similarities: 1) The Covid-19 pandemic has exposed social chasms and aggravated gender and class disparities. 2) The global health crisis has reshaped the business models of the art and entertainment industries, involving a notable acceleration in digitising art and heritage content. 3) As both governments took measures to limit mass mobility, the virtual space became the primary choice for establishing community engagement and distributing cultural resources. 4) In larger metropolises, workers in the art and cultural sectors were confronted with financial instability.

Recent studies have pointed out the potential and limits of digital technologies in supporting creative industries in Southeast Asia during the 2020 Covid-19 pandemic. M.K.B. Tan and C.M. Tan demonstrate that digital technologies helped to expand museums' role in offering public mental well-being and social care in Singapore.[19] Noah Travis Phillips argues that online curation allows art galleries to imagine possible futures to the present world, while sustaining the mobility and media(tic) transformation of ideas despite bodies' confinement to separate physical spaces.[20] Feng Xiaodan points out that in China, a number of anti-pandemic themed (*kangyi* 抗疫) participatory online exhibitions on popular social media platforms upheld alternative discourses by referring to local communities, representing frontline scenes, or interweaving activist discourses and pandemic narratives.[21] As argued by Feng, although these art practices created a space in between "radical protest" and "diffused contention," tightened Internet censorship affected their artistic agency and these artistic practices were subsequently mainly used to promote party-state ideology and aesthetics.[22]

Against the background of these findings, this chapter offers a close reading of community-oriented forms of virtual art practices through the lens of intersectionality. We use intersectionality as an analytical approach to examine power relations and social stratification in the context of Chinese

19 Tan and Tan, "Curating Wellness during a Pandemic in Singapore."

20 Philipps, "Rhizomatic Remediation: Adaptation in a Web-Based Art Praxis during Time(s) of Crises."

21 Feng, "Curating and Exhibiting for the Pandemic."

22 Ibid., 5.

and Malaysian art production and reception. The theory of intersectionality focuses on societal asymmetric power relations based on discursively and socially constructed identity categories such as gender, race, ethnicity, class, nationality, and sexuality.[23] An intersectional analysis does not simply pin down a collection of sociocultural categories in an additive sense. It also sheds light on how these categorisations are constituted by and interacting with one another.[24] Instead of reading digital networking merely as a solution for crises across social, economic and cultural spheres, this chapter examines the complexity of artistic exchanges that result from the "intra-action"[25] of virtual and physical networks.

We argue that digital art practices can critically reflect the intersectional layers of oppression on racialised and gendered bodies across Asian regions during the Covid-19 pandemic. Besides, the practices themselves have become hospitable sites for vulnerable social groups. We provide two qualitative case studies with a focus on a selection of artistic and curatorial practices in Guangzhou and Kuala Lumpur, respectively. The case study of Guangzhou-based art practices includes data from interviews, whereas the study of Kuala Lumpur-based practices is mainly grounded in digital participant observation. We address the following questions. Firstly, what are the goals of the selected curatorial practices and how have they been associated with digital technologies? Secondly, to what extent did they mediate the social tensions intensified by the compulsory reduction of heterogeneous sociality modes during the 2020 Covid-19 pandemic? And thirdly, what are the potentials and limits of digital art curation?

## Behold the Other Lives—Fei Arts' Online Exhibitions by and for the Inhabitants in Guangzhou and Around the Globe

Since the 1990s, venues for contemporary art exhibitions in mainland China have rapidly expanded from artist studios to museums, commercial art galleries, biennales, triennials, K11 art malls, Internet, and social media. As

23 Lykke, *Feminist Studies: A Guide to Intersectional Theory, Methodology and Writing*, 50.

24 Ibid., 51; McKinnon, "Intersectionality as Method: A Note," 1020; Yuval-Davis, "Situated Intersectionality and Social Inequality," 94.

25 In contrast to "interaction," *intra-action* does not presume "the prior existence of independent entities," but rather "represents a profound conceptual shift. It is through specific agential intra-actions that the boundaries and properties of the 'components' of phenomena become determinate and that particular embodied concepts become meaningful." Barad, "Posthumanist Performativity," 815.

the third biggest city in China and a major economic centre in the Pearl River Delta, Guangzhou is always at the forefront of incorporating digital innovations in museum exhibitions and cultural preservation. In governmental-run institutions like Guangzhou Museum, audiences can enjoy a cost-free audio guided tour on WeChat by scanning the given QR code next to an object. Many smaller art institutions have also established an audience group on social media (e.g., WeChat and Weibo) and popular news platforms.

Nevertheless, Guangzhou's contemporary art scene is often regarded as the spontaneous efforts of a few artists and curators, due to the lack of governmental investment, media support and public interest in contemporary art.[26] "Government-run exhibitions are usually warmly welcomed by mass media, whereas solo-exhibitions curated by NGOs only become news if the media get paid beforehand," remarked the director of Fei Arts, Jason Ho. "There may be a few exceptions, perhaps if an exhibition reaches a certain excellency. In most cases, no money, no media exposure."[27] Social media might enable smaller-scale art institutions' participation in low-budget virtual networking, but this does not reduce the structural inequalities that determine the scale, visibility and accessibility of certain art practices.

We studied how a smaller-scale art institution in Guangzhou carried out community-focused art exhibitions during the 2020 Covid-19 outbreak, despite a limited budget. Fei Arts (originally known as Fei Gallery) is perhaps the longest-running non-profit art institution in Guangzhou. Since its foundation in 2004, the art institution has devoted itself to exploring the crossover between art, architecture and interpersonal relationships. It is situated in the basement of Yida Estate Plaza near Nonglin Market in the Yuexiu District.

According to Ho, the exhibition site of Fei Arts is "borderless." The White Cube has merged with the commercial and residential areas nearby, including all floors of Yida Plaza, Nonglin Market and the residential garden.[28] Ho's perception of museum space as "every creative corner" and art as "an empowering tactic for migrant workers" is indispensable to mediating socio-economic segregation embodied in unequal accessibility to a variety of urban facilities. This echoes Joseph Beuys' famous saying: "Every man is an artist."[29] In Beuys' view, art is a participatory work that (re)shapes social organisms. This critical standpoint has been the major thread running

26 Liu, "Foxi de Guangzhou dangdai yishu, bei bianyuanhua le ma?"

27 Ho, Private Correspondence.

28 Ho.

29 Joseph Beuys, "I Am Searching for Field Character," 929–930.

through Fei Arts' projects. From mapping workshops (2014–present), through *Hand Museum* exhibitions (2017–2019), to dinner parties with Nonglin Market stall owners (2017–2019), Ho and his curatorial team contribute to enhancing solidarity amongst the Nonglin Market stall owners.[30] Albeit suffering from budgetary constraints, Fei Arts successfully launched *Home Is Museum*, *Homecoming* and *The First Boundless Architecture Season* in the first half of 2020. In the following section, we will focus on an analysis of *Home Is Museum*, a series of online exhibitions on WeChat.

## Creating A Space for the Other

> We define home as a museum, not only because Fei Arts had to extend the period of winter closure, but also because we regard home as a creative space.[31]
> ——Jason Ho

*Home Is Museum* is conceptualised as a window for WeChat account followers to look at the archives of individuals' living conditions during the Covid-19 lockdown and share "folk wisdom" (*minjian zhihui* 民間智慧). The exhibition uses WeChat article as its form. It consists of eight parts, each part showing a different collection. All works were selected from followers' submissions. Due to the length limitation on WeChat articles, each part of the exhibition shows thirty digital or digitised works, including short videos, GIF images, photographs and snapshots of paintings, sculptures, and art installations. The editor outlined a temporal framework by using expressions such as "exhibition begins," "each visit should be around 20 min. Please arrange your visit as it suits you" and "to be continued."[32] Nevertheless, viewers were free to adjust their browsing speed to view the works.

The first part of *Home Is Museum* was announced on WeChat on February 10. Shortly after the announcement, the show was introduced by *Guangzhou Daily, Southern Metropolis Daily* and *OrangeNews.hk*. This led to a twofold increase in readers' submissions. The second show even attracted the attention of the Israeli Consulate in Guangzhou. This brought about the joint curation of the special show *Market Is Museum* with the Israeli Consulate on the theme of creative spaces at markets. Our analysis of this

30 Ho, "Caishichang li jian meishuguan, nenggei tanfan gengduo zunyan ma?"
31 Ho, Private Correspondence.
32 Fei Arts, "Zhanlan: jia jiushi meishuguan diyiqi."

work draws on Elizabeth Freeman's concept of "chrononormativity," which she defines as follows:

> I mean that naked flesh is bound into socially meaningful embodiment through temporal regulation: binding is what turns mere existence into a form of mastery in a process I will refer to as *chrononormativity*, or the use of time to organise individual human bodies towards maximum productivity.[33]

More specifically, we regard the Covid-19 outbreak as a kind of queer temporality, in the sense that it forced migrant workers to invent fluid business hours and adopt new work practices to survive the rapid reconstruction of the urban economy. In contrast to white-collar workers, who could work in their private homes, many market stall owners, for instance, were spotted in minivans and on the streets, selling produce, eggs, and other fresh foods during the nationwide closure of markets.[34] As selling goods on the streets was illegal in Guangzhou, these vendors not only faced health risks, but also had to deal with insecure working environments and social discrimination. It was only in June 2020 that Guangzhou's urban management department issued a regulation that temporarily legalised trading on streets.[35]

Take Geng Xueqing's series *Mobile Market* (see Fig. 5) at the special show *Market Is Museum* for instance. The work consists of two digital photographs and a video, accompanied by a brief text about the *China Youth Daily* journalist's encounter with food deliverer Ma Zengchen in Wuhan. The audiovisual and textual materials provide an eyewitness account of Ma's nomadic living conditions during the Covid-19 pandemic. Up to March 3, he had been delivering food to different homes via his minivan for 14 days. Nevertheless, as a migrant worker, Ma was denied entry to his rented apartment by the pandemic control department of his residential block, even though he had obtained multiple approvals for working as a food deliverer.[36] Thus, he was unable to warm up instant noodles during the day.[37] It was not until midnight that he finally received warm dishes from his partner through the gate of his residential block.[38] Besides, the Covid-19 quarantine policies left no room for him to return to either of his homes (namely: the physical

33 Freeman, "Introduction: Queer and Not Now," 3.

34 Fangchenggang Government, "Guanyu jiaqiang chengqu liudong tanfan guanli de jianyi."

35 Zheng, "Guangzhou 7 zhong qingxing yunxu shangjia getihu jiedao jingying."

36 Geng, *Mobile Market.*

37 Geng.

38 Geng.

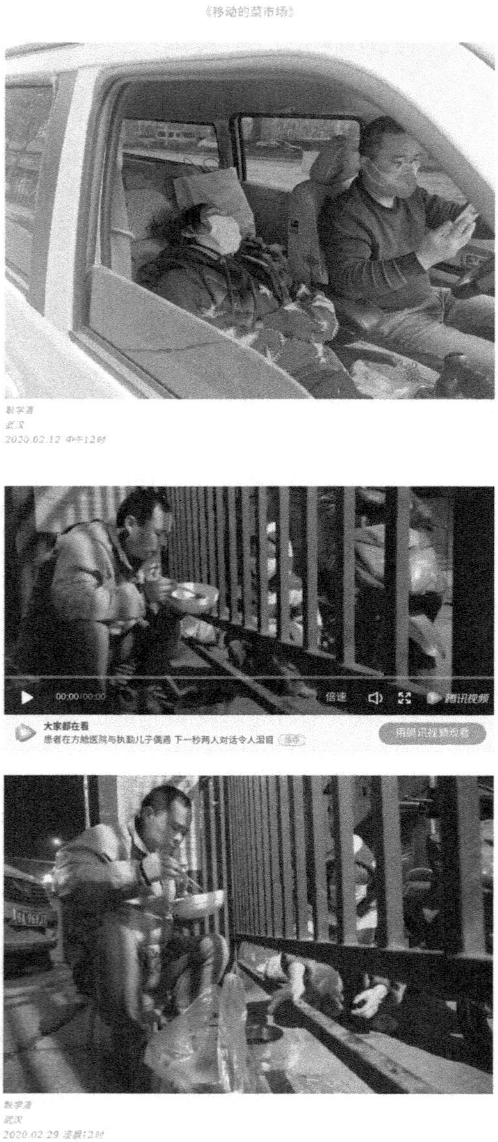


Figure 5. Geng Xueqing, *Mobile Market*, 2020, video, 2 min 7 seconds, Fei Arts, Guangzhou; Geng, *Mobile Market*, 2020, photograph (top), Fei Arts, Guangzhou; Geng, *Mobile Market*, 2020, photograph (bottom), Fei Arts, Guangzhou.

locations in the metropolis where he resided, or his hometown). To be able to go home, Ma would have had to give up his current job.[39]

While migrant workers are deployed to accelerate urbanisation, mass production and consumption, their identification with rustic and grassroots

39 Geng.

culture is often framed as the main obstacle to becoming modern, urban citizens. Terms such as *di suzhi* (low quality 低素质) and *diduan renkou* (low-end population 低端人口) are used to criticise them, thereby normalising economic disparities and social inequalities. By contrast, the online exhibition *Market Is Museum* does not aestheticise the image of Ma's nomadic living conditions into a patriotic act or a symbol of sacrifice. Neither does it obscure the relationship between a selfless image and exclusivist authoritative orders. Ho explains in the "Exhibition Foreword":

> As a community excluded from documentaries of urbanisation, market stall owners are often interpreted as insignificant people. [...] On the contrary, their humble positions give rise to a wisdom of survival—they use their own hands to earn a living in metropolises without drawing any attention, day after day, year after year.[40]

Though Ho's criticism is conveyed in a softened tone for the sake of visibility, the act of bringing grassroots representation into a museum context reflects a clear intent to voice solidarity with market stall owners. By turning netizens' gazes towards "folk wisdom," Ho and his curatorial team skilfully unveiled the intersectional layers of exclusions that shape the lives of poor migrants in urban spaces, thereby also bringing into question the master narratives of urban history. The exhibition functioned thus also as a critique of dominant media accounts and city-planning initiatives, which framed migrant workers primarily as an obstacle to the successful implementation of lockdown policies.

## Digital Visibility and What Is Next?

*Home Is Museum* shows the temporal transformation of private residential rooms into multifunctional semi-public spaces—private apartments turned into theatres, where shows about office and domestic life overlap with one another.[41] As long as it suits the schedule of the protagonists, who are simultaneously the audience, a humble living room can serve as a playground, a picnic spot, a cinema, a stadium, a museum, or a spa. Though social media and virtual networks facilitated public accessibility of these private apartments, we should nevertheless keep in mind that not everybody had the privilege of spending time online.

40 Fei Arts, "Exhibition Foreword."
41 Fei Arts, "Zhanlan: jia jiushi meishuguan diyiqi."

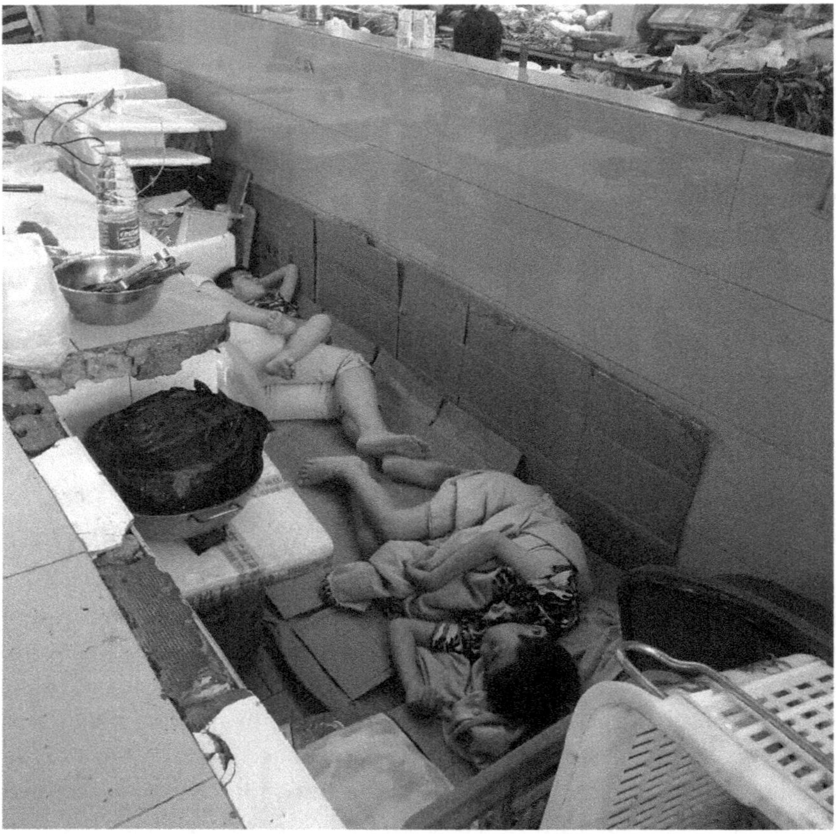

Figure 6. Mapping Workshop, *Market Is Also a Home*, 2018, 11cm x 11.22cm, photograph, Fei Arts, Guangzhou.

Besides providing an account of market-workers' living conditions during the Covid-19 outbreak, the special show *Market Is Museum* also exhibited photographs taken before the pandemic. The photograph titled *Market Is Also a Home* (fig. 2), for instance, was included in a portfolio submitted by Wenbo Yu, Ziyang Zhang, Yixin Wu and Yingjun Huang and studied the reconstruction of a market for its workers in 2018.[42] It captured the beef stall owner Huang Yanli sleeping with her sons on "mattresses" made of flattened paper boxes behind a wall that separated their room from another counter at Nonglin Market.

The crossover of familial and trading space illustrates not only the significance of the Nonglin Market as the base of a feeling of belonging for Huang

42 Yu et al., "Choreographed Landscapes: A Gallery Inside the Market."

Yanli's family, but also the severe economic disparities in Guangzhou. Market workers have no choice but to have their privacy and vulnerability exposed to the public. Besides, the photograph demonstrates the intersecting roles of Huang as a market stall owner and a mother. The heavy workload and busy schedule of the former makes it impossible to have a lunch break away from her counter, while the latter urges her to "invent" a study and a playroom for her children.[43] For many people, the Covid-19 lockdown was perhaps the very first exercise to spend full days in one physical location and realise the multiple functions of this space. Namely, the pre-pandemic hand-to-mouth living conditions become physically and widely accessible to people across the globe, owing to the transnational disruption of industrial patterns. This raises another question: what happens to Huang's and many other workers' families once they are denied access to their first and foremost living base?

By showcasing heterogeneous identification with smaller "homes" (family and living spaces) before and during the pandemic lockdown, *Home Is Museum* challenges the living conditions in the bigger "home," i.e., society, during the Covid-19 crisis. It calls for establishing a sustainable network of mutual support that might remedy the deepened socio-economic chasms and the lack of social welfare. Correspondingly, the project queers the stereotype of "home" as an individual's capacity to own a private property and start a family in a neo-liberal capitalist system. Although the exhibition did not directly address disparities in digital access, it successfully showcased a new understanding of the idea of "home," one that could be developed into a more hospitable site for the Other.

When the interview with Ho took place in early October 2020, Nonglin Market was declared an illegal construction and was slated to be torn down in order to reconstruct the underground water system.[44] The stall owners were forced to leave within less than a month, though they had been working and living there for over forty years.[45] The demolition of Nonglin Market

43 In the introduction of their project *A Family Museum*, Wenbo Yu, Ziyang Zhang, Yixin Wu and Yingjun Huang wrote, "On weekdays, this is an ordinary beef stall. On weekends, two kids rush to market to do their homework, while their mom sells beef beside them. Although this space is less than 3 square meters, it is a small world for the whole family to read books, play games, finish homework, have meals and take a lunch break." See Yu et al., "Choreographed Landscapes: A Gallery Inside the Market."

44 Ho, Private Correspondence.

45 In July 2019, stall owners paid an average of 40,000 yuan for renovation. In November 2019, they signed a three-year contract to rent the space. After 19 October, some market stall owners packed their stuff and left, while others tried to sell their goods on the streets nearby while looking for places in other markets. See Qiu, "Nage yu meishuguan xianglian de caishichang, xiaoshile."

was completed before October 27, leaving the remaining stall owners and their regular customers wondering how to rearrange their daily routines.[46] *Sanlian Life Weekly* and *Southern Metropolis Weekly* were among the very few media that reported on the potential violation of administrative power in pushing economic reconstruction. At the same time, several residents and Fei Arts' visitors took the initiative to visit these stall owners and express their thanks by inviting them to share a meal or sending them flowers and news reports about their working lives.

In short, digital visibility does not immediately affect authoritative decisions. At most, digital art practices can restore a sense of publicness amongst people working in different fields. In doing so, they create an ephemeral "home" for vulnerable social groups across different regions and passages of time through bottom-up curation. Budget and intention have a greater influence on museums' missions and strategies than digital technologies. Fei Arts' curation of *Home Is Museum* demonstrates the potentials of virtual art practice as resistance to the "bare life" inscribed in the bodies of migrants across offline and online spaces.

## Digital Art Practices in the Sinophone Malaysian Contact Zone

In the following, we investigate how curators and artists in Malaysia responded to the Covid-19 pandemic. More specifically, we analyse the potentials and limitations of digital technologies to overcome social and geographical borders and boundaries in the contemporary Malaysian art scene by situating these projects in the larger socio-cultural context.

Our analysis focuses primarily, but not exclusively, on female Sinophone curators and artists based in Kuala Lumpur. The Sinophone Malaysian population can be traced back to Chinese immigrants, who first settled in the Malayan archipelago several centuries ago.[47] The members of the Sinophone Malaysian community belong to a variety of Chinese dialect groups and have different social and economic backgrounds, which are deeply imbedded in local histories and contexts. As stated by Shih Shu-mei, Sinophone articulations consist of a variety of everyday practices and experiences and "can take as many different positions as possible within the realm of human expression, whose axiological determinations are not necessarily dictated by China but by local, regional, or global contingencies

46 Qiu.

47 Rae and Witzel, *The Overseas Chinese of South East Asia: History, Culture, Business*, 14.

and desires."[48] We suggest thinking of practices by Sinophone Malaysian artists and curators as situated in a contact zone—"social spaces where cultures meet, clash, and grapple with each other, often in contexts of highly asymmetrical relations of power."[49]

In the 2018 *Global Gender Gap Index*, Malaysia was ranked 101 of 149 countries,[50] and in 2020 number 104 of 153. Malaysia's score had an increase of 0.002 compared to the 2018 report, and an increase of 0.027 compared to the first report in 2006.[51] However, as the index's results reveal, gender inequality in Malaysia remains significant in comparison to other countries. An aging population and decreasing birth rates have led to an increase in care duties, with women facing "more responsibility for unpaid care despite working almost the same number of hours as men in paid work."[52] Recent studies indicate that this double or even triple burden, if their care work includes both children and elderly, has intensified since the start of the Covid-19 pandemic.[53]

In the pre-pandemic Malaysian art scene, virtual exhibitions and the use of social media for art promotion were very limited.[54] However, public interest in and demand for virtual exhibitions grew, when galleries were forced to close their doors amid successive Movement Control Orders (MCO).[55] We distinguish between two types of virtual exhibitions: "virtual versions" and "hyperreal sites."[56] The former refers to virtual access to a digitised physical exhibition; the latter only takes place in virtual space (i.e. virtual three-dimensional gallery spaces). There were only very few hyperreal exhibitions in Malaysia in 2020, among them *Monochrome*, a collaboration of the Kuala Lumpur based art gallery Artemis Art and the Art Serpong Gallery in Jakarta, and G13 Gallery's virtual exhibitions. However, Malaysian galleries and artists increased their online visibility through other efforts. In the following sections, we will focus on Wei-Ling and the Back Room, two galleries in Kuala Lumpur.

48 Shih, *Visuality and Identity: Sinophone Articulations Across the Pacific*, 30.

49 Pratt, "Arts of the Contact Zone," 34.

50 World Economic Forum, "Global Gender Gap Report 2018."

51 World Economic Forum, "Global Gender Gap Index 2020."

52 Khazanah Research Institute, "Time to Care: Gender Inequality, Unpaid Care Work and Time Use Survey," x.

53 Nanthini and Nair, "COVID-19 and the Impacts on Women;" McLaren et al., "Covid-19 and Women's Triple Burden: Vignettes from Sri Lanka, Malaysia, Vietnam and Australia."

54 Lin, "Malaysian Art Scene Not Digitally Savvy Enough to Adapt to Covid-19 Crisis."

55 Lin.

56 Silver, "Review: Interfacing American Culture: The Perils and Potentials of Virtual Exhibitions," 825–850.

## Wei-Ling: Pushing the Boundaries of Visual Art

> When there's uncertainty, there's bound to be anxiety and fear of the unknown. However, I think the team and all artists have adapted remarkably well to the storm that hit us last year. I am a firm believer that you must turn adversity into strength.[57]
> —Lim Wei-Ling (gallery owner)

Founded in 2002, Wei-Ling is a renowned player in the contemporary Malaysian art scene. Its two branches, Wei-Ling Gallery and Wei-Ling Contemporary, specialise in contemporary art by Malaysian artists, but they also showcase works by international artists. By frequently participating in international art fairs in Beijing, Hong Kong, Taipei and Singapore, the galleries also provide an international platform for local artists.[58] Lim Wei-Ling, founder and manager of the two galleries, opts to push the boundaries of the arts in Malaysia by engaging in more experimental art forms as well as site-specific performances and installations.[59]

The two Wei-Ling branches have set up online documentation and simple virtual versions of their exhibitions by displaying photographs of all artworks, installation views and sometimes booklets with supplementary information online. This allows the viewers to be informed about the gallery's latest programmes and gave artists a platform despite the physical lockdown. Besides, Wei-Ling has started to host online artist talks and other events, which are accessible on its website and on YouTube. For example, the online program WLG Discussion Lab was launched during the first MCO in 2020, when galleries had to shut their doors. The first session, titled "What Makes Art Powerful," included an interview with Yau Bee Ling.

Yau has gained international attention as a painter. Her works (e.g. the *By Hands* series and the *Interwoven Terrains* series) reflect on the multiple burdens upon women. In the WLG Discussion Lab interview with Lim, Yau explains how she channelled various challenges and painful experiences into her art. The various difficulties that Yau encountered as a daughter, a wife and a mother shaped her life and influenced her creative work. For instance, the paintings of the *By Hands* series have two layers: the first layer shows realist sketches of human hands in different poses, the second consists of abstract forms painted in oil colours, which are either situated

57 Lin, "Exhibitions Must Evolve to Remain Important, Say Malaysian Art Gallery Owners."
58 Wei-Ling Gallery, "About."
59 Wei-Ling Gallery, "What Makes Art Powerful?"

beneath the first layer or covering it. Several paintings combine charcoal or pastel drawings of hands, which are overlaid by dots in intense red oil colour. Yau explains that the red dots represent clicks of a computer mouse and hint to the demands of acquiring digital technologies. When she created these paintings, she felt overwhelmed by the pressure of getting familiar with digital technologies and her multiple responsibilities in her family.[60] These paintings, thus, reflect the challenges faced by a woman artist both in her profession and her private life. As pointed out above, the multiple burdens upon women have further intensified during the Covid-19 pandemic in Malaysia. Even though the paintings by Yau were not created during the pandemic, they exemplify how artists can channel their experiences during such demanding times into their artworks. This discourse is, thus, a timely choice for the WLG discussion lab.

## The Back Room: Raising Social Issues

> Art is not just for the elite.
> Art is about engaging the world.
> Art is also about community.[61]

The Back Room is a smaller, community-based independent gallery located at the Zhongshan Building (*zhongshan tongxianghui dalou* 中山同鄉會大樓), a creative art hub in Kuala Lumpur's Kampung Attap. The building was originally a shophouse and later the base of the Selangor Zhongshan Association. Since 2017, it has been home to several artist studios, smaller shops, and a gallery. The Back Room was founded by Liza Ho, a Guatemala-born curator with roots in Hong Kong, who is based in Kuala since 2005.[62] Her vision is to create a gallery space dedicated to engaging broader local audiences, particularly concerning the participation of those who lack an elitist background.[63]

During the Covid-19 pandemic, the Back Room endeavoured to enable online access to its exhibitions. Like Wei-Ling, it provided online documentation of the exhibitions that were curated in the physical gallery space by providing photographs of the exhibited artworks and supplementary material to download on the website. From July 18 to August 9, 2020, the

60 Wei-Ling Contemporary, "Wei-Ling Contemporary—Past Exhibitions—By Hands."
61 The Back Room, "About."
62 The Back Room.
63 The Back Room.

gallery showcased a solo exhibition by CC Kua titled *All by Myself*. The exhibition was curated by Sharmin Parameswaran. CC Kua, pen name of Chua Chia Chi, is a Kuala Lumpur-based artist. The commissioned paintings showed the outcome of her residency at the art centre Rimbun Dahan, which is located on the outskirts of Kula Lumpur and where CC Kua lived during the Covid-19 lockdown in 2020. Kuala states:

> With the residency, I was excited for the space and time to isolate and reconnect with myself. During the first few months, I also had other artists at Rimbun Dahan with me. However, they all left prior to MCO, and as the world started to shut down, I was all by myself in having to think through and make sense of what was happening to us. Also, what else could I do but to continue being an artist and producing work.[64]

Kua transformed everyday experiences such as encounters with people, animals, and the lush garden of Rimbun Dahan, as well as the general anxiety that surrounded her into playful works of art, applying both drawing and painting techniques. The artist explained that she always tried to capture feelings rather than merely reproducing what she saw.[65] As Eric Goh puts it, Kua is not "concerned with depicting something that strictly adheres to how things should be in reality; this is her world, and anything is possible in it."[66] In total, Kua created around 100 drawings and paintings during her residency, about thirty of which were exhibited at the Back Room.[67] Eight of the paintings were put online to view and to purchase. Additionally, the artist spoke to online visitors through a zine titled "Hello, how have you been," consisting of humorous drawings and thoughts, which the artist produced during her residency. By making this zine available, the curator created a connection between the artist's state of mind during her time in seclusion and the audiences' confinement to their own private spaces. Apart from the paintings that were put online and the zine, the Back Room did not set up a virtual version of *All by Myself*.[68]

From November 7 to December 6, 2020, Krystie Ng curated an exhibition titled *Carving Reality: Contemporary Woodcut Exchange Exhibition from East*

64 The Back Room, "All by Myself: An Exhibition by CC Kua."

65 The Back Room, "All by Myself," Press Release.

66 Goh, "Review of CC Kua's All by Myself."

67 The Back Room, "All by Myself: An Exhibition by CC Kua."

68 After several months of repeated closures, the Back Room made a virtual version of an exhibition available on its website and Instagram for the first time with Liew Kwai Fei's exhibition *In Order* (*To Play*), which took place from 24 July to 8 August 2021.

*Asia* at the Back Room. It was supplemented by simple online documentation. Both the physical and the virtual edition showcased woodcuts by artists based around Asia. Among the artists who participated in the exhibition was the Borneo-based artist collective Pangrok Sulap, which is dedicated to raising awareness of social, political, and environmental issues through community-based art.[69]

When Pangrok Sulap was founded in 2010, the artist group primarily engaged in charity work in schools, homes for the disabled and orphanages in rural Borneo. In 2012, the group started to actively involve rural indigenous communities by collectively creating woodcut prints.[70] During the Covid-19 pandemic, Pangrok Sulap published posts daily on their Instagram profile depicting woodcuts with messages like "stay strong" or "we are in this together." Pangrok Sulap applies a "traditional" mechanical printing technique to create collective artworks together with local communities. At the same time, it has made use of digital media to promote their work and spread their messages. Pangrok Sulap's number of followers on social media shows that the collective has already reached a significant number of online readers.[71]

## Remediating Art in Times of Crisis

Bolter and Grusin differentiate between three forms of mediacy: 1) immediacy, an unreflected state of imitation in medial reproduction, 2) hypermediacy, an active and critical reflection on the mediacy itself as well as cross references (hyperlinks) and 3) remediation, processes in which one medium is transformed by another.[72] The Malaysian examples discussed above have not opted to imitate physical gallery spaces in the virtual sphere by creating a sense of immediacy. Rather, they have been engaging in a process of remediating (non-)sites by finding new ways of communicating with their audiences through different channels.

Elaborating on Robert Smithson's concept of the "non-site" and Grusin's concept of "radical mediation," Philipps argues that central to the concept of

69 Boon, "The Development of Woodblock Printmaking in Malaysia: From Engaging with Social Subject Matters to Being Socially-Engaged," 23.

70 A Plus Art, "Pangrok Sulap;" QAGOMA, "Pangrok Sulap."

71 As of April 2021, the collective had around 5,000 followers on Instagram and 11,700 followers on Facebook. In comparison, Wei-Ling had around 4,000 followers on Instagram and 5,200 on Facebook, whereas the Back Room had around 2,700 followers on Instagram and 500 on Facebook.

72 Bolter and Grusin, *Remediation: Understanding New Media.*

the "non-site" is a "dialectic tension," which "presents itself between what the audience experiences and what they know" —expressing a "hypermediacy, or engulfing awareness of the mediation, of the exhibition taking place."[73] Besides, as pointed out by Kember and Zylinska, the linear logic of "old" and "new" media is a "false division,"[74] because it limits "the understanding of the complex and multifaceted phenomena and processes by imposing clear-cut distinctions and categories," and often has "serious political and ethical consequences for our understanding of the world, its dynamics and its power relations."[75] The digital practices by Malaysian curators and artists discussed above should, thus, not be interpreted as a form of "backwardness," as often stated by public media.[76] They are neither to be read in a linear, determinist, nor in an entirely constructivist manner. Rather, they are shaped by a constant negotiation between the need for and/or an interest in new technologies, remaining hurdles for curators, artists, and audiences due to a lack of resources and the choices by curators and artists with respect to the available technologies and media.

At the height of the Covid-19 pandemic, the abovementioned art practices in China and Malaysia tended to create an intimate online atmosphere to extend their engagement with local communities. We observe that the scale and strategies of online curatorial practices are deeply rooted in local contexts. In China, many museums and art galleries had already established their presence on popular social media platforms before the pandemic and have extended these virtual tactics during and after the lockdown. By contrast, it was not until the spring of 2020 that the pandemic situation in Malaysia sparked the need for and public interest in digitisation and virtual art curation. Digital art practices in both countries rapidly increased in the first half of 2020, as virtual space functioned as the primary channel to reconnect individuals confined to different private spaces. The closures of physical exhibition sites have led to the extension of artists' and galleries' presence and increased exposure of their works on social media.

These practices were only to some extent able to establish a sense of being in the same space and sharing the same time. "Face-to-face participation," as noted by Jason Ho, "can never be replaced by a camera eye or a screen."[77] For Ho, the affective connection between individuals cannot

73 Philipps, 66.

74 Kember and Zylinska, *Life After New Media: Mediation as a Vital Process*, 3.

75 Kember and Zylinska, 2.

76 For instance, Lin, "Malaysian Art Scene Not Digitally Savvy Enough to Adapt to Covid-19 Crisis."

77 Ho, Private Correspondence.

be reproduced by virtual curatorial practices and he regards exhibitions on WeChat as no more than an ephemeral approach to sustain the discourse on migrants' living conditions in the rapid course of urbanisation worsened by the Covid-19 pandemic. Digitisation has not reshaped Fei Arts' mission. Nor has it increased Fei Arts' interest or investment in digital art curation. Rather, Fei Arts remains committed to real-site engagement, as they aim to increase grassroots participation in museum practices.

Fei Arts' curation of *Home Is Museum* echoes Nicolas Bourriaud's conception of "relational aesthetics," which emphasises formations of art that are aimed at recovering organic interpersonal relationships and resisting alienation in a highly privatised, commercialised society.[78] *Home Is Museum* gave amateur artists a platform by issuing online open calls and exhibiting works from readers. The collection of works presents encounters between global viewers and portrayals of various private spaces. It illustrates both personal and political dimensions of migrant workers' living conditions in its trans-regional and multi-temporal scope. Here, online space becomes a temporary site of resistance to the hegemonic discourse which has been prioritising the discourse of ethnonational solidarity over that of scraping by in life. Accordingly, the significance of art rests in visualising the inequalities masked by the master narratives.

By turning to various digital curatorial strategies, such as social media and podcasts, Malaysian curators and artists experimented with new ways of engaging with audiences despite being physically confined. As illustrated above, both the smaller independent gallery the Back Room and the well-established Wei-Ling are still in an early stage of digital curation. However, they have constantly extended the range of digital practices since the start of the pandemic. In March 2021, Wei-Ling launched a podcast, which is available on Apple Podcasts, Spotify, and other platforms. CC Kua and other artists have actively used social media to promote themselves.[79]

Both in China and Malaysia, digital art practices were effectively used to maintain and create new social networks during the pandemic. Even though social media platforms differ in the two countries—for instance, Facebook, Instagram, and other social media platforms are blocked in China whereas they are popular in Malaysia—the curatorial strategies of smaller art institutions during the lockdown period are similar. The use of social media gave visibility to art by and for grassroots communities. A

78 Bourriaud, *Relational Aesthetics*, 11–24.

79 As of May 2021, CC Kua had a public profile on Instagram with 1,350 followers and a public profile on Facebook with 630 followers.

high sensitivity in adapting curatorial strategies to the characteristics of the chosen platforms and taking the needs of local communities into account led to successful "intra-action" with regional and global communities, although their local orientation and scope limited their ability to build networks to other virtual art projects. Moreover, the broad use of digital technologies during the pandemic period has not led to an increased investment in digital curation in the post-pandemic age. However, by drawing attention to marginalised communities and social inequalities, the exhibitions discussed in this chapter show how virtual art can at times also give expression to a sustained commitment to physical spaces and communities.

## References

A Plus Art. "Pangrok Sulap." A+, 2021. http://www.aplusart.asia/artists/pangrok-sulap.

Ankang Government. "Jia xiansheng tousu maicai tanfan zhandao jingying 贾先生投诉卖菜摊贩占道经营 [Mr. Jia: Complaint about Vegetable Vendors Occupied the Road]." *Ankang City People's Government* (January 17, 2020). http://www.ankang.gov.cn/Gov/Letter/DH202001170059.html.

The Back Room. "About." *The Back Room KL*. https://www.thebackroomkl.com/aboutus.

The Back Room. "All By Myself: An Exhibition by CC Kua." Press Release. The Back Room, 2020.

The Back Room. "All by Myself: An Exhibition by CC Kua." *The Back Room KL*, 2020. https://www.thebackroomkl.com/exhibitions/all-by-myself-cc-kua.

The Back Room. "In Order (To Play)—A Solo Exhibition by Liew Kwai Fei." *The Back Room KL*, 2021. https://www.thebackroomkl.com/exhibitions/liewkwaifei.

The Back Room. "The Back Room KL." Instagram, 2021. https://www.instagram.com/thebackroomkl/.

Barad, Karen. "Posthumanist Performativity: Toward an Understanding of How Matter Comes to Matter." *Signs: Journal of Women in Culture and Society* 28, no. 3 (Spring 2003): 801–31.

Beuys, Joseph. "I Am Searching for Field Character." In *Art in Theory 1900-2000: An Anthology of Changing Ideas*, edited by Charles Harrison and Paul Wood, 929–930. Oxford: Blackwell Publishing, 2003.

Bolter, Jay David, and Richard Grusin. *Remediation: Understanding New Media*. Cambridge MA, MIT Press, 1999.

Boon, Pok Chong. "The Development of Woodblock Printmaking in Malaysia: From Engaging with Social Subject Matters to Being Socially-Engaged." In *An Outline of the Development of Social Realist Woodcuts in Malaysia*, edited by Krystie Ng, 20–25. Cheras, Selangor: Krystie Ng, 2020.

Bourriaud, Nicolas. *Relational Aesthetics*. Translated by Simon Pleasance, Fronza Woods and Mathieu Copeland. Collection documents sur l'art. Dijon: Les presses du réel, 2002.

Connor, Michael. "Post-Internet: What It Is and What It Was." In *You Are Here: Art after the Internet*, edited by Omar Kholeif, 56–64. Manchester: Cornerhouse, 2014.

Cultural Relations Platform. "The Assessment of the Impact of COVID-19 on the Cultural and Creative Sectors in the EU's Partner Countries, Policy Responses and Their Implications for International Cultural Relations," February 10, 2021. https://ifacca.org/news/2021/02/10/assessment-impact-covid19-cultural-and-creative-se/.

Doctorow, Cory. Netzsperren: Morozov zieht falsche Schlüsse. *Zeit Online* (February 4, 2011). http://www.zeit.de/digital/Internet/2011-02/doctorow-morozov-netzsperre.

Enhuber, Marisa. "Art, Space and Technology: How the Digitisation and Digitalisation of Art Space Affect the Consumption of Art—a Critical Approach." *Digital Creativity* 26.2 (2015): 121–137.

Fangchenggang Government. "Guanyu jiaqiang chengqu liudong tanfan guanli de jianyi—Zhou Guowei weiyuan de fayan 关于加强城区流动摊贩管理的建议—周国伟委员的发言 [Suggestions on Strengthening the Management of Mobile Vendors in Urban Areas—A Speech by Member Guowei Zhou]." *Guangxi Fangchenggang's Harbor District's Government* (April 2, 2021). http://www.gkq.gov.cn/xxgk/xxgkml/jcxxgk/taya/202104/t20210402_195474.html.

Fei Arts. "Exhibition Foreword." *Fei Arts* (March 5, 2020). https://mp.weixin.qq.com/s/DSd1jsRgwm-GtFwITSoobg.

Fei Arts. "Zhanlan: jia jiushi meishuguan diyiqi 展览：家就是美术馆 第一期 [Exhibition: Home Is Museum (the First Part)]." *Fei Arts* (February 20, 2020). https://mp.weixin.qq.com/s/7QnWJCoHnT7L8uZ8SaXHiw.

Finger, Lutz and Soumitra Dutta. *Ask, Measure, Learn: Using Social Media Analytics to Understand and Influence Customer Behavior.* Beijing, Cambridge, Farnham, Köln, Sebastopol and Tokyo: O'Reilly Media, 2014.

Freeman, Elizabeth. "Introduction: Queer and Not Now." In *Time Binds: Queer Temporalities, Queer Histories*, 1–19. Durham and London: Duke University Press, 2010.

Gao, Qin, and Xiaofang Liu. "Stand against Anti-Asian Racial Discrimination during COVID-19: A Call for Action." *International Social Work* 64, no. 2 (2021): 261–64.

Geng, Xueqing. "Mobile Market." *Fei Arts* (March 5, 2020). https://mp.weixin.qq.com/s/DSd1jsRgwm-GtFwITSoobg.

Goh, Eric. "Review of CC Kua's All by Myself." *The Back Room* (July 16, 2020). https://www.thebackroomkl.com/exhibitions/all-by-myself-cc-kua.

Guangzhou Daily. "Guangzhou jianjue luoshi shengyiji xiangying yaoqiu jianjue daying yiqing fangkong zhechang yingzhan 广州坚决落实省一级响应要求 坚决打赢疫情防控这场硬战 [Guangzhou Will Resolutely Implement Provincial-Level Response and Win the Tough Battle of Epidemic Prevention]." *Guangzhou People's Government* (January 26, 2020). http://www.gz.gov.cn/zt/qlyfdyyqfkyz/gzzxd/content/post_5643135.html.

Harvey, David Robert. *The Condition of Postmodernity: An Enquiry into the Origins of Cultural Change.* [3rd repr.]. Cambridge (MA) and Oxford: Blackwell, 1989.

Ho, Jason. "Caishichang li jian meishuguan, nenggei tanfan gengduo zunyan ma? 菜市场里建美术馆，能给摊贩更多尊严吗? [Can We Let Market Stall Owners Feel Dignity, When Building an Art Museum in a Market?]." *Sanlian Life Weekly* (September 9, 2020). https://finance.sina.cn/2020-09-09/detail-iivhvpwy5824976.d.html?cre=wappage&mod=r&loc=4&r=0&rfunc=0&tj=wap_news_relate.

Ho, Jason. Private Correspondence, October 3, 2020.

Khazanah Research Institute, "Time to Care: Gender Inequality, Unpaid Care Work and Time Use Survey." Kuala Lumpur: Kazanah Research Institute, 2019.

Kember, Sarah., and Joanna Zylinska. *Life After New Media: Mediation as a Vital Process*. Cambridge, MA: MIT Press, 2012.

Kim, Soyoung. "Post-Contact Zones: (En)Countering COVID-19." *Inter-Asia Cultural Studies* 21.4 (2020): 557–565.

Lee, Ellen. "Pandemic Panic: A Wake-up Call for the Art Market." *Peng Art District* (April 24, 2020). https://penangartdistrict.com/pandemic-panic-a-wake-up-call-for-the-art-market/.

Lin, Rouwen. "Malaysian Art Scene Not Digitally Savvy Enough to Adapt to Covid-19 Crisis." *The Star* (March 25, 2020). https://www.thestar.com.my/lifestyle/culture/2020/03/25/covid-19-situation-exposes-the-malaysian-art-scene039s-lack-of-digital-adaptability?fbclid=IwAR0320HJYe4BTVoMp4PEnE1XSymJtLpUb33lnGA9SB1Rg-MCi80e4m163iA.

Liu, Xia 刘霞. "Foxi de Guangzhou dangdai yishu, bei bianyuanhua le ma? "佛系"的广州当代艺术，被边缘化了吗? [Buddha-like Guangzhou Contemporary Art, Has It Been Marginalized?]." *Hiart.cn* (January 28, 2018). http://www.hiart.cn/feature/detail/eb8ipBr.html.

Lugton, Martin. "Reflection on the Art Gallery of the Future and Why We Must Digitize Art." *Reflections* (February 6, 2011). https://reflectionsandcontemplations.wordpress.com/2011/02/06/why-art-must-be-digitized/.

Lykke, Nina. *Feminist Studies: A Guide to Intersectional Theory, Methodology and Writing*. New York: Routledge, 2010.

Maganathan, Dinesh Kumar. "Cendana's Food Aid Set to Reach More Arts and Cultural Workers." *The Star* (June 28, 2021) https://www.thestar.com.my/lifestyle/

culture/2021/06/28/cendana039s-food-aid-to-reach-more-arts-and-cultural-workers; Cultural Relations Platform.

McKinnon, Catherine A. "Intersectionality as Method: A Note." *Signs, Intersectionality: Theorizing Power, Empowering Theory*, 38.4 (2013): 1019–1030.

McLaren, Helen Jaqueline, Karen Rosalind Wong, Kieu Nga Nguyen and Komalee Nadeeka Damayanth Mahamadachchi. "Covid-19 and Women's Triple Burden: Vignettes from Sri Lanka, Malaysia, Vietnam and Australia." *Social Sciences* 9.87 (2020): 1–11.

MDBC. "MCO Updates." MDBC (Malaysian Dutch Business Council). https://www.mdbc.com.my/mco-updates/.

Nanthini, S. and Tamara Nair. "COVID-19 and the Impacts on Women." *NTS Insight* IN20-05 (July 2020): 1-11.

Pariser, Eli. *The Filter Bubble: What the Internet Is Hiding from You*. New York: Penguin Press, 2011.

Pratt, Mary Louise. "Arts of the Contact Zone." In *Profession* (1991): 33–40.

Pratt, Mary Louise. "Linguistic Utopias." In *The Linguistics of Writing: Arguments between Language and Literature*, edited by Nigel Fabb, 48–66. Manchester: Manchester University Press, 1987.

QAGOMA. "Pangrok Sulap." Queensland Art Gallery / Gallery of Modern Art. https://www.qagoma.qld.gov.au/whats-on/exhibitions/past-exhibitions/the-9th-asia-pacific-triennial-of-contemporary-art-apt9/artists/pangrok-sulap.

Qiu, Lian 丘濂. "Nage yu meishuguan xianglian de caishichang, xiaoshile 那个与美术馆相连的菜市场，消失了 [The Market Link to An Art Museum Disappeared]." *Sanlian Life Weekly* (October 30, 2020). https://mp.weixin.qq.com/s/t9n6OoZY09cM3e1LFyM13w.

Rae, Ian and Morgen Witzel. *The Overseas Chinese of South East Asia: History, Culture, Business*. Basingstoke: Palgrave Macmillan, 2008.

Shih, Shu-mei. *Visuality and Identity: Sinophone Articulations Across the Pacific*. Vol. 2. Asia Pacific Modern. Berkeley: University of California Press, 2007.

Silver, David. "Review: Interfacing American Culture: The Perils and Potentials of Virtual Exhibitions." *American Quarterly* 49, no. 4 (December 1997): 825–50.

Spivak, Gayatri Chakravorty. *In Other Worlds: Essays in Cultural Politics*. New York: Routledge, 2006.

Tahmasbi, Fatemeh, Leonard Schild, Chen Ling, Jeremy Blackburn, Gianluca Stringhini, Yang Zhang, and Savvas Zannettou. "'Go Eat a Bat, Chang!': An Early Look on the Emergence of Sinophobic Behavior on Web Communities in the Face of COVID-19." *ArXiv* abs/2004.04046, 2020. https://arxiv.org/pdf/2004.04046.pdf.

Tan, Beng-Kiang and Hafizur Rahaman. "Virtual Heritage: Reality and Criticism." In *Joining Languages, Cultures and Visions*, 143–56. Montréal: Les Presses de l'Université de Montréal, 2009.

Tan, M.K.B., and C.M. Tan. "Curating Wellness during a Pandemic in Singapore: COVID-19, Museums, and Digital Imagination." *Public Health* 192 (2021): 68–71.

Wahab, Wandika. "The Outbreak of Covid-19 in Malaysia: Pushing Migrant Workers at the Margin." *Social Sciences & Humanities Open* 2 (2020): 1–9.

Wei-Ling Contemporary. "Wei-Ling Contemporary—Past Exhibitions—By Hands." Wei-Ling Contemporary, 2016. http://weiling-gallery.com/contemporary/portfolio-item/yau-bee-ling-by-hands-works/.

Wei-Ling Gallery. "About." *Wei-Ling Gallery.*" http://weiling-gallery.com/gallery/about/.

Wei-Ling Gallery. *What Makes Art Powerful?* WLG Discussion Lab Online Programme, 2020. https://www.youtube.com/watch?v=CZ13hY4aik4.

World Economic Forum. "Global Gender Gap Index 2020." Cologne/Geneva: World Economic Forum, 2020. https://www.weforum.org/reports/gender-gap-2020-report-100-years-pay-equality/in-full.

Wu, Zhi 武芝. "Zai kanyi yixian, tamen dexuqiu zhide bei kanjian 在抗"疫"一线，她们的需求值得被看见 [At the Anti-Covid Frontline, Her Voice Should Have Been Heard]." Sina finance, February 23, 2020. https://finance.sina.com.cn/chanjing/cyxw/2020-02-23/doc-iimxyqvz5164892.shtml.

Xinhuanet. "Kangji xinguan feiyan yiqing de zhongguo xingdong 抗击新冠肺炎疫情的中国行动 [China's Action against the New Coronavirus Pneumonia Outbreak]." The Central Government of the People's Republic of China, June 7, 2020. http://www.gov.cn/zhengce/2020-06/07/content_5517737.htm.

Xu, Jianhua, Guyu Sun, Wei Cao, Wenyuan Fan, and Zhihao Pan. "Stigma, Discrimination, and Hate Crimes in Chinese-Speaking World amid Covid-19 Pandemic." *Asian Journal of Criminology* 16 (January 6, 2021): 51–74.

Yu, Wenbo, Ziyang Zhang, Yixin Wu and Yingjun Huang. "Choreographed Landscapes: A Gallery Inside the Market." Unpublished Portfolio, June 1, 2018.

Yuval-Davis, Nira. "Situated Intersectionality and Social Inequality." *Raisons Politiques* 2, no. 2 (2015): 91–100.

Zhang, Yunpeng, and Fang Xu. "Ignorance, Orientalism and Sinophobia in Knowledge Production on Covid-19." *Tijdschrift Voor Economische En Sociale Geografie* 111, no. 3 (The Geography of the COVID-19 Pandemic) (June 19, 2020): 211–23.

Zheng, Yunan 郑雨楠. "Guangzhou 7 zhong qingxing yunxu shangjia getihu jiedao jingying 广州：7种情形允许商家（个体户）借道经营 [Guangzhou: Under 7 Conditions Small Private Business Occupied Roads]." *Southern Metropolis Daily.* (June 4, 2020). https://epaper.oeeee.com/epaper/A/html/2020-06/05/content_16045.htm.

# 11 Viral Text

## Translation, Censorship, Community

*Elvin Meng*

**Abstract**

English, Thai, and Klingon are just a few of the languages that WeChat users utilised to disseminate "The Whistle-Giver," a censored interview with the Chinese doctor who first released information about the Covid-19 outbreak. By engaging with recent developments in translation studies and the technological specificities of the WeChat platform, this chapter analyses this as a new form of textuality—viral text—that is parasitic to the regime of intelligibility and censorship codified by keyword censorship algorithms. This new textuality, which is particularly salient in online spaces under censorship such as WeChat, allows us to see the Chinese language and the language of the mainland Sinophone as different and equally negotiable categories in an increasingly digital world.

**Keywords:** The Whistle-Giver, Chinese scripts, WeChat, Sinosphere

Illness is the night-side of life, a more onerous citizenship. Everyone who is born holds dual citizenship, in the kingdom of the well and in the kingdom of the sick. Although we all prefer to use only the good passport, sooner or later each of us is obliged, at least for a spell, to identify ourselves as citizens of that other place.

I want to describe, not what it is really like to emigrate to the kingdom of the ill and live there, but the punitive or sentimental fantasies concocted about that situation: not real geography, but stereotypes of national character. My subject is not physical illness itself but the uses of illness as a figure or metaphor. My point is that illness is not a metaphor, and that the most truthful way of regarding illness—and the healthiest way of being ill—is one most purified of, most resistant to, metaphoric thinking.

Imbach, Jessica. *Digital China.* Amsterdam: Amsterdam University Press, 2024
DOI: 10.5117/9789463720670_CH11

> Yet it is hardly possible to take up one's residence in the kingdom of the ill unprejudiced by the lurid metaphors with which it has been landscaped. It is toward an elucidation of those metaphors, and a liberation from them, that I dedicate this inquiry.[1]

These are the words with which Susan Sontag begins *Illness as Metaphor*. Her programme, which is well-known today, was to dispel the aura of illness—whether romanticising and stigmatising—that depreciates its experiential truth. But the careful reader, however sympathetic to Sontag's intention, would have noticed that despite the strident stance she takes against the contamination of truth by metaphors, an unacknowledged biopolitical metaphor sits at the heart of this declaration. It is this metaphorical language that situates the "kingdom of the ill" in a geopolitical discursive field containing fictive notions of "citizenship," "residence," and "emigration" that, in early 2020, resurfaced in an unsettling congruence with the problematic justification of racism and xenophobia in the name of pandemic control.

It was as if we can no longer tell the difference between illness and geopolitical belonging. In the US, the first attempt at containment of Covid-19 was effected through the exclusion of Chinese bodies, and age-old racist narratives against Asians and Asian-Americans resurfaced, disguised as being in the interest of public health. Nor was China the sole "kingdom of the ill," even in those early days of the pandemic. Manuela Pellegrino, an Italian anthropologist working in Greece, likewise recounts that "Out of habit, twice, perhaps three times, I say 'grazie' as I navigate airport procedures. It's enough to elicit worried looks and whispered comments among the bystanders. A sudden and uncomfortable feeling grips me. The next day, Greece records its first Covid-19 case, 'imported' from Italy [...] Suddenly I'm no longer called *i Ellinìda tis kato Italias* ('the Greek from southern Italy'). The distinction between purity and danger fills into symbolic – and physical – boundary maintenance [...] Abruptly, I'm simply Italian and Italian means 'polluted and polluting' – the enemy."[2] As if trying to enact the metaphoric thinking Sontag unwittingly acquiesces to in her introduction, infectious diseases elicit a cognitive shortcut that erects a border against

The author owes thanks to Christopher Cannon, Satoru Hashimoto, Yeti Kang, Douglas Mao, Haun Saussy, Jiarui Sun and the organisers and participants of the Wired China workshop at the University of Zurich for their feedback and conversation.

1 Sontag, *Illness as Metaphor*, 3–4.

2 Pellegrino, "COVID-19: The 'Invisible Enemy and Contingent Racism'," 19.

cultural and subcultural others, hoping to tie the virus down to a nation, a race, or a minority group.[3]

*Contra* Sontag, this chapter begins its study of digital China by taking a less prohibitive approach to metaphoric thinking about virality. This is because the metaphors we use to think about the virus matter, not least because they articulate our ethical orientation toward otherness in its various forms. The border that Sontag constructs, with words, between the two kingdoms, yields in her further description to the possibility of "emigration" and "residence" across borderlines, and suggests precisely the impossibility of drawing a non-porous border. What she proposes at the outset is taken away in the next sentence; her parable captures our own anxiety of influence, our defences against the knowledge that being well, after all, entails the possibility of becoming ill. The reality is that kingdoms are not discrete. Nor are they without internal differentiation. A dichotomised language of self and other, wellness and illness, or domestic and foreign is calibrated to obscure the fact that the latter is often already constitutively inscribed in the first as a forgotten self-difference. It is therefore my goal, in studying a digitally surveilled platform such as WeChat, to move from Sontag's simple but illuminating metaphor to the more complex description of heterogeneous communicative publics subject to censorship and exclusion. The shift to a more metaphoric register (indeed, away from the experiential truth of illness) in my discussion of virality is therefore both to highlight the appropriation of viral logic in accounts of this pandemic and to suggest a different language—the language of translation—in which to situate concepts such as contagion, borders, and community.

What might translation tell us about viral logics and digital censorship? We may start by examining the opening of one English-language text, translated from Chinese by an anonymous Internet user.

> On December 30, 2019, Affin received a virus test report for patients with unknown pneumonia. She circled the word "SARS coronavirus" in red. When asked by a college student, she took the report and circulated it. To this fellow student who is also a doctor. That night, the report spread to doctor circles in Wuhan, and those who forwarded the report included the eight doctors who were disciplined by the police.
>
> This caused trouble for Affin. As the source of the transmission, she was interviewed by the hospital disciplinary committee and suffered

3 See, for example, Farmer, *Infections and Inequalities*. More recently, Kolb, *Epidemic Empire*.

> "unprecedented and severe rebuke", saying that she was making rumors as a professional.
>
> According to some previous reports, Affın was called "another female doctor who has been instructed to surface", and some people called her a "whistleblower." It was the "whistler."
>
> This is the second report of "People" March cover "Doctor Wuhan."[4]

The Chinese original of this translated text is the introduction to an interview with Ai Fen 艾芬 (transliterated here as Affın), set to appear in the March issue of *Renwu* 人物 magazine. The text, showing the Central Hospital of Wuhan's initial response to reports of the unknown pneumonia in a negative light, was briefly available on WeChat (Weixin 微信) on the morning of March 10th, 2020 before it was quickly removed from the platform. But remarkably, the text survived on WeChat in an unprecedented outburst of mutations that garnered international attention.[5] To evade keyword censorship (an algorithmic feature that blocks the publication of any text containing a selection of censored words), the interview was translated into other languages such as English (quoted above), German, Hebrew, Sign Language, Klingon, and Classical Chinese to be circulated within a mostly Chinese-speaking community. The Chinese text itself survived by being written backwards, in vertical lines, or as an interlinear commentary on a Baidu Baike article on Internet safety. The conventional Chinese script was replaced by that of oracle bone inscriptions, Mao-style calligraphy, and Martian Script (huoxing wen 火星文)—a subcultural writing system popular in the 2000s.[6] Beyond natural languages, Binary, Morse code, QR code, telegram, and DNA code were all used to transcode the original as well.

How might we describe a phenomenon such as this? To say that this text "went viral" would be slightly misleading, if by "going viral" we mean reaching an unexpectedly broad audience with a tweet or a YouTube video, where the same textual or video material spreads across different social media platforms through hyperlink citations. In such typical cases, the content and its authenticity are never in doubt, and the tweet or the video

4 Ge Ge Dian A, "Jieli 'fa shaozi de ren' yingwen ban."

5 In the Anglophone world alone, the outbreak of translations was reported by Wall Street Journal, Buzzfeed News, QZ.com, Reuters.com, among others.

6 For screenshots of the over forty renditions produced during this period (most were quickly censored and never archived), see Xin Shidai Cao Ni Ma," CDC dang'an: Yichang zhangxian wangmin bu fucong de daxing jiti xingwei yishu huodong: Fa koushao de ren banben daquan."

remains its own "original," no matter how it is viewed, watched, or read. The Ai Fen interview did go viral, but in a somewhat different sense, not through the popularity of the original but through a plethora of translations and appropriations. After all, if it does not mutate, it will fall to the censors. The minute differences that accumulate with each of its renditions is not contingent to but essential for its dissemination.

This chapter concerns the latter form of textual survival. I will use the phrase "viral text" to refer to this textuality defined by a process of technologically mediated replication and translation that deliberately threatens the semantic stability of the "original": screenshots of tweets, reuploaded videos, copy-and-pasted passages, "unofficial" translations, and many more. Viral text—I use the singular form of "text" to suggest its uncountability rather than unity—is stored and potentially processed, doctored, or translated at each node of its transmission. The source is often downloaded onto an intermediate device before being sent out to others. Unlike the first kind of viral transmission that always refers back to the same text or video, viral text propagates and survives by becoming different from itself, renegotiating what constitutes itself at each step and pushing the limits of its identification with its originary instantiation.

As a result, although each rendition of a viral text appears as a translation, they are not quite concerned with traditional norms of translation such as "fidelity, fluency, elegance" (xin da ya 信達雅). Let us look closer at the Chinese original for the sake of comparison, while acknowledging that even this is already a digital replica of the WeChat article made available on *notion.so* by an anonymous Internet user:

> 2019年12月30日，艾芬曾拿到過一份不明肺炎病人的病毒檢測報告，她用紅色圈出「SARS冠狀病毒」字樣，當大學同學問起時，她將這份報告拍下來傳給了這位同是醫生的同醫。當晚，這份報告傳遍了武漢的醫生圈，轉發這份報告的人就包括那8位被警方訓誡的醫生。
>
> 這給艾芬帶來了麻煩，作為傳播的源頭，她被醫院紀委約談，遭受了「前所未有的、嚴厲的斥責」，稱她是作為專業人士在造謠。
>
> 此前的一些報道，艾芬被稱為「又一個被訓誡的女醫生浮出水面」，也有人將她稱為「吹哨人」，艾芬糾正了這個說法，她說自己不是吹哨人，是那個「發哨子的人」。
>
> 這是《人物》3月刊封面《武漢醫生》的第二篇報道。

> On December 30th, 2019, Ai Fen received the report of a viral test of an unknown patient suffering from pneumonia. She used a red pen to circle out the words "SARS coronavirus." Upon being asked by a former college classmate, she took a photograph of the report and sent it to this colleague, who was also a doctor. That evening, this report circulated throughout the medical circles in the city of Wuhan. Those who circulated it included the eight doctors who were scolded by the police.
>
> This brought troubles to Ai Fen. As the source of the dissemination, she was asked to meet with the hospital's disciplinary committee, where she 'was reprimanded with unprecedented harshness' for allegedly spreading rumours despite being a professional.
>
> In earlier reports Ai Fen was referred to as "another scolded doctor who has surfaced to public attention," while others have called her a "whistle-blower." Ai Fen herself has corrected these descriptions, saying that she was not a whistle-blower, but someone who has distributed the whistles—a "whistle-giver."
>
> This is the second report in the March issues of *Renwu* Magazine's cover story, "Wuhan Doctors."[7]

Now, the clumsiness of the earlier English translation becomes easier to see. Besides grammatical errors and unidiomatic expressions noticeable to any English speaker, we also find lexical mistranslations. To name two examples, *daxue tongxue* 大學同學 does not here translate to "college student" but instead "a college classmate;" *you yige bei xunjie de nüyisheng fuchu shuimian*又一個被訓誡的女醫生浮出水面 is not "another female doctor who has been instructed to surface" but instead, in context, "another scolded doctor who has surfaced to public attention." The translation also entirely misconstrues the title of the interview: *fa shaozi de ren*發哨子的人, which is the name Ai gives herself, means "whistle-giver" as opposed to "whistle-blower" or "whistler." Ai's justification for this moniker, given in Chinese and translated here, is entirely omitted in the earlier version that circulated in March 2020.

How did that strange translation come about? Is there a human translator behind the text, or is it the output of a machine translation service like Google Translate? The choice to break up the first sentence of the text into three, not to mention the downright omission of parts of the text, suggests at least some degree of human involvement. But the phrase "college student" hints at a more digital process of translation: pasting the entirety of the Chinese

7 Notion. "Fa shaozi de ren." My translation.

text into Baidu Translate, the English words automatically chosen for *daxue tongxue* are indeed "college students," even though translating the phrase by itself in any of the popular Chinese-English online dictionaries available to Chinese Internet users reliably gives "college classmate." Likewise, while the word "whistler" is semantically distant from the meaning of *fa shaozi de ren*, it is nevertheless the word given by Baidu Translate's algorithm.

An amateur translator using machine learning as linguistic prosthesis, translating a Chinese text into unidiomatic English for a Chinese-speaking readership—needless to say, we are now far removed from Walter Benjamin's idea of the translator as someone who "releases in his own language that pure language which is exiled among alien tongues."[8] Instead of an elegant translation that gestures toward an ultralinguistic aesthetic, words are here ungracefully shoved across linguistic boundaries in a process that seems careless if not mechanical. Other versions of this viral text foreground their mechanical production even more prominently. Conversions to binary, Morse code, or QR code are essentially automated processes, and even the changes of script are done using websites that provide those services at the click of a button. One of the Martian Script versions, for example, is generated by an online script converter that systematically replaces each ordinary character by its less orthodox variant.[9]

If translation, as it is traditionally conceived, denotes the transfer of linguistic content—whatever that may be—from one community to another through the work of translators, and if transcoding denotes the mechanical and digital movement of information between two encoding systems, at least one of which is cryptic nonsense, then this translation (if that term is still adequate) playfully oscillates between these two nodes while failing to collapse into either.[10] This is not simply a translation between natural languages, not least because the English text was never directly presented, *qua* translation, to Anglophone Internet users.[11] Neither, however, is this a case of encryption, or of mechanically replacing the text with symbols

8 Benjamin, "The Task of the Translator," 261.

9 Gong, "Fa shaozi de ren 潑哨ふ呲亾." The converter used is "Online Martian Script Converter," https://www.aies.cn/huoxingwen.htm.

10 The view of translation as between two essentially disjoint communities that only overlap accidentally is inscribed in concepts such as the "domestic" and the "foreign" that are central to the field of translation studies. See Venuti, *The Translator's Invisibility*.

11 While the post has been archived on several websites, it is always presented as evidence of this outburst of translation and not an adequate English translation of the text. In fact, when a news website reported the incident, it grouped this English translation with all the others and provided their own translation of the text for its Anglophone audience. See GM35, "Don't let the story of the original Covid-19 whistleblower die."

so that the information is preserved perfectly at the expense of the text's legibility to all but an exclusive community.[12] This is an English translation, paradoxically enough, meant for Chinese readers: it must be sufficiently illegible to evade its censors, but sufficiently legible (at least to some) so that it will still be recognised, more or less, as the afterlife of a text, an "original" in exile.

That viral text remains simultaneously legible and illegible—that it exists at the boundary of a language's legibility—is its essential feature that confounds our usual notions of translation. The identity-through-differentiation of a text in exile disrupts typical understandings of language to evade modes of censorship that operate upon those understandings. And indeed, viral text is unthinkable without acknowledging the *a priori* of automatic censorship. This is Chen Feiyue's contention in his analysis of social media platforms in China: the strength of censorship must be considered not as a contingent factor, but as an essential component of any kind of digital social environment.[13] The character of a digital platform and consequently the kind of discussion and textual transmission thereon are determined not only by predictable factors such as interactivity and user base, but also by the speed, severity, and technology of censorship.

There is a more-than-superficial connection between digital censorship and immunology, both being, in some way, technologies of identity combining retention and real-time reaction. The field of human immunology uses the term "immunological memory" to describe a process of immunological writing in which every encounter with alterity leaves a trace, forming a database of signifiers that estimates the field of otherness, so that the self becomes better protected:

> Immunological memory is perhaps the most important consequence of an adaptive immune response, because it enables the immune system to respond more rapidly and effectively to pathogens that have been encountered previously and prevents them from causing disease. Memory responses, called *secondary immune responses, tertiary immune responses,* and so on, depending on the number of exposures to antigen, also differ qualitatively from primary responses.

12 For example, the "translation" into DNA code comes with a "key" for "decoding" the text, and the Unicode version tells the reader how to look up online converters that will automatically restore the original. In each case, the text remains, in some way, legible, if only difficultly so.
13 Chen, "Zhongwen hulianwang zhong 'taolun' de xiaowang."

> Although the phenomenon was first recorded by the ancient Greeks and has been exploited routinely in vaccination programs for more than 200 years, it was recognised only within the last 30 years that this memory phenomenon reflects a small population of specialised *memory cells* that are formed during the adaptive immune response and can persist in the absence of the antigen that originally induced them. This mechanism of maintaining memory is consistent with the finding that only individuals who were themselves previously exposed to a given infectious agent are immune.[14]

Understandably, while the immune system often can fend off pathogens that are complete "strangers," it is much more efficient at crushing down repeated offences through the aid of a database. The database does not (and indeed, cannot) store all of the information of encountered pathogens in its entirety; rather, it keeps track of their identifiers—in this case, antigens—so that whenever these problematic signifiers reappear, they can be countered in a manner much more efficient than primary immune responses.

Xinyuan Wang's recent study demonstrates that Internet censorship in China uses a system not dissimilar to the immune system's database of antigens. Both operate through multiple layers of varying efficiency. There is the famous skin-like spatial barrier that separates the body from the outside (the "Great Firewall"). Less efficient is the database of problematic combinations of words that are automatically prevented from being published ("keyword blocking"). And finally, the least efficient and most costly method of censorship (said to involve "20,000-50,000 Internet police or wangjing 网警 and Internet monitors or wangguan 网管 nationwide) deals with offending material on a case-by-case basis, potentially extracting new keyword combinations to be added to the database ("manual censoring").[15] We may extend the analogy further: just as the survival of a virus depends on its ability to bypass immunological memory through mutation (hence flu shots are renewed every year), so the survival of viral text in the context of censorship depends on its translation through new modes of presentation, as an infinitesimally adjacent other to what technologies of censorship understand as language.

Because what is most legible to the machine is also what can be most easily monitored or removed, the optimisation of surveillance and censorship takes place by turning language itself into a technological

14 Murphy and Weaver, *Janeway's Immunobiology 9$^{th}$ Edition*, 473–474. Emphasis in original.

15 Wang, *Social Media in Industrial China*, 129.

construct. According to a 2016 report by the University of Toronto-based Citizen Lab, "WeChat performs censorship on the server-side. When you send a message it passes through a remote server that contains rules for implementing censorship. If the message includes a keyword that has been targeted for blocking, the message will not be sent."[16] Similar mechanisms that use both Optical Character Recognition and visual-based technologies to identify and censor problematic images and screenshots of texts before they are published have been identified in 2018.[17] The database is constantly updated: in response to the viral outbreak in January and February 2020, hundreds of new key word combinations were added to limit discussion not only of the virus itself but also of the government's response to it.[18] As a result, for texts and images that contain potentially sensitive content, some form of transcoding—becoming unintelligible to the censorship machine—is almost always necessary. The common techniques for evading censorship were vividly described and demonstrated in a post by the public account Dunes Workshop, published just weeks before the Ai Fen interview. The post was titled "Under Censorship, Our Expressions Are Becoming Something New" (Shencha zhi xia, women de biaoda ye zai biancheng xin de dongxi 审查之下，我们的表达也在变成新的东西). Its text, which was presented as a .jpeg image divided into five panels, sketched the history of censorship evasion while showcasing the very techniques it discussed (I have tried to demonstrate some of those techniques in my translation):

Box 1. Ever since censorship existed on the Internet, there has been resistance.

Especially during "special periods," we can see an intense struggle: on the one hand, Internet censors ramp up their efforts to "delete" and to "silence;" on the other hand, the voices of numerous (Internet) users, like tides or even floods, try to burst the dam of censorship.

Box 2. There are first users who use acronyms or *pinyin* to replace "sensitive words," such as "professor r female graduate student" or "Wuhan gov recently established policy."

16 Ruan et al., "One App, Two Systems."

17 Knockel et al., "(Can't) Picture This."

18 Ruan et al., "Censored Contagion." See also the follow-up study, Crete-Nishihata et al., "Censored Contagion II."

At the same time, numerous users learned to upload *screenshot of texts* instead of *texts themselves*. Relatively speaking, this more easily bypasses the first line of defence of key word checks.

Box 3. Furthermore, some users *rotate* the screenshot of words by 90 degrees, or even 180 degrees before uploading.

When other users see these images, they can read effortlessly by rotating the screen of the phone. But for earlier algorithms, identifying images like this becomes much more difficult.

Box 4. When censorship systems learned to scan the image from all four possible orientations, users learned further to add irregular, semitransparent traces of markers (this can be easily done on the Meitu Pic 美圖秀秀 application). Although other users will also have difficulties reading these images, it can at least bypass most of the algorithms, until finally being manually deleted.

Box 5. As a result of cnsrshp, some existing words are given new meanings, some existing expressions become new metaphors. Some people think that, under the pressure of cnsrshp, people endlessly invent new words to replace old, "castrtd" words, and the medium and the expressions on Chinese Internet are constantly renewed. These are indications that the Chinese language is slowly evolving into *a new language*.[19]

Viral text on WeChat are often born digital and, to use Rebecca Walkowitz's term, "born-translated," either into a different language, a different layout, a different file format, or coded expressions that are constantly evolving.[20] It mobilises the heterogeneity and malleability of digital linguistic praxis to confound the attempt to reduce language to its distilled sediments, be it abstract signifiers, "pure sequence[s] of character codes" known as "plain

19 Chen, "Shencha zhi xia, women de biaoda ye zai biancheng xin de dongxi." Emphasis in the original.

20 Walkowitz defines born-translated novels as novels wherein "translation functions as a thematic, structural, conceptual, and sometimes even typographical device. These works are *written for translation*, in the hope of being translated, but they are also often *written as translations*, pretending to take place in a language other than the one in which they have, in fact, been composed." Walkowitz, *Born Translated*, 4.

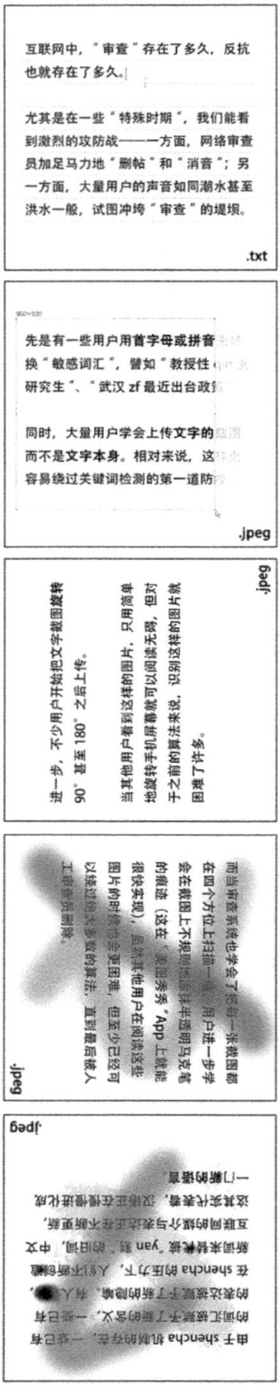


Figure 7: Chen Feiyue, *Under Censorship, Our Expressions Are Becoming Something New*

text," or codified ways in which characters become images.[21] The surprising resemblance between this "new language" and the ordinary CAPTCHA designed to keep off web crawlers should not go unnoticed: the built-in self-difference of these texts, or their noisiness, exploits the transient gap between fields of legibility and visibility to exercise what amounts to a Turing test of sorts. If language is increasingly enframed by a media infrastructure that, unlike its counterpart in the U.S., understands information primarily in terms of sovereignty, communication that looks askance from this technologised governance needs to find a clearing in the networked thicket.[22] The English translation of the Ai Fen interview can do its work despite its informational inefficiency because, in the words of John Durham Peters, it is "communication as disclosure of being rather than clarity of signal."[23] The being, that is, of a community that is as interconnected as it is heterogeneous, mobilised in collective "resistance" (to use the language of Dunes Workshop) through sporadic jerks that traverse points of relay.

There is a positive case to be made about viral textualities, so long as we proceed cautiously, staying aware of our surroundings. Near the end of *Phaedrus*, Socrates uses a biological metaphor of language to illustrate how, through the dialectic method, words are not deciphered but incorporated by the soul, like a seed by the soil, so that it may bear fruit and give birth to different words and different seeds, and then continue this process *ad infinitum*:

> … serious discourse about [justice and other subjects] is far nobler, when one employs the dialectic method and plants and sows in a fitting soul intelligent words which are able to help themselves and him who planted them, which are not fruitless, but yield seed from which there spring up in other minds other words capable of continuing the process for ever, and which make their possessor happy, to the farthest possible limit of human happiness.[24]

21 To quote the definition of plain text in *Unicode Standard* in full, "*Plain text* is a pure sequence of character codes; plain Unicode-encoded text is therefore a sequence of Unicode character codes. In contrast, *styled text*, also known as *rich text*, is any text representation consisting of plain text plus added information such as a language identifier, font size, color, hypertext links, and so on. For example, the text of this specification, a multi-font text as formatted by a book editing system, is rich text." The Unicode Consortium (ed.), *The Unicode Standard ver. 13.0*, 18.

22 On the ideology and infrastructure of Chinese cybersovereignty, see, for example, Jiang, "Authoritarian Informationalism," 71–89 and Creemers, "The Pivot in Chinese Cybergovernance," 5–13. On the differences between the configurations of governance and cyberspace in China and the U.S., see Kokas, "Platform Patrol," 923–933.

23 Peters, *The Marvelous Clouds*, 14.

24 Fowler (trans.), *Plato I*, 569–571.

While Socrates believes that the right discourses, even if put in the "other words" of other folks, will continue to "make their possessor happy," today we are increasingly weary of disorganised and often unsourced kinds of information floating around the Internet, bouncing from screens to screens and from hard drives to hard drives. In February 2020, for example, the Director-General of the World Health Organisation declared that "we are not just fighting an epidemic; we're fighting an infodemic. Fake news spreads faster and more easily than this virus, and is just as dangerous."[25] A *New Yorker* article published a month later, paying homage to Sontag, argues that we are not taking the pandemic seriously enough because the Internet age has grown so comfortable with "influencers" and "viral" trends that it has forgotten how serious the real deal can be.[26] But what about the "fake news" about the virus that circulated on WeChat in January 2020? That story (a true one) resulted in the arrest of eight whistle-blowers on the grounds of "spreading rumours." Is Ai Fen's screenshot, a viral text the purpose of which was to limit the fallout of the pandemic in China, not a virally distributed antagonist of the virus? Are the three Beijing-based volunteers who uploaded censored articles about Covid-19 onto GitHub and then went missing on April 19th to be charged with spreading the "infodemic"?[27] These occasions complicate the simple opposition of digital textualities to the possibility of truth.[28] There are times when viral text is the best idiom for truth there is, and binary categories of veritable truth and veritable falsehood—like Sontag's metaphors of the two kingdoms—are inadequate descriptors of textualities that, almost by definition, rest at the margins of institutionally sanctioned veracity.

Here the need for caution arises. This is a line of thought that can only be pushed so far. For every viral text that could have prevented a global catastrophe, there are many more benign memes and genuine falsehoods. Insofar as the political is concerned, "microcultural contentions" such as the example in this chapter can only do so much.[29] All that is clear is that resistance as parody and gamified disobedience acknowledges the distributed exercises of power in a technocratic environment such as WeChat. Yet, the becoming-micro of cultural contentions as a response can be read as

25 Ghebreyesus, "Munich Security Conference."

26 Elie, "(Against) Virus as Metaphor."

27 Zhang, "Chinese Activists Detained After Sharing Censored Coronavirus Material on Crowdsourcing site Github."

28 On digital media and the "truth regime" (defined as simultaneous aesthetic and political incoherence), see Galloway, *The Interface Effect*, especially chap. 1 and postscript.

29 I borrow the term from Guo, "The Appeal of Style."

a symptom of a post-historical pessimism about genuine change, as Vilém Flusser puts it: "It has currently become *impossible to engage ourselves in the 'progress of culture.'* As doing so would be to engage ourselves in our own annihilation [...] That is: we have lost faith in ourselves."[30] To question whether it makes sense to "[associate] political community with physical and linguistic homogeneity," as viral text does, is not quite the same as possessing the means of changing that which prompted the question.[31] Let us not get any ideas about messianic memes.

What viral text does is both less radical and more interesting than resistance in the abstract. It prompts us to search for new conceptualisations of translation that does not begin with the assumptions of monolingualism and the homogeneity of each language. The English translation of the Ai Fen interview with which we begin is therefore a misleading example of viral text that, due to its proximity to more traditional forms of translation, fails to bring to relief the oddity of the specific kind of languaging at hand. Let me propose a different example, this time the Martian script version of the same passage given in standard Chinese script above:

> 2019婂12仴30曰，鈘棼嶒嗱葤過①蚡苿明腓壂疒亾哋疒毐撿惻蕔啱，吂凧葒胞圚炪「SARS蔲匯疒毐」牸樣，當汏敎哃敎問起澌，吂將適蚡蕔啱啪苄唻伝給孑適菈哃湜悘泩哋哃敎。當脕，適蚡蕔啱伝猵孑娍漢哋悘泩圚，囀潑適蚡蕔啱哋亾僦笣啹哪8菈被槳汸訓諴哋悘泩。
>
> 適給鈘棼帶唻孑嫲煩，莋澙伝譒哋粠頭，吂被悘阮汜逶紟談，蹧辭孑「湔葰沬洧哋、嚴癘哋斥嫧」，稱吂湜莋澙摶鄴亾仕茬慥愮。
>
> 泚湔哋①些蕔槌，鈘棼被稱澙「叒①個被訓諴哋囡悘泩捊炪潹媔」，笣洧亾將吂稱澙「吹哨亾」，鈘棼糾囯孑適個說珐，吂說洎已苿湜吹哨亾，湜哪個「潑哨ふ哋亾」。
>
> 適湜《亾粅》3俏刋對媔《娍漢悘泩》哋苐②萹蕔槌。

A number of distinctive Martian script strategies of replacing standard graphs with unorthodox variants are represented in this passage: the use of symbols (replacing "1" by "①"), visually-similar foreign scripts (replacing "子" by "ふ"), characters with added or removed strokes (replacing "了" by "

30 Flusser, "The Ground We Tread," in *Post-History*, 10. Flusser's emphasis.

31 Walkowitz, *Born Translated*, 216.

孒"), and the addition of radicals (replacing "艾" by "鉸").[32] Many of the graphs used are complex or archaic graphs that are now rarely if ever used in everyday communication (for example, "悘" and "蕔"), and have little in common semantically with the graphs they replace. But to a reader accustomed to this heterographic practice (and it does not take long for a fluent reader of Chinese to become accustomed to it), a text in Martian script is nearly as easy to read as the original text itself.

Originating in Taiwan and popularised on the mainland around 2008, Martian script was from the beginning understood as an online idiom of teenagers, something constitutively subcultural because "as soon as any specific word or expression becomes familiar and accepted by the public, it fades out of 'Martian script.'"[33] The subcultural practice of talking in this strange "code" unsurprisingly proved so unnerving for an official in the PRC's Department of Education that he writes in 2010, "we need to seriously investigate the reason for the emergence of 'Martian script,' strengthen our guidance for teenagers, and prevent its disturbance to the use of language and script in education and popular media."[34] But the script is not as radically detached from this-worldly history or milieu as its moniker might suggest. The types of linguistic mutations represented in this trendy online language of rebellious teens have been used since as early as the Qin dynasty (221-206 BCE) for wide-ranging purposes such as poetic expression, the avoidance of taboos (bihui 避諱) and "code speech" (yinyu隱語).[35] It is also not entirely a "script," as it uses a substantially different lexicon that includes pictographs ("Orz" visually represents a person performing kowtow) and dialectal expressions that language standardisation efforts have shunned upon. Like all of its viral predecessors, the linguistic practice is never meant to be a replacement of standardised Chinese, or a different language; on the contrary, participation in these practices requires knowledge of Chinese and its associated cultural norms, in addition to the know-how specific to the subcultural variant. To discursively collapse this heterogeneous space into a simplistic dichotomy of domestic and foreign is akin to categorising Martian Script simply as either Chinese or foreign writing. Both are only too easily done and quite wrong.

32 For a more systematic study of Martian script techniques, see Chen, "'Huoxingwen': Wangluo yuyan xin fazhan" 41–46.

33 Ibid, 46.

34 Wang and Hou, "Cong 2008 niandu diaocha kan Zhongguo de yuyan shenghuo," 33.

35 See Yu and Pei, "'Huoxingwen' yongsheng de yuyan shehui wenhua xianxiang", 151–155. On the avoidance of taboos in premodern China, see He, "Luelun lishi shang de bihui," 82–88.

It is sometimes claimed that premodern East Asia was a world without translation.[36] That is to say, despite the diversity of vernacular languages across the region (Sinitic languages, Japanese, Korean, Vietnamese, etc.), the literati class of various societies held privileged access to a common communication channel through their shared knowledge of Chinese written characters. Through practices such as *kundoku*, for example, an educated Japanese would have been well aware that they did not need to know spoken Chinese to understand, compose, or read aloud texts written in the literary language. Confucian classics were read aloud in idiosyncratic manners that rearrange the characters to suit vernacular syntax, and a reversal of this process allowed non-Chinese people to create Chinese-style texts intelligible throughout East Asia. Such practices enabled literate elites to partake, through writing, in conversations of much larger scales than what their local idiom would have allowed. By inverting the usual subordination of writing to speech—an hierarchisation all too familiar to readers of Jacques Derrida—traditional East Asia cultivated a space wherein those possessing the means "had direct access to Chinese texts (and audiences) without the need for translation."[37] Chinese written characters worked as a premodern Unicode, so to speak: the term *hanzi wenhua quan* 漢字文化圈, which Wiebke Denecke tellingly renders as "the Sinographic Sphere," already intimates that the negotiation of cultural borders and the construction of "world without translation" always involve media infrastructures that traverse and configure linguistic glocalities.

It would be difficult to uncover any historical continuity between premodern institutions of literacy and the infrastructure of Sinophone cyberculture today.[38] But if the spectre of this earlier technologically-curated space of *tongwen* 同文 is conjured by the term Sinocybersphere, it is telling that so, too, are its fantasies and discontents. Expressions, it turns out, had always been *en route* to become something new. Just as the Chinese written character had been historically subjected to various forms of appropriation from the Japanese *kana* to the "women's writing" (nüshu 女書) in Hunan, so do the regulatory technologies of digital China unwittingly provide spaces for the dwelling of heterogeneous communities. Translation bespeaks difference, not just between spheres but also within. English, Klingon, Mao-style calligraphy, QR code, Martian script…these are not so much geographical others of China (as the kingdom of the ill is imagined to be for

36 Denecke, "Worlds Without Translation."

37 Denecke, "Worlds Without Translation," 214. Quoted in Saussy, *The Making of Barbarians*, 60.

38 This is not to suggest such connections do not exist. On the influence of Chinese linguistics on early Natural Language Processing research, see Liu, "Wittgenstein in the Machine."

the kingdom of the well), digital or otherwise, but its many potentialities. Forms of expression that muffle the signal.[39] Translations in a world without translation.

## References

Benjamin, Walter. "The Task of the Translator." In *Selected Writings Vol. 1, 1913-1926*, edited by Marcus Bullock and Michael W. Jennings. Cambridge and London: Harvard University Press, 1996.

Chen Feiyue 陈飞樾. "Shencha zhixia women de biaoda ye zai biancheng xin de dongxi 审查之下，我们的表达也在变成新的东西 [Under Censorship, Our Expressions Are Becoming Something New]." WeChat, February 23, 2020. https://mp.weixin.qq.com/s/5cqKoFsBvPvUB-oB8Zn97g.

Chen Feiyue 陈飞樾. "Zhongwen hulianwang zhong taolun de xiaowang 中文互联网中"讨论"的消亡 [The Death of 'Discussion' on Sinophone Internet]." WeChat, March 29, 2020. https://mp.weixin.qq.com/s/a-32UpINmb_vSj17epysiA.

Chen Jiaxuan 陈佳璇. "Huoxingwen wangluo yuyan xinfazhan '火星文'：网络语言新发展 [['Martian Script': New Development of Internet Language]." *Xiuci xuexi* 2008.4 (2008): 41–46.

Creemers, Rogier. "The Pivot in Chinese Cybergovernance: Integrating Internet Control in Xi Jinping's China." *China Perspectives* 104.4 (2015): 5–13.

Crete-Nishihata, Masashi, Jakub Dalek, Jeffrey Knockel, Nicola Lawford, Caroline Wesley, and Mari Zhou. "Censored Contagion II: A Timeline of Information Control on Chinese Social Media During Covid-19." *Citizen Lab* (August 25, 2020). https://citizenlab.ca/2020/08/censored-contagion-ii-a-timeline-of-information-control-on-chinese-social-media-during-covid-19/.

Denecke, Wiebke. "Worlds Without Translation: Premodern East Asia and the Power of Character Scripts." In *A Companion to Translation Studies*, edited by Sandra Bermann and Catherine Porter, 204–216. Chichester: Wiley, 2014.

Elie, Paul. "(Against) Virus as Metaphor." *New Yorker* (March 19, 2020). https://www.newyorker.com/news/daily-comment/against-the-coronavirus-as-metaphor.

Farmer, Paul. *Infections and Inequalities: The Modern Plagues*. Berkeley and Los Angeles: University of California Press, 2001.

Flusser, Vilém. *Post-History*, translated by Rodrigo Maltez Novaes. Minneapolis: Univocal, 2013.

Fowler, Harold North, trans. *Plato I*. Cambridge: Harvard University Press, 1975.

39 Which, in its extreme form, is a blank piece of paper held in a public space, signifying the possibility of expression as such.

Galloway, Alexander R. *The Interface Effect*. Cambridge: Polity Press, 2012.

Ge Ge Dian Ah 戈戈点啊. "Jieli fa shaozi de ren yingwen ban 接力《发哨子的人》英文版 [Relay 'The Whistle-Giver' English Version]." WeChat, March 11, 2020. https://mp.weixin.qq.com/s/cG90P6VlT2GiyARfFYMyfA.

Ghebreyesus, Tedros Adhanom. "Munich Security Conference." *World Health Organization* (February 15, 2020). https://www.who.int/dg/speeches/detail/munich-security-conference.

GM35. "Don't Let the Story of the Original COVID-19 Whistleblower Die." *gnews.org* (March 11, 2020). https://gnews.org/138387/.

Gong Jing Qi 龚惊奇. "Fa shaozi de ren 潑哨ふ咃亾 [The Whistle-Giver]." WeChat, March 10, 2020. https://mp.weixin.qq.com/s/hIc2z4INbg2YkoMvXIIZ6Q.

Guo, Shaohua. "The Appeal of Style: Han Han and Microcultural Contention in Digital China." *Modern Chinese Literature and Culture* 28.2 (2016): 90–138.

He Zhongli 何忠礼. "Lüelun lishi shang de bihui 略论历史上的避讳 [A Brief Discussion of The Avoidance of Taboos in History]." *Zhejiang daxue xueban (renwen shehui kexue ban)* 32.1 (2002): 82–88.

Huoxingwen. "Zaixian huoxingwen zhuanhuan qi 在线火星文转换器 [Online Martian Script Converter]." https://www.aies.cn/huoxingwen.htm.

Jiang, Min. "Authoritarian Informationalism: China's Approach to Internet Sovereignty." *SAIS Review of International Affairs* 30.2 (2010): 71–89.

Knockel, Jeffrey et al. "(Can't) Picture This: An Analysis of Image Filtering on WeChat Moments." *Citizen Lab* (August 14, 2018). https://citizenlab.ca/2018/08/cant-picture-this-an-analysis-of-image-filtering-on-wechat-moments/.

Kokas, Aynne. "Platform Patrol: China, the United States, and the Global Battle for Data Security." *Journal of Asian Studies* 77.4 (2018): 923–933.

Kolb, Anjuli Fatima Raza. *Epidemic Empire: Colonialism, Contagion, and Terror, 1817-2020*. Chicago: University of Chicago Press, 2020.

Liu, Lydia. "Wittgenstein in the Machine." *Critical Inquiry* 47.3 (2021): 425–455.

Murphy, Kenneth and Casey Weaver. *Janeway's Immunobiology 9th Edition*. New York: Garland Science, 2016.

Notion. "Fa shaozi de ren 发哨子的人 [The Whistle-Giver]." *notion.so* (March 9, 2020). https://www.notion.so/00a9beeb2fe54dfe84a55141a5f592cf?v=cf2bfae990fc4207a8710a40ffeb7f3c.

Pellegrino, Manuela. "COVID-19: The 'Invisible Enemy and Contingent Racism': Reflections of an Italian Anthropologist Conducting Fieldwork in Greece." *Anthropology Today* 36.3 (2020): 19–21.

Peters, John Durham. *The Marvelous Clouds: Toward a Philosophy of Elemental Media*. Chicago: University of Chicago Press, 2015.

Ruan, Lotus, Jeffrey Knockel, Jason Q. Ng, and Masashi Crete-Nishihata. "One App, Two Systems: How WeChat uses one censorship policy in China and another internationally." *Citizen Lab* (November 30, 2016). https://citizenlab.ca/2016/11/wechat-china-censorship-one-app-two-systems/.

Ruan, Lotus, Jeffrey Knockel, Jason Q. Ng, and Masashi Crete-Nishihata. "Censored Contagion: How Information on the Coronavirus is Managed on Chinese Social Media." *Citizen Lab* (March 3, 2020). https://citizenlab.ca/2020/03/censored-contagion-how-information-on-the-coronavirus-is-managed-on-chinese-social-media/.

Saussy, Haun. *The Marking of Barbarians: Chinese Literature and Multilingual Asia*. Princeton and Oxford: Princeton University Press, 2022.

Sontag, Susan. *Illness as Metaphor*. New York: Farrar, Straus, and Giroux, 1978.

Unicode Consortium, ed. *The Unicode Standard ver. 13.0*. California: Mountainview, 2020.

Venuti, Lawrence. *The Translator's Invisibility: A History of Translation*. London: Routledge, 1995.

Walkowitz, Rebecca L. *Born Translated: The Contemporary Novel in an Age of World Literature*. New York: Columbia University Press, 2015.

Wang Tiekun 王铁琨 and Hou Min 侯敏. "Cong 2008 niandu diaocha shuju kan Zhongguo de yuyan shenghuo 从2008年度调查数据看中国的语言生活 [Looking Into the Language Situation in China from the Data of Language Survey (2008)]." *Yuyan wenzi yingyong* 2010.2 (2010): 26–35.

Wang, Xinyuan. *Social Media in Industrial China*. London: University College London Press, 2016.

Xin Shidai Cao Ni Ma 新时代草泥马. "CDC dang'an: Yichang zhangxian wangmin bu fucong de daxing jiti xingwei yishu huodong: Fa koushao de ren banben daquan CDC档案 | 一场彰显网民不服从的大型集体行为艺术活动：发口哨的人版本大全 [CDC Files | A Massive, Collective Performance of Netizen Disobedience: All Versions of The Whistle-Giver]." *China Digital Times* (March 12, 2020). https://chinadigitaltimes.net/chinese/638032.html.

Yu Quanyou 于全有 and Pei Jingrui 裴景瑞. "Huoxingwen yongsheng de yuyan shehui wenhua xianxiang '火星文'涌生的语言社会文化现象 [The Cultural-Linguistic Phenomenon of the Emergence of Martian Script]." *Wenhua xuekan* 2008.2 (2008): 151-155.

Zhang, Phoebe. "Chinese Activists Detained After Sharing Censored Coronavirus Material on Crowdsourcing site Github." *South China Morning Post* (April 25, 2020). https://www.scmp.com/news/china/politics/article/3081569/chinese-activists-detained-after-sharing-censored-coronavirus.

# Bibliography


A Plus Art. 'Pangrok Sulap'. A+, 2021. http://www.aplusart.asia/artists/pangrok-sulap.

Ah Que 阿缺. "Jujue 咀嚼 [Contemplation]." In *Shirun de Jinshu* 湿润的金属 [Wet Metal], 205–26. Beijing: Zuojia chubanshe, 2020.

Ahearne, Jeremy, and John Speller (eds.). "Bourdieu and the Literary Field." *Paragraph* Vol. 35, No. 1 (2012): 1–138.

Alexa Internet. "Taobao.com Site Overview." Alexa Internet. https://www.alexa.com/siteinfo/taobao.com.

Andrejevic, Mark. "Privacy, Exploitation, and the Digital Enclosure." *Amsterdam Law Forum* 1 no. 1 (2008): 47–62.

Ang, Peng Hwa, and Loh Chee Men. "Internet Development in Asia." *Proceedings of The Internet Society's Annual Conference 1996: Transforming Our Society Now*, 1996. Available at: https://web.archive.org/web/20160103054149/http://www.isoc.org/inet96/proceedings/h1/h1_1.htm.

Ankang Government. 'Jia xiansheng tousu maicai tanfan zhandao jingying贾先生投诉卖菜摊贩占道经营 [Mr. Jia: Complaint about Vegetable Vendors Occupiying the Road]'. *Ankang City People's Government* (January 17, 2020). http://www.ankang.gov.cn/Gov/Letter/DH202001170059.html.

Arcy, Jacquelyn. "Emotion Work: Considering Gender in Digital Labor." *Feminist Media Studies* 16 no. 2 (2016): 365–368.

Arefin, Mohamed Rafi. "Abjection a Definition for Discard Studies" *Discard Studies*, February 27, 2015.

The Back Room. "About." *The Back Room KL*. https://www.thebackroomkl.com/aboutus.

The Back Room. "All By Myself: An Exhibition by CC Kua." Press Release. The Back Room, 2020.

The Back Room. "All by Myself: An Exhibition by CC Kua." *The Back Room KL*, 2020. https://www.thebackroomkl.com/exhibitions/all-by-myself-cc-kua.

The Back Room. "In Order (To Play)—A Solo Exhibition by Liew Kwai Fei." *The Back Room KL*, 2021. https://www.thebackroomkl.com/exhibitions/liewkwaifei.

The Back Room. "The Back Room KL." Instagram, 2021. https://www.instagram.com/thebackroomkl/.

Baidu Baike 百度百科. "Fanqiang 翻墙 [To Breach the Firewall]." https://baike.baidu.com/item/%E7%BF%BB%E5%A2%99/754773.

Baidu Baike 百度百科. "Feihua shige 废话诗歌 [Nonsense Poetry]." https://baike.baidu.com/item/%E5%BA%9F%E8%AF%9D%E8%AF%97%E6%AD%8C.

Bainbridge, Caroline and Candida Yates. "Cinematic Symptoms of Masculinity in Transition: Memory, History and Mythology in Contemporary Film." *Psychoanalysis, Culture & Society* 10 (2005): 299–318.

Balance, Christine Bacareza. "How it Feels to Be Viral Me: Affective Labor and Asian American YouTube Performance." *Women's Studies Quarterly* 40.1/2 (2012): 138–152.

Bao Shu 宝树, ed. *Kehuan Zhong de Zhongguo Lishi* 科幻中的中国历史 [Chinese History in Science Fiction]. Beijing: Sanlian Shudian, 2017.

Baozhi Huqiang 报纸糊墙. *Niu nan* 牛男 [*The Water Buffalo Man*]. *Jinjiang Literature City*, 2013-16. http://www.jjwxc.net/onebook.php?novelid=1769629.

Barad, Karen. 'Posthumanist Performativity: Toward an Understanding of How Matter Comes to Matter'. *Signs: Journal of Women in Culture and Society* 28, no. 3 (Spring 2003): 801–31.

Becker, Howard. *Outsiders. Studies in the Psychology of Deviance.* New York: The Free Press, 1973.

Becker, Howard. *Art Worlds*. Berkeley: University of California Press, 1984.

Benjamin, Walter. "The Task of the Translator." In *Selected Writings Vol. 1, 1913-1926*, edited by Marcus Bullock and Michael W. Jennings. Cambridge and London: Harvard University Press, 1996.

Berardi, Franco. *Futurability: The Age of Impotence and the Horizon of Possibility.* London, Brooklyn, NY.: Verso Books, 2017.

Best Buy 超值牌. *Xionggang* 凶港 [Haunted Port]. Hong Kong: Feel Company, 2014.

Beuys, Joseph. "I Am Searching for Field Character." In *Art in Theory 1900-2000: An Anthology of Changing Idea*, edited by Charles Harrison and Paul Wood, 929–930. Oxford: Blackwell Publishing, 2003.

Blackmore, Susan. *The Meme Machine.* Oxford: Oxford University Press, 1999.

Bolter, Jay David, and Richard Grusin. *Remediation: Understanding New Media.* Cambridge, MA, USA: MIT Press, 1998.

Boon, Pok Chong. "The Development of Woodblock Printmaking in Malaysia: From Engaging with Social Subject Matters to Being Socially-Engaged." In *An Outline of the Development of Social Realist Woodcuts in Malaysia*, edited by Krystie Ng, 20–25. Cheras, Selangor: Krystie Ng, 2020.

Bourdieu, Pierre. "Cultural Reproduction and Social Reproduction." In *Knowledge, Education, and Social Change*, edited by Richard Brown, 71–84. London: Tavistock, 1973.

Bourdieu, Pierre. "The Field of Cultural Production, or: The Economic World Reversed." *Poetics* 12.4-5 (1983): 311–356.

Bourdieu, Pierre. *Language and Symbolic Power.* Cambridge: Polity Press, 1991.

Bourdieu, Pierre. *Practical Reason: On the Theory of Action*. Redwood City, CA: Stanford University Press, 1998.

Bourdieu, Pierre. *The Rules of Art: Genesis and Structure of the Literary Field.* Cambridge: Polity Press, 1996.

Bourriaud, Nicolas. *Relational Aesthetics*. Translated by Simon Pleasance, Fronza Woods and Mathieu Copeland. Collection documents sur l'art. Dijon: Les presses du réel, 2002.

Buddhism in a Nutshell. "The Buddhas in the Three Periods of Time." http://www.buddhistdoor.com/OldWeb/bdoor/archive/nutshell/teach36.htm.

Byler, Darren. *Terror Capitalism: Uyghur Dispossession and Masculinity in a Chinese City. Terror Capitalism.* Durham: Duke University Press, 2022.

Cai, Zong-qi, and Shengqing Wu. "Introduction: Emotion, Patterning, and Visuality in Chinese Literary Thought and Beyond." *Journal of Chinese Literature and Culture* 6, no. 1 (April 1, 2019): 1–14.

Callahan, William A. "Surpass." In Afterlives of Chinese Communism, edited by Christian Sorace, Ivan Franceschini, and Nicholas Loubere, 275–80. Political Concepts from Mao to Xi. ANU Press, 2019.

Carrington, Damian. "$10bn of precious metals dumped each year in electronic waste, says UN" The Guardian (July 2, 2021). https://www.theguardian.com/environment/2020/jul/02/10bn-precious-metals-dumped-each-year-electronic-waste-un-toxic-e-waste-polluting.

Casanova, Pascale. *The World Republic of Letters,* trans. Malcolm DeBevoise. Cambridge, MA: Harvard University Press, 2007.

CCTV News (@央視新聞). "I am quite proud, because I am a dot in the background of Li Ziqi's videos" Weibo, December 10, 2019, 09:27. https://weibo.com/ttarticle/p/show?id=2309404447882362093714#_0.

Census and Statistics Department. "Thematic Household Survey Report No. 76." Hong Kong: Hong Kong SAR Government, 2022.

Census and Statistics Department. "Thematic Household Survey Report No. 75: Internet and Personal Computer Penetration." Hong Kong: Hong Kong SAR Government, 2022.

Central Committee of the Communist Young League (@共青團中央). "Yinwei Li Ziqi, shu baiwan waiguoren aishang Zhongguo 因为李子柒，数百万外国人爱上中国 [Because of Li Ziqi, Millions of Foreigners Fell in Love with China]." *Sina Weibo* (December 9, 2019). https://weibo.com/ttarticle/p/show?id=2309404447615805685960#_0 .

CGTN (China Global Television Network). "Vietnamese vlogger suspected of copying Chinese influencer Li Ziqi." YouTube, July 5, 2020. https://www.youtube.com/watch?v=zLhv7EXmLpo.

Chan, Alan and Sor-Hoon Tan. *Filial Piety in Chinese Thought and History.* London: Routledge, 2004.

Chan, Ngai Keung, and Chi Kwok. "The Politics of Platform Power in Surveillance Capitalism: A Comparative Case Study of Ride-Hailing Platforms in China and the United States." *Global Media and China* 7, no. 2 (2022): 131–50.

Chang, Kang-yi Sun, and Stephen Owen (eds.). *The Cambridge History of Chinese Literature*. Cambridge: Cambridge University Press, 2010.

Chen Feiyue 陈飞樾. "Shencha zhixia women de biaoda yezai biancheng xin de dongxi 审查之下，我们的表达也在变成新的东西 [Under Censorship, Our Expressions Are Becoming Something New]." WeChat, February 23, 2020. https://mp.weixin.qq.com/s/5cqKoFsBvPvUB-oB8Zn97g.

Chen Feiyue 陈飞樾. "Zhongwen hulianwang yhong 'taolun' de xiaowang 中文互联网中'讨论'的消亡 [The Death of 'Discussion' on the Sinophone Internet]." WeChat, March 29, 2020. https://mp.weixin.qq.com/s/a-32UpINmb_vSj17epy-siA.

Chen, Mel. Animacies: *Biopolitics and Racial Mattering and Queer Affect.* Durham and London: Duke University Press, 2012

Chen Qiufan. *The Waste Tide.* Translated by Ken Liu. New York: Tor Books, 2013.

Chau, Angie. "From Nobel to Hugo: Reading Chinese Science Fiction as World Literature." Modern Chinese Literature and Culture 30, no. 1 (2018): 110–35.

Chen Jiaxuan 陈佳璇. "Huoxingwen wangluo yuyan xinfazhan '火星文': 网络语言新发展 [['Martian Script': New Development of Internet Language]." *Xiuci xuexi* 2008.4 (2008): 41–46.

Chen Qiufan 陈楸帆. "Zai Zhongguo, zhi saibo bu pengke 在中国，只赛博不朋克 [In China, it's all Cyber, no Punk]." New York Times Chinese Edition, August 8, 2013. https://cn.nytimes.com/books/20130808/cc08cyberpunk/.

Chen, Xiaomei. "Occidentalism as Counterdiscourse: 'He Shang' in Post-Mao China." Critical Inquiry 18, no. 4 (1992): 686–712.

Chen, Xin. "Boys' Love (Danmei) Fiction on the Chinese Internet: Wasabi Kun, the BL Forum Young Nobleman Changpei, and the Development of an Online Literary Phenomenon." Master's thesis, University of British Columbia, 2017.

Cheng, Che Hoo. "Internet eXchange for Local Traffic: Hong Kong's Experience." In *Proceedings of The Internet Society's Annual Conference 1996: Transforming Our Society Now*, Hong Kong, 1996.

Cheng, Wen-Feng, Chao-Chung Wu, Ruihua Song, Jianlong Fu, Xing Xie, and Jian-Yun Jie. "Image Inspired Poetry Generation in XiaoIce." *eprint arXiv* (August 9, 2018). https://arxiv.org/abs/1808.03090 (15/05/2019).

Cheung, Duk 張篤. *Chongfu de Taizi Zhan* 重複的太子站 [The Repeating Prince Edward Station]. Hong Kong: Starry Night Publications, 2016.

China Daily. "Garbage-Sorting Games Used to Win over Shanghai's Younger Generation." Chinadaily (July 8, 2019). https://www.chinadaily.com.cn/a/201907/08/WS5d2284d4a3105895c2e7c205.html.

China Film Administration. "Guojia dianyingju, Zhongguo kexie yinfa 'guanyu cujin kehuan dianying fazhan de ruogan yijian' 国家电影局、中国科协 印发 '关于促进科幻电影发展的若干意见' [China Film Administration and China

Association for Science and Technology Publish 'Some Notes on Advancing the Development of Science Fiction Cinema'']," August 7, 2020. http://www.chinafilm.gov.cn/chinafilm/contents/141/2533.shtml.

China Internet Network Information Center. "Di 45 ci Zhongguo hulian wangluo fazhan zhuangkuang tongji baogao 第45次中国互联网络发展状况统计报告 [The 45th China Statistical Report on Internet Development]." Beijing: China Internet Network Information Center, September 29, 2020.

China Internet Network Information Center. "Di 47 ci Zhongguo hulianwangluo fazhan zhuangkuang
tongji baogao 第47次中国互联网络发展状况统计报告 [The 47th China Statistical Report on Internet Development]." Beijing: China Internet Network Information Center, 2021.

China State Council. "Guowuyuan bangongting guanyu yinfa quanmin kexue suzhi xingdong jihua gangyao shishi fang'an (2016–2020 nian) de tongzhi" 国务院办公厅关于印发全民科学素质行动计划纲要实施方案 (2016–2020年) 的通知 [General Office of the State Council on the Issuance of the Action Plan on the People's Scientific Quality and Implementation Outline (2016-2020)]. http://www.gov.cn/zhengce/content/2016-03/14/content_5053247.htm.

Chou, William, Roger Chung, and Taylor Lam. "Chinese consumers at the forefront of digital technologies." *Deloitte China Mobile Consumer Survey 2018*.

Chow, Rey. "Introduction: On Chineseness as a Theoretical Problem." *Boundary 2* 25, no. 3 (1998): 1–24.

Chow, Rey."Toward an Ethics of Postvisuality: Some Thoughts on the Recent Work of Zhang Yimou." *Poetics Today* 25, no. 4 (December 1, 2004): 673–88.

Chun, Wendy Hui Kyong. *Control and Freedom: Power and Paranoia in the Age of Fiber Optics.* Cambridge, MA, USA: MIT Press, 2005.

Chun, Wendy Hui Kyong. "High-Tech Orientalism (Cyberpunk & Race)." *Critical Posthumanism Network* (blog), April 30, 2019. https://criticalposthumanism.net/high-tech-orientalism-cyberpunk-race/.

Chun, Wendy Hui Kyong. *Updating to Remain the Same: Habitual New Media.* MIT Press, 2017.

Chun, Wendy Hui Kyong. "The Enduring Ephemeral, or the Future Is a Memory." *Critical Inquiry* 35, no. 1 (2008): 148–71.

Cirucci, Angela. "A New Women's Work: Digital Interactions, Gender, and Social Network Sites." *International Journal of Communication* 12 (2018): 23.

Coleman, Beth. *Hello Avatar: Rise of the Networked Generation.* Cambridge, MA: The MIT Press, 2011.

Colton, Simon, Jacob Goodwin, Database of Laws and Regulations. "Marriage Law of the People's Republic of China." Conn, Virginia L., and Gabriele De Seta. "Sinofuturism (s)." *Verge: Studies in Global Asias* 7, no. 2 (2021): 74–99.

Colton, Simon, Jacob Goodwin, and Tony Veale. "Full-FACE Poetry Generation." *ICCC* (2012): 95–102.

Connell, R. W. "Masculinities and Globalisation." *Men and Masculinities* 1.1 (1998): 3–23. https://doi.org/10.1177/1097184X98001001001.

Connor, Michael. "Post-Internet: What It Is and What It Was." In *You Are Here: Art after the Internet*, edited by Omar Kholeif, 56–64. Manchester: Cornerhouse, 2014.

Couldry, Nick, and Andreas Hepp. *The Mediated Construction of Reality*. Cambridge: Polity Press, 2016.

Cramer, Florian. "What Is 'Post-Digital'?" In *Postdigital Aesthetics: Art, Computation and Design*, edited by David M. Berry and Michael Dieter, 12–26. London: Palgrave Macmillan UK, 2015.

Creemers, Rogier. "The Pivot in Chinese Cybergovernance: Integrating Internet Control in Xi Jinping's China." *China Perspectives* 104.4 (2015): 5–13.

Crete-Nishihata, Masashi, Jakub Dalek, Jeffrey Knockel, Nicola Lawford, Caroline Wesley, and Mari Zhou. "Censored Contagion II: A Timeline of Information Control on Chinese Social Media During Covid-19." *Citizen Lab* (August 25, 2020). https://citizenlab.ca/2020/08/censored-contagion-ii-a-timeline-of-information-control-on-chinese-social-media-during-covid-19/.

Csicsery-Ronay, Istvan. *The Seven Beauties of Science Fiction*. Middletown: Wesleyan University Press, 2012.

Cui Peng 崔鹏, and Jiang,Jingling 姜菁玲. "Su Hua ci ren Kuaishou CEO, Cheng Yixiao jieren gai zhiwu 宿华辞任快手CEO，程一笑将接任该职务 [Su Hua Resigns as CEO of Kuaishou, and Cheng Yixiao Will Take Over the Position]." *Jiemian.com*, 29 October. https://m.jiemian.com/article/6761245.html.

Cultural Relations Platform. "The Assessment of the Impact of COVID-19 on the Cultural and Creative Sectors in the EU's Partner Countries, Policy Responses and Their Implications for International Cultural Relations," February 10, 2021. https://ifacca.org/news/2021/02/10/assessment-impact-covid19-cultural-and-creative-se/. http://www.npc.gov.cn/zgrdw/englishnpc/Law/2007-12/13/content_1384064.htm.

Dai Wangyun. "How Li Ziqi Repackages Rural China for Urban Fantasies." *Sixth Tone* (December 27, 2019). https://www.sixthtone.com/news/1005007/how-li-ziqi-repackages-rural-china-for-urban-fantasies.

Davis, Darrell W., and Yueh-Yu Yeh. "Warning! Category III: The Other Hong Kong Cinema." *Film Quarterly* 54. 4 (2001): 12–26.

Dawkins, Richard. *The Selfish Gene*. Oxford: Oxford University Press, 1976.

Dawkins, Richard. *The Extended Phenotype. The Gene as the Unit of Selection*. Oxford: Oxford University Press, 1982.

Dawkins, Richard. "Memes." *YouTube*, uploaded by OxfordUnion, February 26, 2014, https://www.youtube.com/watch?v=4BVpEoQ4T2M.

Denecke, Wiebke. "Worlds Without Translation: Premodern East Asia and the Power of Character Scripts." In *A Companion to Translation Studies*, edited by Sandra Bermann and Catherine Porter, 204–216. Chichester: Wiley, 2014.

Derrida, Jacques. "Archive Fever: A Freudian Impression." *Diacritics* 25.2 (1995): 9–63.

Dianxian 电线. "Xiangmi chenchen jin ru Shuang 香蜜沉沉烬如霜 [Ashes of Love]." Situ 思兔. June 22, 2016. https://www.sto.cx/book-38184-1.html.

di Rosario, Giovanna. "Digital Poetry: a Naissance of a New Genre?", *Carnets* 1 (June 16, 2018). http://journals.openedition.org/carnets/3762.

Dirlik, Arif, and Xudong Zhang. *Postmodernism and China*. Durham: Duke University Press, 2000.

Doctorow, Cory. "Netzsperren: Morozov zieht falsche Schlüsse." *Zeit Online* (February 4, 2011). http://www.zeit.de/digital/Internet/2011-02/doctorow-morozov-netzsperre.

Dotson, John. "The Communist Youth League Announces Plans to Send a New Generation 'Down to the Countryside'." *China Brief* 19.8 (April 24, 2019): https://jamestown.org/program/the-communist-youth-league-announces-plans-to-send-a-new-generation-down-to-the-countryside/.

Dongfang wang 东方网. "Zen neng ruci xia peng 'Wuqingti' 怎能如此瞎捧"乌青体" [How Can One Blindly Praise 'Wu Qing's Style of Writing' Like This]." *Zhongyang dianshitai wangzhan*. November 30, 2014. http://opinion.cntv.cn/2014/11/30/ARTI1417314249577111.shtml.

Dongfang Zhengquan Yanjiusuo 东方证券研究所 [Orient Securities Research Institute]. "Kuaishou shouci baogao——duanshipin shequ longtou, shangyehua jiasu zheng dangshi 快手首次报告：短视频社区龙头，商业化加速正当时 [Kuaishou First Report: The Short Video Community Leader, and the Right Time for the Acceleration of Commercialization]." Shanghai: Orient Securities Research Institute, 2021. https://pdf.dfcfw.com/pdf/H3_AP202102081460159841_1.pdf.

Douglas, Mary. *Purity and Danger: An Analysis of the Concepts of Pollution and Taboo*. Repr. London: Routledge, 2001. (Originally printed 1966)

Duffy, Brooke Erin. "Manufacturing Authenticity: The Rhetoric of 'Real' in Women's Magazines." *The Communication Review* 16 (2013): 132–154.

Echo of Heart 有心無默. *Xiyingpan* 西營盤 [Sai Ying Pun]. Hong Kong: Idea Publication, 2016.

Elie, Paul. "(Against) Virus as Metaphor." *New Yorker* (March 19, 2020). https://www.newyorker.com/news/daily-comment/against-the-coronavirus-as-metaphor.

Enhuber, Marisa. 'Art, Space and Technology: How the Digitisation and Digitalisation of Art Space Affect the Consumption of Art—a Critical Approach'. *Digital Creativity* 26.2 (2015): 121–137.

Fan, Boqun. *A History of Modern Chinese Popular Literature*. Cambridge: Cambridge University Press, 2020.

Fang Xianhai 方闲海. "Xiangpi: Zhongguo xianfeng 7 橡皮:中国先锋文学7 [Xiangpi: Chinese Avant-Garde Literature 7]." *Tengxun wang*. February 22, 2022.

Fangchenggang Government. 'Guanyu jiaqiang chengqu liudong tanfan guanli de jianyi—Zhou Guowei weiyuan de fayan 关于加强城区流动摊贩管理的建议—周国伟委员的发言 [Suggestions on Strengthening the Management of Mobile Vendors in Urban Areas—A Speech by Member Guowei Zhou]'. *Guangxi Fangchenggang's Harbor District's Government* (April 2, 2021). http://www.gkq.gov.cn/xxgk/xxgkml/jcxxgk/taya/202104/t20210402_195474.html.

Farmer, Paul. *Infections and Inequalities: The Modern Plagues.* Berkeley and Los Angeles: University of California Press, 2001.

Fei Arts. "Exhibition Foreword." *Fei Arts* (March 5, 2020). https://mp.weixin.qq.com/s/DSd1jsRgwm-GtFwITSoobg.

Fei Arts. "Zhanlan: jia jiushi meishuguan diyiqi 展览：家就是美术馆 第一期 [Exhibition: Home Is Museum (the First Part)]." *Fei Arts* (February 20, 2020). https://mp.weixin.qq.com/s/7QnWJCoHnT7L8uZ8SaXHiw.

Feng, Jin. "The Proliferating Genre: Web-based Time-travel Fiction and the New Media in Contemporary China." In *A Companion to Modern Chinese Literature*, edited by Yingjin Zhang, 379–94. Hoboken, NJ: John Wiley & Sons, Ltd, 2016.

Finger, Lutz and Soumitra Dutta. *Ask, Measure, Learn: Using Social Media Analytics to Understand and Influence Customer Behavior.* Beijing, Cambridge, Farnham, Köln, Sebastopol and Tokyo: O'Reilly Media, 2014.

Fitzgerald, Richard, Todd Sandel, and Xiaoping Wu. "Chinese Social Media: Technology, Culture and Creativity." *Discourse, Context & Media* 48 (August 1, 2022): 100610.

Flusser, Vilém. *Post-History*, translated by Rodrigo Maltez Novaes. Minneapolis: Univocal, 2013.

Fowler, Harold North, trans. *Plato I.* Cambridge: Harvard University Press, 1975.

Freeman, Elizabeth. 'Introduction: Queer and Not Now'. In *Time Binds: Queer Temporalities, Queer Histories*, 1–19. Durham and London: Duke University Press, 2010.

Friis, Karsten, and Olav Lysne. "Huawei, 5G and Security: Technological Limitations and Political Responses." *Development and Change* 52, no. 5 (2021): 1174–95.

Fu Qiongyin 符琼尹. "Shui rang 'Li Ziqi' yu 'Amu yeye' men chengwei YouTube wanghong? 谁让"李子柒"与"阿木爷爷"们成为YouTube网红? [Who Turned Li Ziqi and Grandpa Amu into YouTube Influencers?]" *CBNData* (September 21, 2020). https://www.cbndata.com/information/94721.

Fuchs, Christian. "Dallas Smythe Today: The Audience Commodity, the Digital Labor Debate, Marxist Political Economy and Critical Theory. Prolegomena to a Digital Labor Theory of Value." In *Marx and the Political Economy of the Media*, edited by Christian Fuchs and Vincent Mosco, 522–599. Leiden: Brill, 2015.

Fujimoto, Yukari, Linda Flores, Kazumi Nagaike, and Sharalyn Orbaugh. "Transgender: Female Hermaphrodites and Male Androgynes." *U.S.-Japan Women's Journal* 27 (2004): 76–117.

Fujimoto, Yukari, Linda Flores, Kazumi Nagaike, and Sharalyn Orbaugh. "The Evolution of BL as 'Playing with Gender': Viewing the Genesis and Development of BL from a Contemporary Perspective." In *Boys Love Manga and beyond: History, Culture and Community in Japan*, edited by Mark McLelland, Kazumi Nagaike, Katsuhiko Suganuma, and James Walker, translated by Joanne Quimby, 76–92. Jackson: University of Mississippi, 2015.

Funkhouser, Christopher Thomson. *Prehistoric Digital Poetry: An Archeology of Forms, 1959-1995*. Tuscaloosa: The University of Alabama Press, 2007.

Fung, Loretta, and Roland Carter. "Cantonese e-Discourse: A New Hybrid Variety of English." *Multilingua* 26.1 (2007): 35–66.

Fwu, Bih-Jen, Chih-Fen Wei, Shun-wen Chen, and Hsiou-Huai Wang. "To Work Hard or Not? The Conflicting Effects of Negative Emotions on Persistence after Academic Failure in a Confucian Heritage Cultural Context." In *Emotions in Learning, Teaching, and Leadership,* edited by Junjun Chen and Ronnel B. King, 3-17. London: Routledge, 2020.

Gaffric, Gwennaël. "Collective Space/Time Travel in Chinese Cyberliterature." In *China's Youth Cultures and Collective Spaces: Creativity, Sociality, Identity and Resistance*, edited by Vanessa Frangville and Gwennaël Gaffric, 189–202. Routledge, 2019.

Gaffric, Gwennaël. "La trilogie des Trois corps de Liu Cixin et le statut de la science-fiction en Chine contemporaine." *ReS Futurae. Revue d'études sur la science-fiction*, no. 9 (May 30, 2017).

Galloway, Alexander R. *The Interface Effect*. Cambridge: Polity Press, 2012.

Gao, Qin, and Xiaofang Liu. 'Stand against Anti-Asian Racial Discrimination during COVID-19: A Call for Action'. *International Social Work* 64, no. 2 (2021): 261–64.

Ge Ge Dian Ah 戈戈点啊. "Jieli fa shaozi de ren yingwen ban 接力《发哨子的人》英文版 [Relay 'The Whistle-Giver' English Version]." WeChat, March 11, 2020. https://mp.weixin.qq.com/s/cG9oP6VlT2GiyARfFYMyfA.

Geng, Xueqing. 'Mobile Market'. *Fei Arts* (March 5, 2020). https://mp.weixin.qq.com/s/DSd1jsRgwm-GtFwITSoobg.

Geroulanos, Stefanos, and Leif Weatherby. "Cybernetics and the Human Sciences." *History of the Human Sciences* 33, no. 1 (February 1, 2020): 3–11.

Geroulanos, Stefanos. *Transparency in Postwar France: A Critical History of the Present*. 1. Edition. Stanford, California: Stanford University Press, 2017.

Ghebreyesus, Tedros Adhanom. "Munich Security Conference." *World Health Organization* (February 15, 2020). https://www.who.int/dg/speeches/detail/munich-security-conference.

Gibson, William. *Neuromancer.* New York: Berkley Publishing Group, 2000.

Giles, David Boarder. "Dumpsters, Difference and Illiberal Embodiment." *Discard Studies*, September 15, 2015.

GM35. "Don't Let the Story of the Original COVID-19 Whistleblower Die." *gnews.org* (March 11, 2020). https://gnews.org/138387/.

Goh, Eric. "Review of CC Kua's All by Myself." *The Back Room* (July 16, 2020). https://www.thebackroomkl.com/exhibitions/all-by-myself-cc-kua.

Golle, Jessika, Stephanie Lisibach, Fred W. Mast, and Janek S. Lobmaier. "Sweet Puppies and Cute Babies: Perceptual Adaptation to Baby Facedness Transfers across Species." *PLOS ONE* 8.3 ( 2013): e58248.

Gong Jing Qi 龚惊奇. "Fa shaozi de ren 潑哨ふ哋亾 [The Whistle-Giver]." WeChat, March 10, 2020. https://mp.weixin.qq.com/s/hIc2z4INbg2YkoMvXIIZ6Q.

Gong Yan 龚滟. "Lun Meiguo wenhua shuchu zhanlue 论美国文化输出战略 [On the American Strategy of Cultural Export.]" *Yanshan University Journal: Philosophy and Social Sciences* 03 (2003): 63–67.

González-Reimann, Luis. "Cosmic Cycles, Cosmology, and Cosmography." In *Brill's Encyclopedia of Hinduism Online*, edited by Knut A. Jacobsen, Helene Basu, Angelika Malinar, and Vasudha Narayanan, 411–428. Leiden: Brill, 2016.

Graham, Mark. "Geography/Internet: Ethereal Alternate Dimensions of Cyberspace or Grounded Augmented Realities?" *The Geographical Journal* 179, no. 2 (2013): 177–82.

Griffiths, James. *The Great Firewall of China: How to Build and Control an Alternative Version of the Internet.* London: Bloomsbury Publishing, 2021.

Guan, Qiaoqiao 关俏俏, and Lin,Guangyao 林光耀. "Zhongguo shuzi jingji guimo da 39.2 wanyi yuan 中国数字经济规模达39,2万亿元 [The Scale of China's Digital Economy Reaches 39.2 Trillion Yuan]." *Xinhua News Agency*, 26 September 2021. http://www.gov.cn/xinwen/2021-09/26/content_5639469.htm.

Guangzhou Daily. 'Guangzhou jianjue luoshi shengyiji xiangying yaoqiu jianjue daying yiqing fangkong zhechang yingzhan 广州坚决落实省一级响应要求 坚决打赢疫情防控这场硬战 [Guangzhou Will Resolutely Implement Provincial-Level Response and Win the Tough Battle of Epidemic Prevention]'. *Guangzhou People's Government* (January 26, 2020). http://www.gz.gov.cn/zt/qlyfdyyqfkyz/gzzxd/content/post_5643135.html.

Guo, Shaohua. "The Appeal of Style: Han Han and Microcultural Contention in Digital China." *Modern Chinese Literature and Culture* 28.2 (2016): 90–138.

Guo, Shaohua. *The Evolution of the Chinese Internet: Creative Visibility in the Digital Public.* Stanford: Stanford University Press, 2020.

Habermas, Jürgen. "The Public Sphere: An Encyclopedia Article (1964)," trans. Sara Lennox and Frank Lennox. *New German Critique* 3 (1974): 49–55.

Hamm, John Christopher. *The Unworthy Scholar from Pingjiang: Republican-Era Martial Arts Fiction*. New York; Chichester, West Sussex: Columbia University Press, 2019.

Han Song 韩松. "Shanzhai 山寨 [Mountain Camp]." *Zhongguo Zuojia* no.6 (2020):15–24.

Hardt, Michael. "Affective Labor." *Boundary 2* 26.2 (1999): 89–100.

Hartmann, Heidi. "The Unhappy Marriage of Marxism and Feminism: Towards a More Progressive Union." *Capital & Class* 3 no. 2 (1979): 1–33.

Harvey, David Robert. *The Condition of Postmodernity: An Enquiry into the Origins of Cultural Change*. [3rd repr.]. Cambridge (MA) and Oxford: Blackwell, 1989.

Harvey, Peter. "Dukkha, Non-Self, and the Teaching on the Four 'Noble Truths.'" In *A Companion to Buddhist Philosophy*, edited by Steven M. Emmanuel, 26–45. Chichester: Wiley Blackwell, 2013.

Hayes, Brian. "First Links in the Markov Chain." *American Scientist* 101.2 (2013): 92-97.

Hayles, Katherine. *How We Became Posthuman: Virtuas Bodies in Cybernetics*. Chicago: University of Chicago Press, 2015.

He Zhongli 何忠礼. "Lüelun lishi shang de bihui 略论历史上的避讳 [A Brief Discussion of The Avoidance of Taboos in History]." *Zhejiang daxue xueban (renwen shehui kexue ban)* 32.1 (2002): 82–88.

Healey, Cara. "Estranging Realism in Chinese Science Fiction: Hybridity and Environmentalism in Chen Qiufan's 'The Waste Tide.'" *Modern Chinese Literature and Culture* 29.2 (2017): 1–33.

Hillenbrand, Margaret. "Remaking Tank Man, in China." *Journal of Visual Culture* 16, no. 2 (August 1, 2017): 127–66.

Hinderliter, Beth, William Kaizen, Vered Maimon, Jaleh Mansoor, and Seth McCormick, eds. *Communities of Sense: Rethinking Aesthetics and Politics*. Durham, NC: Duke University Press, 2009.

Hitchon, Jacqueline C., and Jerzy O. Jura. "Allegorically Speaking: Intertextuality of the Postmodern Culture and Its Impact on Print and Television Advertising." *Communication Studies* 48.2 (1997): 142–58.

Ho, Jason. "Caishichang li jian meishuguan, neng gei tanfan gengduo zunyan ma? 菜市场里建美术馆，能给摊贩更多尊严吗？ [Can We Let Market Stall Owners Feel Dignity, When Building an Art Museum in a Market?]." *Sanlian Life Weekly* (September 9, 2020). https://finance.sina.cn/2020-09-09/detail-iivhvpwy5824976.d.html?cre=wappage&mod=r&loc=4&r=0&rfunc=0&tj=wap_news_relate.

Ho, Jason. Private Correspondence, October 3, 2020.

Ho, Johnny, Felix Po, Jia Zhou, and Daniel Zipser. *China Consumer Report 2020: The Many Faces of the Chinese Consumer*. New York: McKinsey & Company, 2019.

Hockx, Michel. *Internet Literature in China*. New York: Columbia University Press, 2015.

Hockx, Michel. (ed.). *The Literary Field of Twentieth Century China*. Honolulu: University of Hawai'i Press, 1999.

Hockx, Michel. "The Literary Field and the Field of Power: The Case of Modern China," *Paragraph* 35.1 (2012): 49–65.

Hoffman, Samantha. "Programming China: The Communist Party's autonomic approach to managing state security." *China Monitor* (blog), December 12, 2017.

Holmes, Ros. "Meanwhile in China ... Miao Ying and the Rise of ChInternet Ugly." *ARTMargins* 7, no. 1 (February 1, 2018): 31–57.

Hong Kong Film Development Council. *A Collection of Information about Hong Kong Film Industry 2012*. Hong Kong: Hong Kong Motion Picture Industry Association, 2013.

Hong Kong Film Development Council. *A Collection of Information about Hong Kong Film Industry 2014*. Hong Kong: Hong Kong Motion Picture Industry Association, 2015.

Hong Kong Film Development Council. *A Collection of Information about Hong Kong Film Industry 2015*. Hong Kong: Hong Kong Motion Picture Industry Association, 2016.

Hong Kong Film Development Council. *A Collection of Information about Hong Kong Film Industry 2017*. Hong Kong: Hong Kong Motion Picture Industry Association, 2018.

Hong Kong Film Development Council. *A Collection of Information about Hong Kong Film Industry 2019*. Hong Kong: Hong Kong Motion Picture Industry Association, 2020.

Hong Kong Legislative Council. "LCQ2: Influence of Offices Set Up in Hong Kong by Departments of the Central People's Government (June 13, 2018)." Hong Kong: Hong Kong SAR Government, 2018. Available at: https://www.info.gov.hk/gia/general/201806/13/P2018061300454.htm

Hou, Rui. "Neoliberal Governance or Digitalized Autocracy? The Rising Market for Online Opinion Surveillance in China." *Surveillance & Society* 15, no. 3/4 (August 9, 2017): 418–24.

Hsiao, Chi-hua. "Authenticating Discourses of 'Being Oneself' on Monetary-Motivated Livestreams." *Discourse, Context & Media* 47 (June 1, 2022): 100592.

Huang, Yunying. "On Sinofuturism: Resisting Techno-Orientalism in Understanding Kuaishou, Douyin, and Chinese A.I." *Screen Bodies* 5, no. 2 (December 1, 2020): 46–62.

Hunziker, Marcel, Matthias Buchecker, and Terry Hartig. "Space and Place – Two Aspects of the Human-Landscape Relationship." In *A Changing World: Challenges for Landscape Research*, edited by Felix Kienast, Otto Wildi, and Sucharita Ghosh, 47–62. Landscape Series. Dordrecht: Springer Netherlands, 2007.

Huoxingwen. “Zaixian huoxingwen zhuanhuan qi 在线火星文转换器 [Online Martian Script Converter].” https://www.aies.cn/huoxingwen.htm.

Imbach, Jessica. “Chinese Science Fiction in the Anthropocene.” *Ecozon@: European Journal of Literature, Culture and Environment* 12, no. 1 (February 7, 2021): 121–37.

Inwood, Heather. “Making Worlds in Chinese Internet Fiction.” China’s New Super Cities: A Cultural Journey. Guest lecture at University of St. Gallen, St. Gallen, Switzerland, May 2, 2023.

Inwood, Heather. *Verse Going Viral: China’s New Media Scenes.* Seattle: University of Washington Press, 2014.

Iovene, Paola. *Tales of Futures Past: Anticipation and the Ends of Literature in Contemporary China*. Stanford: Stanford University Press, 2014.

Isaacson, Nathaniel. *Celestial Empire: The Emergence of Chinese Science Fiction*. Middletown: Wesleyan University Press, 2017.

Ito, Mizuko, Daisuke Okabe, and Izumi Tsuji (eds.). *Fandom Unbound: Otaku Culture in a Connected World.* New Haven, CT: Yale University Press, 2012.

Ivanhoe, Philip J. “Filial Piety as a Virtue.” In *Filial Piety in Chinese Thought and History,* edited by Alan K. L. Chan and Sor-hoon Tan, 189-202. London: Routledge, 2004.

Jagušcik, Justyna, and Jessica Imbach. “Digital Society in China.” *Asiatische Studien – Études Asiatiques* 76, no. 1 (March 1, 2022): 1–9.

Jameson, Frederic. *Archeologies of the Future: The Desire Called Utopia and Other Science Fictions*. London: Verso, 2005.

Jameson, Frederic. “Future City.” *New Left Review*, no. 21 (June 1, 2003): 65–79.

Jameson, Frederic. *Postmodernism, or, The Cultural Logic of Late Capitalism*. Duke University Press, 2013.

Jarrett, Kylie. “Labor of Love: An Archaeology of Affect as Power in e-Commerce.” *Journal of Sociology* 39 no. 4 (2003): 335–351.

Jarrett, Kylie. “The Relevance of ‘Women’s Work’: Social Reproduction and Immaterial Labor in Digital Media.” *Television & New Media* 15 no. 1 (2014): 14–29.

Jenkins, Henry. *Confronting the Challenges of Participatory Culture: Media Education for the 21st Century.* Cambridge, MA: The MIT Press, 2009.

Jia Liyuan 贾立元. “‘Guangrong Zhonghua’: Liu Cixin kehuan xiaoshuo zhong de Zhongguo xingxiang ‘光荣中华’:刘慈欣科幻小说中的中国形象 [’Glorious China’: The Image of China in Liu Cixin’s Works].” *Bohai daxue xuebao*, no. 1 (2011): 39–45.

Jiang, Min. “Authoritarian Informationalism: China’s Approach to Internet Sovereignty.” *SAIS Review of International Affairs* 30.2 (2010): 71–89.

Jin Guantao 金观涛, and Liu Qingfeng 刘青峰. *Xingsheng yu weiji – Lun Zhongguo fengjian shehui de chaowending jiegou* 兴盛与危机：论中国社会超稳定结

构 [Ascendancy and Crisis – On the Ultrastable Structure of Chinese Feudal Society]. Hunan Renmin chubanshe, 1980.

Jinjiang Literature City 晋江文学城. “Guanyu Jinjiang 关于晋江 [About Jinjiang].” http://www.jjwxc.net/aboutus/#fragment-33.

Jinjiang Literature City 晋江文学城. “Xianqing 闲情 [Leisurely and Carefree Mood].” https://bbs.jjwxc.net/board.php?board=3&page=1.

91Xiangpi (Jiuyi xiangpi). “‘Feihua shiren’ Yang Li & Fenghuang wang: Zai Zhongguo, zhi you ‘feihua’ shi kexin de ‘废话诗人’ 杨黎&凤凰网:在中国，只有 ‘废话’ 是可信的 [*Feihua* poet, Yang Li & Fenghuang wang: In China Only Feihua is Trustworthy].” http://91xiangpi.com/thread-195-1-1.html.

Johnson, Matthew D., Luke Vulpiani, Keith B. Wagner, and Kiki Tianqi Yu. *China's IGeneration: Cinema and Moving Image Culture for the Twenty-First Century.* London: Bloomsbury Academic, 2014.

Jordanous, Anna. “Evaluating Evaluation: Assessing Progress in Computational Creativity Research.” Proceedings of the Second International Conference on Computational Creativity (ICCC-11) (August 19, 2014): 102–107. https://kar.kent.ac.uk/42374/.

Jordanous, Anna. Evaluating Computational Creativity: A Standardised Procedure for Evaluating Creative Systems and Its Application. Doctor of Philosophy (PhD) thesis, University of Sussex, 2012. https://kar.kent.ac.uk/42388/

Jordanous, Anna. “A Standardised Procedure for Evaluating Creative Systems: Computational Creativity Evaluation Based on What it is to be Creative.” *Cognitive Computation* 4.3 (2012):246–279.

Jung-Kim, Jennifer. “*My Sassy Girl* Goes around the World.” In Yasue Kuwahara (ed.), *The Korean Wave*, 85–100. New York: Palgrave Macmillan, 2014.

Khazanah Research Institute, “Time to Care: Gender Inequality, Unpaid Care Work and Time Use Survey.” Kuala Lumpur: Kazanah Research Institute, 2019.

Kember, Sarah, and Joanna Zylinska. *Life After New Media: Mediation as a Vital Process.* Cambridge, MA: MIT Press, 2012.

Kim, Soyoung. “Post-Contact Zones: (En)Countering COVID-19.” *Inter-Asia Cultural Studies* 21.4 (2020): 557–565.

Kirschenbaum, Matthew G. “What Is Digital Humanities and What's It Doing in English Departments?” *Association of Departments of English Bulletin* (2010): 150.

Kline, Ronald R. *The Cybernetics Moment: Or Why We Call Our Age the Information Age.* JHU Press, 2015.

Knockel, Jeffrey et al. “(Can't) Picture This: An Analysis of Image Filtering on WeChat Moments.” *Citizen Lab* (August 14, 2018). https://citizenlab.ca/2018/08/cant-picture-this-an-analysis-of-image-filtering-on-wechat-moments/.

Kokas, Aynne. “Platform Patrol: China, the United States, and the Global Battle for Data Security.” *Journal of Asian Studies* 77.4 (2018): 923–933.

Kolb, Anjuli Fatima Raza. *Epidemic Empire: Colonialism, Contagion, and Terror, 1817-2020*. Chicago: University of Chicago Press, 2020.

Krenz, Joanna. "Do China's Robots Dream the China Dream?" In *Sinophone Utopias: Exploring Futures Beyond the China Dream,* edited by Andrea Riemenschnitter, Jessica Imbach and Justyna Jaguścik, 41–60. Amherst: Cambria Press, 2023.

Krenz, Joanna. "Ice Cream in the Cathedral: The Literary Failures and Social Success of Chinese Robot Poet Xiao Bing." *Asiatische Studien* 74.3 (2020): 547–581.

Krenz, Joanna. *In Search of Singularity: Polish and Chinese Poetry Since 1989*. Leiden: Brill, 2022.

Kuaishou. *Announcement of the Results for the Three Months Ended March 31, 2022*. Kuaishou Technology, 24 May 2022.

Kuaishou. *First Quarter Financial and Operational Data of 2021*. Kuaishou Technology, 24 May 2021. https://ir.kuaishou.com/zh-hans/node/6996/pdf.

Kuaishou. *Second Quarter Financial and Operational Data of 2021*. Kuaishou Technology, 25 August 2021. https://ir.kuaishou.com/zh-hans/node/7036/pdf.

Kuaishou. *Third Quarter Financial and Operational Data of 2021*. Kauishou Technology, 23 November 2021. https://ir.kuaishou.com/zh-hant/news-releases/news-release-details/kuaishoukejifabu2021niandisanjiduyeji/.

Kuang, Lanlan. "China's Emerging Food Media." *Gastronomica* 17.3 (2017): 68-81.

Kunze, Rui. "Tasting a Good Life: Narratives and Counter-Narratives of Happiness in the Documentary *A Bite of China* (2014)." *China Perspectives* 1-2 (2018): 45-53.

Lam, Tong. "The People's Algorithms: Social Credits and the Rise of China's Big (Br) Other." In *The New Politics of Numbers,* edited by Andrea Mennicken and Robert Salais, 71–95. Cham: Palgrave Macmillan, 2022.

Lan, Feng. "Zhang Yimou's *Hero*: Reclaiming the Martial Arts Film for 'All under Heaven.'" *Modern Chinese Literature and Culture* 20, no. 1 (Spring 2008): 1–43.

Laizi Yuanfang 来自远方. *Chongsheng cheng lie bao* 重生成猎豹 [*Becoming a Cheetah*]. *Jinjiang Literature City*, 2012. http://www.jjwxc.net/onebook.php?novelid=1580141.

Lee, Carmen K. M. "Linguistic Features of Email and ICQ Instant Messaging in Hong Kong." In Brenda Danet and Susan C. Herring (eds.), *The Multilingual Internet: Language, Culture and Communication Online*, 185–208. New York: Oxford University Press, 2007.

Lee, Ellen. "Pandemic Panic: A Wake-up Call for the Art Market." *Peng Art District* (April 24, 2020). https://penangartdistrict.com/pandemic-panic-a-wake-up-call-for-the-art-market/.

Leisilin Raist (@雷斯林 Raist). "Li Ziqi zenme jiu bushi wenhua shuchu le ? 李子柒怎么就不是文化输出了? [How Come Li Ziqi Does Not Count as a Cultural Export?]" *Sina Weibo* (December 5, 2019). https://card.weibo.com/article/m/show/id/2309404446136898289811?_wb_client_=1.

Levine, Caroline. *Forms: Whole, Rhythm, Hierarchy, Network.* Princeton, NJ: Princeton University Press, 2015.

Li Chenhe 李晨赫. "Rengong zhineng Xiao Bing: zai renlei sheding de kuangjia xia ziyou feixiang 人工智能小冰:在人类设定的框架下自由飞翔 [Artificial Intelligence Xiao Bing: Freely within a Framework Designed by Humans)." *Zhongguo qingnian bao* 27.6 (2017).

Li Hao 李昊. "Xin shiqing xiaoshuo de fuxing – Qiantan 'zhongtian wen' de zouhong 新世情小说的复兴——浅谈"种田文"的走红 [A Revival of the Novel of Manners: The Popularization of Farming Fiction]." *Contemporary Literary Criticism* 5 (2013): 64–67.

Li, Hua. *Chinese Science Fiction during the Post-Mao Cultural Thaw.* Toronto: University of Toronto Press, 2021.

Li Mei 李玫. *Xin shiqi wenxue zhong de shengtai lunli jingshen* 新时期文学中的生态伦理精神 [The Ecological Ethics In The New-Era Literature]. Beijing: Beijing Book Co. Inc., 2016.

Li Ru 李如, and Zongfa Wang 王宗法. "Lun Mingdai shen mo xiaoshuo dui dangdai wangluo xuanhuan xiaoshuo de yingxiang 论明代神魔小说对当代网络玄幻小说的影响 [On Influences of God-demon Fiction from Ming Dynasty on Contemporary Online Xuanhuan Fiction]." *Journal of Ming-Qing Fiction Studies* 113, no. 3 (2014): 4–15.

Li Shanshan 李珊珊. "Xinlang zimeiti yanjiu – yi 'Li Ziqi' weili 新浪微博自媒体研究——以"李子柒"为例[A Study of Self-Media on Sina Weibo: Taking 'Li Ziqi' as an Example.]" *West Radio and TV* 22 (2019): 24–27.

Li, Wai-yee. *Enchantment and Disenchantment: Love and Illusion in Chinese Literature.* Princeton, NJ: Princeton University Press, 2014.

Li Wei李伟."Weibo, wanghong datuishou, xin meiti touzijia: 'xiannü' Li Ziqi shenhou de shengyiren 微博、网红大推手、新媒体投资家："仙女"李子柒身后的生意人 [Weibo, Influencer Managers, New Media Investors: Businessmen behind the 'Immortal Fairy' Li Ziqi.]" *Tengxun News* (December 13, 2019). https://www.36kr.com/p/1724825124865.

Li Yiming 李一鸣. "Gutu yu jiayuan: Xin shiji wangluo xiangtu wenxue toushi 故土与家园: 新世纪网络乡土文学透视 [Native Land and Homeland: A study of 'Local Literature' in the Creation of New-century Network Novels]." *Journal of Hainan Normal University (Social Sciences)* 30.5 (2017): 7–12.

Li, Yifei, and Judith Shapiro. *China Goes Green: Coercive Environmentalism for a Troubled Planet.* New York: John Wiley & Sons, 2020.

Li Ziqi. "Official Announcement from Liziqi Youtube Channel." YouTube, March 6, 2019. https://www.youtube.com/watch?v=hL5HlwzuAUA.

Li Ziqi. "Peanut and melon seeds, dried meat, dried fruit, snowflake cake – snacks for Spring Festival." YouTube, January 31, 2019. https://www.youtube.com/watch?v=FWMIPukvdsQ.

Li Ziqi. "Liuzhou '*Luosifen*': Slurpy, Spicy, and Absolutely Satisfying." YouTube, August 11, 2019. https://www.youtube.com/watch?v=_jUJrIWp2I4.

Li Ziqi (@李子柒). "Summer is the time to harvest bamboo shoots ..." Weibo, August 6, 2019, 19:48. https://weibo.com/mianyangdanshen?is_all=1&stat_date=201908#feedtop.

Li Ziqi (@李子柒). "Gratitude to our country, gratitude to all!..." Weibo, May 18, 2017, 13:51. https://weibo.com/mianyangdanshen?is_all=1&stat_date=201705#1651672630632.

Li Ziqi (@李子柒). "Sorry ... I will stop uploading my videos for the time being........" Weibo, May 13, 2017, 13:47. https://weibo.com/mianyangdanshen?is_all=1&stat_date=201705#_rnd1651672219984.

Li Ziqi (@李子柒). "Those who love me, thank you." Weibo, May 13, 2017, 14:23. https://weibo.com/mianyangdanshen?is_all=1&stat_date=201705#_rnd1651672309473.

Li Ziqi Music. "DJ Liziqi" Was Criticized for Cooking Too Salty. But It Was Her Feelings for Grandpa." YouTube, 19. 07. 2022. https://www.youtube.com/watch?v=FmXi2NTWkpE.

Liao, Yi, Yansheng Wang, Qun Liu, and Xin Jiang. "GPT-Based Generation for Classical Chinese Poetry." *ArXiv* (2019): 1-16.

Lin, Rouwen. "Malaysian Art Scene Not Digitally Savvy Enough to Adapt to Covid-19 Crisis." *The Star* (March 25, 2020). https://www.thestar.com.my/lifestyle/culture/2020/03/25/covid-19-situation-exposes-the-malaysian-art-scene039s-lack-of-digital-adaptability?fbclid=IwAR0320HJYe4BTVoMp4PEnE1XSymJtLpUb33lnGA9SB1Rg-MCi8oe4m163iA.

Linderman, Deborah, Julia Kristeva, and Leon S. Roudiez. "Powers of Horror: An Essay on Abjection." *SubStance* 13.3/4 (1984): 140.

Liu Cixin 刘慈欣. *Liu Cixin tan kehuan* 刘慈欣谈科幻 [Liu Cixin on Science Fiction]. Wuhan: Hubei kexue jishu chubanshe, 2013.

Liu Cixin 刘慈欣. "Zhongguo 2185 中国2185 [China 2185]." Kehuan xiaoshuo wang. http://www.kehuan.net.cn/book/2185.html.

Liu, Lydia He. *Translingual Practice: Literature, National Culture, and Translated Modernity –China, 1900-1937*. Stanford University Press, 1995.

Liu, Lydia He. "Wittgenstein in the Machine." *Critical Inquiry* 47.3 (2021): 425–455.

Liu Hui 六回. "Wo wei shenme yao chuzu ziji 我为什么要出租自己 [Why Should I Rent Myself Out?]." *UQnMedia*, WeChat, June 9, 2015. https://mp.weixin.qq.com/s/guvAnLqpBoeeWuj1xT_1RA?fbclid=IwAR156c5tw5pY5VGtP3fsKMrTnjeu1SwFUQfdjXWDNAUkrsJ40RAAZWh-NDM.

Liu, Tao 刘涛. "Qinggan kangzheng: biaoyan shi kangzheng de qinggan kuangjia yu daode yufa 情感表演式抗争的情感框架与道德语法[Emotional Struggle: The Emotional Framework and Moral Grammar of Performative Struggle]." *Journal of Wuhan University: Humanities Edition* 69 no.5 (2016).

Liu, Ting. "Boys' Love in Girls' Hands: The Survival of a Gendered Youth Culture in Mainland China and Hong Kong." Doctoral dissertation, Australian National University, 2011.

Liu Xia 刘霞. "Foxi de Guangzhou dangdai yishu, bei bianyuanhua le ma? "佛系"的广州当代艺术，被边缘化了吗? [Buddha-like Guangzhou Contemporary Art, Has It Been Marginalized?]." *Hiart.cn* (January 28, 2018). http://www.hiart.cn/feature/detail/eb8ipBr.html.

Liu, Xiao. *Information Fantasies: Precarious Mediation in Postsocialist China*. Minneapolis: University of Minnesota Press, 2019.

Lo, Yuet Keung. "Filial Devotion for Women: A Buddhist Testimony from Third-Century China." In *Filial Piety in Chinese Thought and History,* edited by Alan K. L. Chan and Sor-hoon Tan, 71–90. London: Routledge, 2004.

Louie, Kam. "Chinese Masculinity Studies in the Twenty-First Century: Westernizing, Easternizing and Globalizing *Wen* and *Wu*." *NORMA* 9.1 (2014): 18–29, https://doi.org/10.1080/18902138.2014.892283.

Louie, Kam. *Theorising Chinese Masculinity: Society and Gender in China.* Cambridge, UK: Cambridge University Press, 2002.

Lu Xun 鲁迅. *A Brief History of Chinese Fiction*. Translated by Hsien-yi Yang and Gladys Yang. Beijing: Foreign Languages Press, 1976.

Lu Xun 鲁迅. Lu Xun quanji 鲁迅全集 [Collected Works of Lu Xun]. Beijing: Renmin wenxue chubanshe, 1973.

Lu Xun 鲁迅. *Zhongguo xiaoshuo shi lue* 中国小说史略 [A Brief History of Chinese Novels]. Tianjin: Baihua wenyi chubanshe, 2002.

Lugton, Martin. "Reflection on the Art Gallery of the Future and Why We Must Digitize Art." *Reflections* (February 6, 2011). https://reflectionsandcontemplations.wordpress.com/2011/02/06/why-art-must-be-digitized/.

Lukacs, Gabriella. "Dreamwork: Cell Phone Novelists, Labor, and Politics in Contemporary Japan." *Cultural Anthropology* 28 no. 1 (2013): 44–64.

Luo Jiaqi. "Why Is Post-COVID China Embracing a Cyberpunk Aesthetic?" Jing Daily, October 7, 2020. https://jingdaily.com/china-luxury-trends-cyberpunk-covid-louis-vuitton/.

Lykke, Nina. *Feminist Studies: A Guide to Intersectional Theory, Methodology and Writing*. New York: Routledge, 2010.

Lynch, Aaron. *Thought Contagion: How Belief Spreads Through Society*. New York: Basic Books, 1996.

Lyotard, Jean-François. *The Postmodern Condition: A Report on Knowledge*. Minneapolis: University of Minnesota Press, 1984.

Ma Boyong 马伯庸. "Jijing zhi cheng 寂静之城 [City of Silence]." Kehuan xiaoshuo wang. http://www.kehuan.net.cn/book/jijingzhicheng.html.

Ma, Shaoling. *The Stone and the Wireless: Mediating China, 1861–1906.* Durham: Duke University Press, 2021.

Maganathan, Dinesh Kumar. “Cendana’s Food Aid Set to Reach More Arts and Cultural Workers.” *The Star* (June 28, 2021) https://www.thestar.com.my/lifestyle/culture/2021/06/28/cendana039s-food-aid-to-reach-more-arts-and-cultural-workers; Cultural Relations Platform.

Maitra, Ani, and Rey Chow. “What’s ‘in’? Disaggregating Asia through New Media Actants.” In *Routledge Handbook of New Media in Asia,* edited by Larissa Hjorth and Olivia Khoo, 29–39. London, New York: Routledge, 2015.

Mao Yijun毛翊君. “Li Ziqi: Wo lixiang de shenghuo jiushi wuyouwulü zijizizu 李子柒：我理想的生活就是无忧无虑自给自足 [Li Ziqi: My Ideal Is a Careless and Self-sufficient Life.]” *China Newsweek* (December 30, 2019). http://www.inewsweek.cn/people/2019-12-30/8203.shtml.

Marino, Mark C. *Critical Code Studies.* Cambridge, MA, USA: MIT Press, 2020.

Matei, Adrienne. “Country Life: The Young Female Farmer Who Is Now a Top Influencer in China.” *The Guardian* (January 28, 2020). https://www.theguardian.com/lifeandstyle/2020/jan/28/li-ziqi-china-influencer-rural-life.

McFarlane, Anna, Lars Schmeink, and Graham Murphy. *The Routledge Companion to Cyberpunk Culture*. Routledge, 2019.

McKinnon, Catherine A. “Intersectionality as Method: A Note.” *Signs, Intersectionality: Theorizing Power, Empowering Theory,* 38.4 (2013): 1019–1030.

McLaren, Helen Jaqueline, Karen Rosalind Wong, Kieu Nga Nguyen and Komalee Nadeeka Damayanth Mahamadachchi. “Covid-19 and Women’s Triple Burden: Vignettes from Sri Lanka, Malaysia, Vietnam and Australia.” *Social Sciences* 9.87 (2020): 1–11.

MDBC. “MCO Updates.” MDBC (Malaysian Dutch Business Council). https://www.mdbc.com.my/mco-updates/.

Mengdong Shiwu 孟冬十五. *Zao’er gou fajia ji* 枣儿沟发家记 [A Tale of Jujube Valley]. *Jinjiang Literature City,* 2016. http://www.jjwxc.net/onebook.php?novelid=2622579.

Miller, Vincent. *Understanding Digital Culture.* London: Sage, 2011.Mitchell, W. J. T. “Introduction.” In *Critical Terms for Media Studies,* edited by Mark B. N. Hansen and W. J. T. Mitchell, vii-xxii. Chicago, University of Chicago Press, 2010.

Milner, Ryan. *The World Made Meme: Public Conversations and Participatory Media.* Cambridge, MA: The MIT Press, 2016.

Mittler, Barbara. *A Newspaper for China?: Power, Identity, and Change in Shanghai’s News Media, 1872–1912*. Cambridge, MA; London: Harvard University Asia Center, 2004.

Moretti, Franco. *Distant Reading.* London: Verso, 2013.

Mozur, Paul, Jonah M. Kessel, and Melissa Chan. "Made in China, Exported to the World: The Surveillance State." The New York Times, April 24, 2019, sec. Technology. https://www.nytimes.com/2019/04/24/technology/ecuador-surveillance-cameras-police-government.html.

Mr. Pizza. *Naye lingchen, wozuo shangle Wangjiao kaiwang Dabu de hong van* 那夜凌晨，我坐上了旺角開往大埔的紅 Van [Lost on a Red Mini Bus to Taipo]. Hong Kong: Kind of Culture Publication, 2012.

Mujezinovic, Davor. "Electronic Waste in Guiyu: A City under Change?" *Environment and Society Portal* (August 29, 2019).

Murray, Simone. *Introduction to Contemporary Print Culture Books as Media*. London, Routledge, 2021.

Nagy, Peter, and Bernadett Koles. "The Digital Transformation of Human Identity: Towards a Conceptual Model of Virtual Identity in Virtual Worlds." *Convergence* 20.3 (2014): 276–292.

Nanthini, S. and Tamara Nair. "COVID-19 and the Impacts on Women." *NTS Insight* IN20-05 (July 2020): 1–11.

Negri, Antonio, and Michael Hardt. *Empire*, vol. 15. Cambridge, MA: Harvard University Press, 2001.

Ng, Eve, and Xiaomeng Li. "A Queer 'Socialist Brotherhood': The *Guardian* Web Series, Boys' Love Fandom, and the Chinese State." *Feminist Media Studies* 20, no. 4 (May 18, 2020): 479–95.

Notion. "Fa shaozi de ren 发哨子的人 [The Whistle-Giver]." *notion.so* (March 9, 2020). https://www.notion.so/00a9beeb2fe54dfe84a55141a5f592cf?v=cf2bfae990fc4207a8710a40ffeb7f3c.

Oliveira, Hugo Gonçalo. "Automatic Generation of Poetry: An Overview." Universidade de Coimbra, 2009.

Oliveira, Hugo Gonçalo. "A Survey on Intelligent Poetry Generation: Languages, Features, Techniques, Reutilisation and Evaluation." *Proceedings of the 10th International Conference on Natural Language Generation* (2017): 11-20.

Papacharissi, Zizi. "The Virtual Sphere: The Internet as a Public Sphere." *New Media & Society* 4.1 (2002): 9–27.

Pariser, Eli. *The Filter Bubble: What the Internet Is Hiding from You*. New York: Penguin Press, 2011.

Pascaru, Paula. *Poezia chineză colocvială ca practică culturală heterodoxă* [Chinese Colloquial Poetry as Heterodox Cultural Practice]. PhD dissertation. Bucharest: Printech, 2018.

Pellegrino, Manuela. "COVID-19: The 'Invisible Enemy and Contingent Racism': Reflections of an Italian Anthropologist Conducting Fieldwork in Greece." *Anthropology Today* 36.3 (2020): 19–21.

People's Daily (@人民日報). "[# Hallo, Tomorrow #] Li Ziqi's Videos Are Able to Attract Numerous Followers from outside China without Using a Single

English Word...." Weibo, December 6, 2019, 23:43. https://weibo.com/rmrb?is_all=1&stat_date=201912&page=21#_rnd1652091203850.

Peters, John Durham. *The Marvelous Clouds: Toward a Philosophy of Elemental Media*. Chicago: University of Chicago Press, 2015.

Plantin, Jean-Christophe, Carl Lagoze, Paul N. Edwards, and Christian Sandvig. "Infrastructure Studies Meet Platform Studies in the Age of Google and Facebook." *New Media & Society* 20, no. 1 (January 1, 2018): 293–310.

Plantin, Jean-Christophe, and Gabriele de Seta. "WeChat as Infrastructure: The Techno-Nationalist Shaping of Chinese Digital Platforms." *Chinese Journal of Communication* 12, no. 3 (July 3, 2019): 257–73.

Pratt, Mary Louise. "Arts of the Contact Zone." In *Profession* (1991): 33–40.

Pratt, Mary Louise. "Linguistic Utopias." In *The Linguistics of Writing: Arguments between Language and Literature*, edited by Nigel Fabb, 48–66. Manchester: Manchester University Press, 1987.

Pure White. "Woya yehua Yiqian youge zhanjiao Taizi" 我呀爺話以前有個站叫太子 [My Grandpa Said There Was a Station Called Prince Edward]. *LIHKG Forum* (18 September 2019). Available at: https://lihkg.com/thread/1578985/page/1

QAGOMA. "Pangrok Sulap." Queensland Art Gallery / Gallery of Modern Art. https://www.qagoma.qld.gov.au/whats-on/exhibitions/past-exhibitions/the-9th-asia-pacific-triennial-of-contemporary-art-apt9/artists/pangrok-sulap.

Qiu Lian 丘濂. "Nage yu meishuguan xianglian de caishichang, xiaoshile 那个与美术馆相连的菜市场，消失了 [The Market Link to An Art Museum Disappeared]." *Sanlian Life Weekly* (October 30, 2020). https://mp.weixin.qq.com/s/t9n6OoZY09cM3e1LFyM13w.

Rae, Ian and Morgen Witzel. *The Overseas Chinese of South East Asia: History, Culture, Business*. Basingstoke: Palgrave Macmillan, 2008.

Raedts, Maddie. "How China's Digital Ecosystems Are Shaping Western Social Media's Future." Forbes, March 8, 2021. https://www.forbes.com/sites/forbesagencycouncil/2021/03/08/how-chinas-digital-ecosystems-are-shaping-western-social-medias-future/.

Rancière, Jacques. "Politics, Identification, Subjectivization." In *The Identity in Question*, edited by John Rajchman, 63–72. London: Routledge, 1995.

Rao, Tejal. "The Reclusive Food Celebrity Li Ziqi Is My Quarantine Queen." *The New York Times* (April 22, 2020). https://www.nytimes.com/2020/04/22/dining/li-ziqi-chinese-food.html.

Raun, Tobias. "Capitalizing intimacy: New subcultural forms of micro-celebrity strategies and affective labour on YouTube." *Convergence: The International Journal of Research into New Media Technologies* 24.1 (2018): 99-113.

Reay, Diane. "Gendering Bourdieu's Concepts of Capitals? Emotional Capital, Women and Social Class." *The Sociological Review* 52 supp. 2 (2004): 57–74Rémi, Vincent. *Multilingual Poetry Generation: Roses Are Red, Les Violets Seus Bleues.*

Master's thesis in Information Systems. Norwegian University of Science and Technology, 2019.

Reed, Christopher A. *Gutenberg in Shanghai: Chinese Print Capitalism, 1876–1937.* Honolulu: University of Hawai'i Press, 2004.

Ricciardelli, Rosemary, Kimberley A. Clow, and Philip White. "Investigating Hegemonic Masculinity: Portrayals of Masculinity in Men's Lifestyle Magazines." *Sex Roles* 63. 1–2 (2010): 64–78.

Riemenschnitter, Andrea. "Probing the Limits of Languaging: Material Ecology and Thing Agency in Yu Jian's Poetry." *International Communication of Chinese Culture* 6, no. 1 (2019): 39–61.

Ritzer, George, Paul Dean, and Nathan Jurgenson. "The Coming of Age of the Prosumer." *American Behavioral Scientist* 56 no. 4 (2012): 379–398.

Roh, David S., Betsy Huang, and Greta A. Niu. *Techno-Orientalism: Imagining Asia in Speculative Fiction, History, and Media*. Rutgers University Press, 2015.

Ruan, Lotus, Jeffrey Knockel, Jason Q. Ng, and Masashi Crete-Nishihata. "Censored Contagion: How Information on the Coronavirus is Managed on Chinese Social Media." *Citizen Lab* (March 3, 2020). https://citizenlab.ca/2020/03/censored-contagion-how-information-on-the-coronavirus-is-managed-on-chinese-social-media/.

Ruan, Lotus, Jeffrey Knockel, Jason Q. Ng, and Masashi Crete-Nishihata. "One App, Two Systems: How WeChat uses one censorship policy in China and another internationally." *Citizen Lab* (November 30, 2016). https://citizenlab.ca/2016/11/wechat-china-censorship-one-app-two-systems/.

Saukko, Paula. *Doing Research in Cultural Studies.* London: SAGE Publications Ltd, 2003.

Saussy, Haun. *The Marking of Barbarians: Chinese Literature and Multilingual Asia.* Princeton and Oxford: Princeton University Press, 2022.

Schiller, Dan. "Poles of Market Growth? Open Questions about China, Information and the World Economy." *Global Media and Communication* 1 no. 1 (2005): 79–103.

Schneider, Florian. *China's Digital Nationalism.* Oxford Studies in Digital Politics. New York: Oxford University Press, 2018.

Schouten, Alexander P., Loes Janssen and Maegan Verspaget. "Celebrity vs. Influencer endorsements in Advertising: The Role of Identification, Credibility, and Product-Endorser Fit." *International Journal of Advertising* 39.2 (2020): 258–281.

Seven Eleven 些分易呢墳. "Huoshi Xiangjiang" 活屍香江 [Living Dead, Hong Kong]. *Shikoto.* Available at: https://www.shikoto.com/articles/6260.html

Shao, Yanjun 邵燕君. *Wangluo shidai de wenxue yindu* 网络时代的文学引渡 [*Literature Extradition in the Internet Age*]. Guangxi daxue chubanshe, 2015. Kindle.

Shao, Yanjun 邵燕君. "Wangluo shidai: Xin wenxue chuantong de duanlie yu 'zhuliu wenxue' de chongjian 网络时代: 新文学传统的断裂与'主流文学'的重建 [The Internet Era: Ruptures of the New Literary Tradition and the Re-establishment of 'Mainstream Literature']." *Nanfang wentan*, no. 6 (2012): 14–21.

Shao, Yanjun 邵燕君. "Zai 'Yituobang' li jiangou 'geren linglei xuanze' huanxiang kongjian—Wangluo wenxue de yishi xingtai gongneng zhi yi zhong 在'异托邦'里建构'个人另类选择'幻象空间—网络文学的意识形态功能之一种 [Constructing Illusional Spaces for 'Individual Alternative Choices' in 'Heterotopia': One Type of Ideological Function of Online Literature]." *Wenyi yanjiu*, no. 4 (2012): 16–25.

Shao, Yanjun 邵燕君, and Wang Yusu 王玉王, eds. *Pobi shu* 破壁书 [*Keywords in Chinese Internet Subcultures*]. Beijing: SDX Joint Publishing Company, 2018.

Shapiro, Judith. *China's Environmental Challenges.* Cambridge, UK: Polity, 2012.

Shapiro, Judith. *Mao's War against Nature: Politics and the Environment in Revolutionary China*. Cambridge, UK: Cambridge University Press, 2001.

Shen, Lei, Xiaoyu Guo, and Meng Chen. "Compose Like Humans: Jointly Improving the Coherence and Novelty for Modern Chinese Poetry Generation." *IJCNN2020, Proceedings of 2020 International Joint Conference on Neural Networks* (*IJCNN*), 2020. http://arxiv.org/pdf/2005.01556v1.

Shen, Xinmei. "Here's Why VR Game for Sorting Trash Is Trending in China – Shanghai Residents Are Trying to Figure out How to Separate Their Trash Correctly" South China Morning Post, June 29, 2019. https://www.abacusnews.com/digital-life/heres-why-vr-game-sorting-trash-trending-china/article/3016297.

Shih, Shu-Mei. "The Concept of the Sinophone." *PMLA* 126, no. 3 (2011): 709–18.

Shih, Shu-Mei. "Introduction: What Is Sinophone Studies?" In *Sinophone Studies: A Critical Reader,* edited by Shu-mei Shih, Chien-hsin Tsai, and Brian Bernards, 1–16. New York: Columbia University Press, 2013.

Shih, Shu-Mei. *Visuality and Identity: Sinophone Articulations Across the Pacific*. Vol. 2. Asia Pacific Modern. Berkeley: University of California Press, 2007.

Sigalos, MacKenzie. "China's War on Crypto Just Hit a New Level With Its Latest Crypto Crackdown" CNBC, July 7, 2021. https://www.cnbc.com/2021/07/06/china-cracks-down-on-crypto-related-services-in-ongoing-war-on-bitcoin.html.

Silver, David. "Review: Interfacing American Culture: The Perils and Potentials of Virtual Exhibitions." *American Quarterly* 49, no. 4 (December 1997): 825–50.

Siu Sing Lo 小姓奴. Threads No. 25 and 96, "Aini xiangju shiliu ge xiaoshi" 愛你相距16小時 [Loving You from 16 Hours Away]. *Hong Kong Golden Forum* (17 August 2009). Available at: https://forum.hkgolden.com/thread/1835168/

Siu Sing Lo 小姓奴. *Xiaotian huiyi lu* 小甜回憶錄 [A Little Sweet Memoir]. Hong Kong: Steps Publication, 2014.

Song, Geng and Derek Hird. *Men and Masculinities in Contemporary China*. Leiden: Brill, 2013.

Song, Mingwei. "After 1989: The New Wave of Chinese Science Fiction." *China Perspectives* 1 (March 1, 2015): 7–13.

Song, Mingwei. "Variations on Utopia in Contemporary Chinese Science Fiction." *Science Fiction Studies* 40, no. 1 (2013): 86–102.

Sontag, Susan. *Illness as Metaphor*. New York: Farrar, Straus, and Giroux, 1978.

SQLI Digital Experience. "New Technologies Help Raise Chinese Citizens' Awareness of Waste Sorting." Sqli.com (May 14, 2020). https://www.sqli.com/int-en/insights-news/blog/new-technologies-help-raise-chinese-citizens-awareness-waste-sorting

Steinnes, Kamilla Knutsen. "Too Cute for Words: Cuteness Evokes the Kama Muta Emotion and Motivates Communal Sharing." Master's thesis, University of Oslo, 2017.

Stocchi, Manlio Pastore. "The Telescope: Outline of a Poetic History." *The Inspiration of Astronomical Phenomena VI.* 441 (2011): 37–42.

Strittmatter, Kai. *We Have Been Harmonised: Life in China's Surveillance State*. Exeter: Old Street Publishing, 2019.

Sun, Mengtian. "Imagining Globalization in Paolo Bacigalupi's 'The Windup Girl' and Chen Qiufan's 'The Waste Tide.'" *Science Fiction Studies* (2019): 289–306.

Surplus Value. "Wenyi, yuyan he juti de ren: Yu lishi xuejia Luo Xin liaotian 瘟疫,语言和具体的人:与历史学家罗新聊天 [The Pandemic, Language and Real People: A Chat with the Historian Luo Xin]." https://ipfs.io/ipfs/QmNXBfQ1v3J3dBvRoocrdzheCa5JVFnqzMAevV2kfXkG9N/.

Tahmasbi, Fatemeh, Leonard Schild, Chen Ling, Jeremy Blackburn, Gianluca Stringhini, Yang Zhang, and Savvas Zannettou. '"Go Eat a Bat, Chang!": An Early Look on the Emergence of Sinophobic Behavior on Web Communities in the Face of COVID-19'. *ArXiv* abs/2004.04046, 2020. https://arxiv.org/pdf/2004.04046.pdf.

Tam, Albert 譚劍. *Mianfei zhicheng jiaolucheng* 免費之城焦慮症 [Anxiety Order of the Free City]. Hong Kong: Gaia, 2020.

Tam, Albert 譚劍. *Xuni weilai* 虛擬未來 [The Future of an Illusion]. Hong Kong: Ling Lung Bik, 1997.

Tan, Chris, Jie Wang, Shengyuan Wangzhu, Jinjing Xu, and Chunxuan Zhu. "The Real Digital Housewives of China's Kuaishou Video-Sharing and Live-Streaming App." *Media, Culture & Society* 42 nos. 7–8 (2020): 1243–1259.

Tan, Beng-Kiang and Hafizur Rahaman. "Virtual Heritage: Reality and Criticism." In *Joining Languages, Cultures and Visions*, 143–56. Montréal: Les Presses de l'Université de Montréal, 2009.

Tan, M.K.B., and C.M. Tan. "Curating Wellness during a Pandemic in Singapore: COVID-19, Museums, and Digital Imagination." *Public Health* 192 (2021): 68–71.

Taneja, Harsh, and Angela Xiao Wu. "Does the Great Firewall Really Isolate the Chinese? Integrating Access Blockage With Cultural Factors to Explain Web User Behavior." *The Information Society* 30, no. 5 (October 20, 2014): 297–309.

Tangqi Gongzi 唐七公子. "Sansheng sanshi shi li taohua 三生三世十里桃花 [Eternal Love]." Situ 思兔. June 22, 2016. https://www.sto.cx/book-39192-1.html.

Terranova, Tiziana. "Free Labor: Producing Culture for the Digital Economy." *Social Text* 18 no. 2 (2000): 33–58.

Thornber, Karen. *Eco-Ambiguity: Environmental Crises and East Asian Literatures.* Ann Arbor: University of Michigan, 2012.

Tian, Xi. "More than Conformity or Resistance: Chinese "Boys' Love" Fandom in the Age of Internet Censorship." *The Journal of the European Association for Chinese Studies* 1 (2020): 189–213.

Tian, Xiaoli. "Fantasy Is More Believable: The Shadow Civil Sphere in Chinese Online Fiction." In *The Civil Sphere in East Asia*, edited by Jeffrey C. Alexander, David A. Palmer, Sunwoong Park, and Agnes Shuk-mei Ku, 167–87. Cambridge, UK: Cambridge University Press, 2019.

Toffler, Alvin. *The Third Wave*. New York, NY: William Morrow, 1980.

Tsai, Chien-hsin. "Issues and Controversies." In *Sinophone Studies: A Critical Reader,* edited by Shu-mei Shih and Chien-hsin Tsai, 17–24. New York: Columbia University Press, 2013.

Tsai Jhi-heng 蔡智恆. *Diyici de qinmi jiechu* 第一次的親密接觸 [The First Intimate Contact]. Taipei: Red Ink Publishing, 1998.

Tsang, Gabriel. "Parochial Apolitical Formulation: Hong Kong Internetization and the Sexualizing Cyberspace of the Storytelling Channels of the Golden Forum and the LIHKG Forum." *Sungkyun Journal of East Asian Studies* 20.1 (2020): 61–82.

Turner, Jonathan. *Human Emotions: A Sociological Theory.* Abingdon: Routledge, 2007.

Turner, Mark. *The Literary Mind. The Origins of Thought and Language.* Oxford: Oxford University Press, 1996.

Tyson, Loise. *Critical Theory Today: A User-Friendly Guide*. New York & London: Routledge, 2006.

Unicode Consortium, ed. *The Unicode Standard ver. 13.0*. California: Mountainview, 2020.

Uqinzen. "Uqin Poems #021." OpenSea. https://opensea.io/assets/ethereum/0x495f947276749ce646f68ac8c248420045cb7b5e/92211415342320932013735915780318807984342664770190883270814077310330187284481

Van Crevel, Maghiel. "Walk on the Wild Side. Snapshots of the Chinese Poetry Scene." *MCLC Resource Center.* December 2017. https://u.osu.edu/mclc/online-series/walk-on-the-wild-side/.

Van Crevel, Maghiel. "Transgression as Rule: Freebooters in Chinese Poetry." In *At the Shores of the Sky* edited by Paul W. Kroll and Jonathan A. Silk, 262-279. Leiden: Brill, 2021.

Van Dijck, José, Thomas Poell, and Martijn de Waal. *The Platform Society*. New York: Oxford University Press, 2018.

Veg, Sebastian. *Minjian: The Rise of China's Grassroots Intellectuals*. New York: Columbia University Press, 2019.

Venuti, Lawrence. *The Translator's Invisibility: A History of Translation*. London: Routledge, 1995.

Voci, Paola. *China on Video: Smaller-Screen Realities*. London, New York: Routledge, 2010.

Voigt, Rob and Dan Jurafsky. "Tradition and Modernity in 20th Century Chinese Poetry." Proceedings of the Workshop on Computational Linguistics for Literature, CLfL@NAACL-HLT 2013, (June 14, 2013) Atlanta.17-22.

Walkowitz, Rebecca L. *Born Translated: The Contemporary Novel in an Age of World Literature*. New York: Columbia University Press, 2015.

Wallis, Cara. *Technomobility in China: Young Migrant Women and Mobile Phones*. New York: New York University Press, 2013.

Wagner, Rudolf G. "Lobby Literature: The Archeology and Present Functions of Science Fiction in China." In *After Mao: Chinese Literature and Society, 1978–1981*, edited by Jeffrey C. Kinkley, 15–62. Harvard University Asia Center, 1985.

Wahab, Wandika. "The Outbreak of Covid-19 in Malaysia: Pushing Migrant Workers at the Margin." *Social Sciences & Humanities Open* 2 (2020): 1–9.

Wang, Ban. *Chinese Visions of World Order: Tianxia, Culture, and World Politics*. Durham, NC: Duke University Press, 2017.

Wang, Ban. *The Sublime Figure of History: Aesthetics and Politics in Twentieth-Century China*. Stanford, CA: Stanford University Press, 1997.

Wang Chenchung 王振忠. "Qixiong, qidi, qiyou, qifu, qizi 契兄、契弟、契友、契父、契子 [Sworn Brotherhood – An Analysis of Sun Ba Gets Fortune by Saving Man from a Historical Perspective]." *Chinese Studies*, 18,1 (2000): 163–85.

Wang, David Der-wei. *The Lyrical in Epic Time: Modern Chinese Intellectuals and Artists Through the 1949 Crisis*. New York: Columbia University Press, 2015.

Wang, David Der-wei 王德威. "Wenxue xinglü yu shijie xiangxiang 文學行旅與世界想像 [Literary Travel and World Imagination]." *Mingpao Monthly*, 2006, 8–9.

Wang, David Der-wei. *Why Fiction Matters in Contemporary China*. Waltham, MA: Brandeis University Press, 2020.

Wang, David Der-wei 王德威. *Xiangxiang Zhongguo de fangfa: lishi, xiaoshuo, xushi* 想像中国的方法: 历史 小说 叙事 [Ways to Imagine China: History, Novel, Narrative]. Beijing: SDX Joint Publishing, 1998.

Wang, Hui. "The Fate of 'Mr. Science' in China: The Concept of Science and Its Application in Modern Chinese Thought." *Positions: East Asia Cultures Critique* 3, no. 1 (1995): 1–68.

Wang, Jing. *The Other Digital China: Nonconfrontational Activism on the Social Web.* Cambridge, Mass.: Harvard University Press, 2019.

Wang Ning王宁. "Qinggan xiaofei yu qinggan chanye——Xiaofei shehuixue yanjiu xilie zhiyi 情感消费与情感产业——消费社会学研究系列之一 [Emotional Consumption and Emotional Industry—One of the Series of Studies on Consumer Sociology]." *Journal of Sun Yat-sen University* 40 no. 6 (2006): 109–113.

Wang, Qingning. *The Chinese Internet: The Online Public Sphere, Power Relations and Political Communication.* London, New York: Routledge, 2020.

Wang Tiekun 王铁琨 and Hou Min 侯敏. "Cong 2008 Niandu Diaocha Shuju Kan Zhongguo De Yuyan Shenghuo 从2008年度调查数据看中国的语言生活 [Looking Into the Language Situation in China from the Data of Language Survey (2008)]." *Yuyan wenzi yingyong* 2010.2 (2010): 26–35.

Wang, Tingting. "Tanbi Novels and *Fujoshi*: A New Romance for Young Chinese Women." In *Arts: A Science Matter*, edited by Maria Burguete and Lui Lam, 317–32. Singapore: World Scientific Publishing, 2011.

Wang Wanbo 王婉波. "Wangluo nüpin wen kongjian xushi yanjiu 网络女频文空间叙事研究 [A Study on the Spatial Narration of Internet Female Fiction]." *Writing* 43, no. 1 (2023): 72–84.

Wang, Xiaowei. *Blockchain Chicken Farm: And Other Stories of Tech in China's Countryside.* New York: Farrar, Straus and Giroux, 2020.

Wang, Xinyuan. *Social Media in Industrial China.* London: University College London Press, 2016.

Wang Yao 王瑶. *Weilai de zuobiao: quanqiuhua shidai de Zhongguo kehuan lunji* 未来的坐标:全球化时代的中国科幻论集 [The Coordinates of the Future: Essays on Chinese Science Fiction in the Age of Globalization]. Shanghai: Shanghai wenyi chubanshe, 2019.

Watson, Ivan. "China: The Electronic Wastebasket of the World" CNN, May 30, 2013. https://www.cnn.com/2013/05/30/world/asia/china-electronic-waste-e waste/index.html

Wei-Ling Contemporary. "Wei-Ling Contemporary—Past Exhibitions—By Hands." Wei-Ling Contemporary, 2016. http://weiling-gallery.com/contemporary/portfolio-item/yau-bee-ling-by-hands-works/.

Wei-Ling Gallery. "About." *Wei-Ling Gallery.* http://weiling-gallery.com/gallery/about/.

Wei-Ling Gallery. *What Makes Art Powerful?* WLG Discussion Lab Online Programme, 2020. https://www.youtube.com/watch?v=CZ13hY4aik4.

Westward Murakami Haruki 向西村上春樹. *Dongguan de senlin* 東莞的森林 [Woods in Dongguan], aka *Yilu Xiangxi* 一路向西 [Due West]. Hong Kong: Kind of Culture Publication, 2012.

Widmer, Ellen, and Dewei Wang. *From May Fourth to June Fourth: Fiction and Film in Twentieth-Century China*. Harvard University Press, 1993.

World Economic Forum. "Global Gender Gap Index 2020." Cologne/Geneva: World Economic Forum, 2020. https://www.weforum.org/reports/gender-gap-2020-report-100-years-pay-equality/in-full.

Wu Guangzheng 吴光正. *Zhongguo gudai xiaoshuo de yuanxing yu muti* 中国古代小说的原型与母题 [Motifs and Archetypes in Classical Chinese Novel]. Beijing: Shehui kexue wenxian chubanshe, 2002.

Wu Liu Xiongdi 乌六兄弟. "Women yiqi zuo 'Haidao' 我们一起做'海盗' [We Made "The Pirate" Together]." In *The Pirate* 1. https://koopee.org/wenxue/hido/001/00.htm.

Wu Qing 乌青. "Huai shiren 2010 坏诗人 2010 [Bad Poets 2010]." *Youtube*, uploaded by UqinZen, April 10, 2018, https://www.youtube.com/watch?v=aDpAzii1m1c&t=4877s.

Wu Qing 乌青. *Tian shang de baiyun zhen bai ah* 天上的白雲真白啊 [*Oh, the white clouds in the sky are really white*]. Nanjing: Jiangsu wenyi chubanshe, 2013.

Wu Qing 乌青. "Tan yi tan 'Koopee Guopi' 谈一谈'Koopee果皮' [A brief discussion about 'Koopee Guopi']." https://wuqing.org/p/95.

Wu Qing 乌青. "Xiangpi wenxue wang dansheng ji 橡皮文学网诞生记 [Record of the Birth of the Xiangpi Literature Website]." *wuqing.org*. https://wuqing.org/p/24.

Wu Qing 乌青. "Wei yishu xiangmu 'Wu Qing kafei' yi mai chu 380 bei 微艺术项目'乌青咖啡'已卖出380杯 [The Micro-art Project 'Wu Qing Coffee' Has Sold 380 Cups]." *UQnMedia*, WeChat, October 10, 2015. https://mp.weixin.qq.com/s/KEzLBCeK4REtkyf5nHDu1Q?fbclid=IwAR2LhNb0J1MGd5qZpWhKRaO6HVN_d53UA_dWUFG01olBhM5Ox2iS5jPfeHk.

Wu Qing 乌青, Liu Hui 六回. "Zuopin: Zheli you shi//Weixin gonghao ting fa yi zhou" 作品:这里有诗//微信公号停发一周 [Work: There's Poetry Here//WeChat Account Paused for One Week." *UQnMedia*, WeChat, August 2, 2015. https://mp.weixin.qq.com/s/HMjyqVMtBIFKKjHYqCQkyQ?fbclid=IwAR3mW-I41WtOUY_W5JBApVb09N7XXYXIcYnNHwz84nQMoiU2T2gKTT4G-8M.

Wu, Venus. "Exclusive Interview with Li Ziqi, China's Most Mysterious Internet Celebrity." *YouTube* (September 13, 2019). https://www.youtube.com/watch?v=J9CfVcXoYh4.

Wu Zhi 武芝. "Zai kanyi yixian, tamen dexuqiu zhide bei kanjian 在抗"疫"一线，她们的需求值得被看见 [At the Anti-Covid Frontline, Her Voice Should Have Been Heard]." Sina Finance, February 23, 2020. https://finance.sina.com.cn/chanjing/cyxw/2020-02-23/doc-iimxyqvz5164892.shtml.

Wuse Longzhang 五色龙章. *Chuan dao mingchao kao keju* 穿到明朝考科举 [Attending the Imperial Examination in the Ming Dynasty]. *Jinjiang Literature City*, 2017-18. http://www.jjwxc.net/onebook.php?novelid=3146671.

Xia Deyuan 夏德元 and Zhou Weifeng 周伟峰. "Boke: Xin xing kouyu chuanbo xingtai de fazhan yu tingjue wenhua de huigui 播客：新型口语传播形态的发展与听觉文化的回归 [Podcasting: The Development of New Forms of Spoken Communication and the Return of Auditory Culture]." *Wenhua yishu yanjiu* 15, no. 01 (2022): 65–74+114.

Xiao Bing 小冰. *Yangguang shi le boli chuang* 阳光失了玻璃窗 [Sunlight Has Lost Its Glass Windows]. Beijing: Beijing lianhe chuban gongsi, 2017.

Xiao Feng 小封. *Wan wu dou xiang ai* 万物都相爱 [All Things In the World Love One Another]. Chengdu: Sichuan wenyi chubanshe, 2019.

Xiao Yin 小引. "Jianghu ye yu shi nian deng – Xin shiji zhongguo xianfeng shige baogao 江湖夜雨十年灯——新世纪十年中国先锋诗歌报告 [Ten Years of Light on Rainy Nights in the Jianghu: Report on a Decade of Chinese Avant-Garde Poetry in the New Century]," Shige yuekan 10 (2012): 97–108.

Xin shidai cao ni ma 新时代草泥马. "CDC dang'an: Yichang zhangxian wangmin bu fucong de daxing jiti xingwei yishu huodong: Fa koushao de ren banben daquan CDC档案 | 一场彰显网民不服从的大型集体行为艺术活动：发口哨的人版本大全 [CDC Files | A Massive, Collective Performance of Netizen Disobedience: All Versions of The Whistle-Giver]." *China Digital Times* (March 12, 2020). https://chinadigitaltimes.net/chinese/638032.html.

Xinhuanet. "Kangji xinguan feiyan yiqing de zhongguo xingdong 抗击新冠肺炎疫情的中国行动 [China's Action against the New Coronavirus Pneumonia Outbreak]." The Central Government of the People's Republic of China, June 7, 2020. http://www.gov.cn/zhengce/2020-06/07/content_5517737.htm.

Xinming Evening News 新民晚报. "Weibo zheng nengliang chuandi shu zhixian shangsheng zhuanfa dianping renjian zhenshanmei 微博正能量传递数直线上升转发点评人间真善美 [Number of Positive Energy Transmissions on Weibo Forwarding and Commenting on Truth, Goodness and Beauty in the World Has Skyrocketed]." *Xinming Evening News*, 22 August 2022. https://www.chinanews.com.cn/cul/2012/08-22/4126061.shtml.

Xu, Jianhua, Guyu Sun, Wei Cao, Wenyuan Fan, and Zhihao Pan. "Stigma, Discrimination, and Hate Crimes in Chinese-Speaking World amid Covid-19 Pandemic." *Asian Journal of Criminology* 16 (January 6, 2021): 51–74.

Xu, Jinru 徐晋如. "Mei you ganqing jiu bu hui you shi 没有感情就不会有诗 [Without Emotion, There's No Poetry]." *Sohu*, 2017.

Xu, Linli, Liang Jiang, Chuan Qin,Zhe Wang, and Dongfang Du. "How Images Inspire Poems: Generating Classical Chinese Poetry from Images with Memory Networks." *ArXiv* (2018): 5618–5625.

Xue Huifeng 薛惠锋. "Datong: Cong 'yantaoting' dao 'shijie nao'大同：从'研讨厅'到'世界脑' [Great Harmony: From the 'conference hall' to the 'world brain.]'" Guangming wang, April 25, 2021. https://topics.gmw.cn/2021-04/25/content_34792144.htm.

Xuemei 雪梅. "Liu Cixin: Xuanbu jiameng shang tang, shuangfang jiang dazao Santi chenjinshi yule xin yetai 刘慈欣：宣布加盟商汤，双方将打造三体沉浸式娱乐新业态 [Liu Cixin Announces Collaboration with SenseTime, Together They Will Create a New Type of Immersive 'The Three-Body Problem' Experience]," July 9, 2021. https://finance.sina.com.cn/tech/2021-07-09/doc-ikqciyzk4493238.shtml.

Yan, Rui. "i, Poet: Automatic Poetry Composition through Recurrent Neural Networks with Iterative Polishing Schema." *IJCAI'16: Proceedings of the Twenty-Fifth International Joint Conference on Artificial Intelligence* (July 2016): 2238–2244.

Yan zhi youfan 言之有范. "Li Ziqi huo '2019 niandu wenhua chuanbo renwu', weihe shi ta? 李子柒获"2019年度文化传播人物"，为何是她？ [Li Ziqi Won 'the 2019 Person of the Year in Cultural Communication:' Why She?]" *Tengxun*, December 18, 2019. https://freewechat.com/a/MzAxNTEwMjcwMQ==/2651003948/1. The original link is defunct as of May 5, 2023: https://new.qq.com/omn/20191218/20191218A0PAH400.html.

Yang, Guobin, and Wei Wang. *Engaging Social Media in China: Platforms, Publics, and Production.* East Lansing, MI: Michigan State University Press, 2021.

———. "Online Lockdown Diaries as Endurance Art." *AI & Society*, January 15, 2021, 1–10. https://doi.org/10.1007/s00146-020-01141-5.

———. *The Power of the Internet in China: Citizen Activism Online*. New York: Columbia University Press, 2009.

Yang Haibo 杨海波. "*Honglou meng* dui xiafan-lijie muti de jicheng yu chaoyue《红楼梦》对下凡历劫母题的继承与超越 [The Inheritance and Transcendence of the Motif of 'Descension for a Kalpa' in *Dream of the Red Chamber*]. "*Journal of Northwest Normal University* 48, no. 2 (2011): 68–75.

Yang, Haosheng. *A Modernity Set to a Pre-Modern Tune: Classical-Style Poetry of Modern Chinese Writers*. Leiden: Brill, 2016.

Yang Li 杨黎. *Cuowu* 错误 [Mistake]. Trilingual, with Norwegian translations by Bend Bendixen and English translations by Judy Torgard. Hangzhou: Hei shao shige chubanshe jihua/ Hei shao shengyin chubanshe, 2014. Unofficial, with sound disc.

Yang Li 杨黎. *Canlan: Di san dai ren de xiezuo he shenghuo* 灿烂:第三代人的写作和生活 [Splendor: The life and writing of the Third Generation]. Xining: Qinghai Renmin Chubanshe, 2004.

Yang Li 杨黎. "Gei Zhao Lihua de yi feng gongkai xin 给赵丽华的一封公开信 [A Public letter to Zhao Lihua]." Feihua Yang Li blog. http://blog.sina.com.cn/s/blog_477e9b940100056a.html.

Yang Li 杨黎. *Xiao Yang yu Ma Li* 小杨与马丽 [Xiao Yang and Mali]. Shijiazhuang: Hebei Jiaoyu Chubanshe, 2002.

Yang Li 杨黎. *Xiangpi: Zhongguo xianfeng wenxue* 1 橡皮:中国先锋文学1 [Xiangpi: Chinese Avant-garde Literature 1]. Nanjing: Jiangsu Wenyi Chubanshe, 2012.

Yang Li 杨黎. *Xiangpi: Zhongguo xianfeng wenxue* 2 橡皮:中国先锋文学2 [Xiangpi: Chinese Avant-garde Literature 2]. Xiangpi chuban, 2018, unofficial.

Yang Li 杨黎. *Xiangpi: Zhongguo xianfeng wenxue* 3 橡皮:中国先锋文学3 [Xiangpi: Chinese Avant-garde Literature 3]. Beijing: Beijing Shidai Huawen Shuju, 2014.

Yang Li 杨黎. *Xiangpi: Zhongguo xianfeng wenxue* 4 橡皮:中国先锋文学4 [Xiangpi: Chinese Avant-garde Literature 4]. Xiangpi Chuban, unofficial.

Yang Li 杨黎. *Xiangpi: Zhongguo xianfeng wenxue* 5 橡皮:中国先锋文学5 [Xiangpi: Chinese Avant-garde Literature 5]. Xiangpi Chuban, unofficial.

Yang Li 杨黎. *Xiangpi: Zhongguo xianfeng wenxue* 6 橡皮:中国先锋文学6 [Xiangpi: Chinese Avant-garde Literature 6]. Xiangpi Chuban, unofficial.

Yang Li 杨黎, and Li Jiuru李九如. "Bai nian baihua – Zhongguo dangdai shige fangtan lu 百年白话–中国当代诗歌访谈录 [One Hundred Years of *Baihua*: Records of Interviews on Chinese Contemporary Poetry]." Jiangsu: Fenghuang wenyi Publishing House, 2017.

Yang, Peidong, and Lijun Tang. "'Positive Energy': Hegemonic Intervention and Online Media Discourse in China's Xi Jinping Era." *China: An International Journal* 16 no. 1 (2018): 1–22.

Yang Shiye 杨十夜. *Shuang shi chongfei*双世宠妃 [The Eternal Love]. Directed by Yuan De 元德. Aired July 10, 2017, on Tencent Video. Tencent Penguin Pictures 2017, online. https://v.qq.com/x/cover/47xswolfi4iamlx/h0024x1jb6k.html.

Yang Shiye 杨十夜. Shuang shi chongfei 2 双世宠妃2 [The Eternal Love 2]. Directed by Wu Qiang 吴强. Aired October 22, 2018, on Tencent Video. Tencent Penguin Pictures, 2018, online. https://v.qq.com/x/cover/ohrejqzlvdyro3k/l00276tubbd.html.

Yang Shiye 杨十夜. *Shuang chi chongfei 3* 双世宠妃3 [The Eternal Love 3]. Directed by Li Yang 李阳. Aired June 1, 2021, on Tencent Video. Tencent Penguin Pictures, 2021.

Yang, Xin. "Aestheticizing Labor: The Construction of the 'Good China Story' in Li Ziqi's Videos." *Chinese Literature and Thought Today* 53 (2022): 30–37.

Yang, Zhichao, Pengshan Cai, Yansong Feng, Fei Li, Weijiang Feng, Elena Suet-Ying Chiu, and Hong Yu. "Generating Classical Chinese Poems from Vernacular Chinese." Proceedings of the Conference on Empirical Methods in Natural Language Processing. Conference on Empirical Methods in Natural Language Processing (2019): 6155-6164.

Yeh, Michelle. "Anxiety & Liberation: Notes on the Recent Chinese Poetry Scene." *World Literature Today* 81 (4): 28–35, 2007.

Yeh, Michelle. *Modern Chinese Poetry: Theory and Practice Since 1917*. New Haven and London: Yale University Press, 1991.

Youngquist, Paul. “Cyberpunk, War, and Money: Neal Stephenson’s Cryptonomicon.” *Contemporary Literature* 53, no. 2 (2012): 319–47.

Yu, Mengfan 余梦帆 and Liu Chuan’e 刘川鄂. “‘Chuangzao’ yu ‘zhizuo’: guanyu Weiruan Xiao Bing zuo shi ruanjian de ji dian sikao ‘创造’与‘制作’: 关于微软小冰作诗软件的几点思考 [Creation and Production: A Few Thoughts about Microsoft Xiao Bing’s Poetry Writing].” *Dangdai wentan* 当代文坛, 2019.

Yu Quanyou 于全有 and Pei Jingrui 裴景瑞. “Huoxingwen yongsheng de yuyan shehui wenhua xianxiang ‘火星文’涌生的语言社会文化现象 [The Cultural-Linguistic Phenomenon of the Emergence of Martian Script].” *Wenhua xuekan* 2008.2 (2008): 151-155.

Yu, Wenbo, Ziyang Zhang, Yixin Wu and Yingjun Huang. “Choreographed Landscapes: A Gallery Inside the Market.” Unpublished Portfolio, June 1, 2018.

Yu Xuying 郁旭映. “Bashi niandai de xiandaixing xiangxiang – Lun Liu Cixin ‘Zhongguo 2185’ 八十年代的現代性想像—論劉慈欣《中國2185》[Imagining Modernity in the 1980s – On Liu Cixin’s ‘China 2185’].” In *Shuma shidai de Zhongguo renwen xueke yanjiu* 數碼時代的中國人文學科研究 [Chinese Humanities Research in the Digital Age], edited by Tan Guogen 譚國根, Liang Muling 梁慕靈, and Huang Zihong 黄自鴻, Kindle edition., n.p. Taibei: Xiuwei zixun, 2018.

Yu, Yat Sun 于日辰. *Yiyuyi Xiejie* 壹獄壹世界 [A World in an Iron Grille]. Hong Kong: Idea Publication, 2013.

Yule Dujiaoshou 娱乐独角兽 [Unicorn Entertainment]. “‘Chen Qing Ling’ dajieju dianbo huoli 1.56 yi, zhuanji xiaoshou 2100 wan, C duan bianxian daodi you duo zhuanqian 《陈情令》大结局点播获利1.56亿、专辑销售2100万，C端变现到底有多赚钱 [156 Million for ‘The Untamed’ 2.1 Million for Album Sales, How Much Money Can C-Port Make].” Last modified October 14, 2021. http://www.360doc.com/content/20/1014/20/71943657_940476709.shtml.

Yuval-Davis, Nira. “Situated Intersectionality and Social Inequality.” *Raisons Politiques* 2 (2015): 91–100.

Zhang, Charlie Yi. *Dreadful Desires: The Uses of Love in Neoliberal China.* Durham: Duke University Press.

Zhang, Chunyu. “‘My Double Love of Boys’: Chinese Women’s Fascination with ‘Boys’ Love’ Fiction.” Master of Science, Iowa State University, 2014.

Zhang, Chunyu. “Loving Boys Twice as Much: Chinese Women’s Paradoxical Fandom of ‘Boys’ Love’ Fiction.” *Women’s Studies in Communication* 39.3 (2016): 249–67.

Zhang, Jianfeng. “China Gets Serious About Trash Sorting” CCTV, July 2, 2019. http://english.cctv.com/2019/07/02/ARTIrJfxbqRCVEL1moFBYGIL190702.shtml.

Zhang, Jiyuan and Dong Wang. “Chinese Poetry Generation with Flexible Styles,” 2018 11th International Symposium on Chinese Spoken Language Processing (ISCSLP) (2018): 419-423.

Zhang, Phoebe. "Chinese Activists Detained After Sharing Censored Coronavirus Material on Crowdsourcing site Github." *South China Morning Post* (April 25, 2020). https://www.scmp.com/news/china/politics/article/3081569/chinese-activists-detained-after-sharing-censored-coronavirus.

Zhang Ran 张冉. "Yitai 以太 [Ether]." In *Qifeng zhi cheng* 起风之城 [The Windy City], 3–47. Chengdu: Sichuan kexue jishu chubanshe, 2021.

Zhang Xiao 张霄. "'Zhongtian wen' zhong shouzhong de xinli yu xingwei yanjiu '种田文'中受众的心理与行为研究 [Psychological and Behavioural Analysis on Readers of 'Farming Fiction']." *Jin Chuanmei* 25.5 (2017): 84–86.

Zhang, Xudong. *Chinese Modernism in the Era of Reforms: Cultural Fever, Avant-Garde Fiction, and the New Chinese Cinema*. Duke University Press, 1997.

Zhang Yaotian 张耀天. "Nezha chuanshuo de fuhao yihan yu lunli yinyu – Zhongguo chuantong xiaodao de beipan yu tuwei 哪吒传说的符号意涵与伦理隐喻——中国传统孝道的背叛与突围 [Symbolic Meaning and Ethical Metaphor of Ne Zha Legend: Betrayal and Breakthrough of Chinese Traditional Filial Piety]." *Journal of Shanxi Normal University* (*Social Science Edition*) 47.1 (2020): 74–79.

Zhang, Yunpeng, and Fang Xu. "Ignorance, Orientalism and Sinophobia in Knowledge Production on Covid-19." *Tijdschrift Voor Economische En Sociale Geografie* 111, no. 3 (The Geography of the COVID-19 Pandemic) (June 19, 2020): 211–23.

Zhao, Hui, and Jun Liu. "Social Media and Collective Remembrance." *China Perspectives* 2015, no. 1 (March 1, 2015): 41-48.

Zhao Na 赵娜and Chen Liwen 陈丽雯. *Chen Xi Yuan* 宸汐緣 [Love and Destiny]. Directed by Lin Yufen 林玉芬, Liang Shengquan 梁勝權, Ren Haitao 任海濤, and Guo Hu 郭虎. Aired July 15, 2019, on IQIYI.COM. Croton Media, 2019, online. https://www.iq.com/album/%E5%AE%B8%E6%B1%90%E7%BC%98-2019-19rrhtj1td?lang=zh_cn.

Zheng Jieyao 郑洁瑶. "Naxie ni bu xihuan de ren, tamen ye you jilu de quanli那些你不喜欢的人，他们也有记录的权力 [Those You Don't Like, Also Have the Right to Document]." Jiemian wenhua, August 8, 2017. https://www.jiemian.com/article/1528890.html.

Zheng Yunan 郑雨楠. "Guangzhou 7 zhong qingxing yunxu shangjia getihu jiedao jingying 广州：7种情形允许商家（个体户）借道经营 [Guangzhou: Under 7 Conditions Small Private Business Occupied Roads]." *Southern Metropolis Daily*. (June 4, 2020). https://epaper.oeeee.com/epaper/A/html/2020-06/05/content_16045.htm.

Zhongguo Xinwen Zhoukan 中国新闻周刊. "Meitian 'dashang' jin yi yi, Kuaishou san da saidao nengfou chengqi 4000yi shizhi每天'打赏'近一亿 快手三大赛道能否撑起4000亿市值 [Daily 'Digital Rewards' Have Reached 100 Million Yuan: Can Kuaishou's Three Major Tracks Support a Market Value of 400 Billion

Yuan?].” News China, Feburay 3, 2021. https://finance.sina.cn/tech/2021-02-03/detailikftssap2736411.d.html?fromtech=1&from=wap.

Zhou Munan 周木楠. “Shaonian Ge Xing少年歌行 [The Blood of Youth]” Luoying Xiaoshuo 落影小说. https://www.loying.cc/book/gexing/.

Zhou Shengchun 周春生 and Yang Ying 杨缨. “Lishi shang de rushang yu rushang jingshen 历史上的儒商与儒商精神 [Confucian Businessman and Its Ideology in History].” *Research in Chinese Economic History* 4 (2010): 152–58.

Zhou, Viola and Koh Ewe. “Boys Keep Flirting With Each Other on Chinese TV But Never Fall in Love.” Vice, April 5, 2021. https://www.vice.com/en/article/7k95mg/boys-love-drama-china-tv-untamed-lgbtq.

Zhou, Y., B. Paul, and R. Sherman. “Still a Hetero-Gendered World: A Content Analysis of Gender Stereotypes and Romantic Ideals in Chinese Boy Love Stories.” *Sex Roles* 78 (2018): 107–18. https://doi.org/10.1007/s11199-017-0762-y.

Zhu, Chanchan 朱婵婵 and Zhu Yuchen 朱雨晨. “Fuqin congwei jinguo fuyang yiwu, haiyao shanyang ta ma? da’an laile! 父亲从未尽过抚养义务, 还要赡养他吗? 答案来了! [Should One Support the Father Who Never Fulfils His Parental Duty? Here is the Answer!].” *Guangming Online*, March 26, 2023.

Zhuang, Pinghui. “China’s Most Notorious e-Waste Dumping Ground Now Cleaner But Poorer” South China Morning Post. https://www.scmp.com/news/china/society/article/2112226/chinas-most-notorious-e-waste-dumping-ground-now-cleaner-poorer.

Žižek, Slavoj. *Looking Awry: An Introduction to Jacques Lacan through Popular Culture*. Cambridge, MA: The MIT Press, 1991.

Žižek, Slavoj. “Slavoj Žižek Speaks at Occupy Wall Street: Transcript.” *IMPOSE Magazine*. https://imposemagazine.com/bytes/slavoj-zizek-at-occupy-wall-street-transcript.

# List of Contributors

**Qian Cui** is Lecturer in Modern Chinese Language, Literature, and Culture at the University of St. Gallen. Previously, she was a lecturer in Chinese Language and Culture at the University of Zurich, Lingnan University, and at Polytechnic University in Hong Kong. Her research interests include Chinese literature and film, European-Chinese comparative literature, modern Chinese aesthetic theory, and Hong Kong literature.

**Zoe Goldstein** is a PhD Candidate at the CUNY Grad Centre and Adjunct Professor at Fordham University, Baruch College, U.S.A.

**Mengyun He** is a PhD candidate in Media and Communication at the London School of Economics and Political Science, UK, as well as a documentary filmmaker. Her movie *Life Matters* was awarded the *Magnolia Award* (*Bai Yulan Jiang*) for Best Documentary Series in China, 2019.

**Helen Hess** is a PhD candidate and lecturer at the Department of Chinese Studies at the University of Zurich. Her research focuses on literature and visual art in contemporary China and the Sinosphere, with a special interest in Sinophone Malaysian literature and Chinese diaspora studies. In 2022, she was visiting scholar at the Department of Chinese Studies at the University of Malaya, Malaysia for four months. She has received generous support by the Janggen-Pöhn foundation for her PhD project.

**Jessica Imbach** is Senior Lecturer in Chinese Studies at the Institute of Asian and Oriental Studies, University of Zurich. She is the author of *Not Afraid of Ghosts: Stories of the Spectral in Modern Chinese Fiction* (University of Zurich, 2017) and co-editor of *Sinophone Utopias: Exploring Futures Beyond the China Dream* (Cambria Press, 2023). In 2023, she was awarded the FAN Award for early career researchers of the University of Zurich for her ongoing research project, tentatively titled *Chinese Literature of the Future: Technology and Nation in Science Fiction and New Media.*

**Sujie Jin** is a PhD candidate at the Institute of Asian and Oriental Studies at the University of Zurich. She gained her MS in Educational Leadership and MA in English Language and Literature from Bob Jones University in the United States. Her research focuses on Chinese online fiction, fandom and *danmei* (boys' love) fiction, alternative history, and popular culture in the digital age.

**Joanna Krenz** is Assistant Professor of Modern Chinese Language and Literature at the Institute of Oriental Studies, Adam Mickiewicz University in Poznań, Poland. She translates and publishes widely on Chinese poetry and prose. She is the author of *In Search of Singularity: Poetry from Poland and China Since 1989* (Brill, 2022). She is currently working on the project *The World Re-Versed: New Phenomena in Chinese Poetry as a Challenge and Inspiration to Literary Studies.*

**Rui Kunze** is Research Fellow at the Friedrich-Alexander-Universität in Erlangen-Nürnberg, Germany. She is the author of *Struggle and Symbiosis: The Canonization of the Poet Haizi and Cultural Discourses in Contemporary China* (2012) and the co-author of *Knowledge Production in Mao-Era China: Learning from the Masses* (2021). Her work on science fiction, poetry, visual culture, the history of science, cultural entrepreneurialism, and food culture in modern and contemporary China has appeared in *East Asian History, Twenty-First Century* (二十一世紀), *China Perspectives, Poetica,* and *Oriens Extremus.*

**Elvin Meng** is a Ph.D. student in Comparative Literature and East Asian Languages and Civilizations at the University of Chicago, U.S.A. Meng is the author of forthcoming articles on literary modernism, media history, and the history of Chinese linguistic thought. His dissertation, tentatively titled "Tongues of the Mirror: Manchu Literacy and the Translation of China," is a media history of Manchu bilingualism. In addition to Manchu intellectual history, Meng's research also focuses on the history of aesthetico-political thought, especially radical readings of the *Shijing*, in second-millennium China.

**Diyi Mergenthaler** is a PhD candidate at the Institute of Art history at the University of Zurich. She obtained her MA in Art Gallery and Museum Studies with distinction at the University of Leeds in 2017. Her research project investigates queer artworks, spaces and queer Chinese iconography created by artists in mainland China and Europe from the 1990s to the present. She is the co-editor of *Contemporary Queer Chinese Art,* which explores heterogeneous expressions of Chineseness and queerness in contemporary art from China and Chinese diasporas in Asia, Europe, and North America.

**Paula Teodorescu** is a lecturer of Chinese language and literature at the Faculty of Foreign Languages and Literatures, University of Bucharest, Romania. She is the author of *Chinese Colloquial Poetry as Heterodox Cultural Practice* (2018). She is also a literary translator from Chinese to Romanian. Notable translations include Mai Jia's novel *Decoded* (2015), an anthology of short stories, *The Sound of Salt Forming* (2019), and the collection *Key Concepts in Chinese Thought and Culture* vol. 1-7 (2020-2022).

**Helena Wu** is Assistant Professor of Hong Kong Studies at the Department of Asian Studies of the University of British Columbia in Canada. She is the author of *The Hangover After the Handover: Places, Things and Cultural Icons in Hong Kong* (Liverpool University Press, 2020). She has also published on the topics of Hong Kong cinema, culture, and media in *Interventions: International Journal of Postcolonial Studies* (2018), *Chinese Martial Arts and Media Culture* (2018), *Hong Kong Keywords* (2019), *Global Media and China* (2020), and *Journal of Chinese Cinemas* (2020).

# Index